Da-na-na, da-na-na,
da-na-na-na-
na-na-na

冨樫義博

A little late to the party… *Shin Godzilla* was awesome!! Hooray for Japanese cinema!!

Yoshihiro Togashi

Yoshihiro Togashi's manga career began in 1986 at the age of 20, when he won the coveted Osamu Tezuka Award for new manga artists. He debuted in the Japanese **Weekly Shonen Jump** magazine in 1989 with the romantic comedy **Tende Shôwaru Cupid**. From 1990 to 1994 he wrote and drew the hit manga **YuYu Hakusho**, which was followed by the dark comedy science-fiction series **Level E**, and finally this adventure series, **Hunter x Hunter**, available from VIZ Media's SHONEN JUMP Advanced imprint. In 1999 he married the manga artist Naoko Takeuchi.

HUNTER X HUNTER Volume 34
SHONEN JUMP ADVANCED Manga Edition

STORY AND ART BY
YOSHIHIRO TOGASHI

English Adaptation & Translation/Lillian Olsen
Touch-up Art & Lettering/Mark McMurray
Design/Matt Hinrichs
Editor/Urian Brown

HUNTERxHUNTER © POT (Yoshihiro Togashi) 2016
All rights reserved. First published in Japan in 2016 by SHUEISHA Inc.,
Tokyo. English translation rights arranged by SHUEISHA Inc.

The stories, characters and incidents mentioned in this publication are
entirely fictional.

Printed in the U.S.A.

Published by VIZ Media, LLC
P.O. Box 77010
San Francisco, CA 94107

10 9 8 7 6 5 4 3 2 1
First printing, March 2018

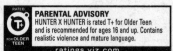

[redacted] MANGA

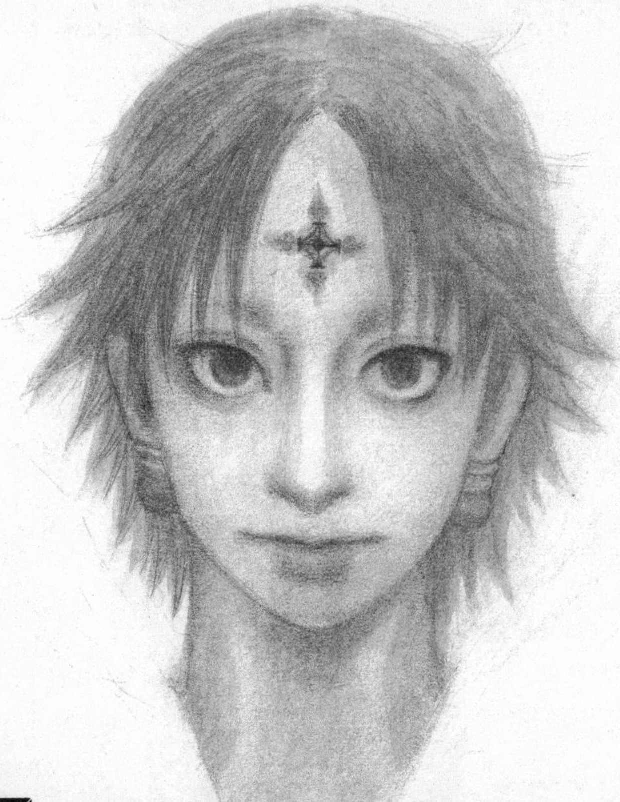

HUNTER × HUNTER

ハンター × ハンター

Story & Art by
Yoshihiro Togashi

Volume 34

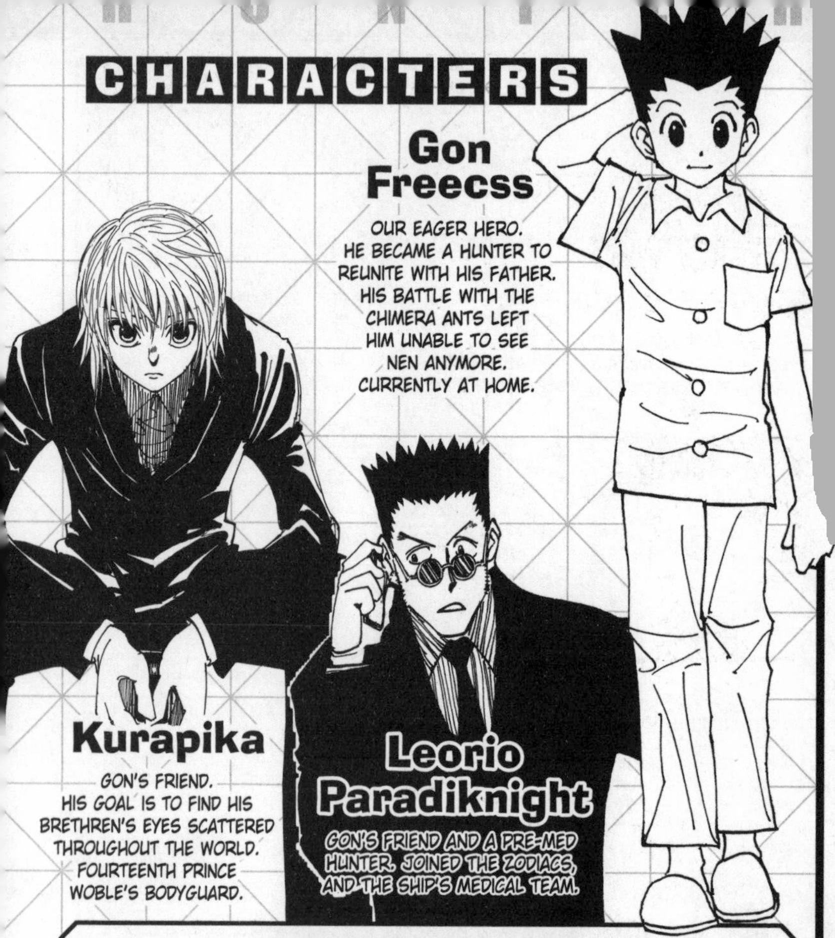

CHARACTERS

Gon Freecss

OUR EAGER HERO. HE BECAME A HUNTER TO REUNITE WITH HIS FATHER. HIS BATTLE WITH THE CHIMERA ANTS LEFT HIM UNABLE TO SEE NEN ANYMORE. CURRENTLY AT HOME.

Kurapika

GON'S FRIEND. HIS GOAL IS TO FIND HIS BRETHREN'S EYES SCATTERED THROUGHOUT THE WORLD. FOURTEENTH PRINCE WOBLE'S BODYGUARD.

Leorio Paradiknight

GON'S FRIEND AND A PRE-MED HUNTER. JOINED THE ZODIACS, AND THE SHIP'S MEDICAL TEAM.

The Story Thus Far

GON DREAMS OF BEING A HUNTER LIKE THE FATHER HE HARDLY REMEMBERS, THE GREAT GING FREECSS.

GON REUNITES WITH GING'S OLD FRIEND KITE AND ENCOUNTERS THE CHIMERA ANTS, WHICH CAME FROM THE OUTSIDE WORLD. THE HUNTER ASSOCIATION SENDS OUR HEROES TO STORM THE PALACE IN E. GORTEAU TO DEFEAT THE ANTS. MANKIND IS VICTORIOUS, BUT AT THE COST OF HUNTER ASSOCIATION CHAIRMAN NETERO'S LIFE. AN ELECTION IS HELD TO PICK THE NEXT CHAIRMAN, AND CHEADLE OF THE ZODIACS IS PICKED. GON, CRITICALLY WOUNDED, IS HEALED BY ALLUKA, KILLUA'S SISTER.

NETERO'S SON, BEYOND, ANNOUNCES A VOYAGE TO THE DARK CONTINENT TO THE ENTIRE WORLD, WHICH WAS SUPPOSED TO BE TABOO. WHILE EVERYONE PREPARES FOR THE JOURNEY, THE BATTLE FOR THE THRONE OF THE KAKIN KINGDOM IS SET TO TAKE PLACE DURING THE VOYAGE...

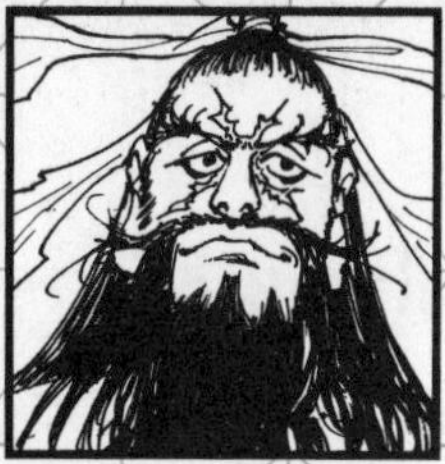

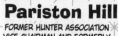

Beyond Netero

NETERO'S SON. PLANNING THE FORBIDDEN JOURNEY TO THE DARK CONTINENT.

Pariston Hill

FORMER HUNTER ASSOCIATION VICE CHAIRMAN AND FORMERLY ONE OF THE ZODIACS. INTRICATELY INVOLVED IN BEYOND'S JOURNEY PLANS.

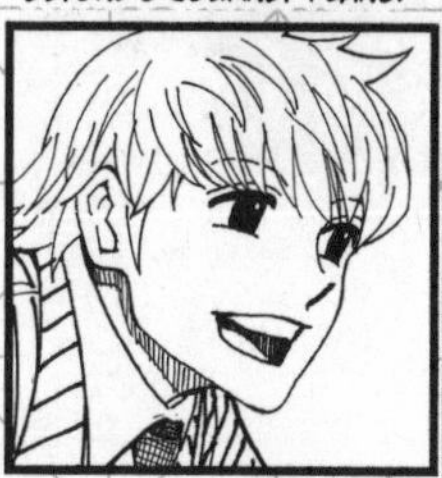

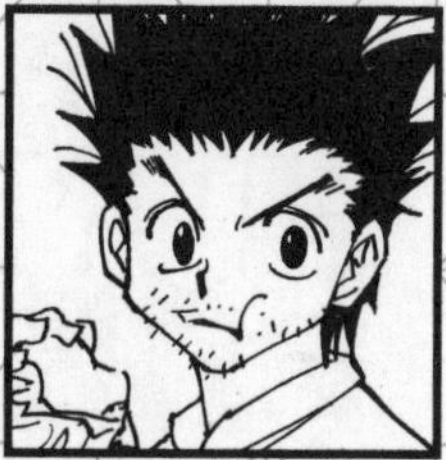

Ging Freecss

GON'S FATHER, ONE OF THE TOP FIVE NEN USERS IN THE WORLD. SAILING TO THE DARK CONTINENT WITH PARISTON.

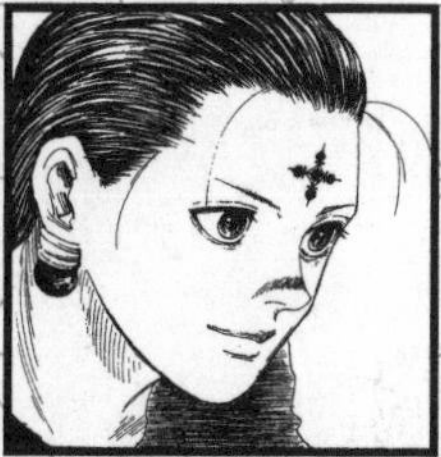

Chrollo

THE LEADER OF THE PHANTOM TROUPE. ONCE DENIED HIS NEN ABILITIES, HE IS NOW ABLE TO FIGHT HISOKA.

Hisoka

SO BATTLE-OBSESSED THAT HE TRACKED DOWN AN EXORCIST FOR CHROLLO SO HE COULD FIGHT HIM.

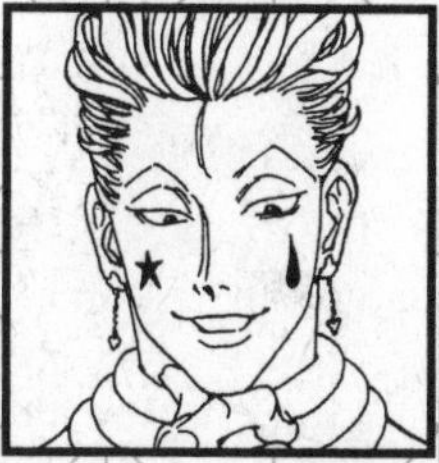

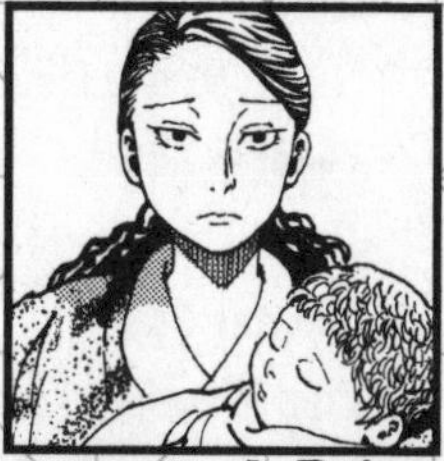

Fourteenth Prince Woble and Oito

THE FOURTEENTH PRINCE OF KAKIN AND HER MOTHER. KURAPIKA'S CLIENTS WHO HIRED HIM AS A BODYGUARD.

The Zodiacs

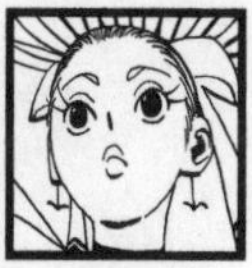

CLUCK (BIRD)

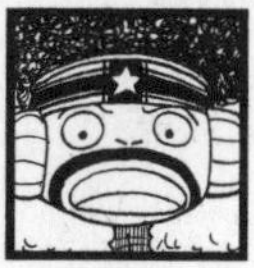

GINTA (RAM)

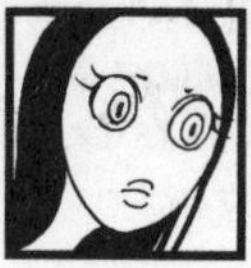

GEL (SNAKE)

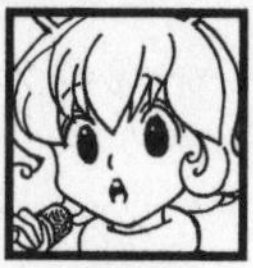

PYON (RABBIT)

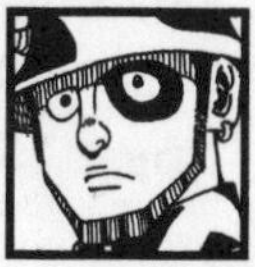

MIZAISTOM (COW)

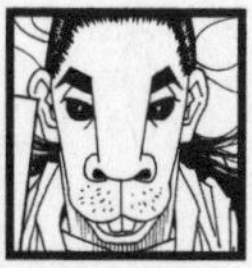

SATCHO (HORSE)

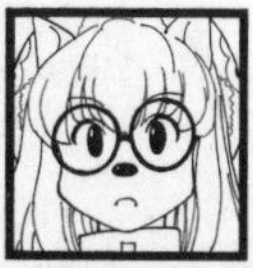

CHEADLE (DOG)

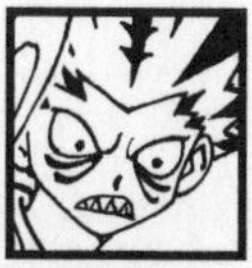

KANZAI (TIGER)

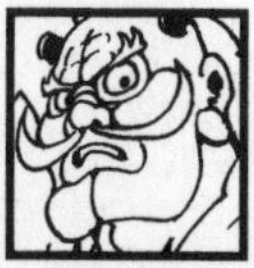

BOTOBAI (DRAGON)

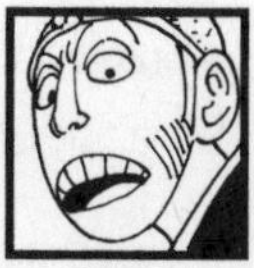

SAIYU (MONKEY)

HUNTER×HUNTER

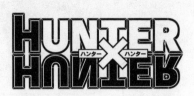

Volume 34

CONTENTS

Chapter 351: Battle to the Death

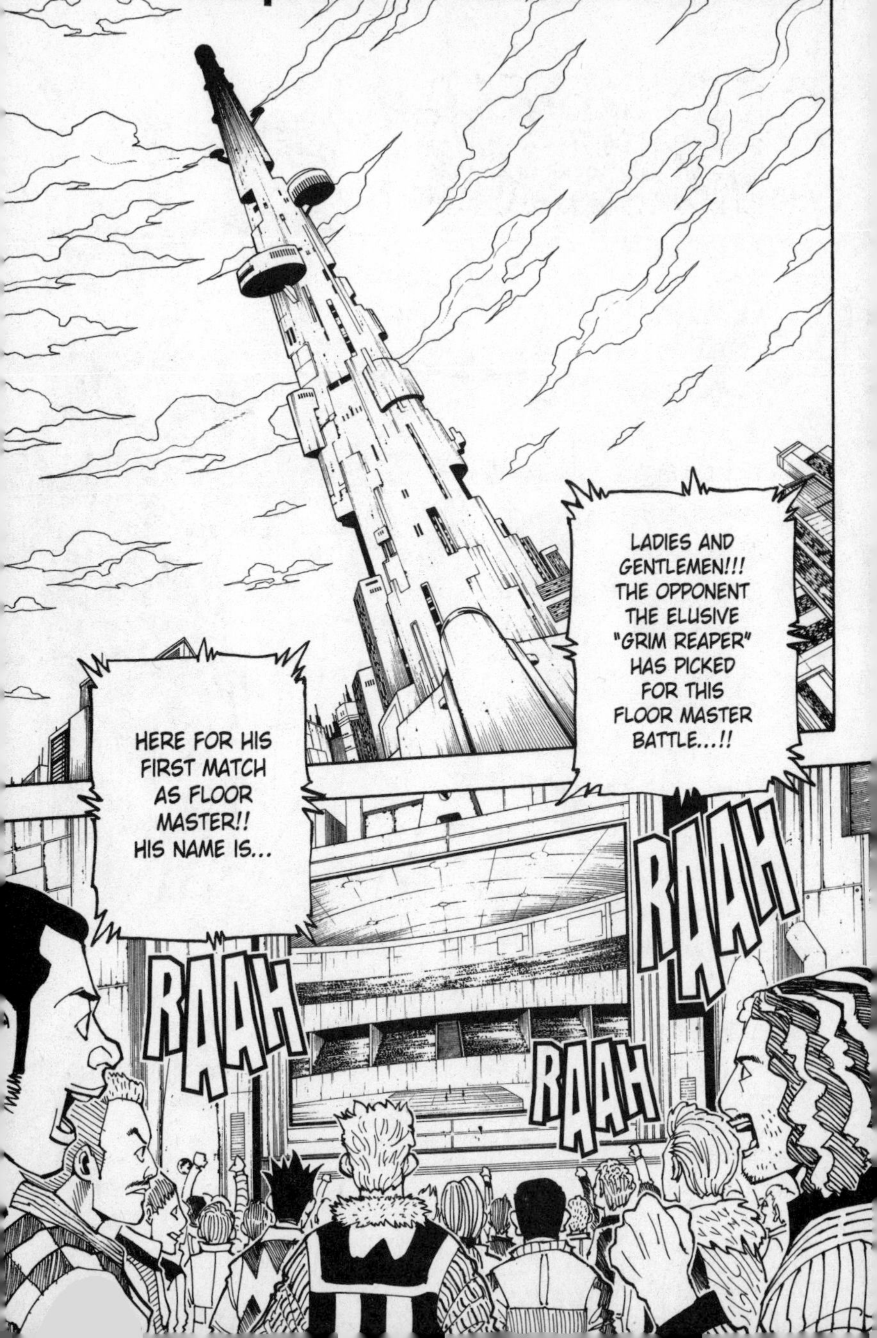
LADIES AND GENTLEMEN!!! THE OPPONENT THE ELUSIVE "GRIM REAPER" HAS PICKED FOR THIS FLOOR MASTER BATTLE...!!
HERE FOR HIS FIRST MATCH AS FLOOR MASTER!! HIS NAME IS...
RAAH
RAAH
RAAH

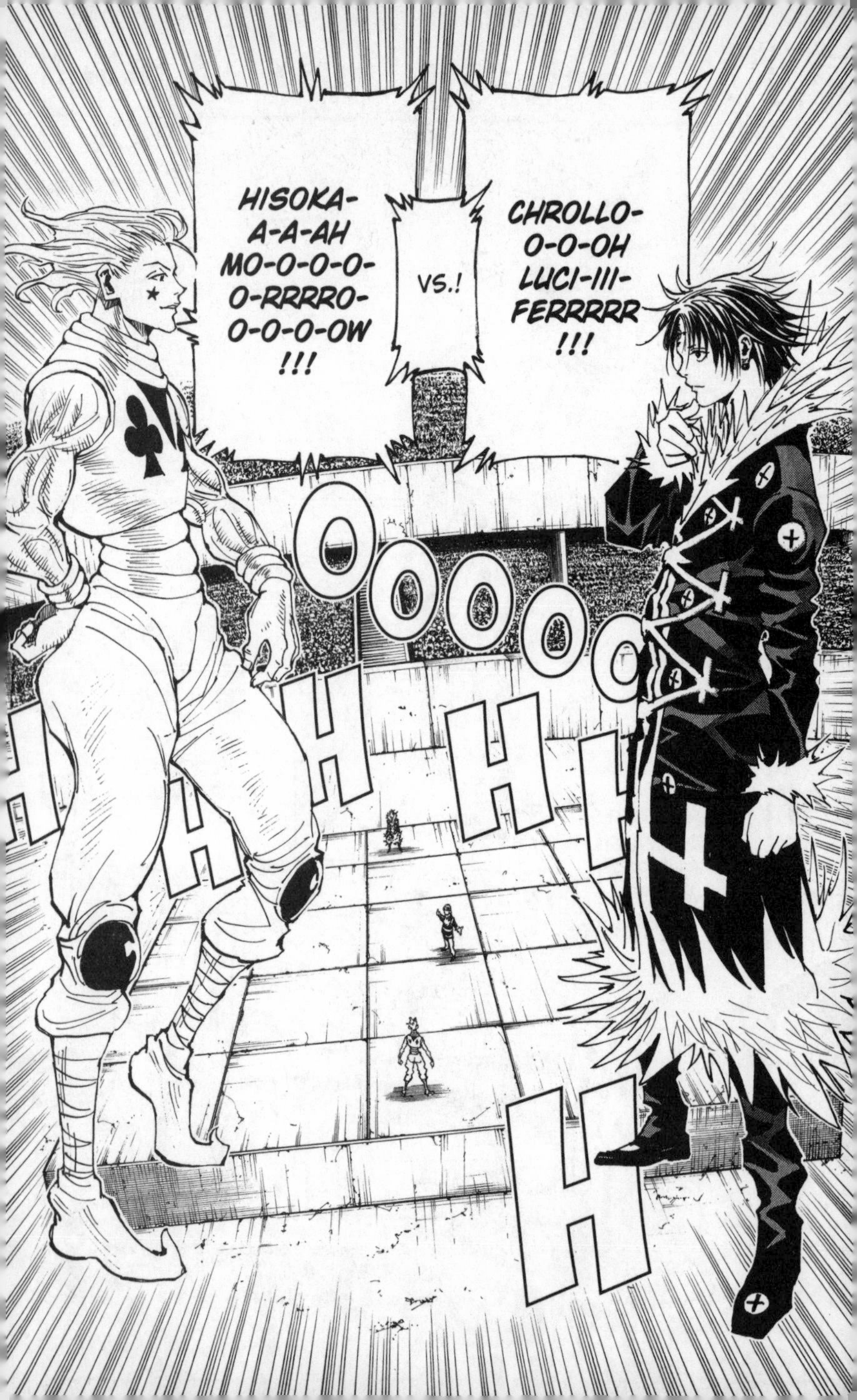
CHROLLO-O-O-OH LUCI-III-FERRRRR!!!
VS.!
HISOKA-A-A-AH MO-O-O-O-O-RRRRO-O-O-O-OW!!!
OOOOOOHHHHHH

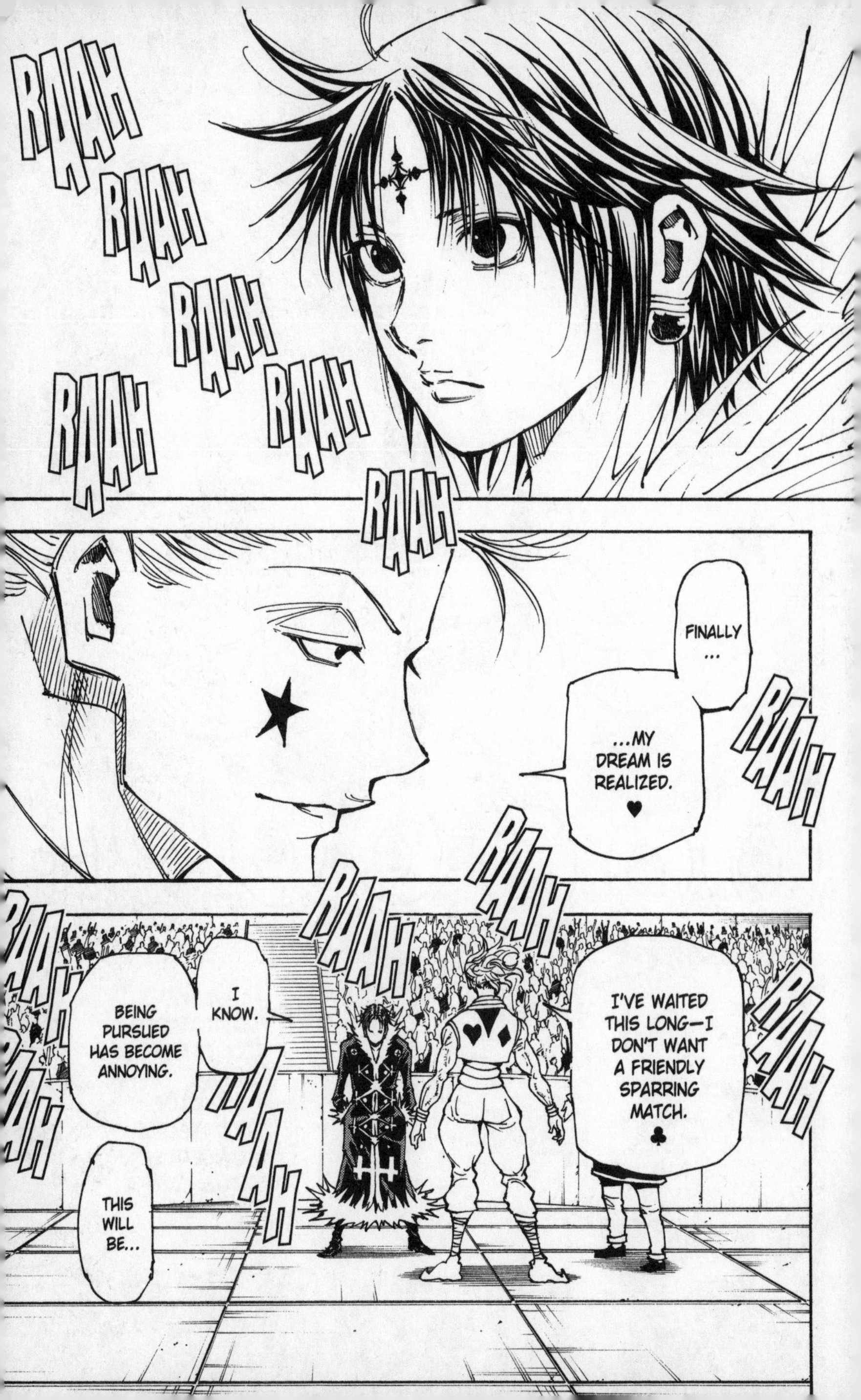
RAAH
RAAH
RAAH
RAAH
RAAH
RAAH
FINALLY ...
...MY DREAM IS REALIZED. ♥
RAAH
RAAH
RAAH
RAAH
I'VE WAITED THIS LONG—I DON'T WANT A FRIENDLY SPARRING MATCH. ♣
I KNOW.
BEING PURSUED HAS BECOME ANNOYING.
THIS WILL BE...
RAAH
RAAH
RAAH

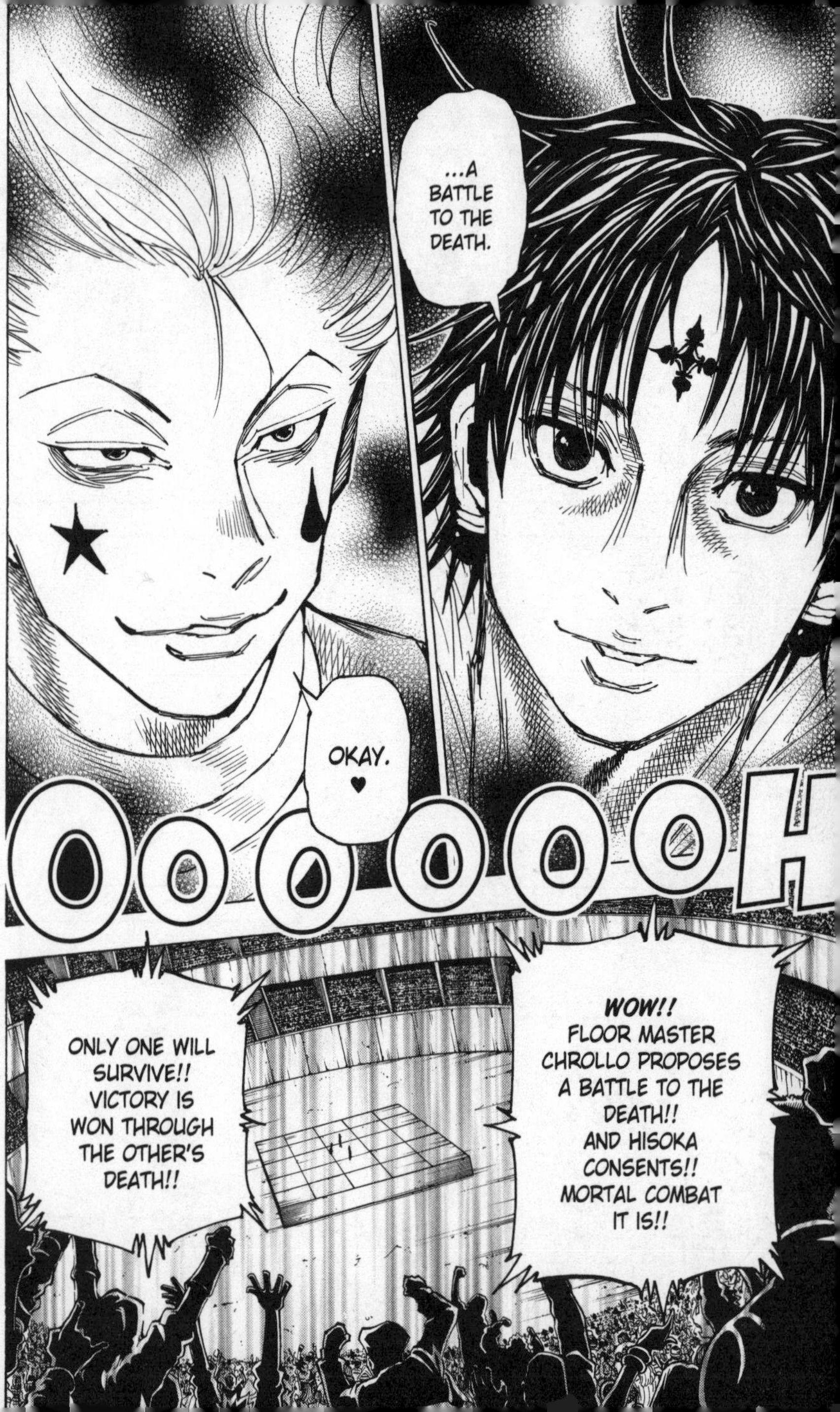
...A BATTLE TO THE DEATH.
OKAY. ♥
OOOOOOH
WOW!! FLOOR MASTER CHROLLO PROPOSES A BATTLE TO THE DEATH!! AND HISOKA CONSENTS!! MORTAL COMBAT IT IS!!
ONLY ONE WILL SURVIVE!! VICTORY IS WON THROUGH THE OTHER'S DEATH!!

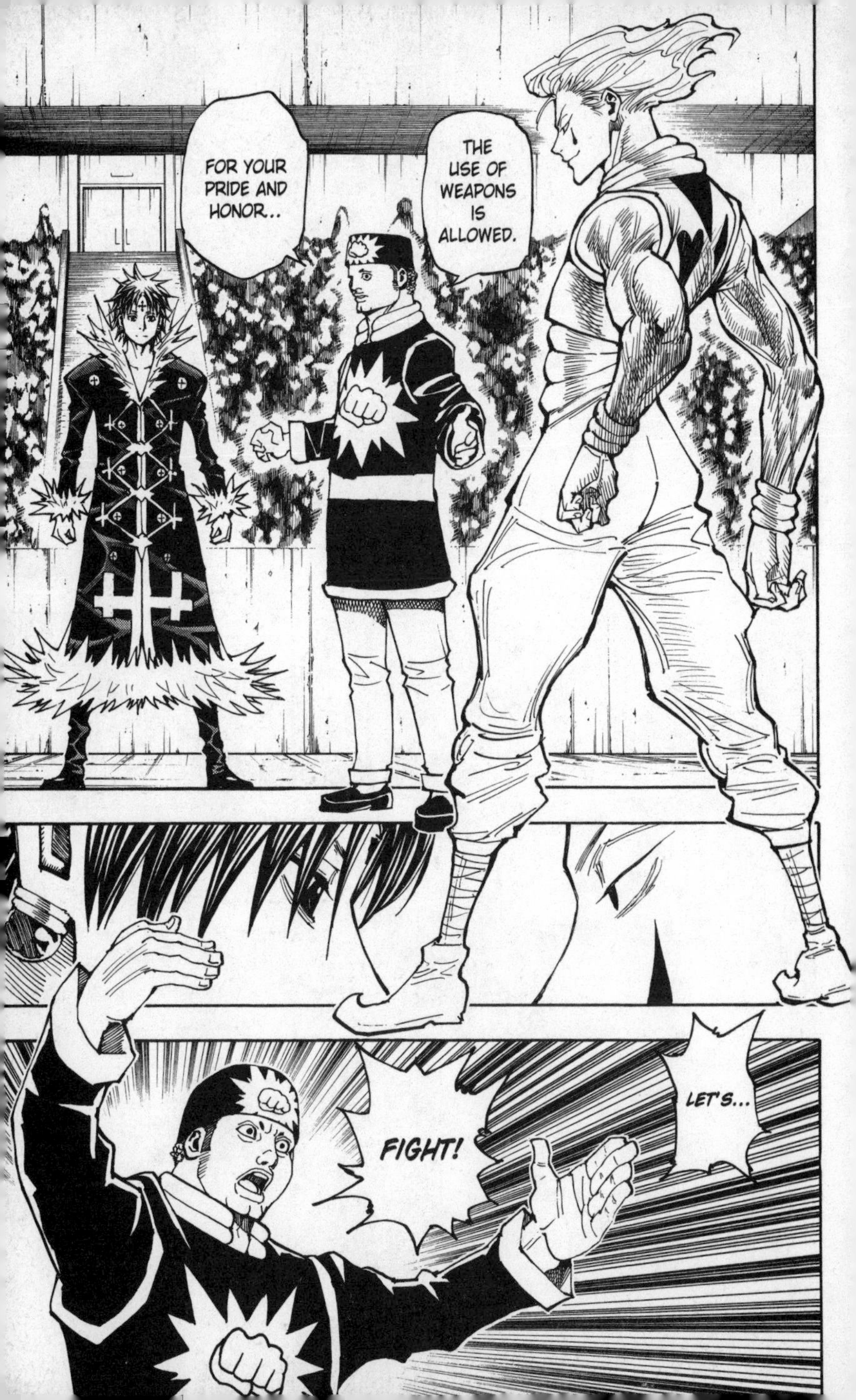
THE USE OF WEAPONS IS ALLOWED.
FOR YOUR PRIDE AND HONOR...
LET'S...
FIGHT!

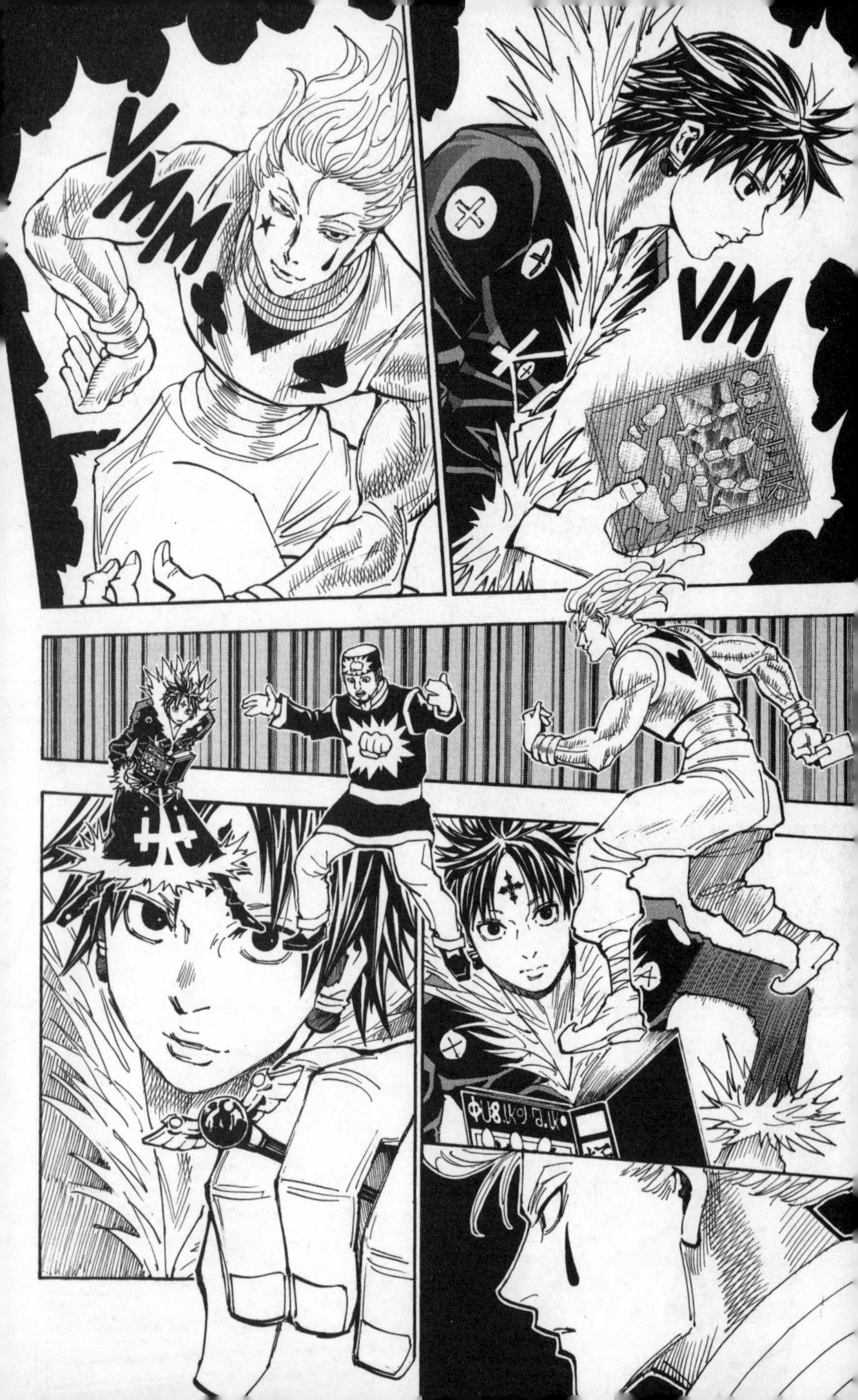
VM
VMM

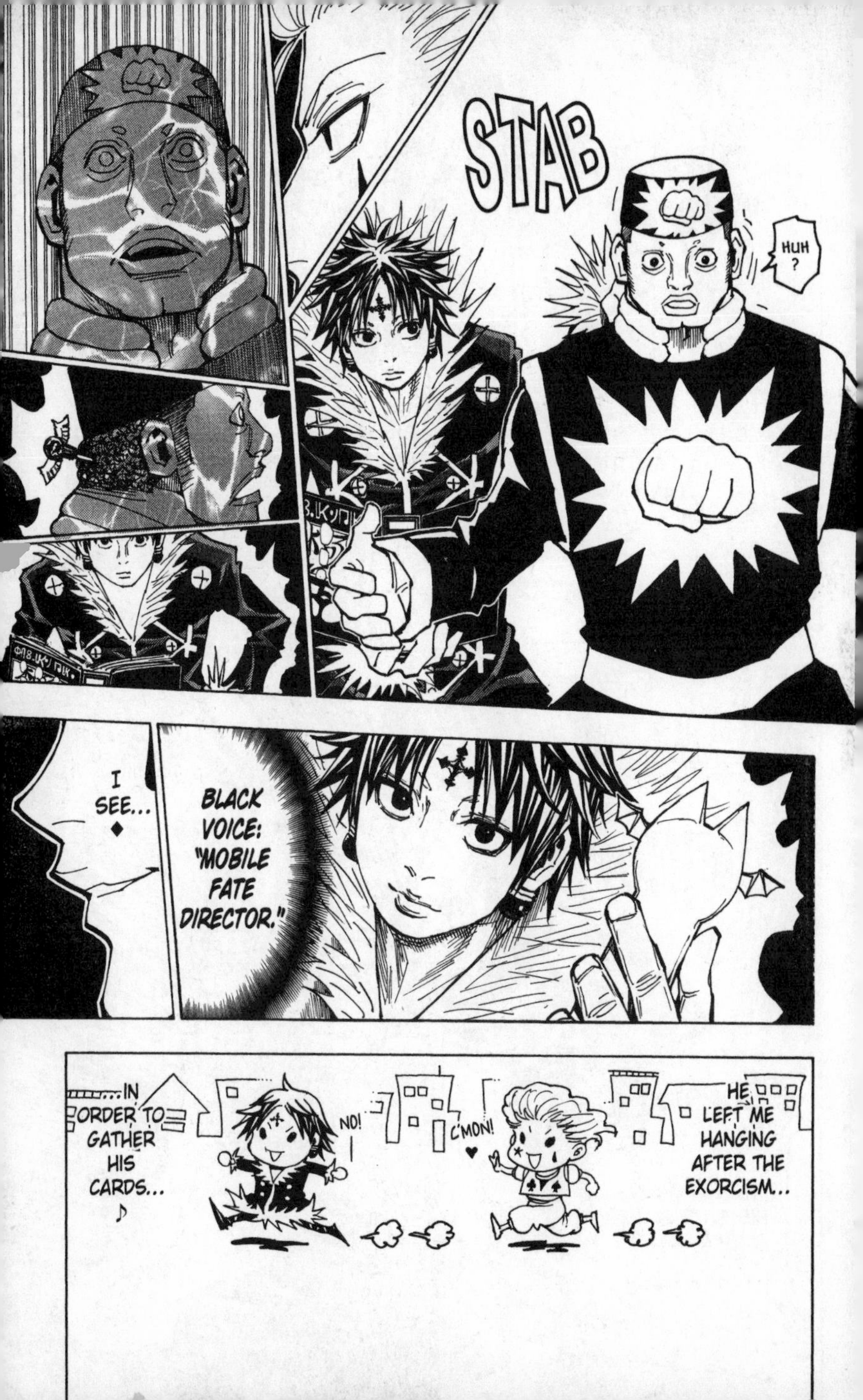
STAB
HUH ?
BLACK VOICE: "MOBILE FATE DIRECTOR."
I SEE... ♦
HE LEFT ME HANGING AFTER THE EXORCISM...
C'MON! ♥
NO!
...IN ORDER TO GATHER HIS CARDS... ♪

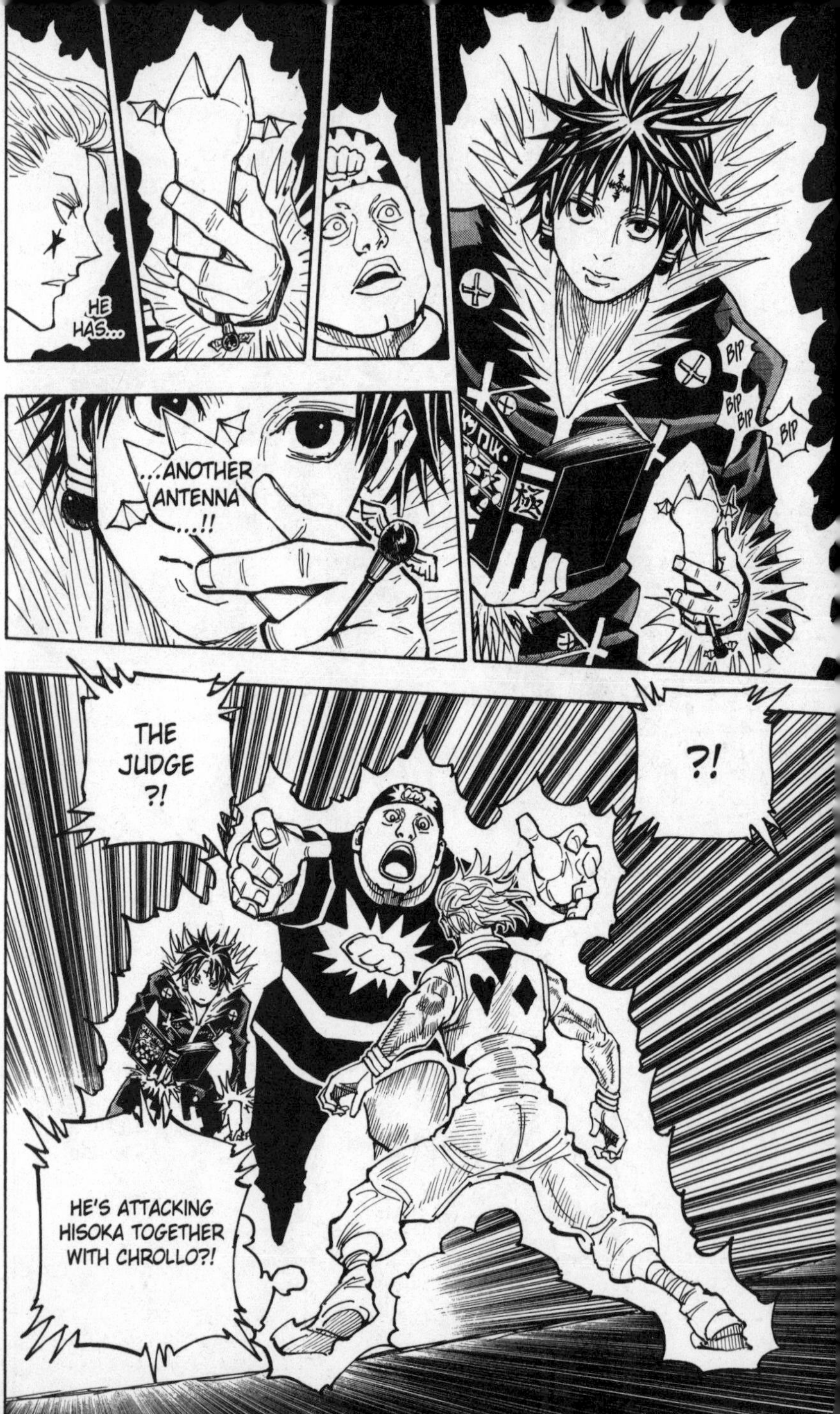
BIP
BIP
BIP
BIP
HE HAS...
...ANOTHER ANTENNA ...!!
?!
THE JUDGE ?!
HE'S ATTACKING HISOKA TOGETHER WITH CHROLLO?!

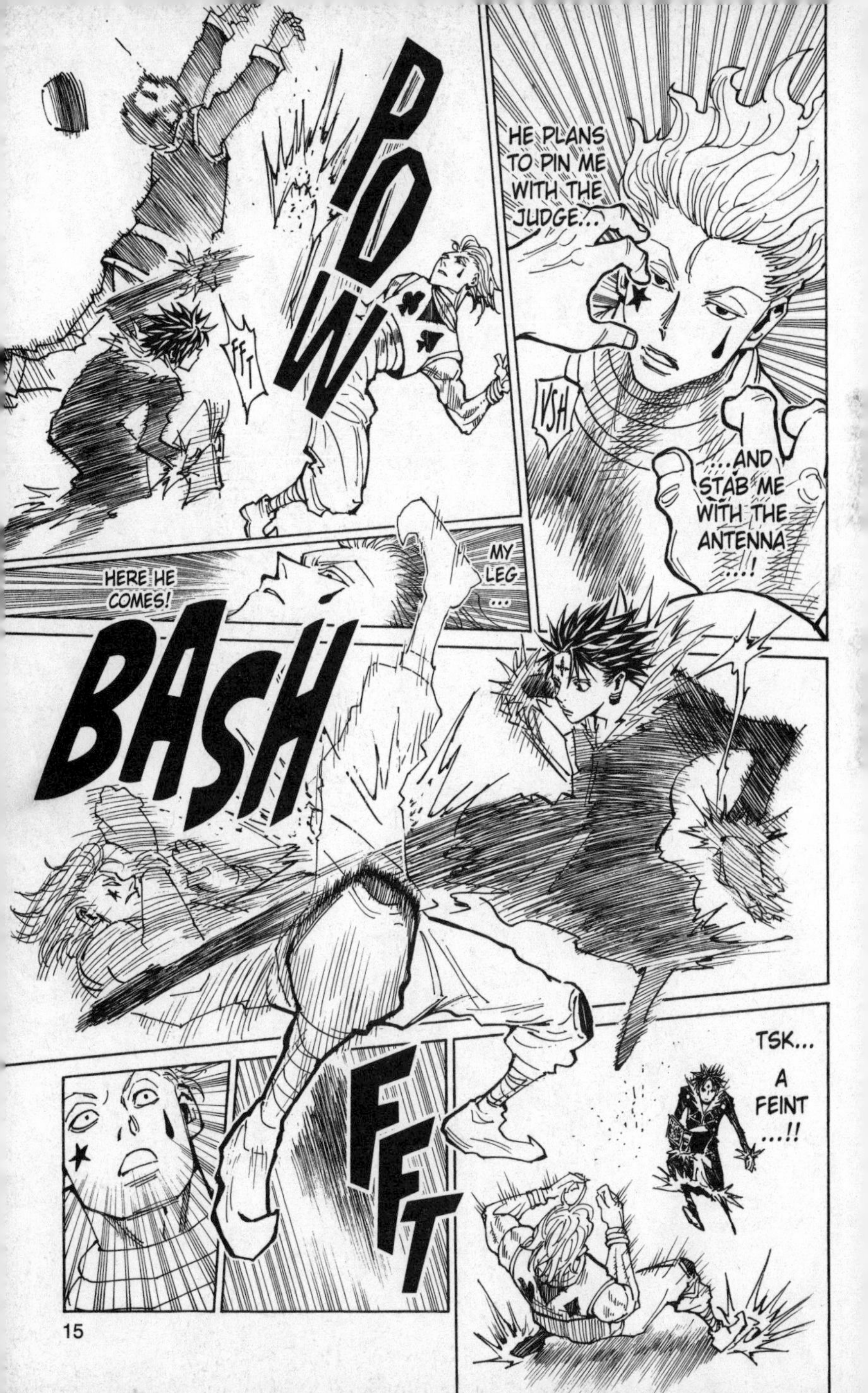
HE PLANS TO PIN ME WITH THE JUDGE...
VSH
...AND STAB ME WITH THE ANTENNA ...!
POW
FFT
MY LEG ...
HERE HE COMES!
BASH
TSK... A FEINT ...!!
FFT

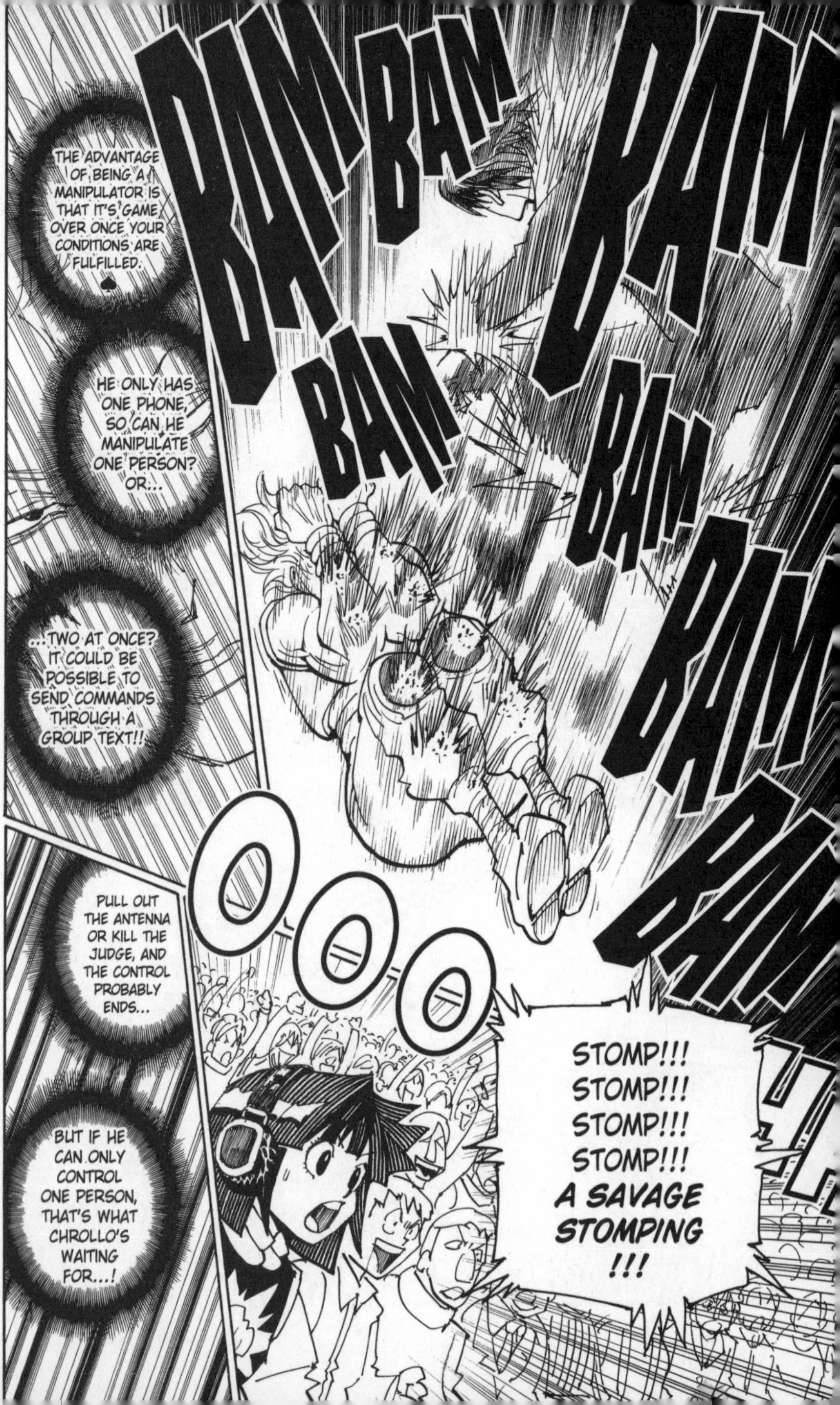
BAM BAM BAM
BAM BAM BAM BAM
THE ADVANTAGE OF BEING A MANIPULATOR IS THAT IT'S GAME OVER ONCE YOUR CONDITIONS ARE FULFILLED. ♠
HE ONLY HAS ONE PHONE, SO CAN HE MANIPULATE ONE PERSON? OR...
...TWO AT ONCE? IT COULD BE POSSIBLE TO SEND COMMANDS THROUGH A GROUP TEXT!!
OOO
STOMP!!! STOMP!!! STOMP!!! STOMP!!! A SAVAGE STOMPING !!!
PULL OUT THE ANTENNA OR KILL THE JUDGE, AND THE CONTROL PROBABLY ENDS...
BUT IF HE CAN ONLY CONTROL ONE PERSON, THAT'S WHAT CHROLLO'S WAITING FOR...!

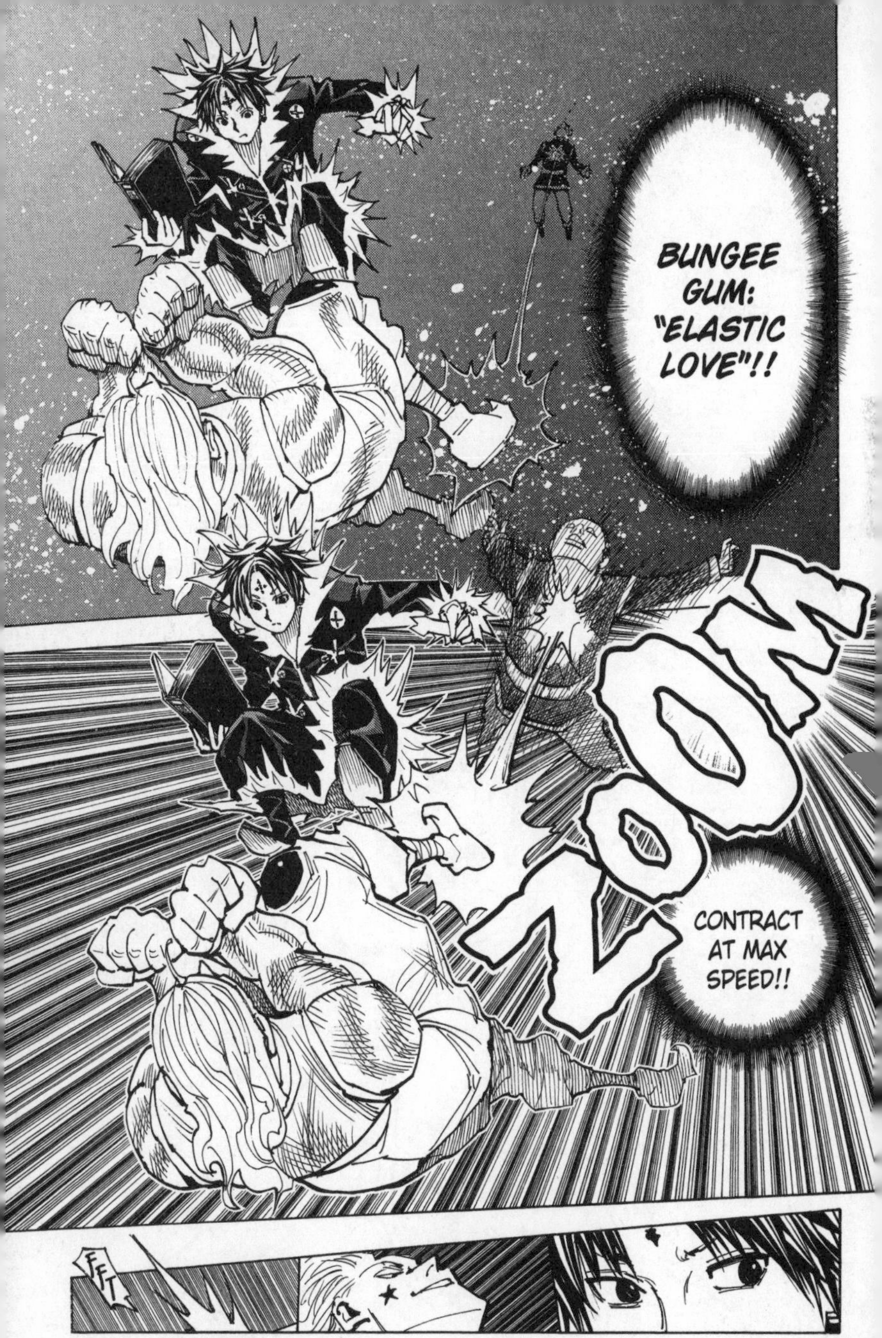
BUNGEE GUM: "ELASTIC LOVE"!!
ZOOM
CONTRACT AT MAX SPEED!!
FFFT

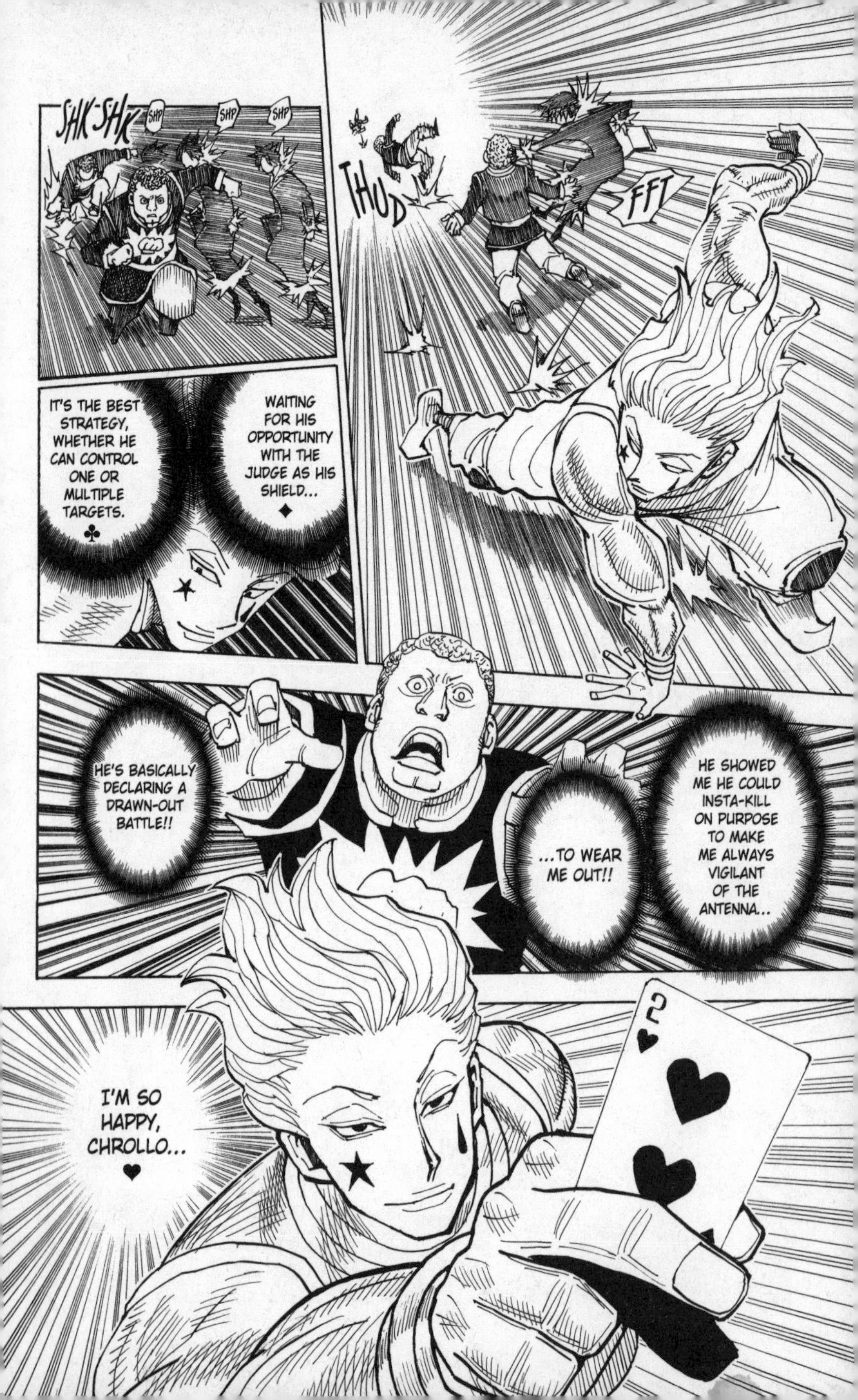
THUD
FFT
SHK-SHK
SHP
SHP
SHP
WAITING FOR HIS OPPORTUNITY WITH THE JUDGE AS HIS SHIELD... ♦
IT'S THE BEST STRATEGY, WHETHER HE CAN CONTROL ONE OR MULTIPLE TARGETS. ♣
HE SHOWED ME HE COULD INSTA-KILL ON PURPOSE TO MAKE ME ALWAYS VIGILANT OF THE ANTENNA...
...TO WEAR ME OUT!!
HE'S BASICALLY DECLARING A DRAWN-OUT BATTLE!!
I'M SO HAPPY, CHROLLO... ♥

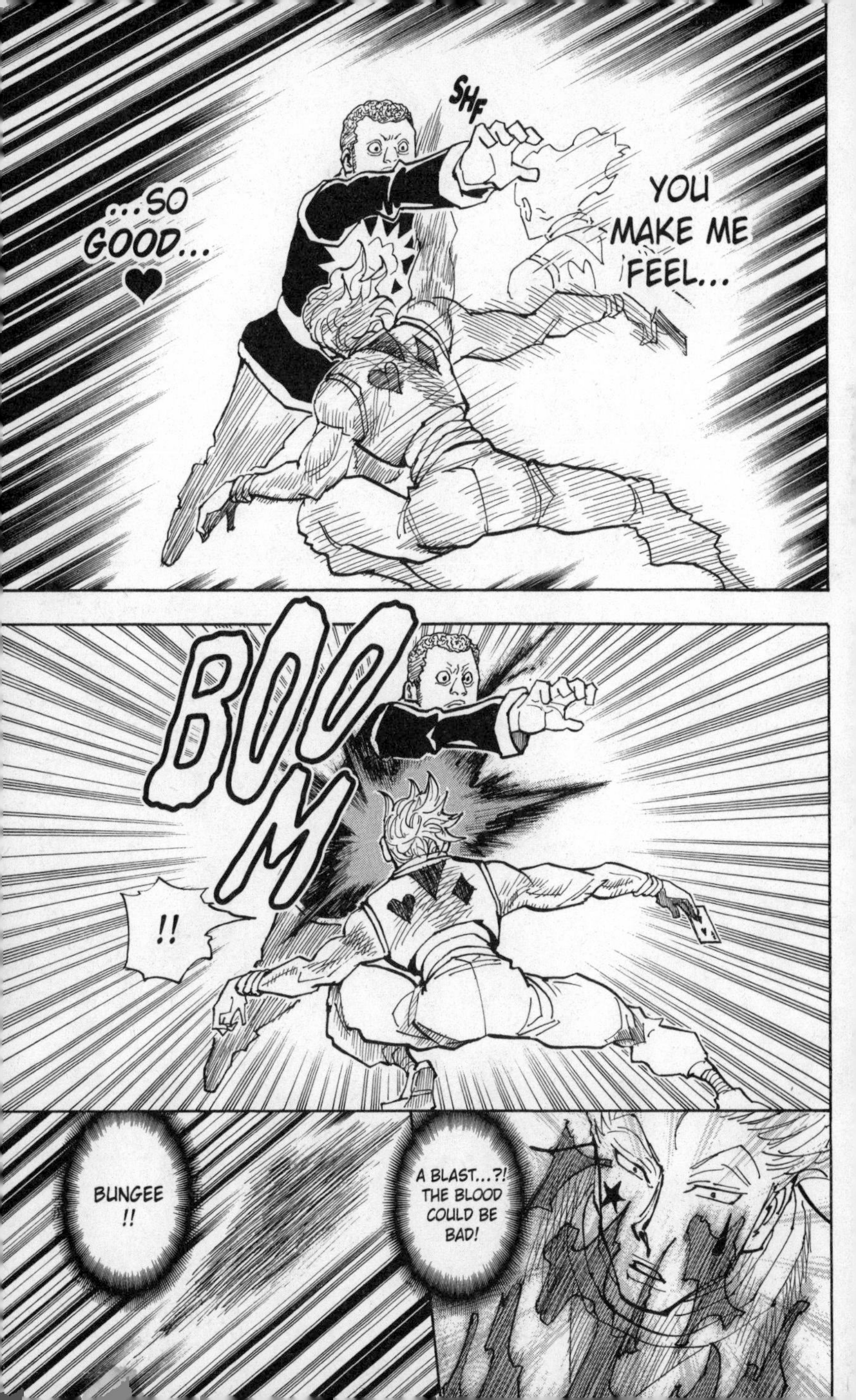
SHF
YOU MAKE ME FEEL...
...SO GOOD... ♥
BOOM
!!
A BLAST...?! THE BLOOD COULD BE BAD!
BUNGEE !!

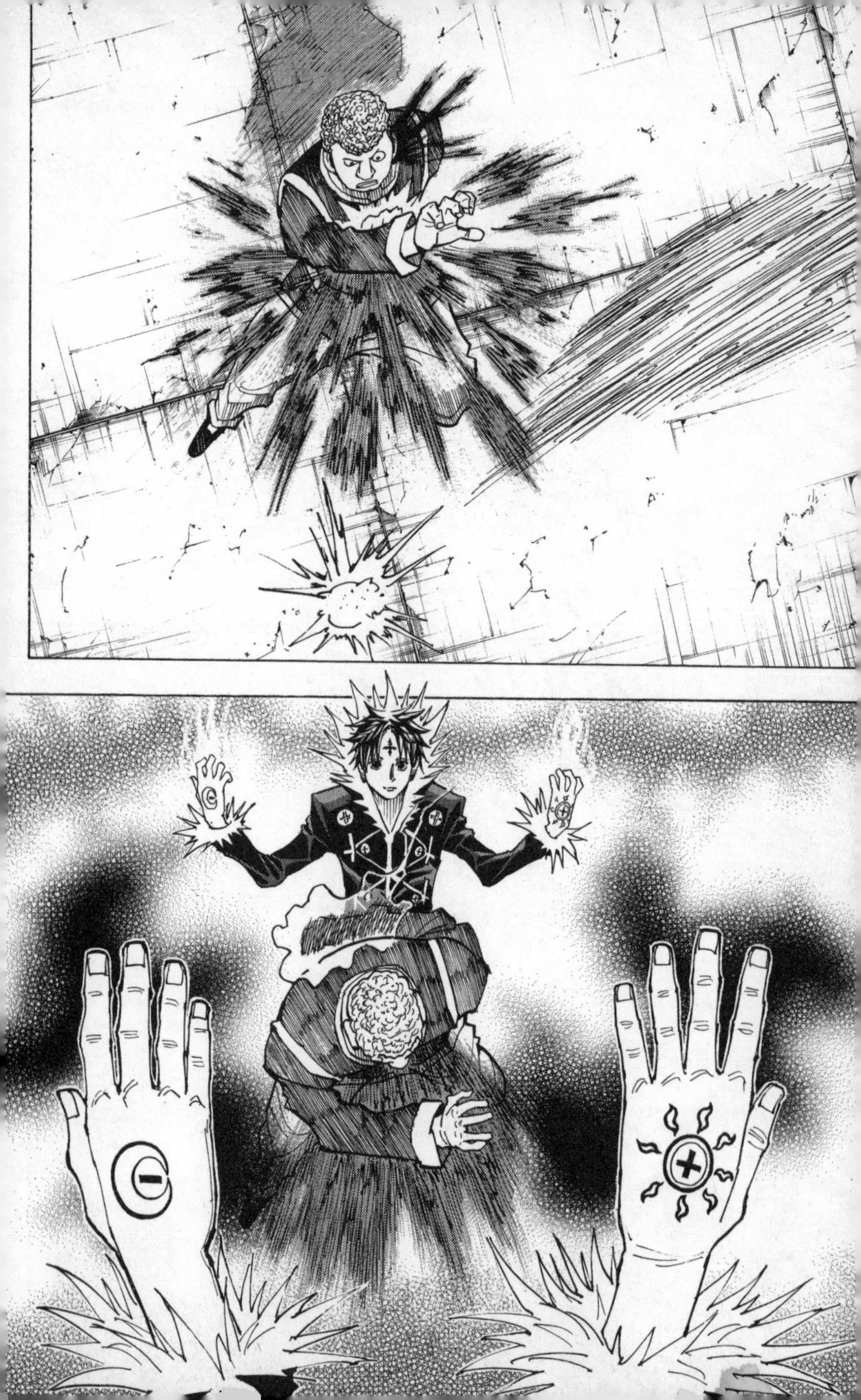

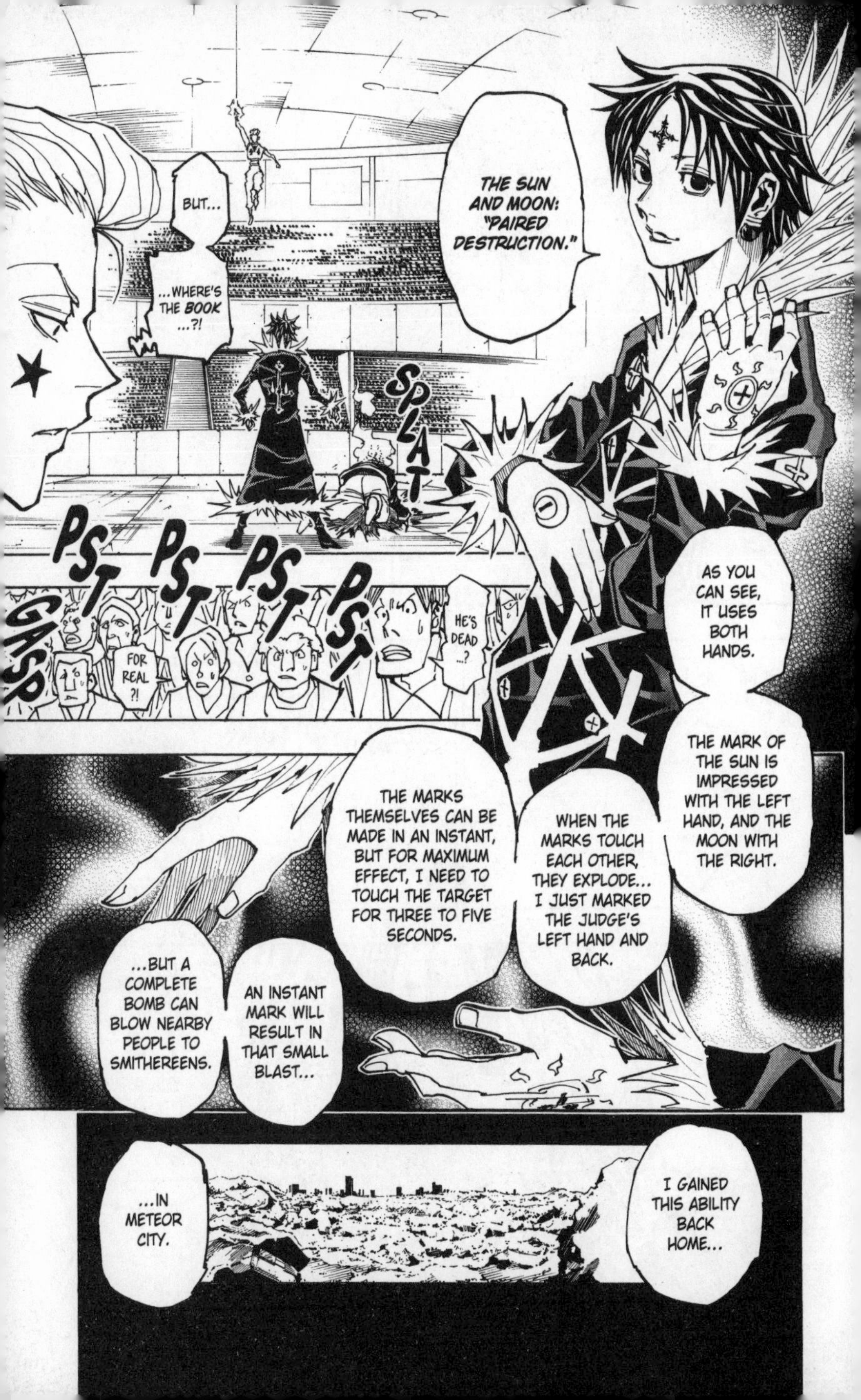
THE SUN AND MOON: "PAIRED DESTRUCTION."
BUT...
...WHERE'S THE BOOK...?!
SPLAT
HE'S DEAD...?
PST PST PST PST
FOR REAL?!
GASP
AS YOU CAN SEE, IT USES BOTH HANDS.
THE MARK OF THE SUN IS IMPRESSED WITH THE LEFT HAND, AND THE MOON WITH THE RIGHT.
WHEN THE MARKS TOUCH EACH OTHER, THEY EXPLODE... I JUST MARKED THE JUDGE'S LEFT HAND AND BACK.
THE MARKS THEMSELVES CAN BE MADE IN AN INSTANT, BUT FOR MAXIMUM EFFECT, I NEED TO TOUCH THE TARGET FOR THREE TO FIVE SECONDS.
AN INSTANT MARK WILL RESULT IN THAT SMALL BLAST...
...BUT A COMPLETE BOMB CAN BLOW NEARBY PEOPLE TO SMITHEREENS.
I GAINED THIS ABILITY BACK HOME...
...IN METEOR CITY.

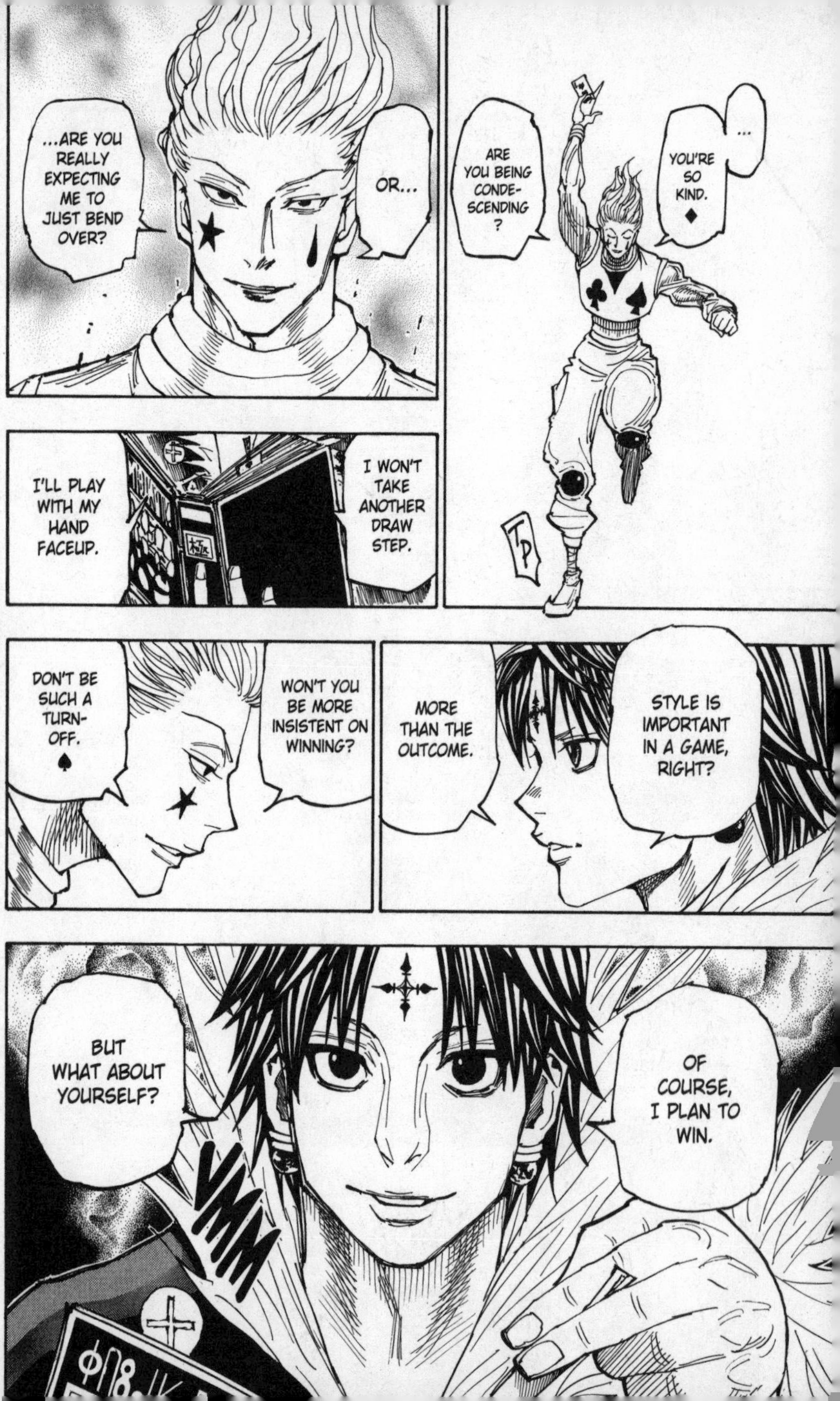
...
YOU'RE SO KIND. ♦
ARE YOU BEING CONDESCENDING?
OR...
...ARE YOU REALLY EXPECTING ME TO JUST BEND OVER?
TP
I WON'T TAKE ANOTHER DRAW STEP.
I'LL PLAY WITH MY HAND FACEUP.
STYLE IS IMPORTANT IN A GAME, RIGHT?
MORE THAN THE OUTCOME.
WON'T YOU BE MORE INSISTENT ON WINNING?
DON'T BE SUCH A TURN-OFF. ♠
OF COURSE, I PLAN TO WIN.
BUT WHAT ABOUT YOURSELF?
VMM

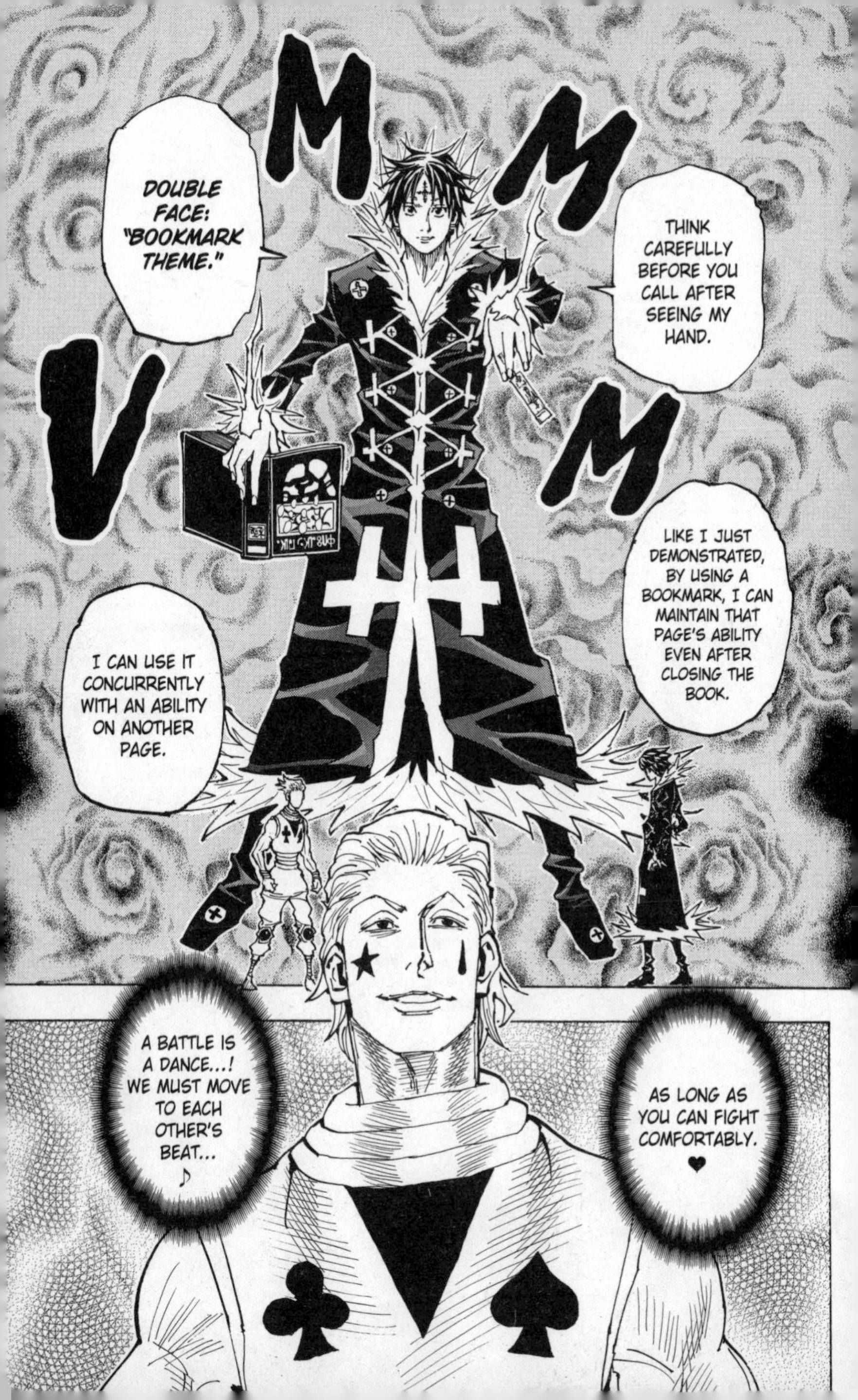
DOUBLE FACE: "BOOKMARK THEME."
VMMMM
THINK CAREFULLY BEFORE YOU CALL AFTER SEEING MY HAND.
LIKE I JUST DEMONSTRATED, BY USING A BOOKMARK, I CAN MAINTAIN THAT PAGE'S ABILITY EVEN AFTER CLOSING THE BOOK.
I CAN USE IT CONCURRENTLY WITH AN ABILITY ON ANOTHER PAGE.
AS LONG AS YOU CAN FIGHT COMFORTABLY. ♥
A BATTLE IS A DANCE...! WE MUST MOVE TO EACH OTHER'S BEAT... ♪

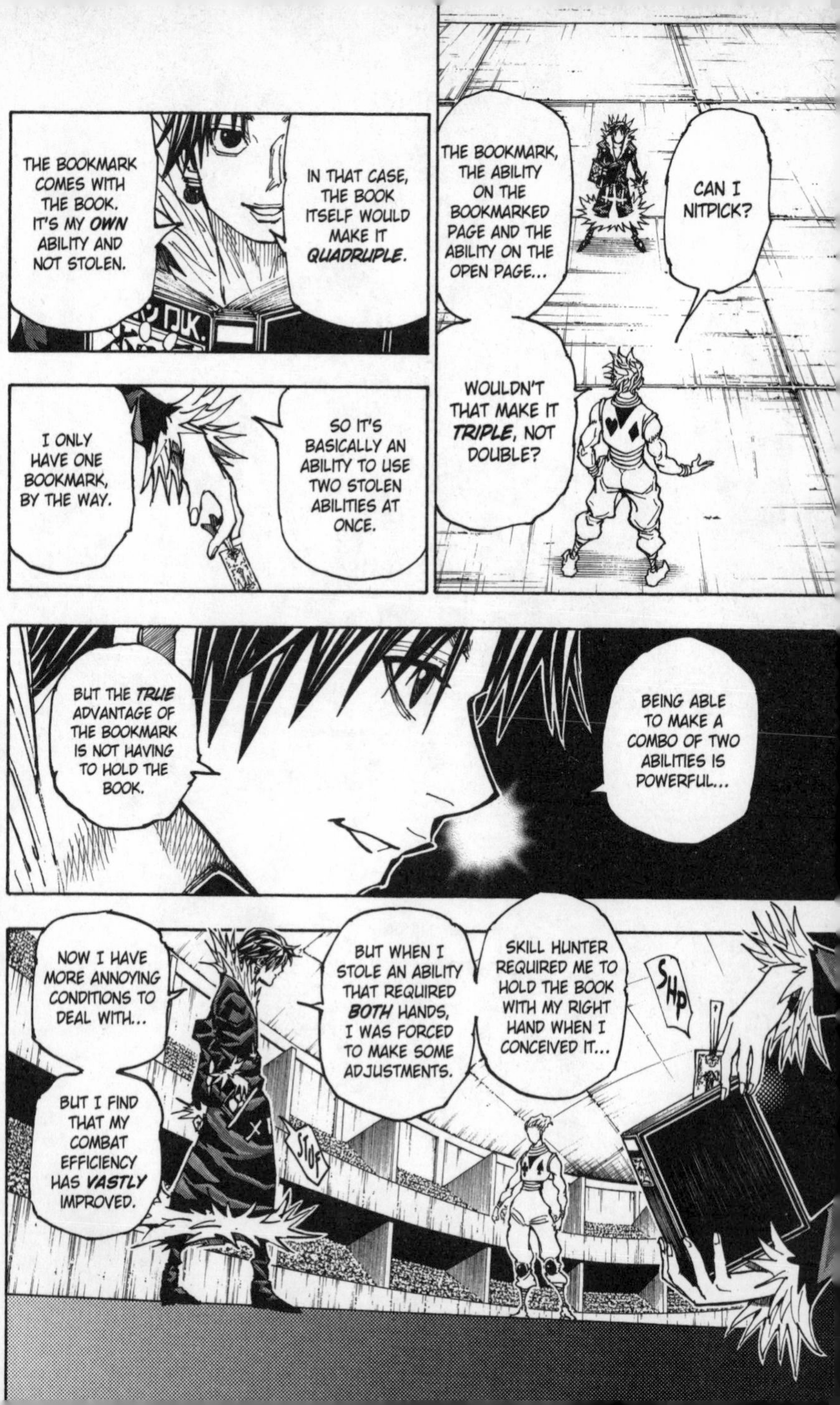
CAN I NITPICK?
THE BOOKMARK, THE ABILITY ON THE BOOKMARKED PAGE AND THE ABILITY ON THE OPEN PAGE...
WOULDN'T THAT MAKE IT *TRIPLE*, NOT DOUBLE?
IN THAT CASE, THE BOOK ITSELF WOULD MAKE IT *QUADRUPLE*.
THE BOOKMARK COMES WITH THE BOOK. IT'S MY *OWN* ABILITY AND NOT STOLEN.
SO IT'S BASICALLY AN ABILITY TO USE TWO STOLEN ABILITIES AT ONCE.
I ONLY HAVE ONE BOOKMARK, BY THE WAY.
BEING ABLE TO MAKE A COMBO OF TWO ABILITIES IS POWERFUL...
BUT THE *TRUE* ADVANTAGE OF THE BOOKMARK IS NOT HAVING TO HOLD THE BOOK.
SHP
SKILL HUNTER REQUIRED ME TO HOLD THE BOOK WITH MY RIGHT HAND WHEN I CONCEIVED IT...
BUT WHEN I STOLE AN ABILITY THAT REQUIRED *BOTH* HANDS, I WAS FORCED TO MAKE SOME ADJUSTMENTS.
NOW I HAVE MORE ANNOYING CONDITIONS TO DEAL WITH...
BUT I FIND THAT MY COMBAT EFFICIENCY HAS *VASTLY* IMPROVED.

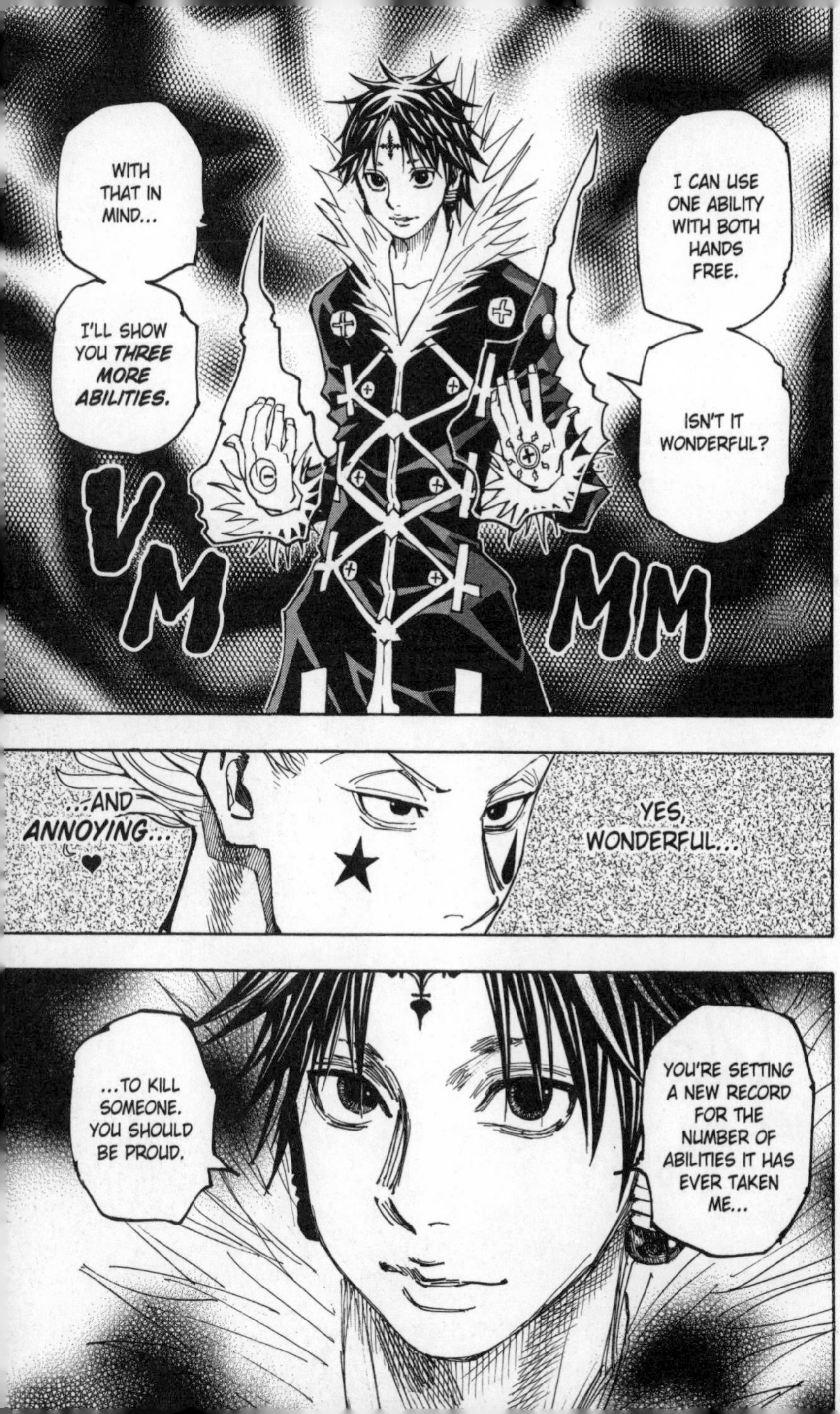

I CAN USE ONE ABILITY WITH BOTH HANDS FREE.
ISN'T IT WONDERFUL?
WITH THAT IN MIND...
I'LL SHOW YOU *THREE MORE ABILITIES.*
VMMM
YES, WONDERFUL...
...AND *ANNOYING...*
YOU'RE SETTING A NEW RECORD FOR THE NUMBER OF ABILITIES IT HAS EVER TAKEN ME...
...TO KILL SOMEONE. YOU SHOULD BE PROUD.

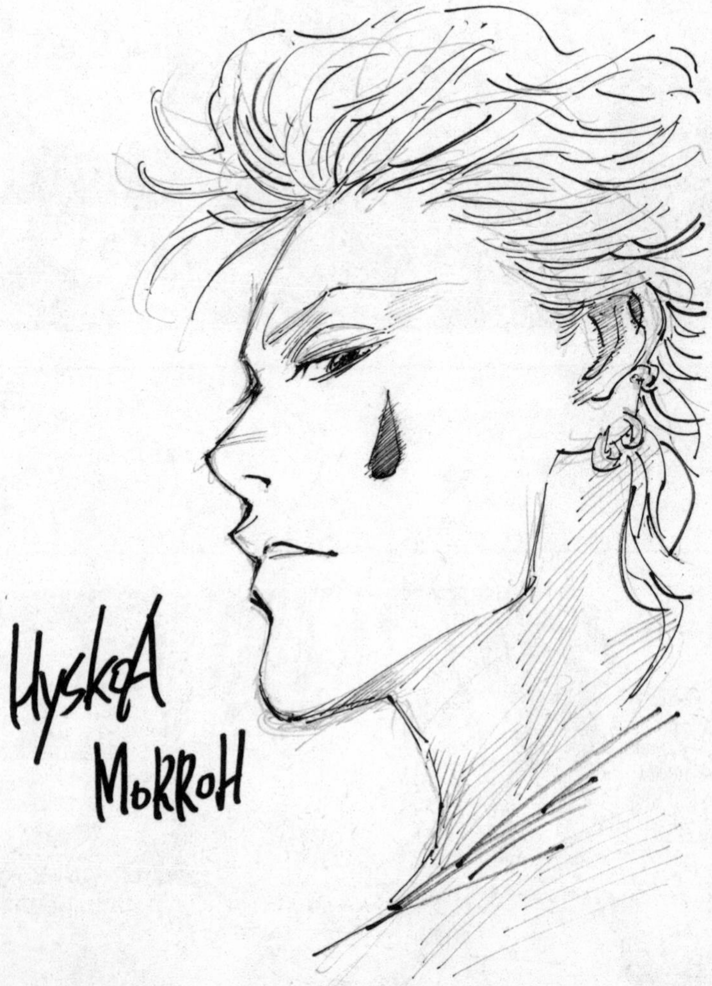
HyskoA
MoRRoH

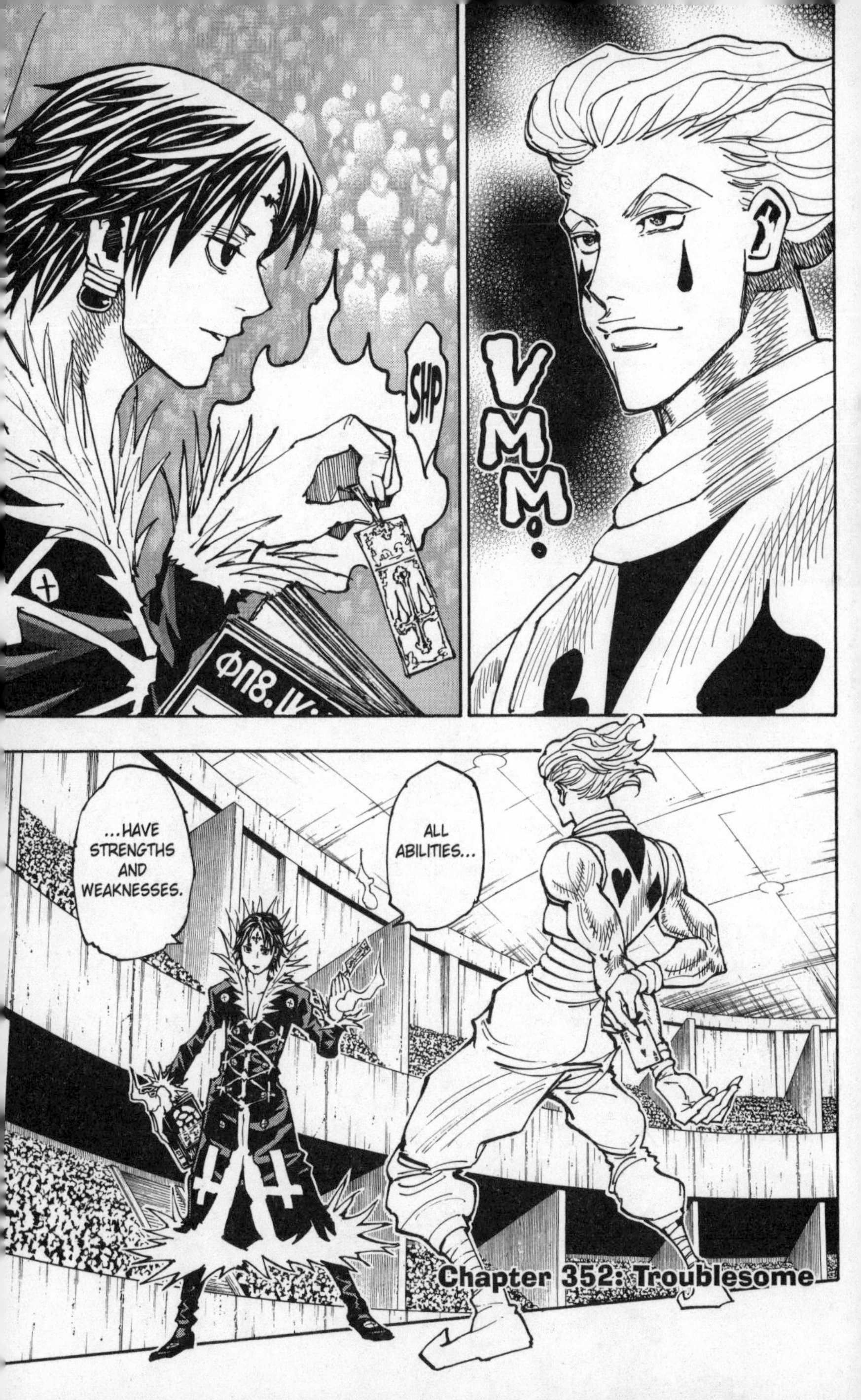
VMM...
SHP
ALL ABILITIES...
...HAVE STRENGTHS AND WEAKNESSES.
Chapter 352: Troublesome

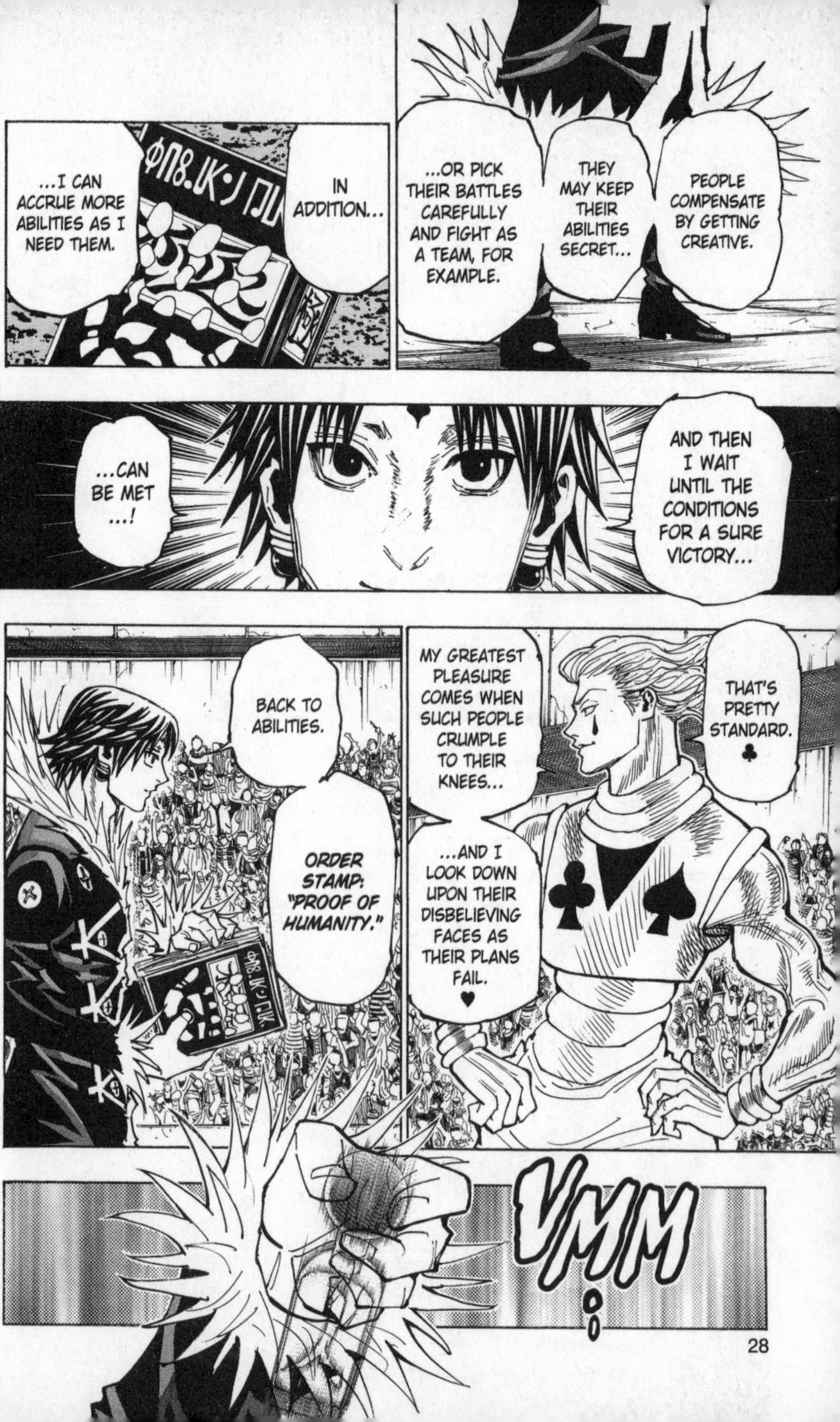
PEOPLE COMPENSATE BY GETTING CREATIVE.
THEY MAY KEEP THEIR ABILITIES SECRET...
...OR PICK THEIR BATTLES CAREFULLY AND FIGHT AS A TEAM, FOR EXAMPLE.
IN ADDITION...
...I CAN ACCRUE MORE ABILITIES AS I NEED THEM.
AND THEN I WAIT UNTIL THE CONDITIONS FOR A SURE VICTORY...
...CAN BE MET ...!
THAT'S PRETTY STANDARD. ♣
MY GREATEST PLEASURE COMES WHEN SUCH PEOPLE CRUMPLE TO THEIR KNEES...
...AND I LOOK DOWN UPON THEIR DISBELIEVING FACES AS THEIR PLANS FAIL. ♥
BACK TO ABILITIES.
ORDER STAMP: "PROOF OF HUMANITY."
VMM

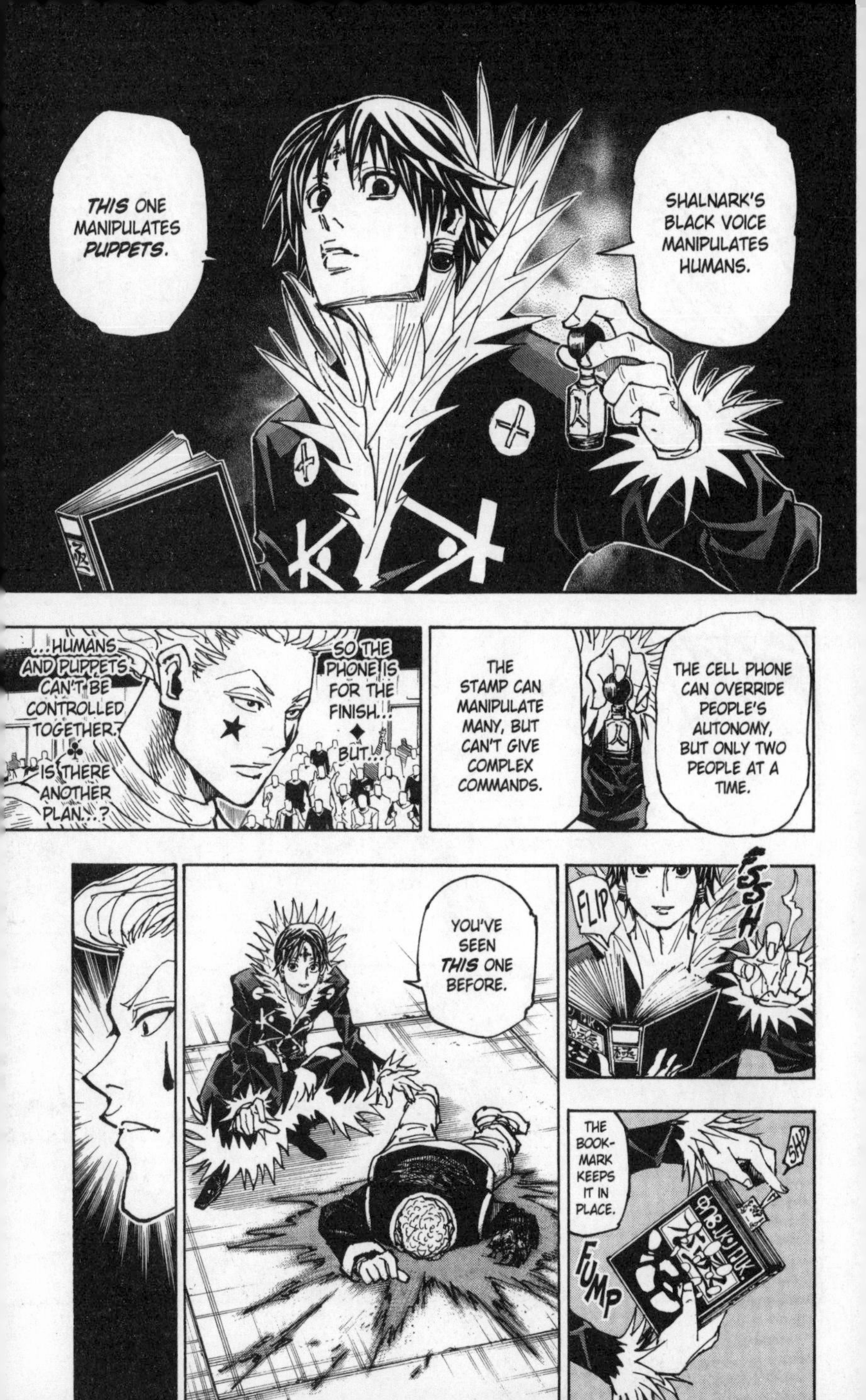
SHALNARK'S BLACK VOICE MANIPULATES HUMANS.
THIS ONE MANIPULATES PUPPETS.
THE CELL PHONE CAN OVERRIDE PEOPLE'S AUTONOMY, BUT ONLY TWO PEOPLE AT A TIME.
THE STAMP CAN MANIPULATE MANY, BUT CAN'T GIVE COMPLEX COMMANDS.
SO THE PHONE IS FOR THE FINISH...
BUT...
...HUMANS AND PUPPETS CAN'T BE CONTROLLED TOGETHER.
IS THERE ANOTHER PLAN...?
FSSH
FLIP
SHP
THE BOOK-MARK KEEPS IT IN PLACE.
FUMP
YOU'VE SEEN THIS ONE BEFORE.

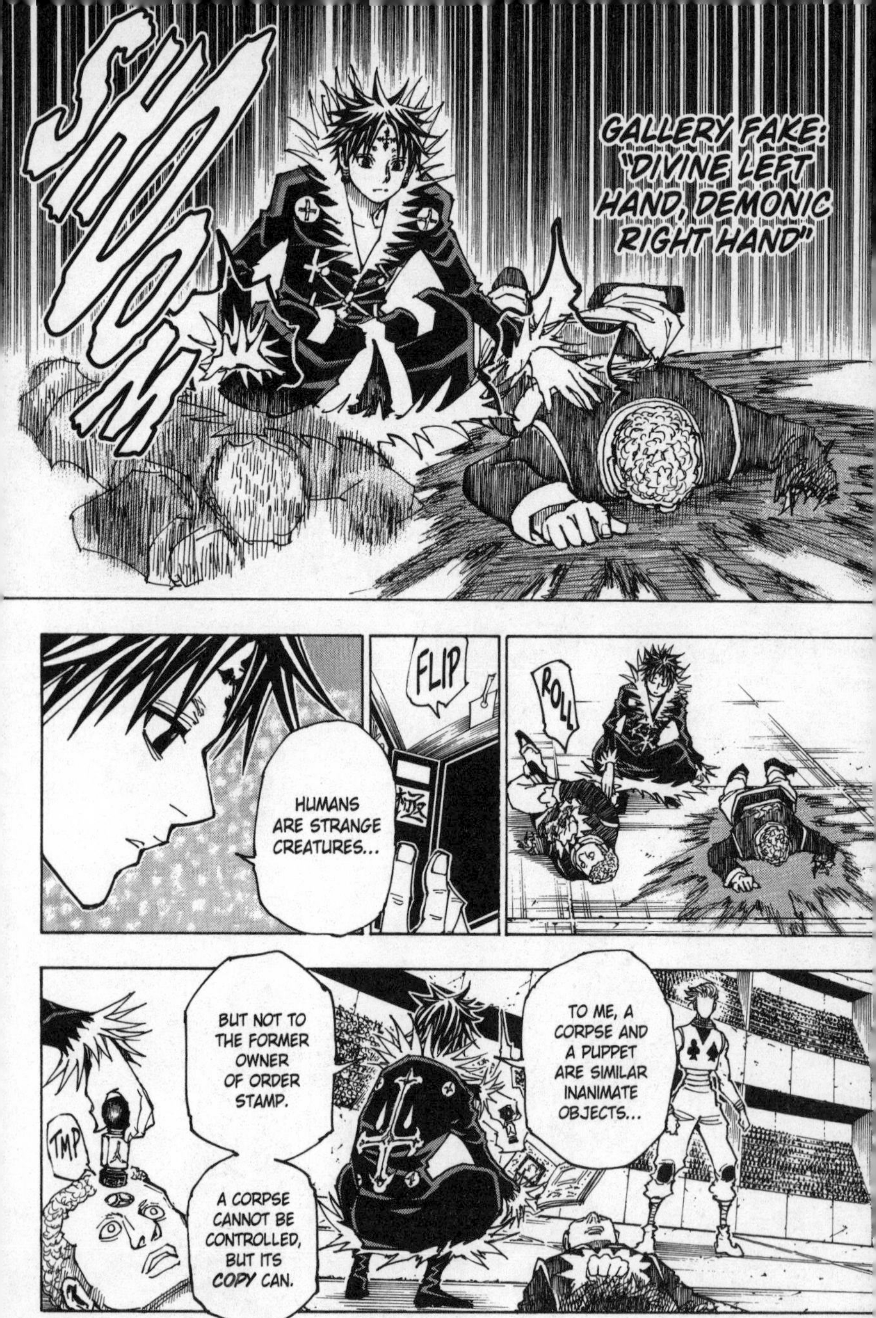
GALLERY FAKE: "DIVINE LEFT HAND, DEMONIC RIGHT HAND"
SHOOM
ROLL
FLIP
HUMANS ARE STRANGE CREATURES...
TO ME, A CORPSE AND A PUPPET ARE SIMILAR INANIMATE OBJECTS...
BUT NOT TO THE FORMER OWNER OF ORDER STAMP.
A CORPSE CANNOT BE CONTROLLED, BUT ITS *COPY* CAN.
TMP

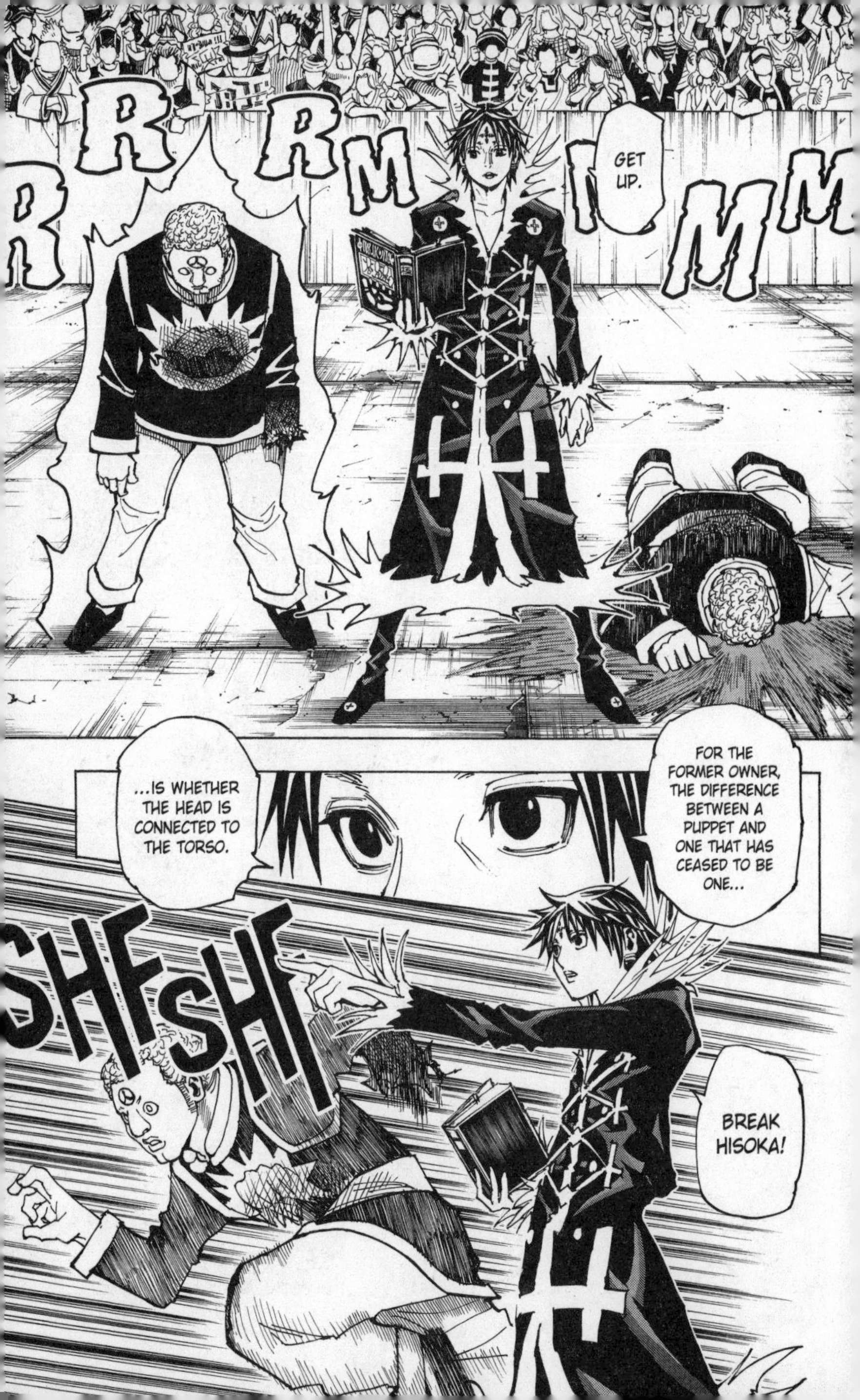
GET UP.
RRRMMMM
FOR THE FORMER OWNER, THE DIFFERENCE BETWEEN A PUPPET AND ONE THAT HAS CEASED TO BE ONE...
...IS WHETHER THE HEAD IS CONNECTED TO THE TORSO.
BREAK HISOKA!
SHFSHF

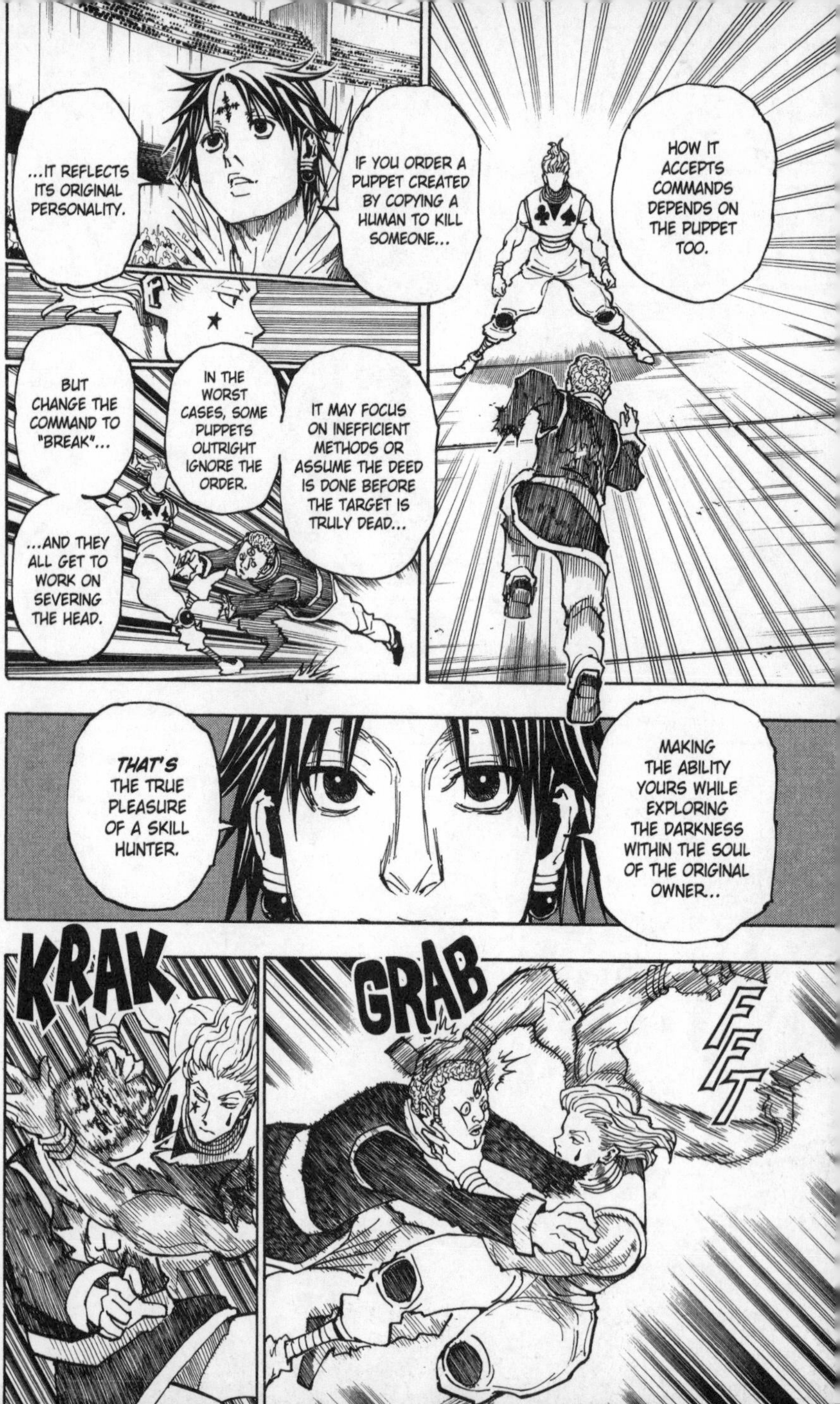
HOW IT ACCEPTS COMMANDS DEPENDS ON THE PUPPET TOO.
IF YOU ORDER A PUPPET CREATED BY COPYING A HUMAN TO KILL SOMEONE...
...IT REFLECTS ITS ORIGINAL PERSONALITY.
IT MAY FOCUS ON INEFFICIENT METHODS OR ASSUME THE DEED IS DONE BEFORE THE TARGET IS TRULY DEAD...
IN THE WORST CASES, SOME PUPPETS OUTRIGHT IGNORE THE ORDER.
BUT CHANGE THE COMMAND TO "BREAK"...
...AND THEY ALL GET TO WORK ON SEVERING THE HEAD.
MAKING THE ABILITY YOURS WHILE EXPLORING THE DARKNESS WITHIN THE SOUL OF THE ORIGINAL OWNER..
THAT'S THE TRUE PLEASURE OF A SKILL HUNTER.
FFT
GRAB
KRAK

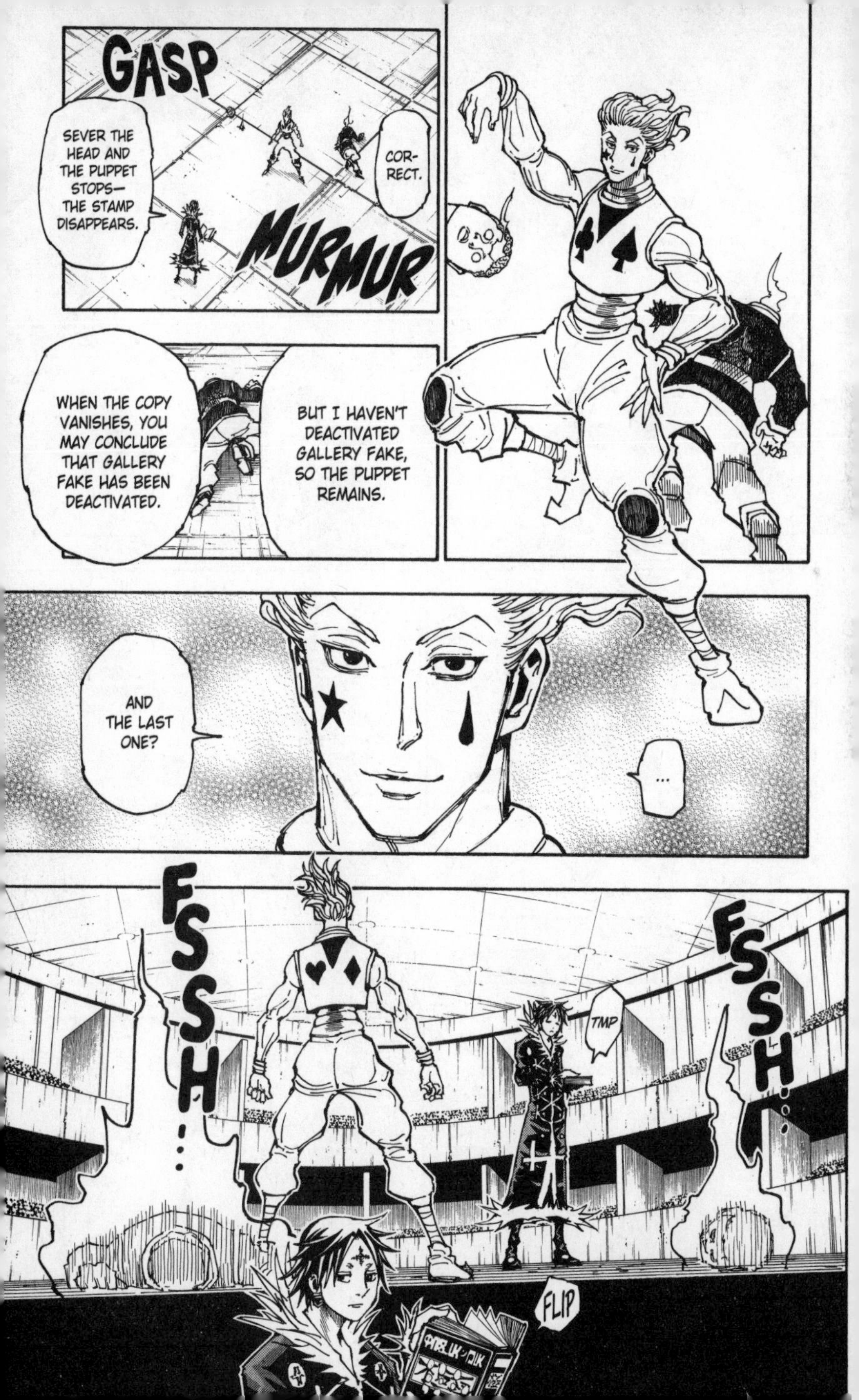
GASP
SEVER THE HEAD AND THE PUPPET STOPS— THE STAMP DISAPPEARS.
CORRECT.
MURMUR
WHEN THE COPY VANISHES, YOU MAY CONCLUDE THAT GALLERY FAKE HAS BEEN DEACTIVATED.
BUT I HAVEN'T DEACTIVATED GALLERY FAKE, SO THE PUPPET REMAINS.
...
AND THE LAST ONE?
FSSH...
TMP
FSSH...
FLIP

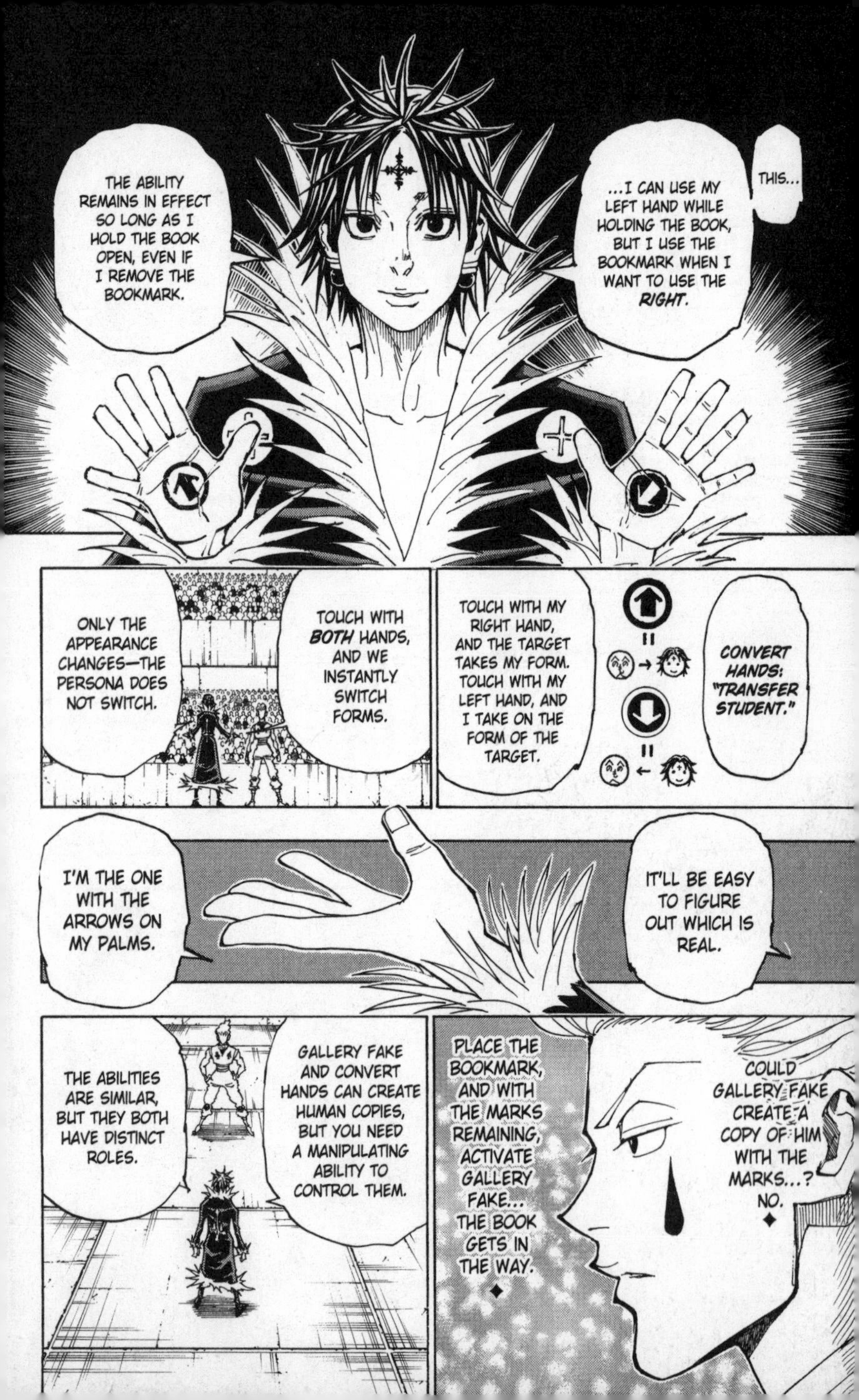
THIS...
...I CAN USE MY LEFT HAND WHILE HOLDING THE BOOK, BUT I USE THE BOOKMARK WHEN I WANT TO USE THE *RIGHT*.
THE ABILITY REMAINS IN EFFECT SO LONG AS I HOLD THE BOOK OPEN, EVEN IF I REMOVE THE BOOKMARK.
CONVERT HANDS: "TRANSFER STUDENT."
TOUCH WITH MY RIGHT HAND, AND THE TARGET TAKES MY FORM. TOUCH WITH MY LEFT HAND, AND I TAKE ON THE FORM OF THE TARGET.
TOUCH WITH *BOTH* HANDS, AND WE INSTANTLY SWITCH FORMS.
ONLY THE APPEARANCE CHANGES—THE PERSONA DOES NOT SWITCH.
IT'LL BE EASY TO FIGURE OUT WHICH IS REAL.
I'M THE ONE WITH THE ARROWS ON MY PALMS.
COULD GALLERY FAKE CREATE A COPY OF HIM WITH THE MARKS...? NO.
PLACE THE BOOKMARK, AND WITH THE MARKS REMAINING, ACTIVATE GALLERY FAKE... THE BOOK GETS IN THE WAY.
GALLERY FAKE AND CONVERT HANDS CAN CREATE HUMAN COPIES, BUT YOU NEED A MANIPULATING ABILITY TO CONTROL THEM.
THE ABILITIES ARE SIMILAR, BUT THEY BOTH HAVE DISTINCT ROLES.

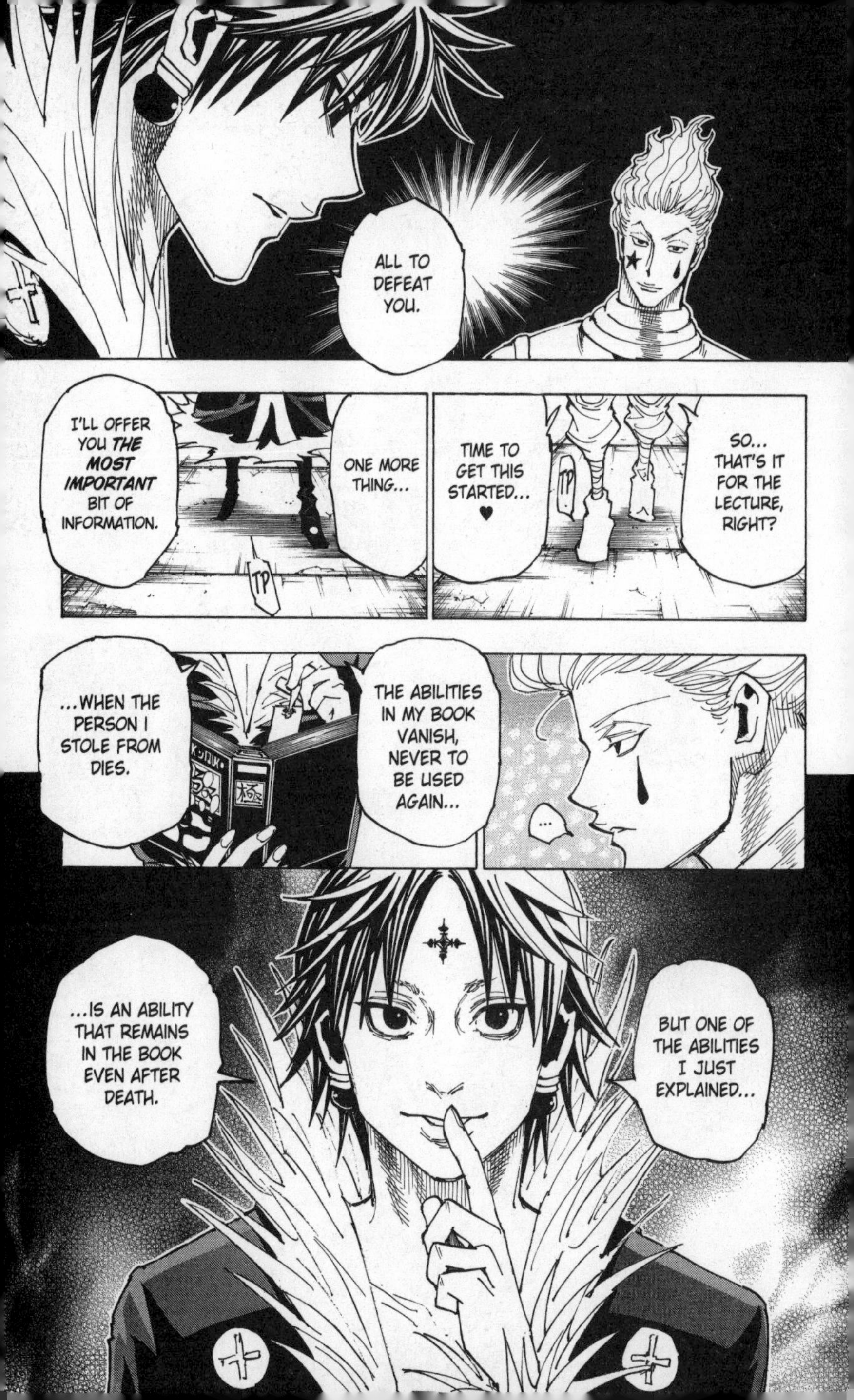
ALL TO DEFEAT YOU.
SO... THAT'S IT FOR THE LECTURE, RIGHT?
TIME TO GET THIS STARTED... ♥
TP
ONE MORE THING...
I'LL OFFER YOU *THE MOST IMPORTANT* BIT OF INFORMATION.
TP
...
THE ABILITIES IN MY BOOK VANISH, NEVER TO BE USED AGAIN...
...WHEN THE PERSON I STOLE FROM DIES.
BUT ONE OF THE ABILITIES I JUST EXPLAINED...
...IS AN ABILITY THAT REMAINS IN THE BOOK EVEN AFTER DEATH.

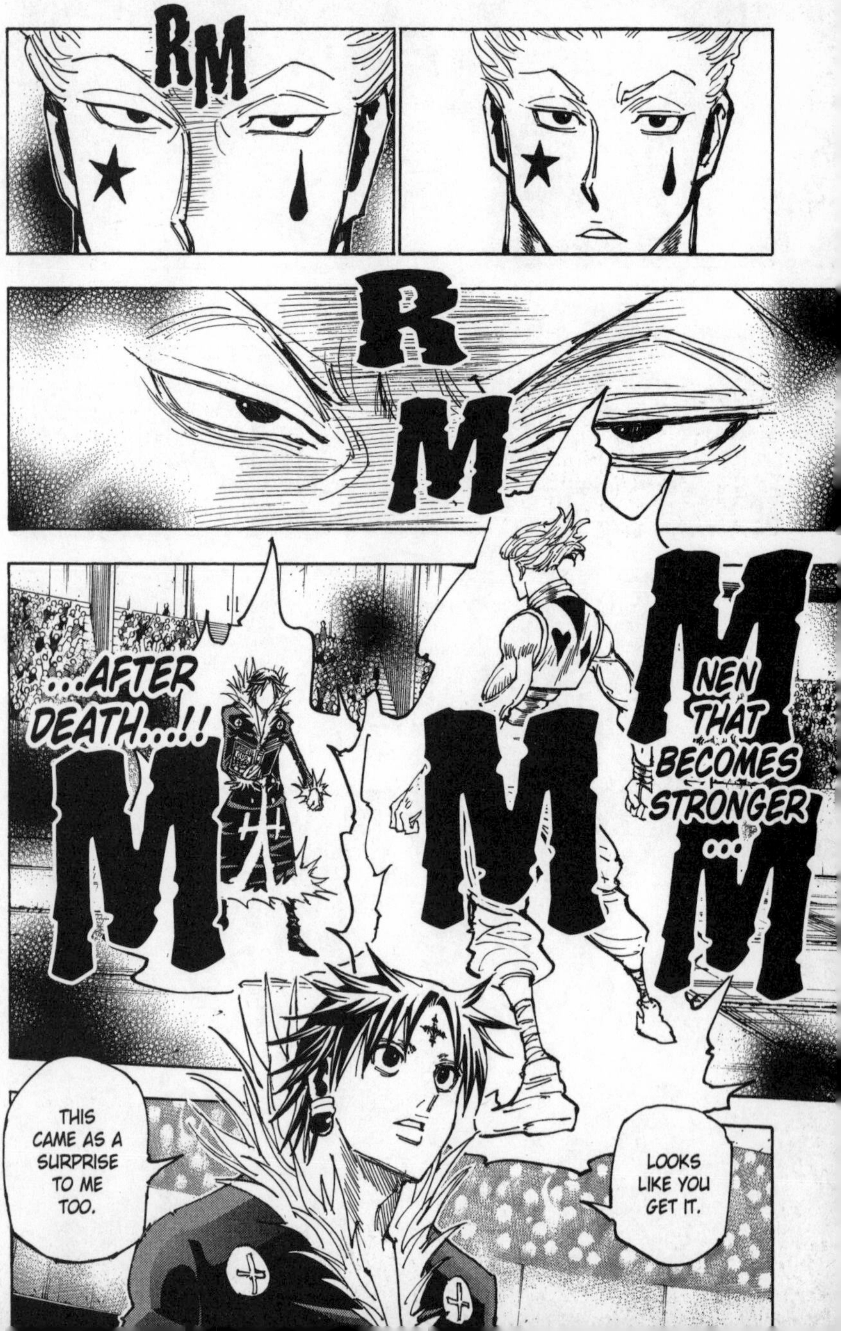
RM
R
M
NEN THAT BECOMES STRONGER...
...AFTER DEATH...!!
MMMM
LOOKS LIKE YOU GET IT.
THIS CAME AS A SURPRISE TO ME TOO.

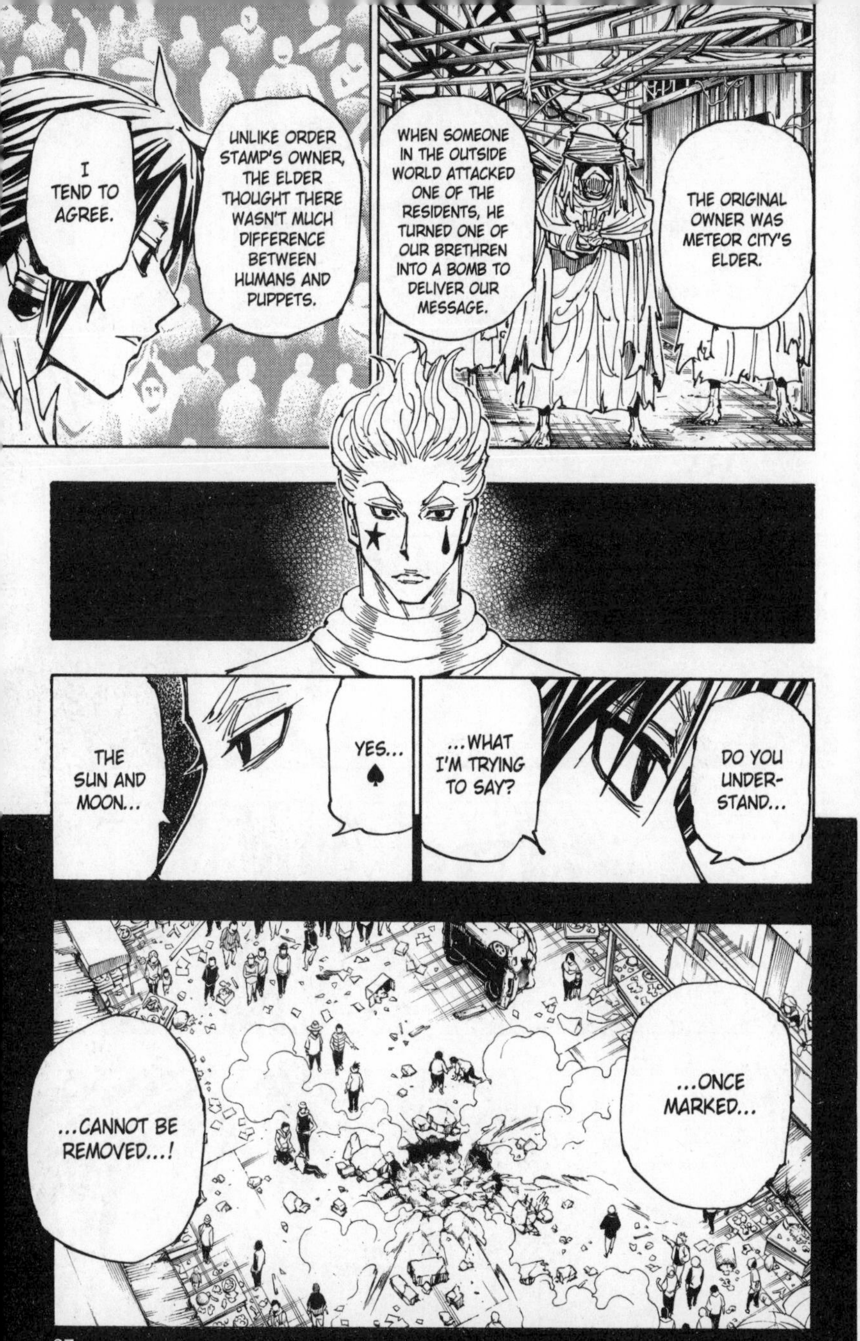
THE ORIGINAL OWNER WAS METEOR CITY'S ELDER.
WHEN SOMEONE IN THE OUTSIDE WORLD ATTACKED ONE OF THE RESIDENTS, HE TURNED ONE OF OUR BRETHREN INTO A BOMB TO DELIVER OUR MESSAGE.
UNLIKE ORDER STAMP'S OWNER, THE ELDER THOUGHT THERE WASN'T MUCH DIFFERENCE BETWEEN HUMANS AND PUPPETS.
I TEND TO AGREE.
DO YOU UNDERSTAND...
...WHAT I'M TRYING TO SAY?
YES... ♠
THE SUN AND MOON...
...ONCE MARKED...
...CANNOT BE REMOVED...!

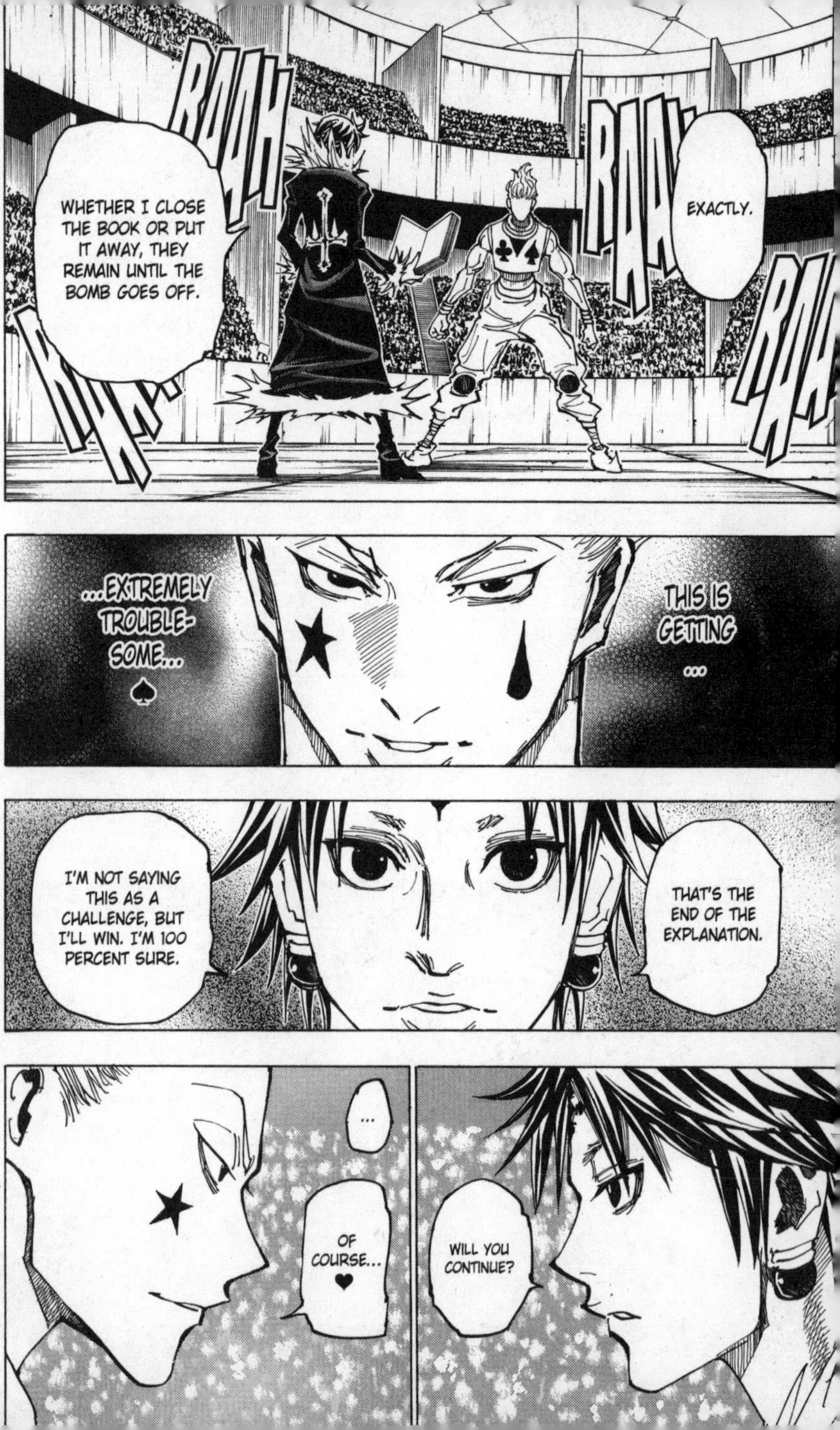
RAAH
EXACTLY.
RAAH
RAAH
WHETHER I CLOSE THE BOOK OR PUT IT AWAY, THEY REMAIN UNTIL THE BOMB GOES OFF.
RAAH
THIS IS GETTING...
...EXTREMELY TROUBLE-SOME... ♠
THAT'S THE END OF THE EXPLANATION.
I'M NOT SAYING THIS AS A CHALLENGE, BUT I'LL WIN. I'M 100 PERCENT SURE.
WILL YOU CONTINUE?
...
OF COURSE... ♥

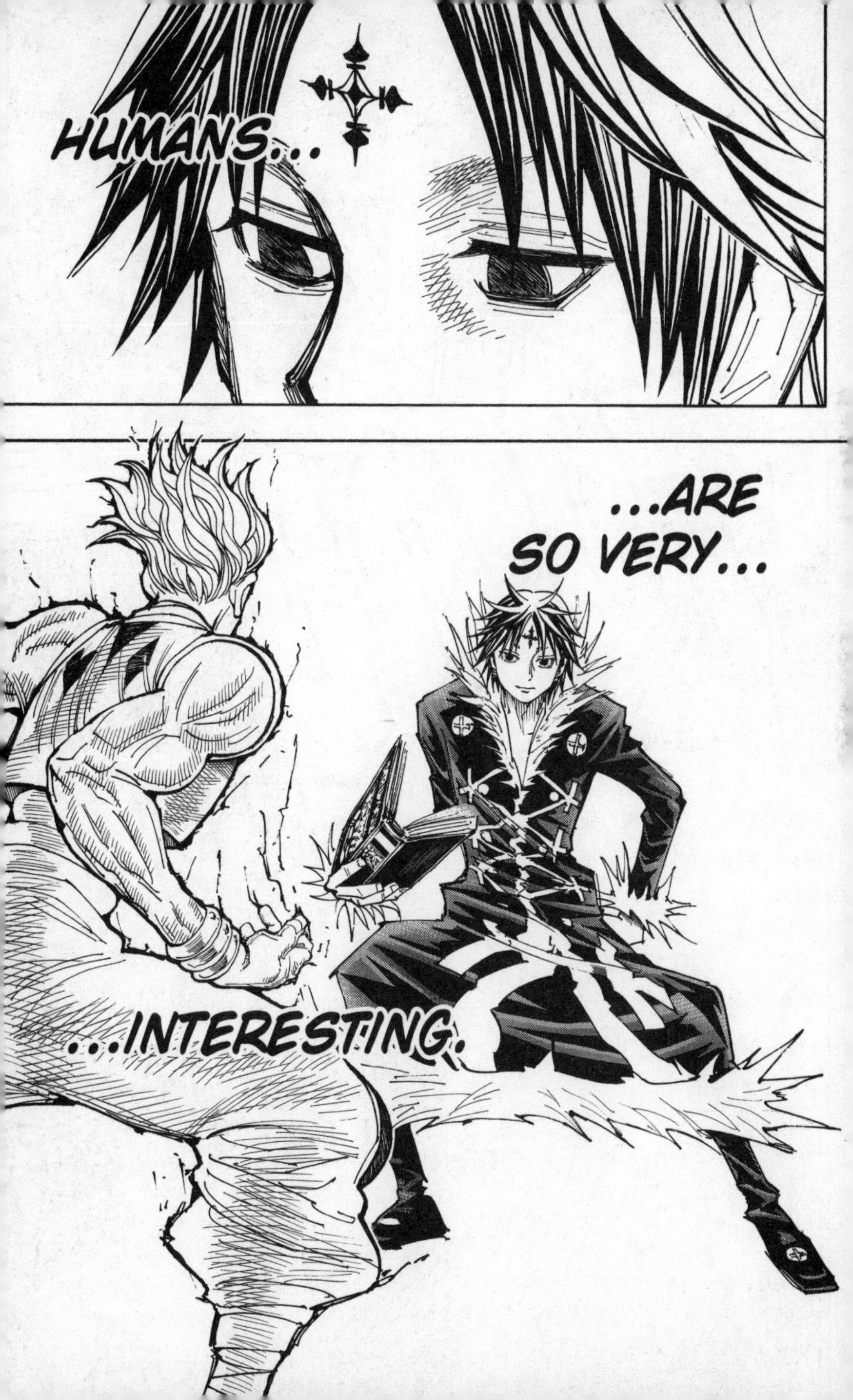
HUMANS...
...ARE SO VERY...
...INTERESTING.

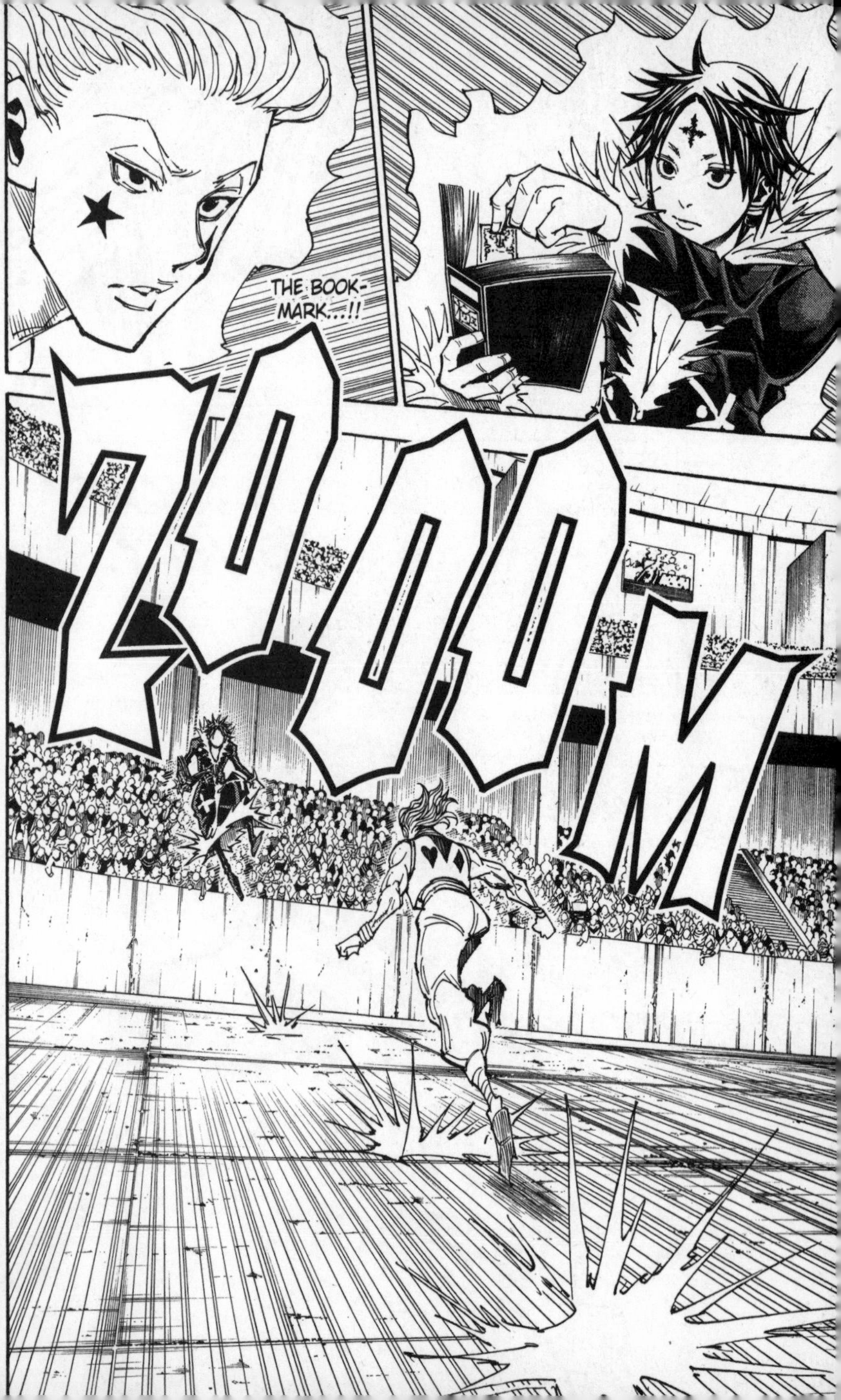
THE BOOK-
MARK...!!
ZOOOM

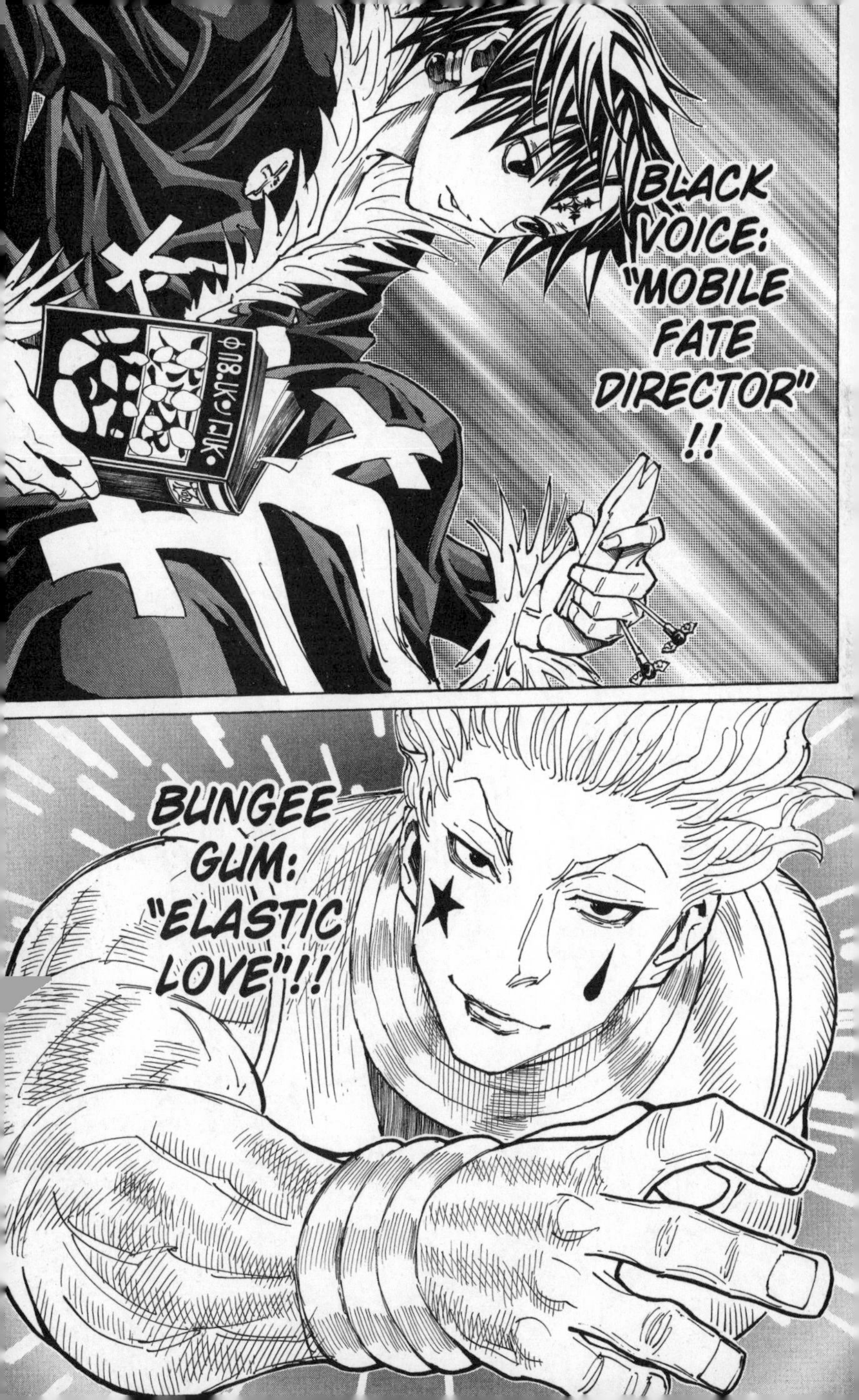
BLACK VOICE: "MOBILE FATE DIRECTOR"!!
BUNGEE GUM: "ELASTIC LOVE"!!

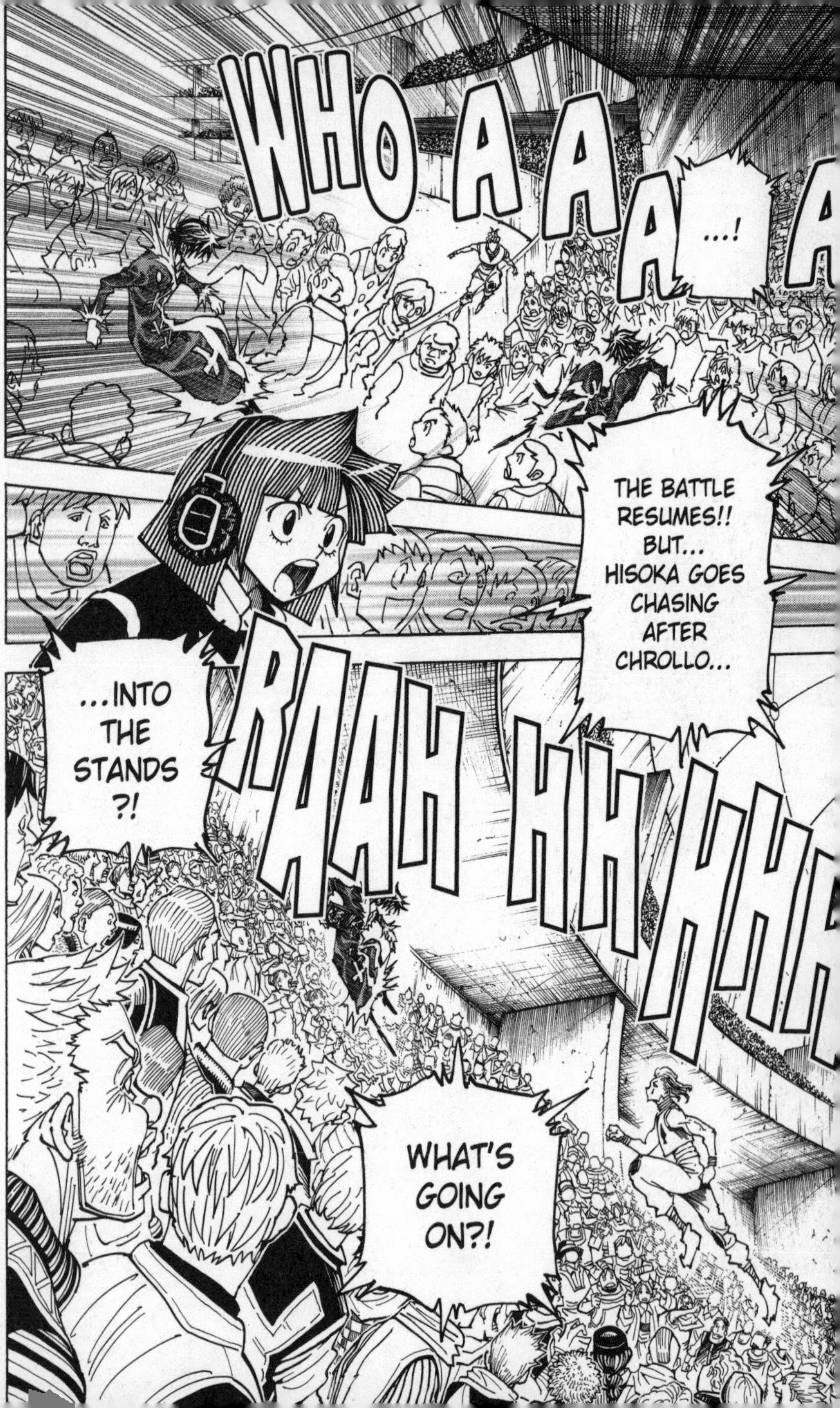
WHOAAAAA
...!
THE BATTLE RESUMES!! BUT... HISOKA GOES CHASING AFTER CHROLLO...
...INTO THE STANDS?!
RAAHHHHH
WHAT'S GOING ON?!

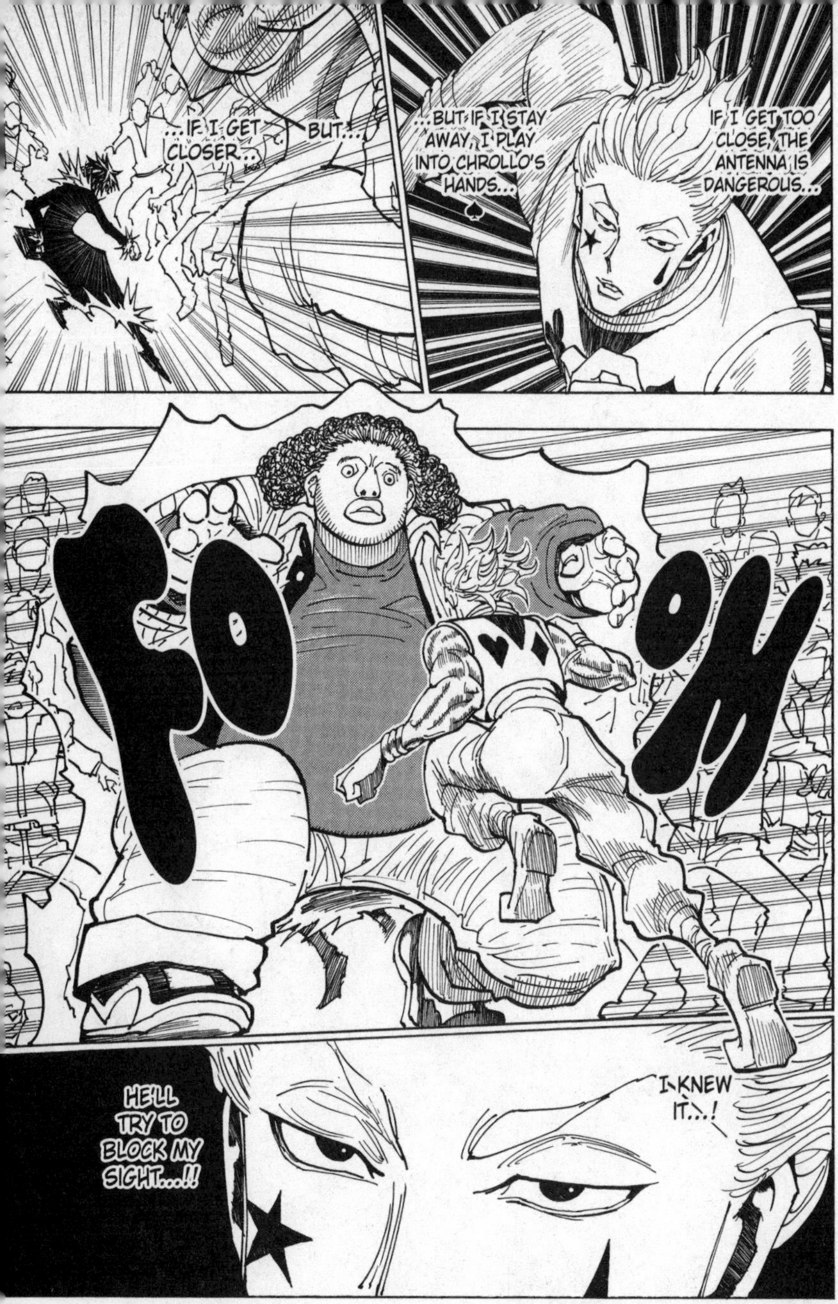
IF I GET TOO CLOSE, THE ANTENNA IS DANGEROUS...
...BUT IF I STAY AWAY, I PLAY INTO CHROLLO'S HANDS...
BUT...
...IF I GET CLOSER...
FOOM
I KNEW IT...!
HE'LL TRY TO BLOCK MY SIGHT...!!

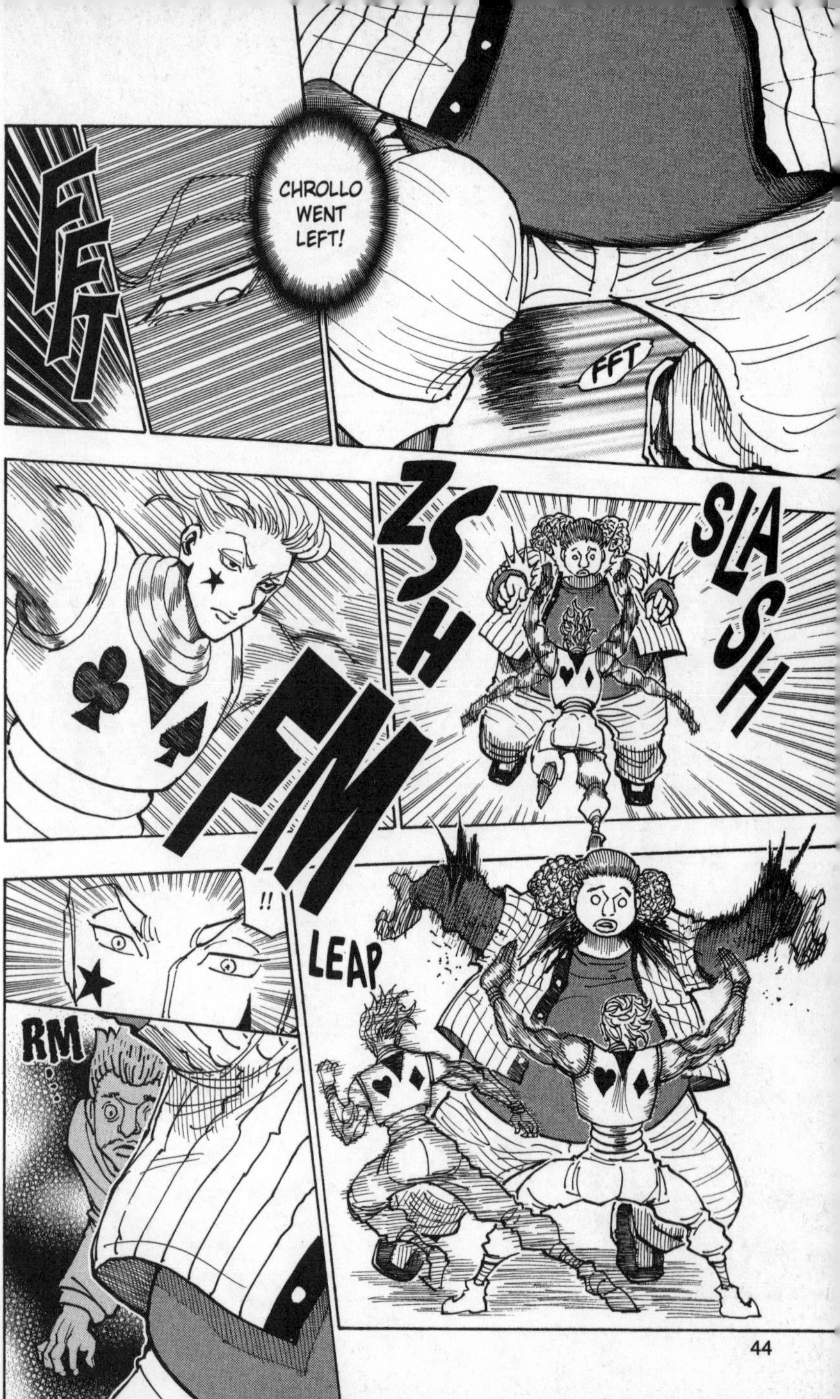

CHROLLO WENT LEFT!
FFT
FFFT
SLASH
ZSH
FM
LEAP
!!
RM

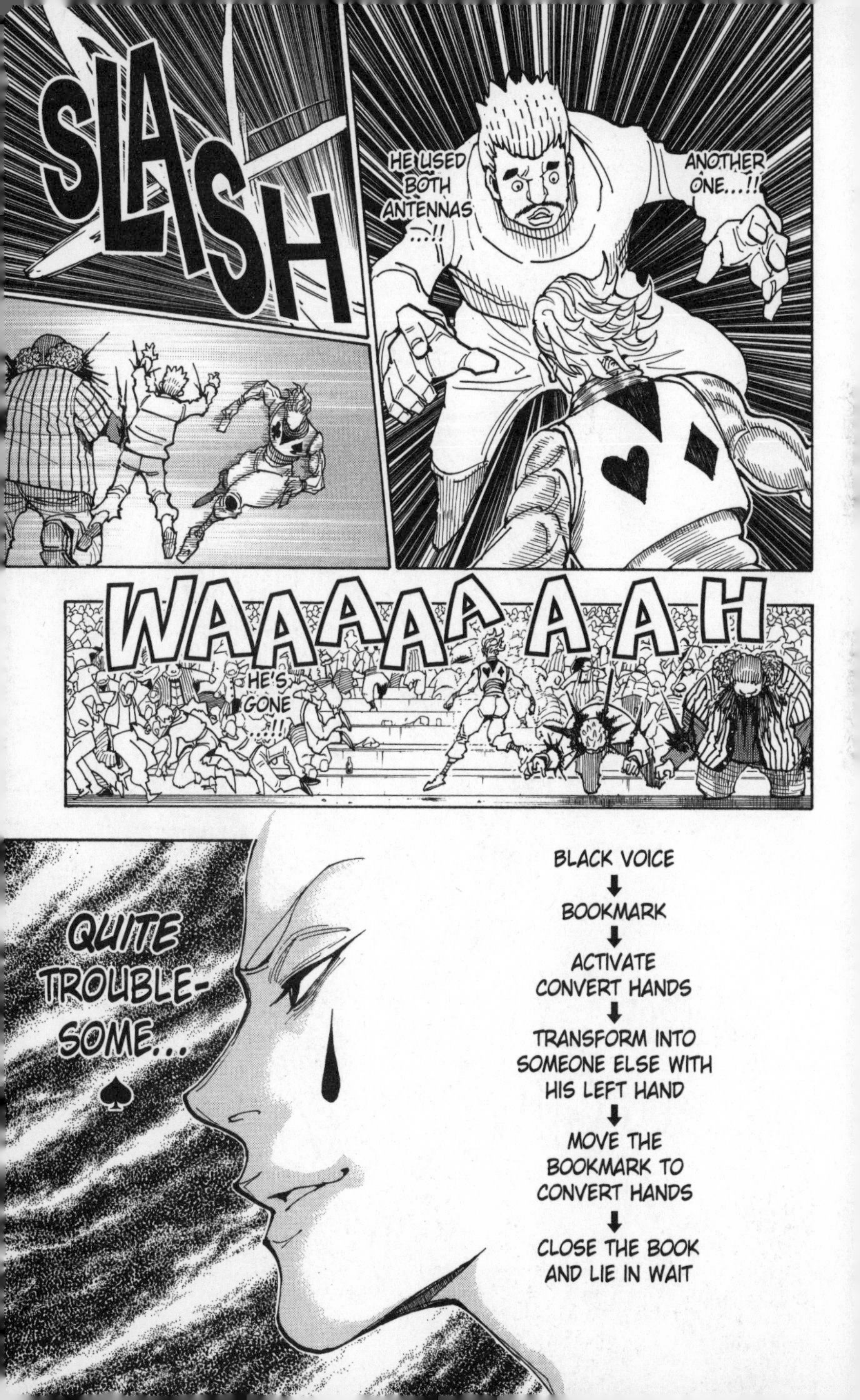
ANOTHER ONE...!!
HE USED BOTH ANTENNAS ...!!
SLASH
WAAAAA A A H
HE'S GONE ...!!
BLACK VOICE
BOOKMARK
ACTIVATE CONVERT HANDS
TRANSFORM INTO SOMEONE ELSE WITH HIS LEFT HAND
MOVE THE BOOKMARK TO CONVERT HANDS
CLOSE THE BOOK AND LIE IN WAIT
QUITE TROUBLE-SOME... ♠

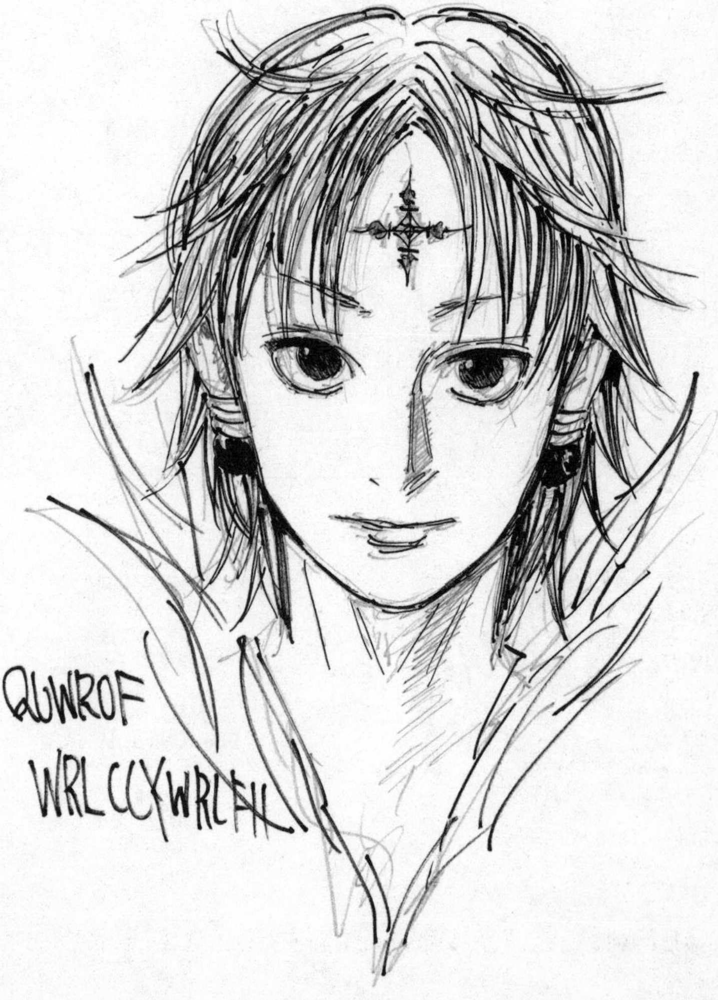
QUWROF
WRLCCXWRLFIL

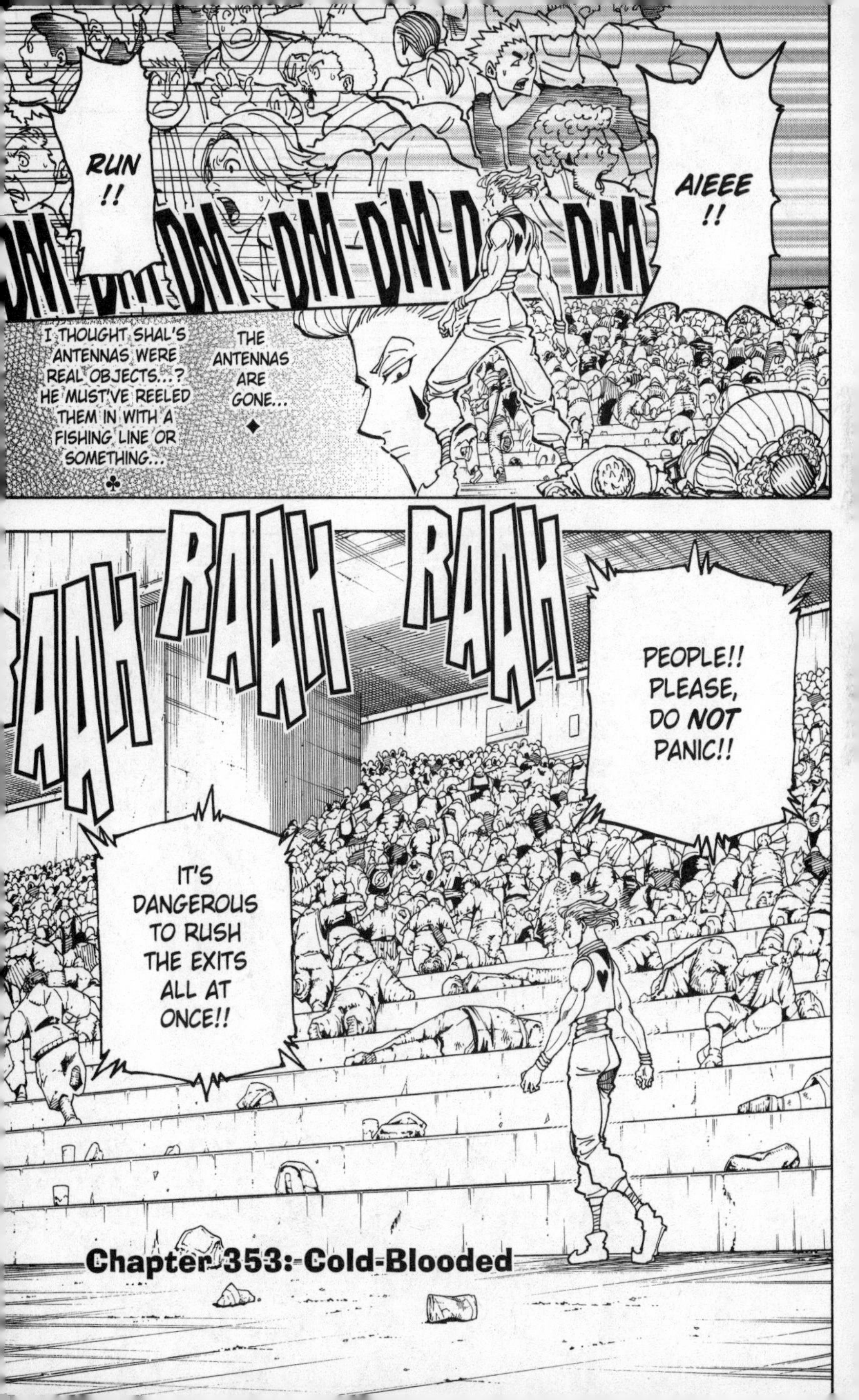
AIEEE !!
RUN !!
DM DM DM-DM-DM DM DM
THE ANTENNAS ARE GONE... ◆
I THOUGHT SHAL'S ANTENNAS WERE REAL OBJECTS...? HE MUST'VE REELED THEM IN WITH A FISHING LINE OR SOMETHING... ♣
RAAH RAAH RAAH
PEOPLE!! PLEASE, DO NOT PANIC!!
IT'S DANGEROUS TO RUSH THE EXITS ALL AT ONCE!!

Chapter 353: Cold-Blooded

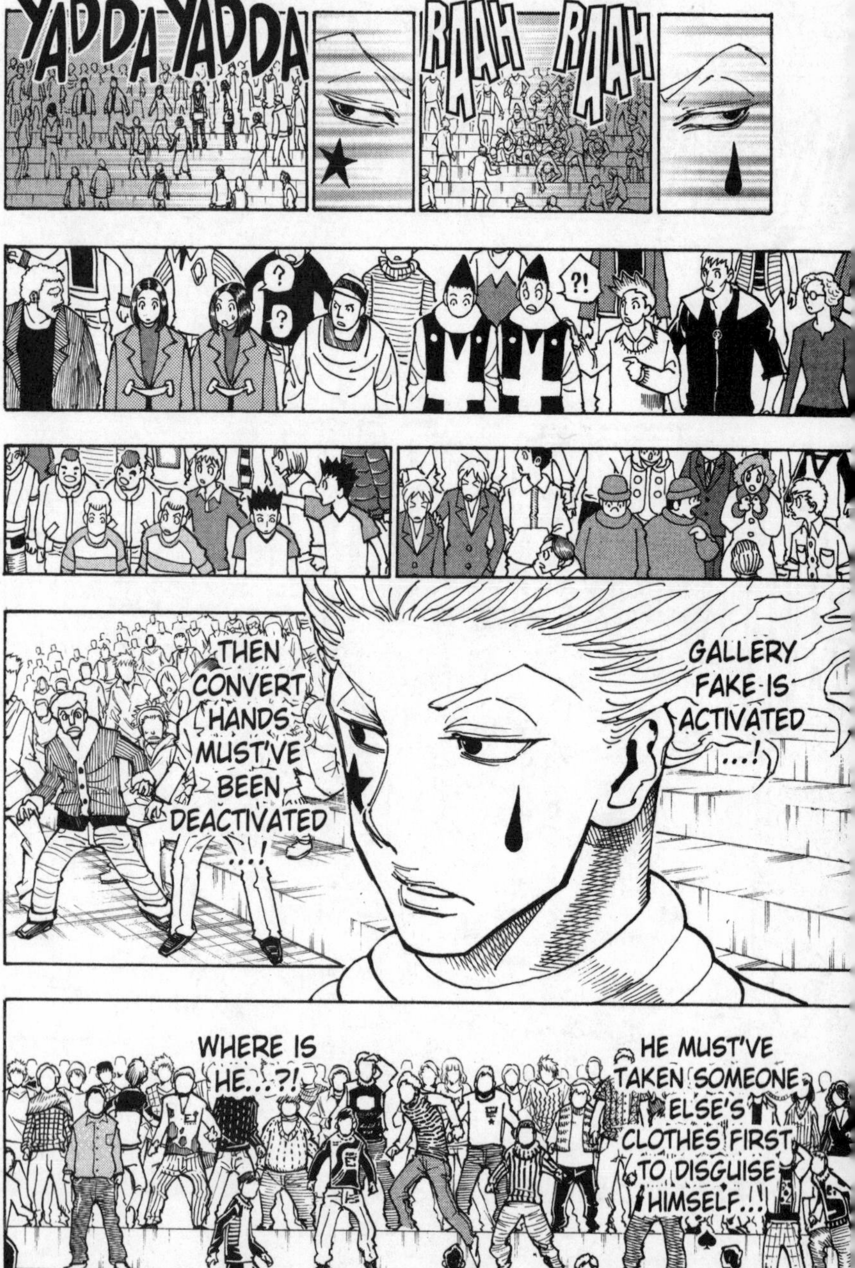
RAAH RAAH
YADDA YADDA
?!
?
?
GALLERY FAKE IS ACTIVATED ...!
THEN CONVERT HANDS MUST'VE BEEN DEACTIVATED ...!
HE MUST'VE TAKEN SOMEONE ELSE'S CLOTHES FIRST TO DISGUISE HIMSELF..!!
WHERE IS HE...?!

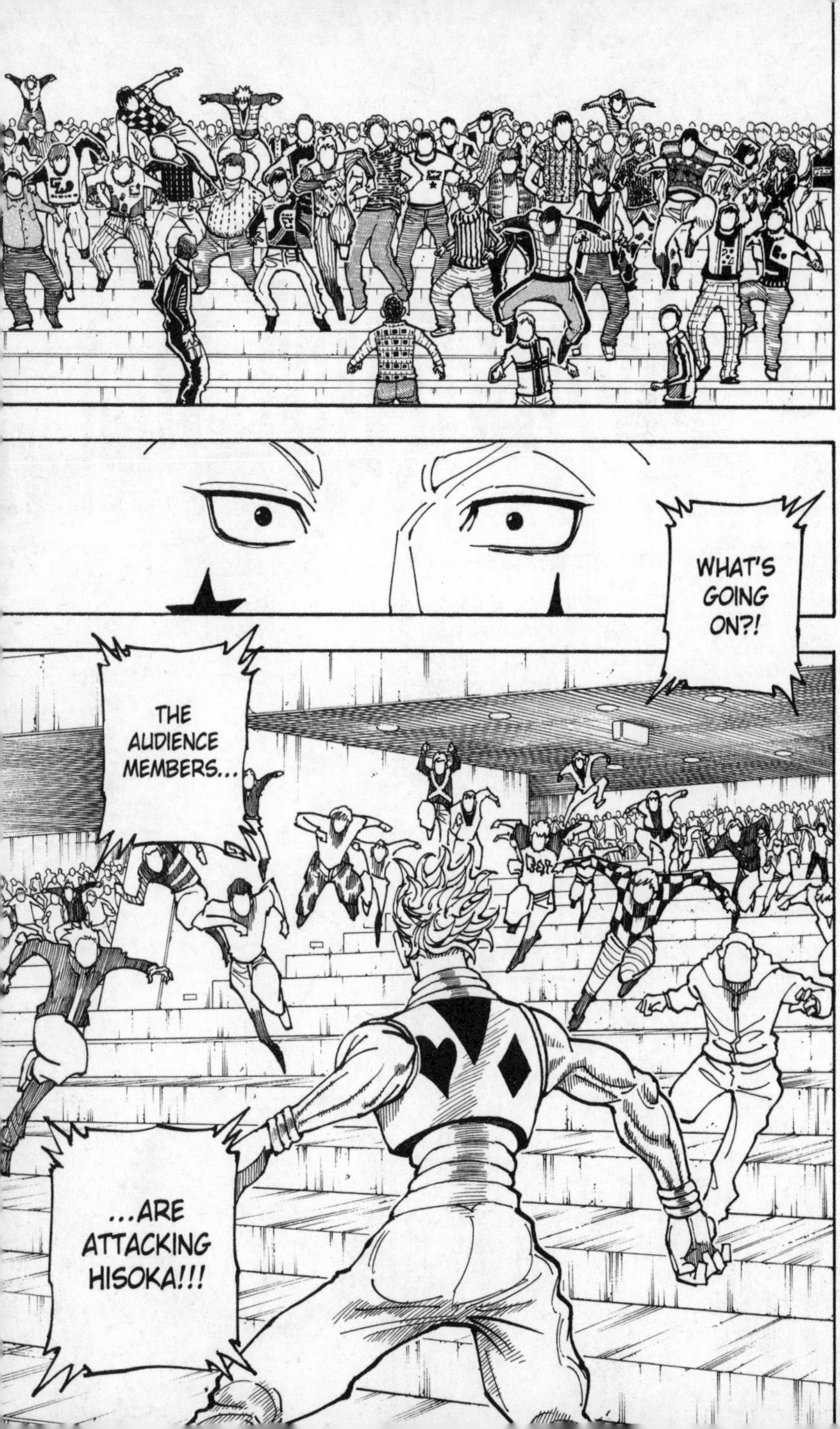
WHAT'S GOING ON?!
THE AUDIENCE MEMBERS...
...ARE ATTACKING HISOKA!!!

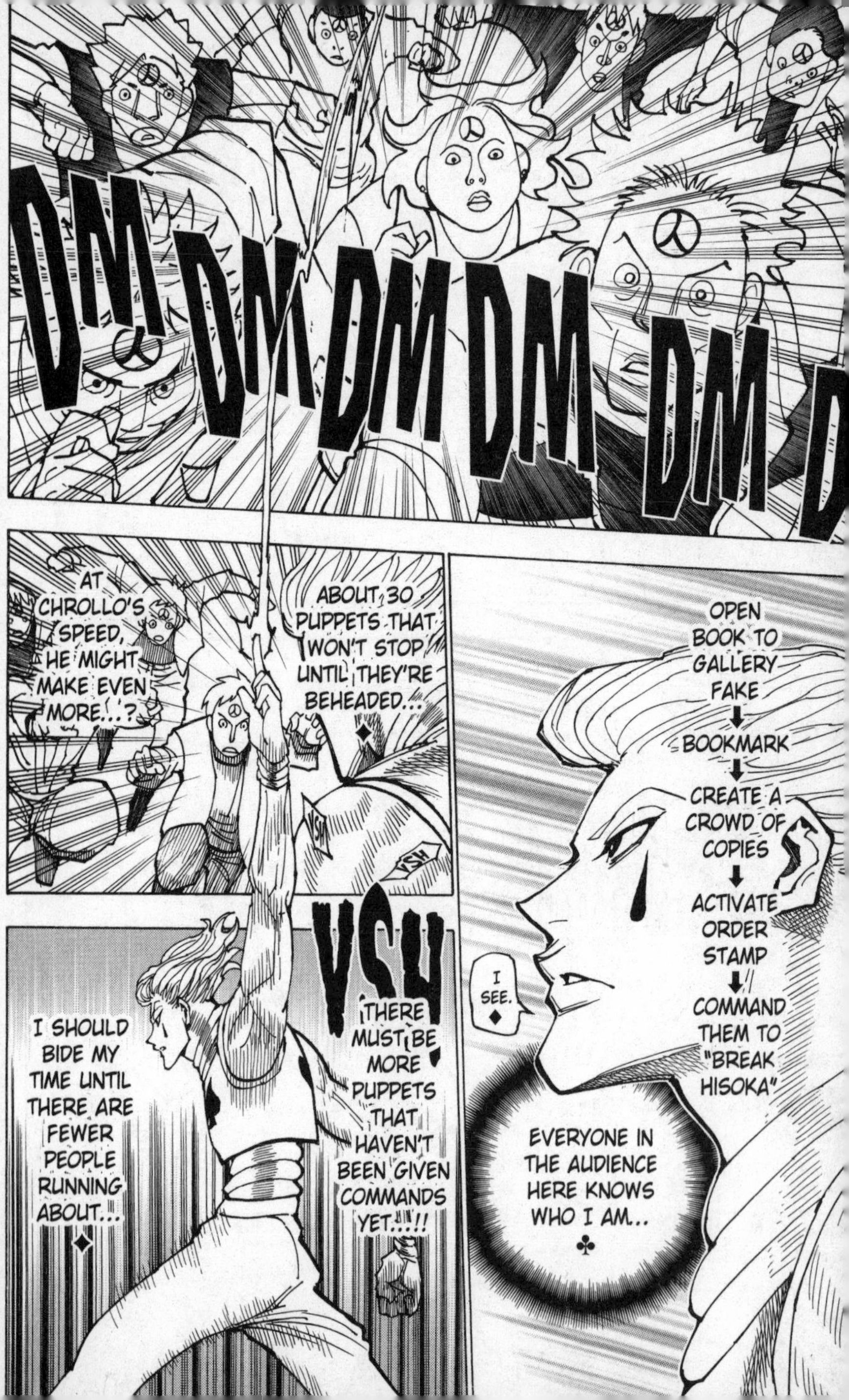
DM DM DM DM DM D
OPEN BOOK TO GALLERY FAKE ↓ BOOKMARK ↓ CREATE A CROWD OF COPIES ↓ ACTIVATE ORDER STAMP ↓ COMMAND THEM TO "BREAK HISOKA"
I SEE.
EVERYONE IN THE AUDIENCE HERE KNOWS WHO I AM...
ABOUT 30 PUPPETS THAT WON'T STOP UNTIL THEY'RE BEHEADED...
AT CHROLLO'S SPEED, HE MIGHT MAKE EVEN MORE...?
VSH
VSH
VSH
THERE MUST BE MORE PUPPETS THAT HAVEN'T BEEN GIVEN COMMANDS YET...!!
I SHOULD BIDE MY TIME UNTIL THERE ARE FEWER PEOPLE RUNNING ABOUT...

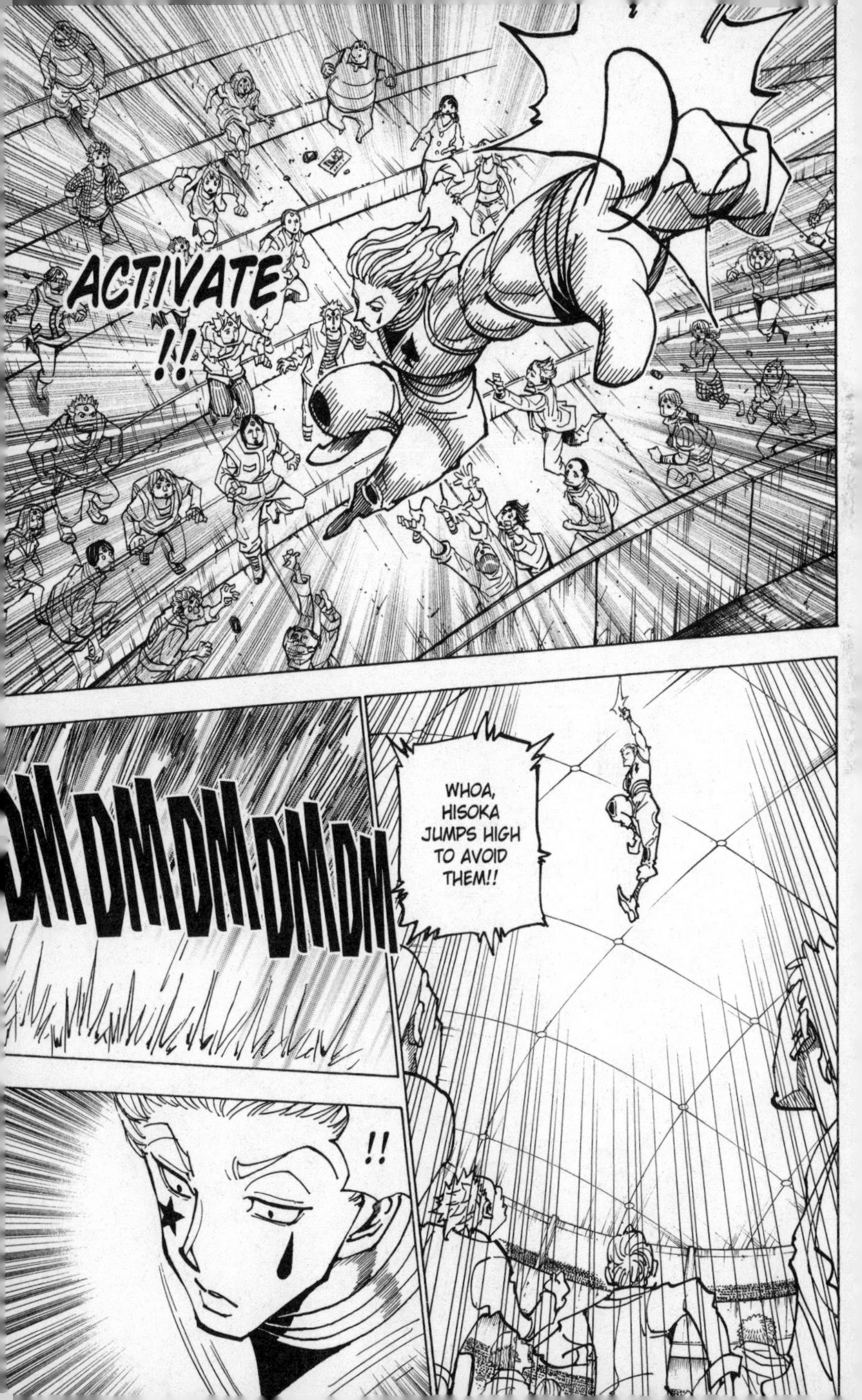
ACTIVATE!!
WHOA, HISOKA JUMPS HIGH TO AVOID THEM!!
DM DM DM DM DM DM
!!

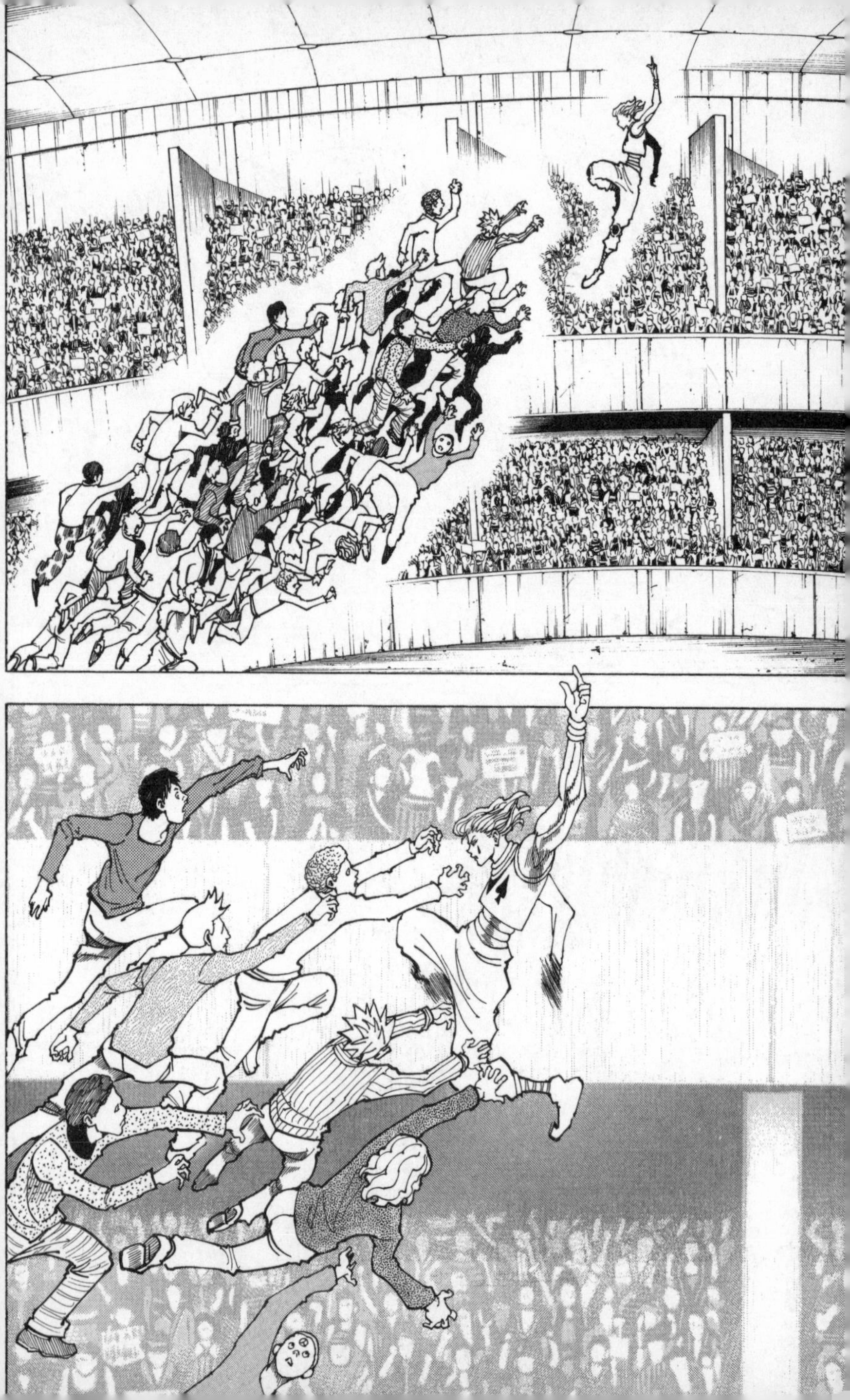

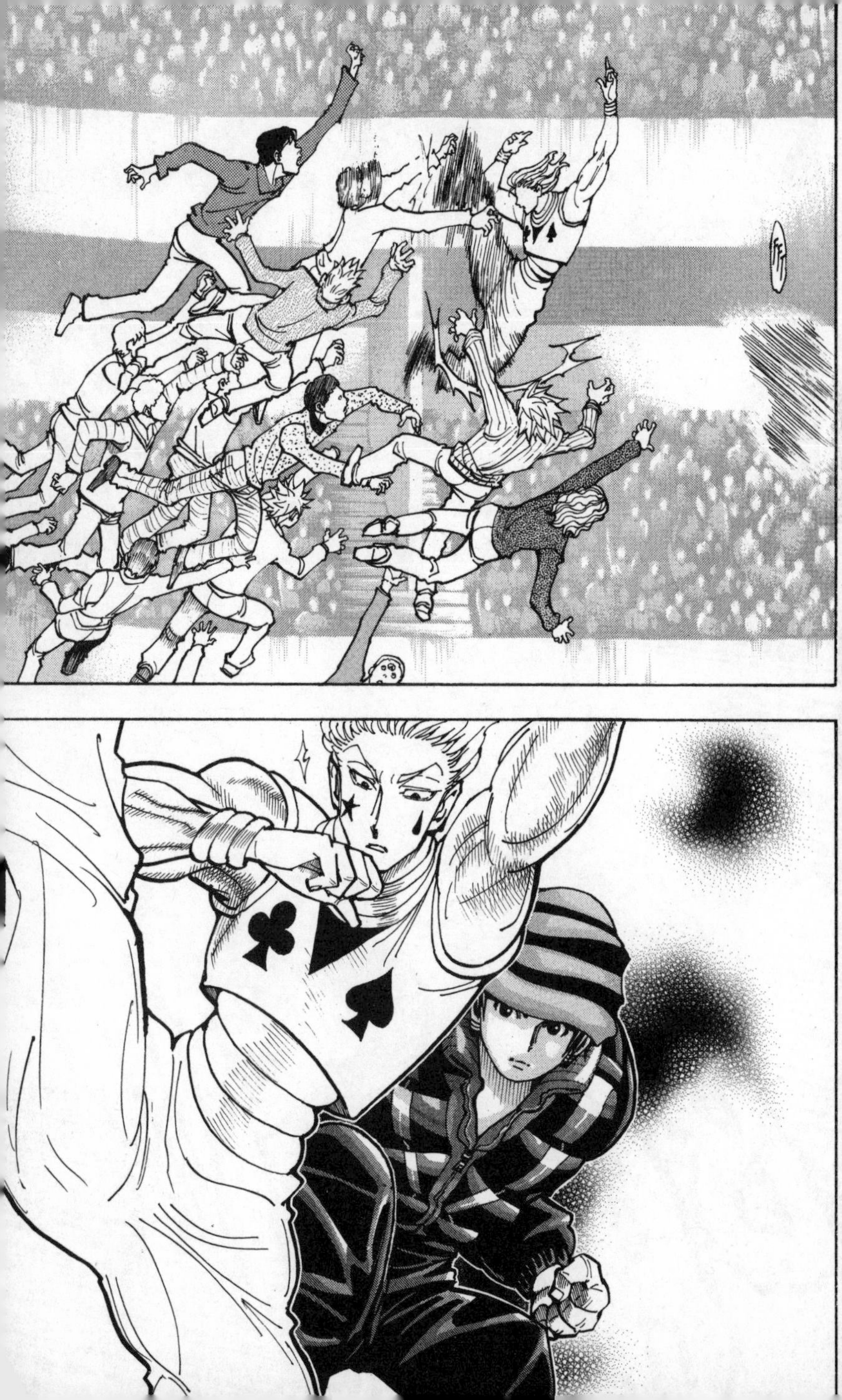
FFF

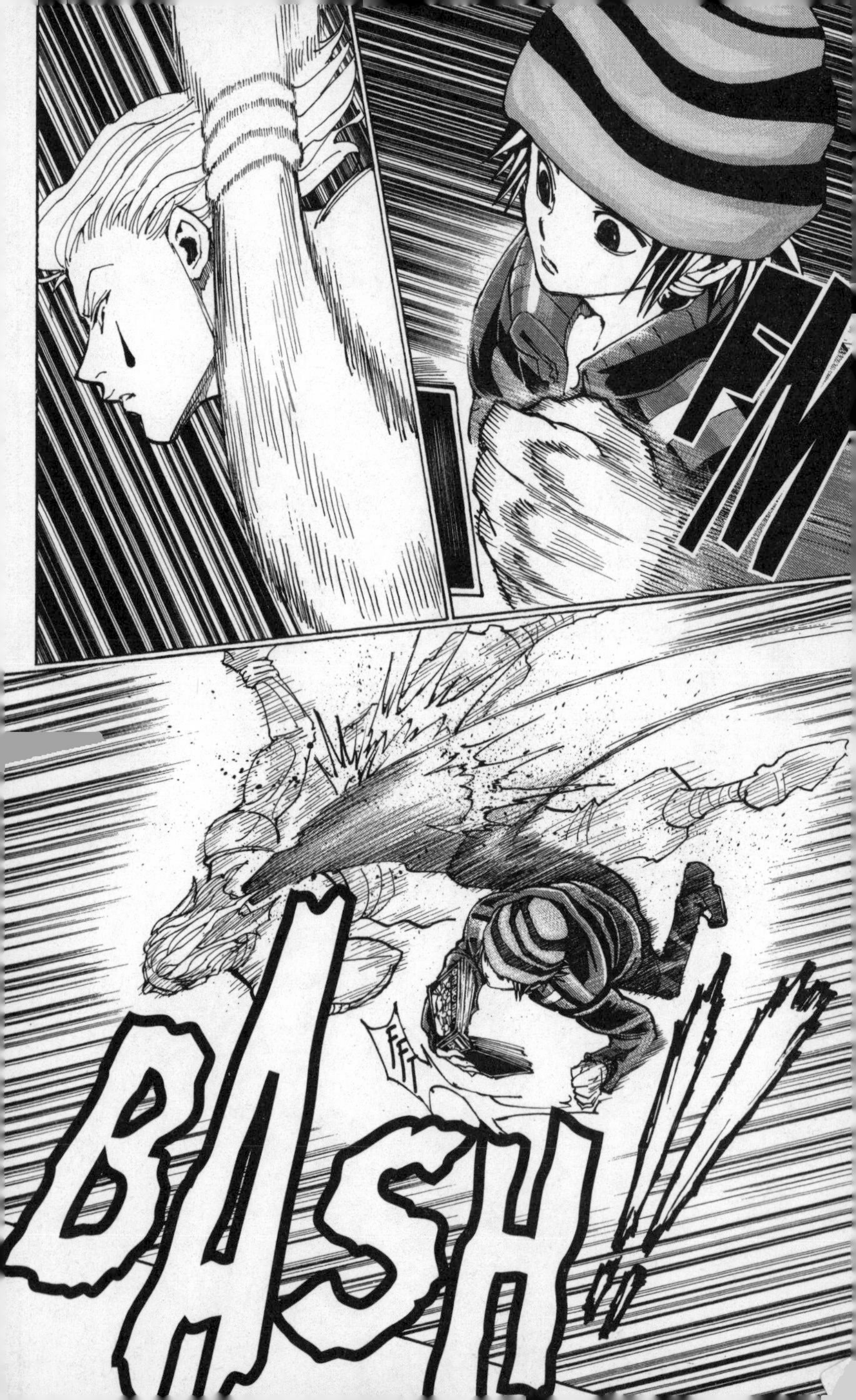
FFT
BASH!!

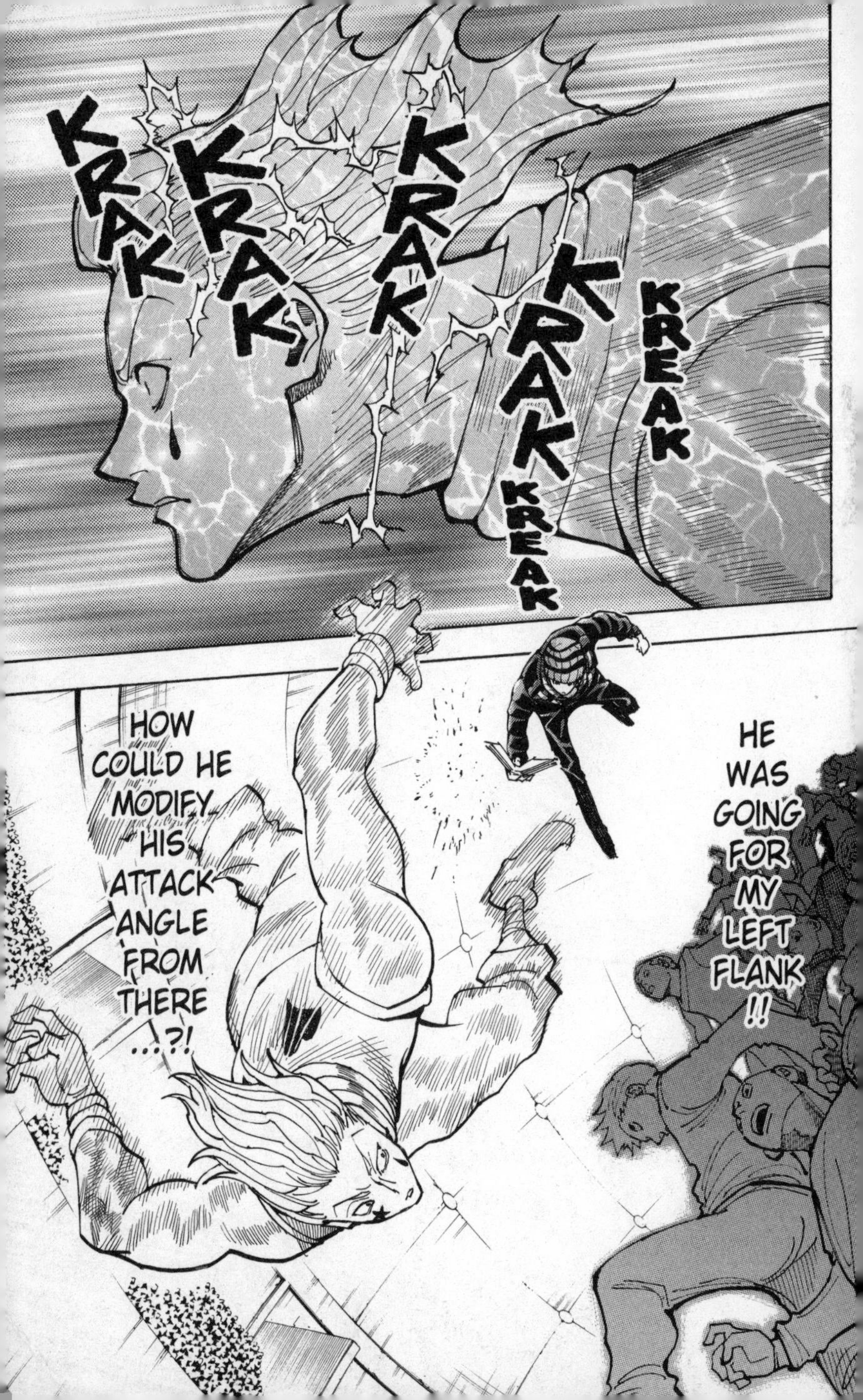
KREAK
KRAK
KREAK
KRAK
KRAK
KRAK
HE WAS GOING FOR MY LEFT FLANK!!
HOW COULD HE MODIFY HIS ATTACK ANGLE FROM THERE...?!

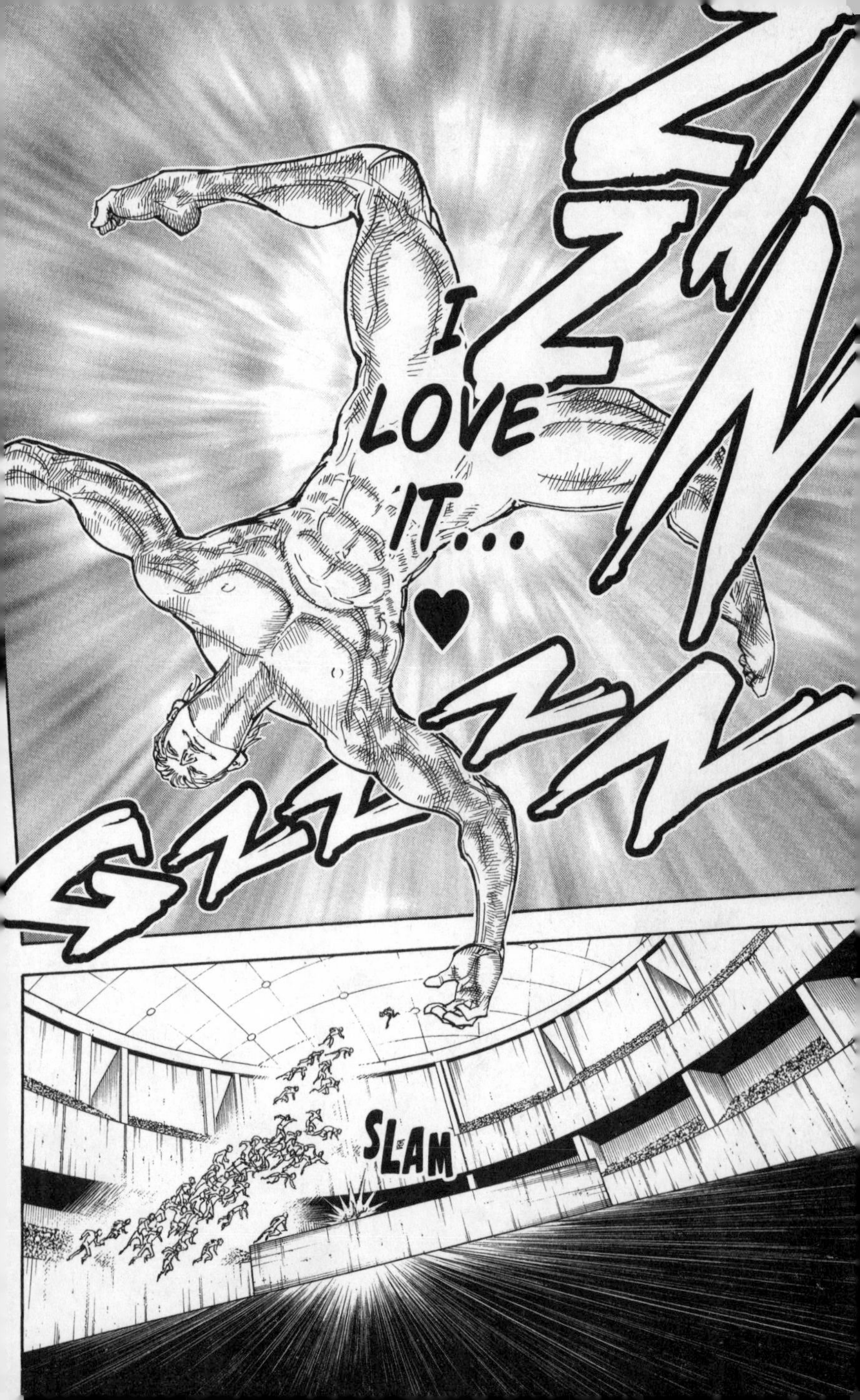
I LOVE IT... ♥
GZZN
GZZZN
SLAM

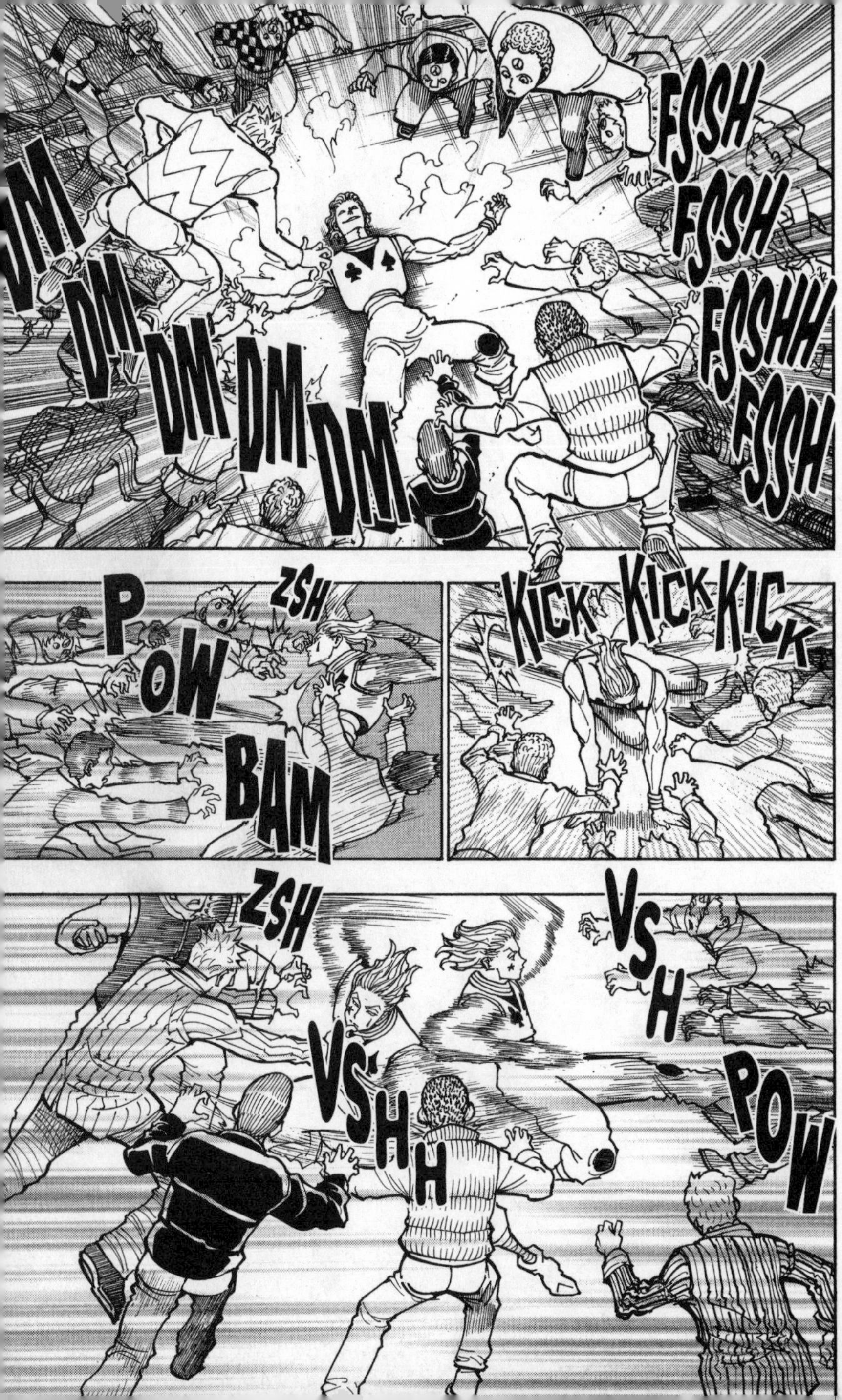
FSSH
FSSH
FSSHH
FSSH
DM
DM
DM
DM
DM
DM
KICK KICK KICK
ZSH
POW
BAM
VSH
POW
ZSH
VSHH

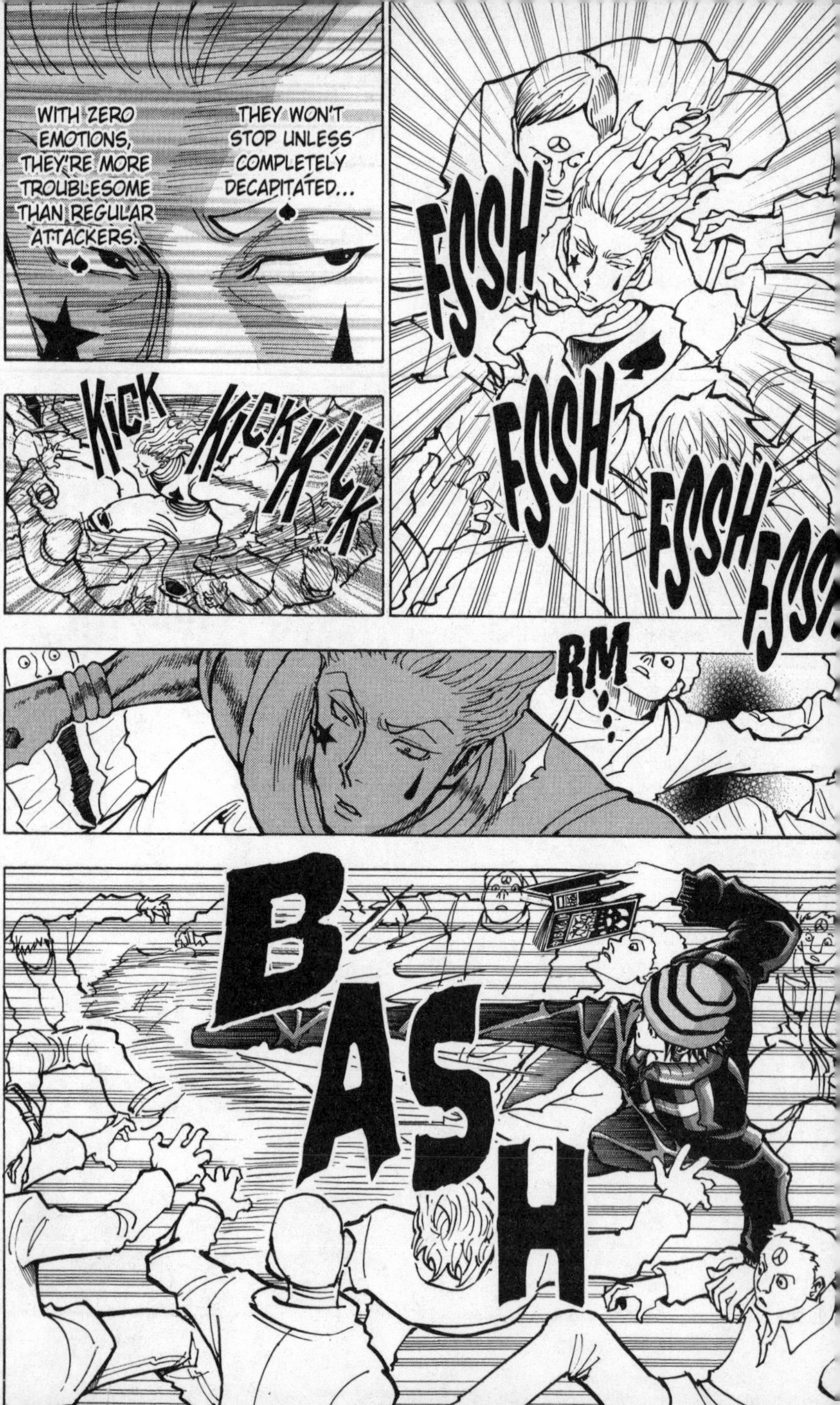
FSSH
FSSH
FSSH
FSS
THEY WON'T STOP UNLESS COMPLETELY DECAPITATED...
WITH ZERO EMOTIONS, THEY'RE MORE TROUBLESOME THAN REGULAR ATTACKERS.
KICK
KICK
KICK
KICK
RM
BASH

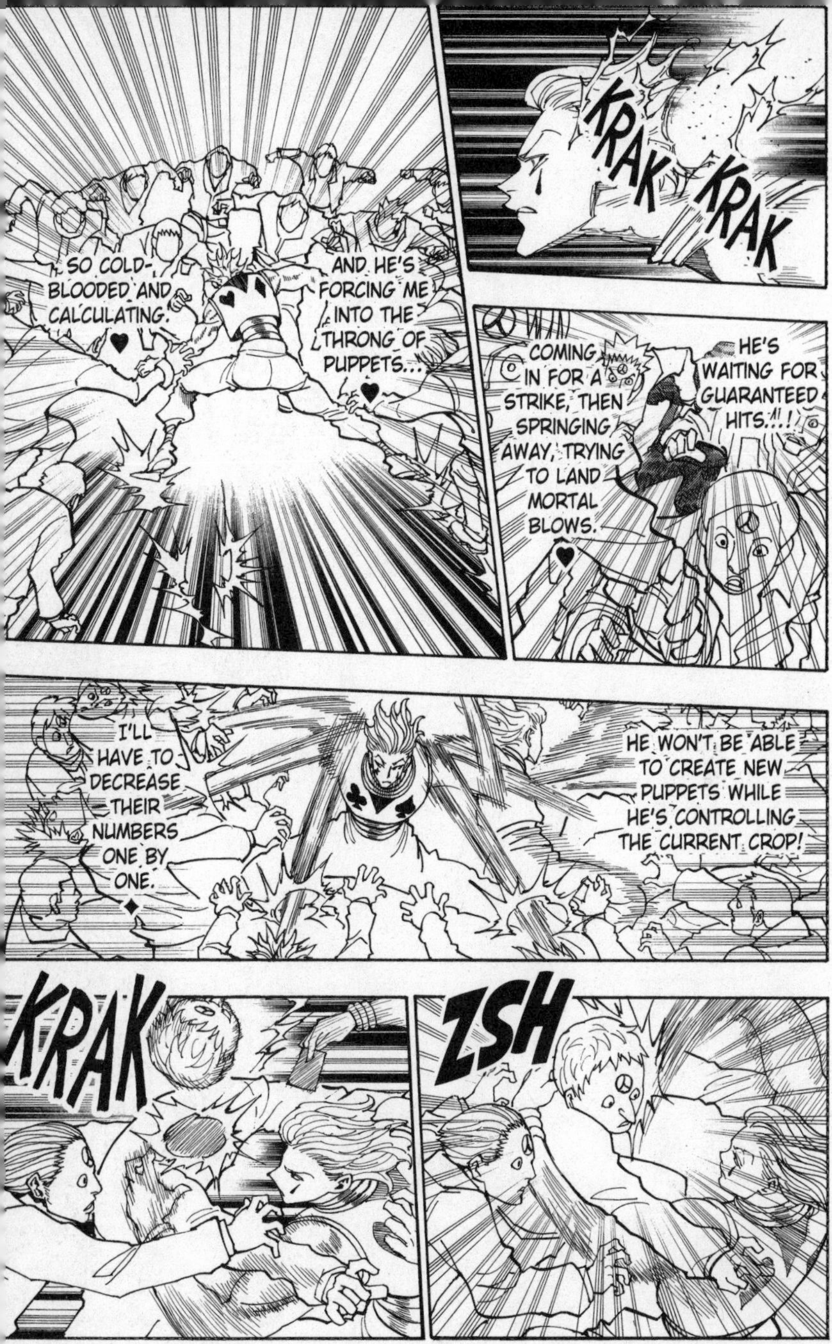
KRAK KRAK
HE'S WAITING FOR GUARANTEED HITS...!
COMING IN FOR A STRIKE, THEN SPRINGING AWAY, TRYING TO LAND MORTAL BLOWS. ♥
AND HE'S FORCING ME INTO THE THRONG OF PUPPETS... ♥
SO COLD-BLOODED AND CALCULATING. ♥
HE WON'T BE ABLE TO CREATE NEW PUPPETS WHILE HE'S CONTROLLING THE CURRENT CROP!
I'LL HAVE TO DECREASE THEIR NUMBERS ONE BY ONE. ♦
ZSH
KRAK

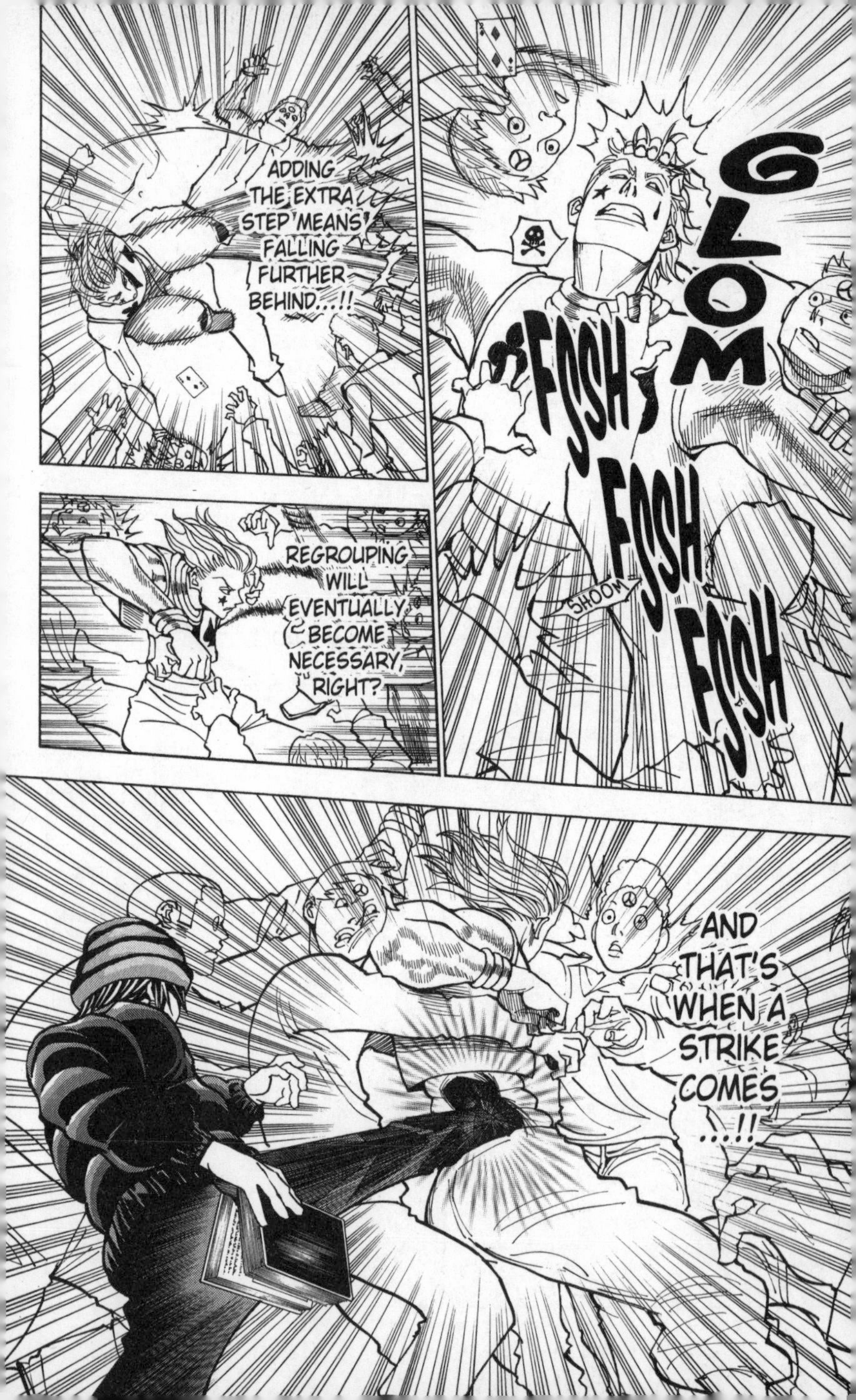
GLOM
FOSH FOSH FOSH FOSH
SHOOM
ADDING THE EXTRA STEP MEANS FALLING FURTHER BEHIND...!!
REGROUPING WILL EVENTUALLY BECOME NECESSARY, RIGHT?
AND THAT'S WHEN A STRIKE COMES...!!

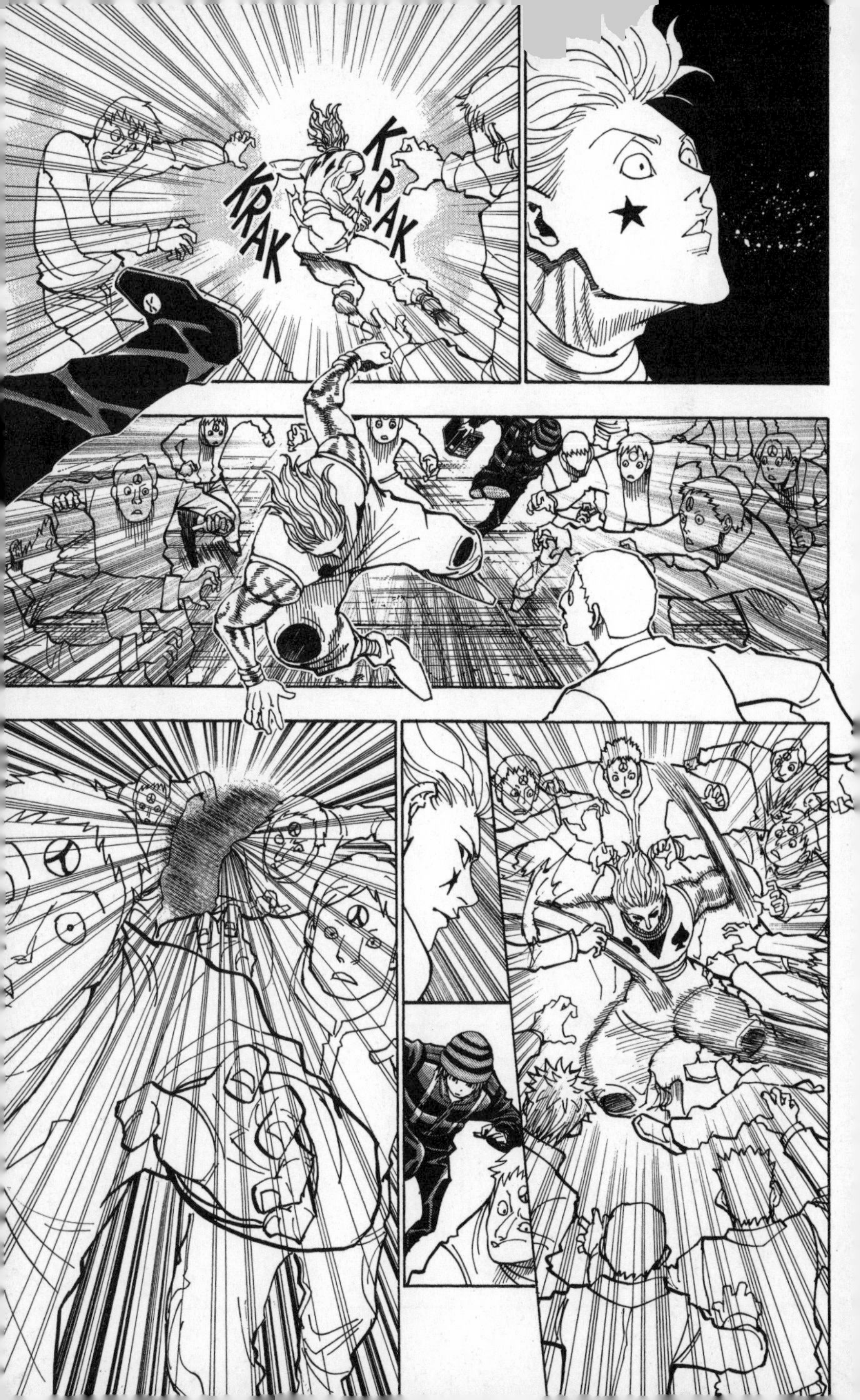
KRAK
KRAK

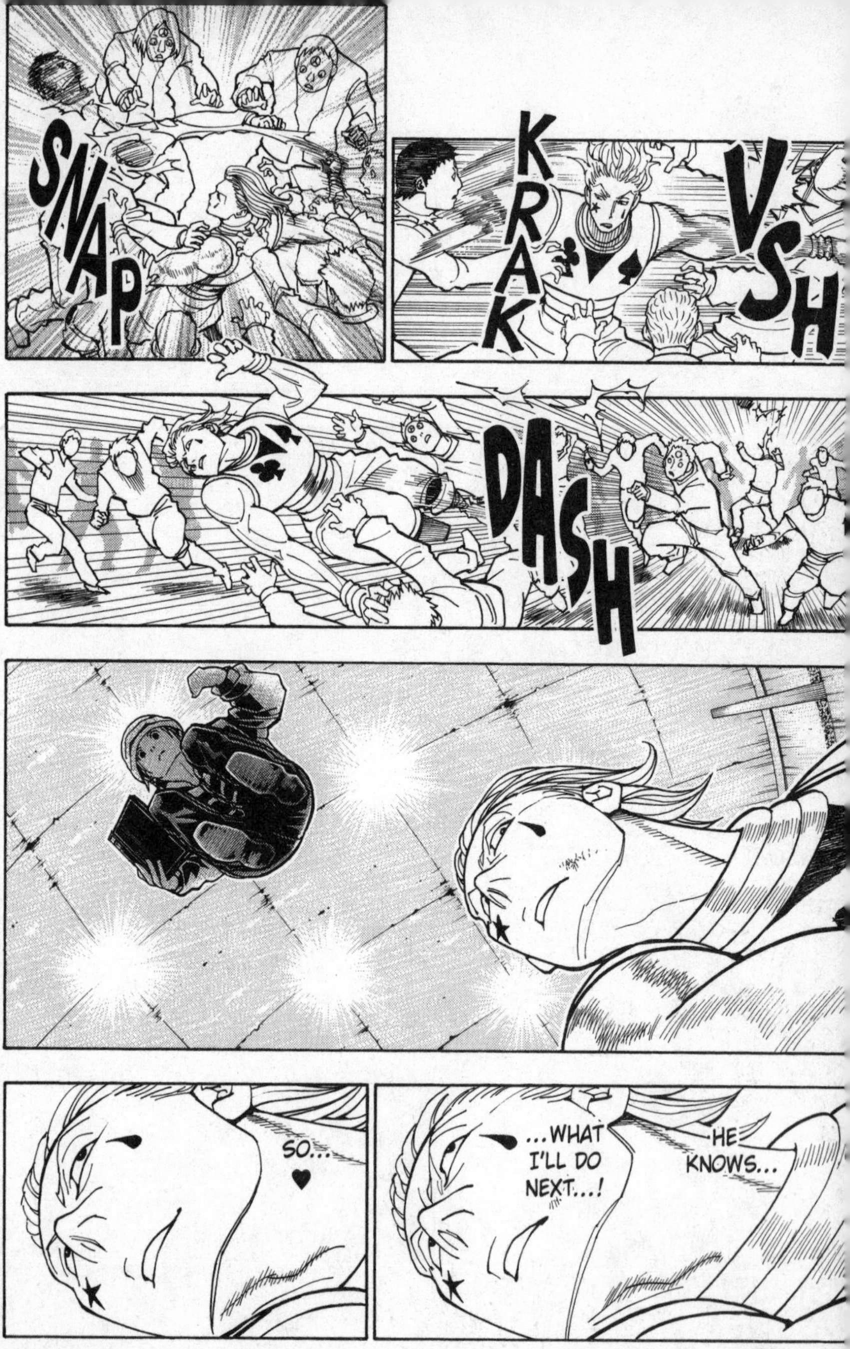
VSH
KRAK
SNAP
DASH
HE KNOWS...
...WHAT I'LL DO NEXT...!
SO... ♥

READ THIS WAY

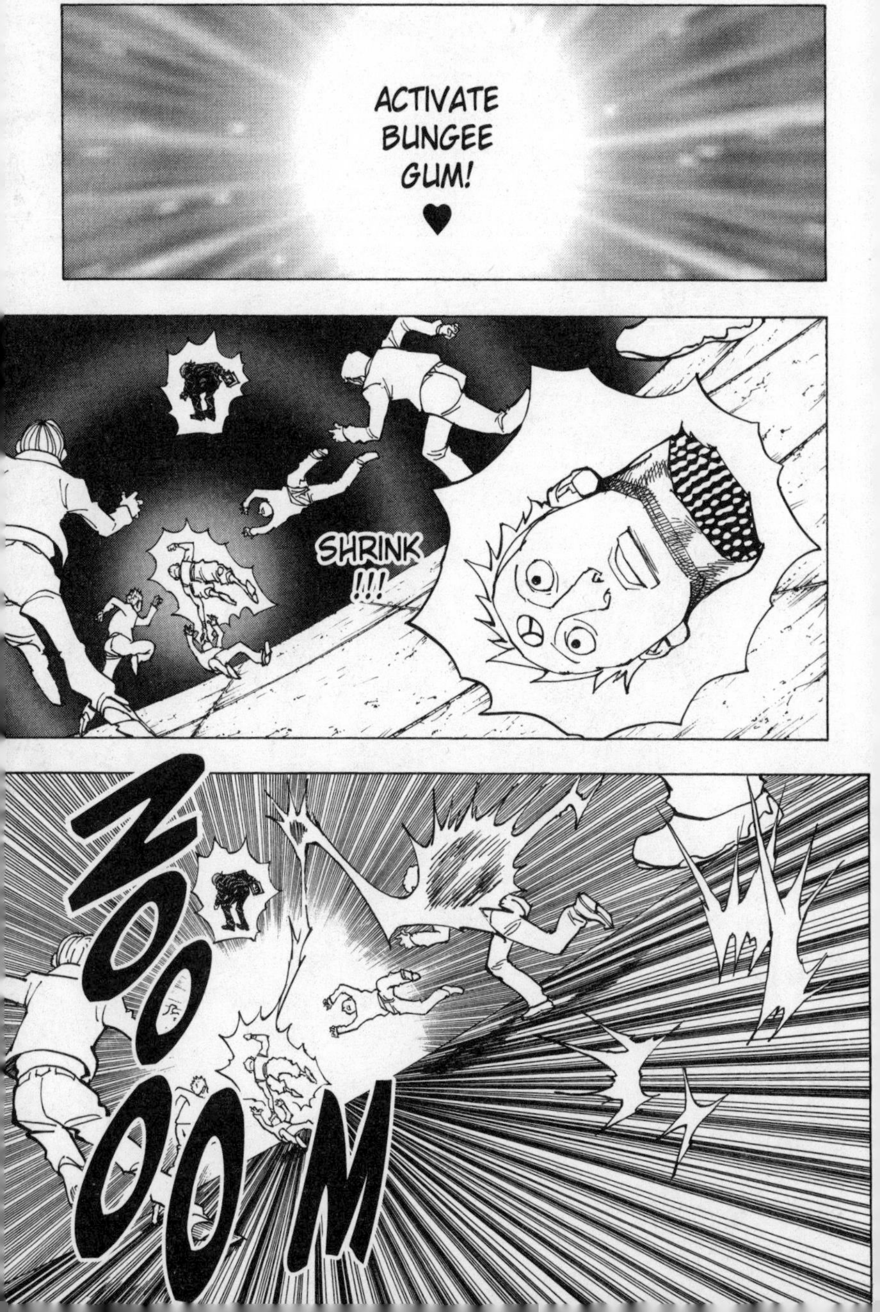
ACTIVATE BUNGEE GUM! ♥
SHRINK !!!
NOOOOM

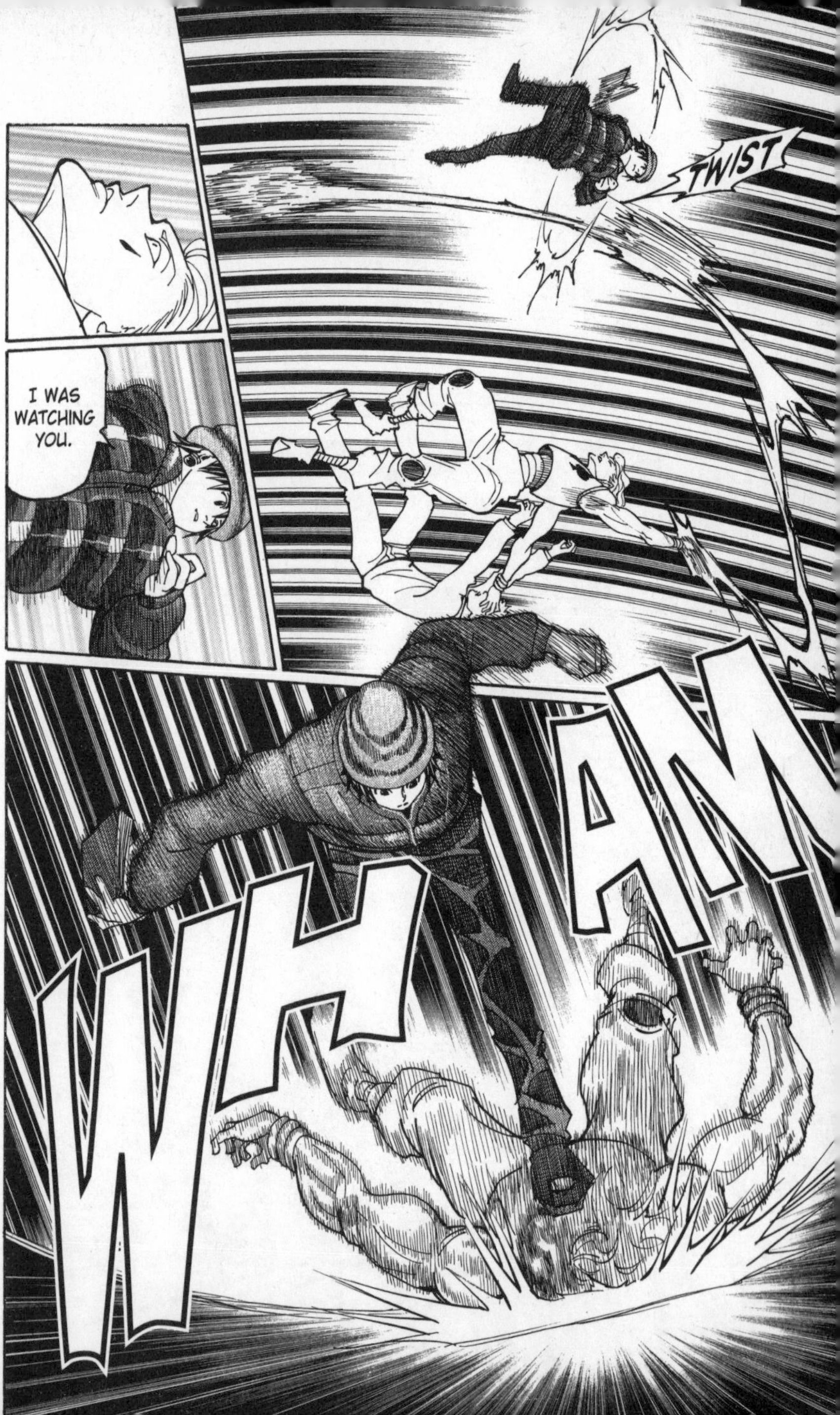
TWIST
I WAS WATCHING YOU.
WHAM

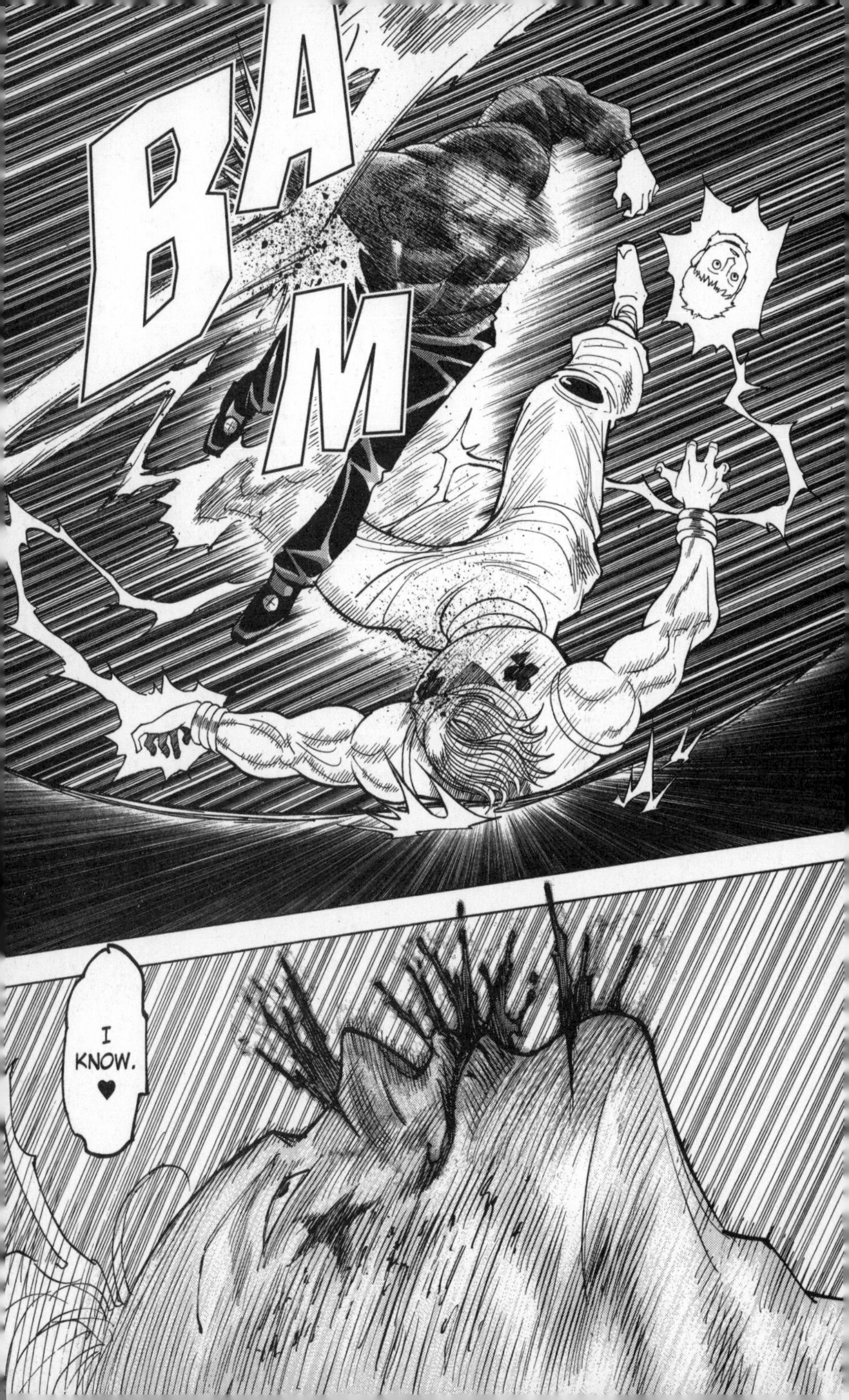
BAM
I KNOW. ♥

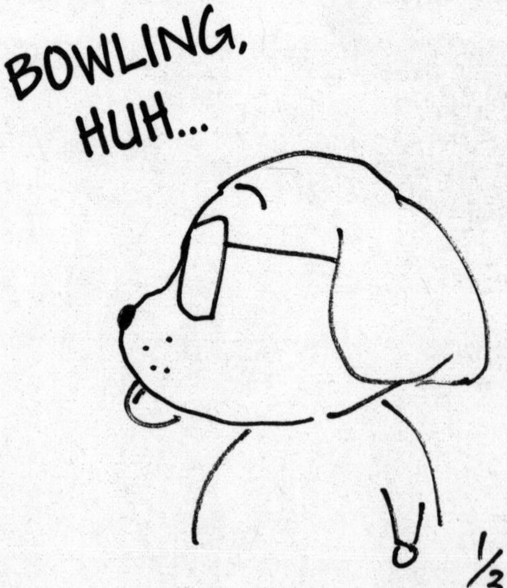
BOWLING, HUH...
1/3

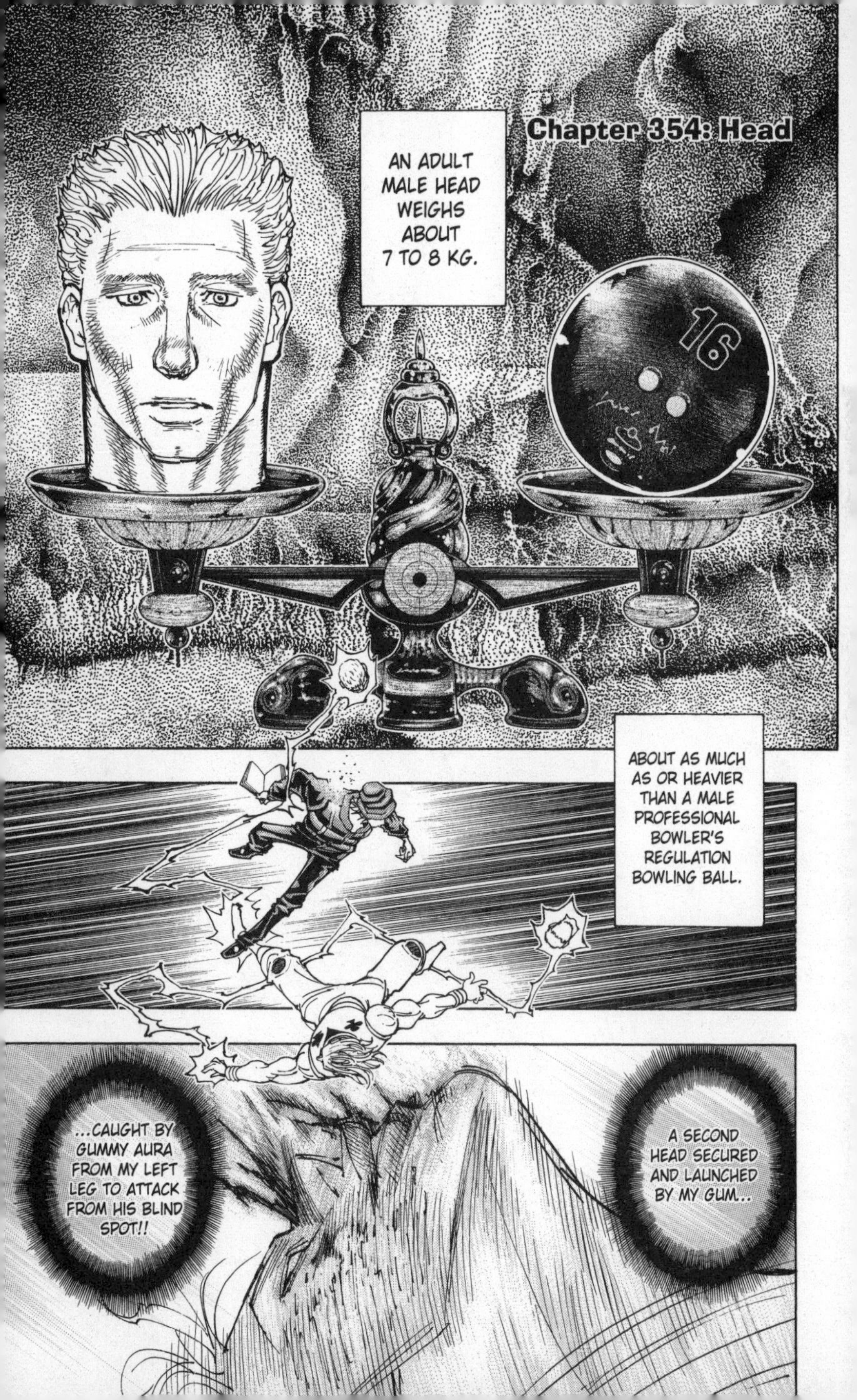
Chapter 354: Head
AN ADULT MALE HEAD WEIGHS ABOUT 7 TO 8 KG.
16
ABOUT AS MUCH AS OR HEAVIER THAN A MALE PROFESSIONAL BOWLER'S REGULATION BOWLING BALL.
A SECOND HEAD SECURED AND LAUNCHED BY MY GUM..
...CAUGHT BY GUMMY AURA FROM MY LEFT LEG TO ATTACK FROM HIS BLIND SPOT!!

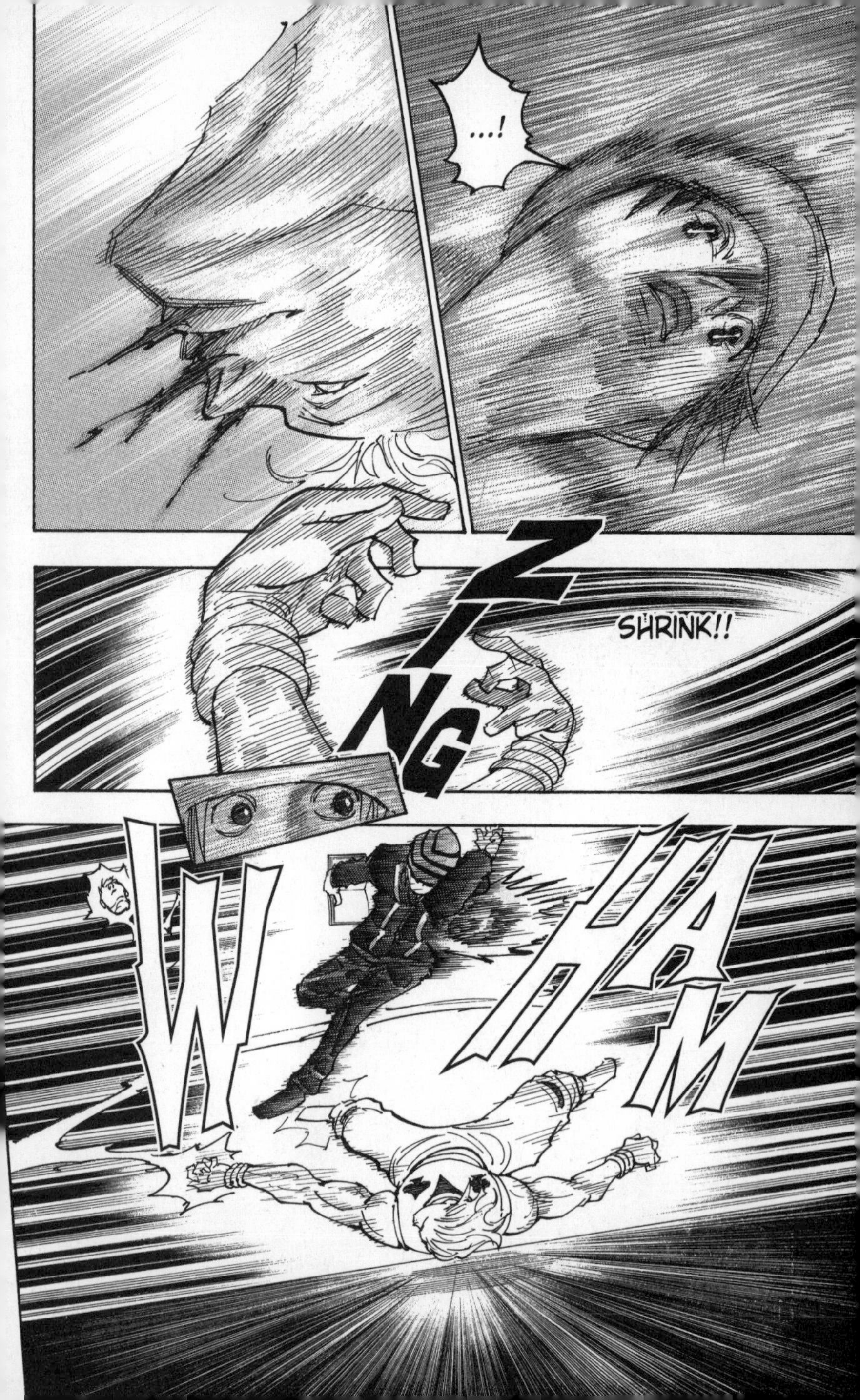
...!
ZING
SHRINK!!
WHAM

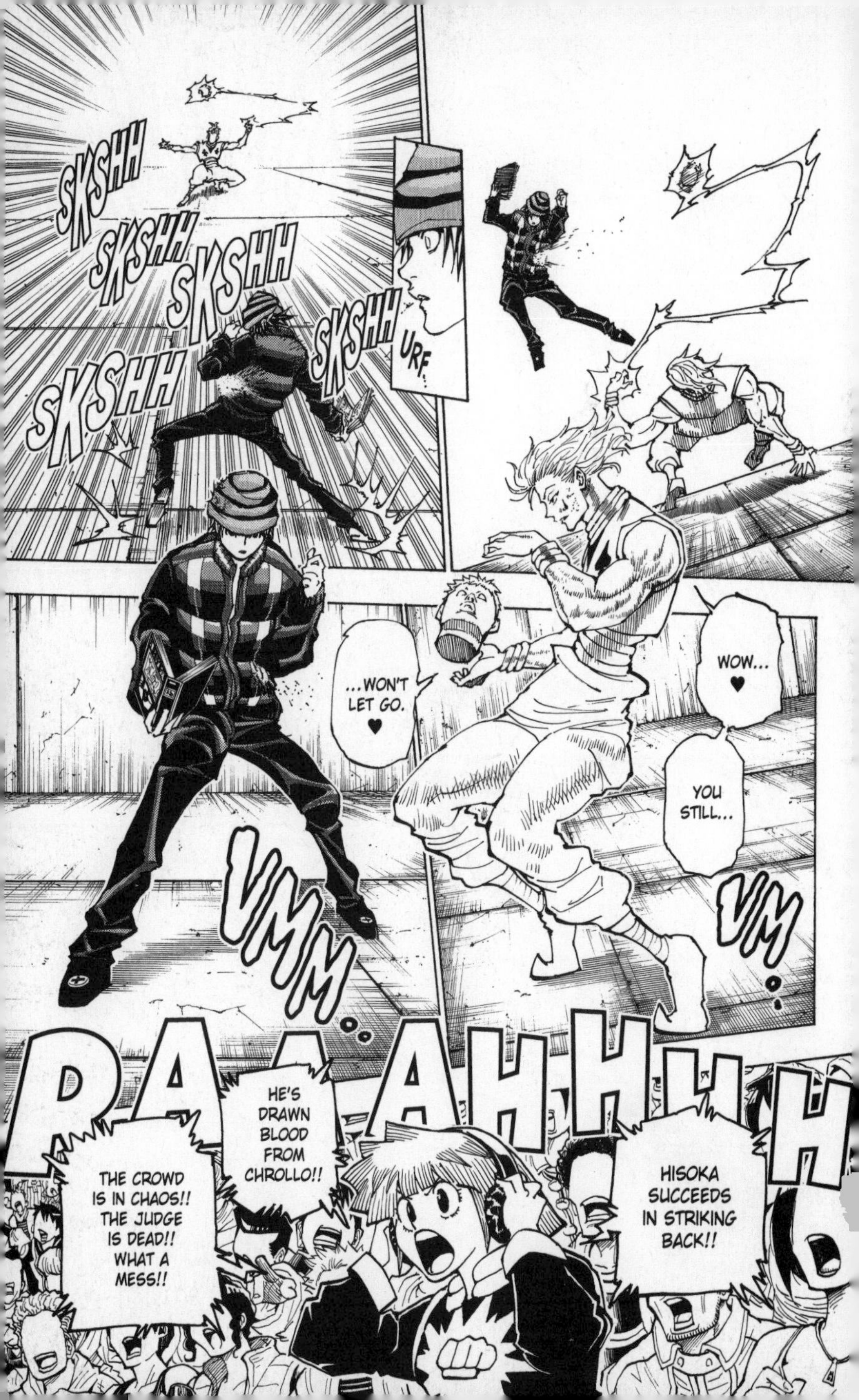
SKSHH
SKSHH
SKSHH
SKSHH
SKSHH
URF
WOW... ♥
YOU STILL...
...WON'T LET GO. ♥
VM
VMMM
RAAAHHHH
HISOKA SUCCEEDS IN STRIKING BACK!!
HE'S DRAWN BLOOD FROM CHROLLO!!
THE CROWD IS IN CHAOS!! THE JUDGE IS DEAD!! WHAT A MESS!!

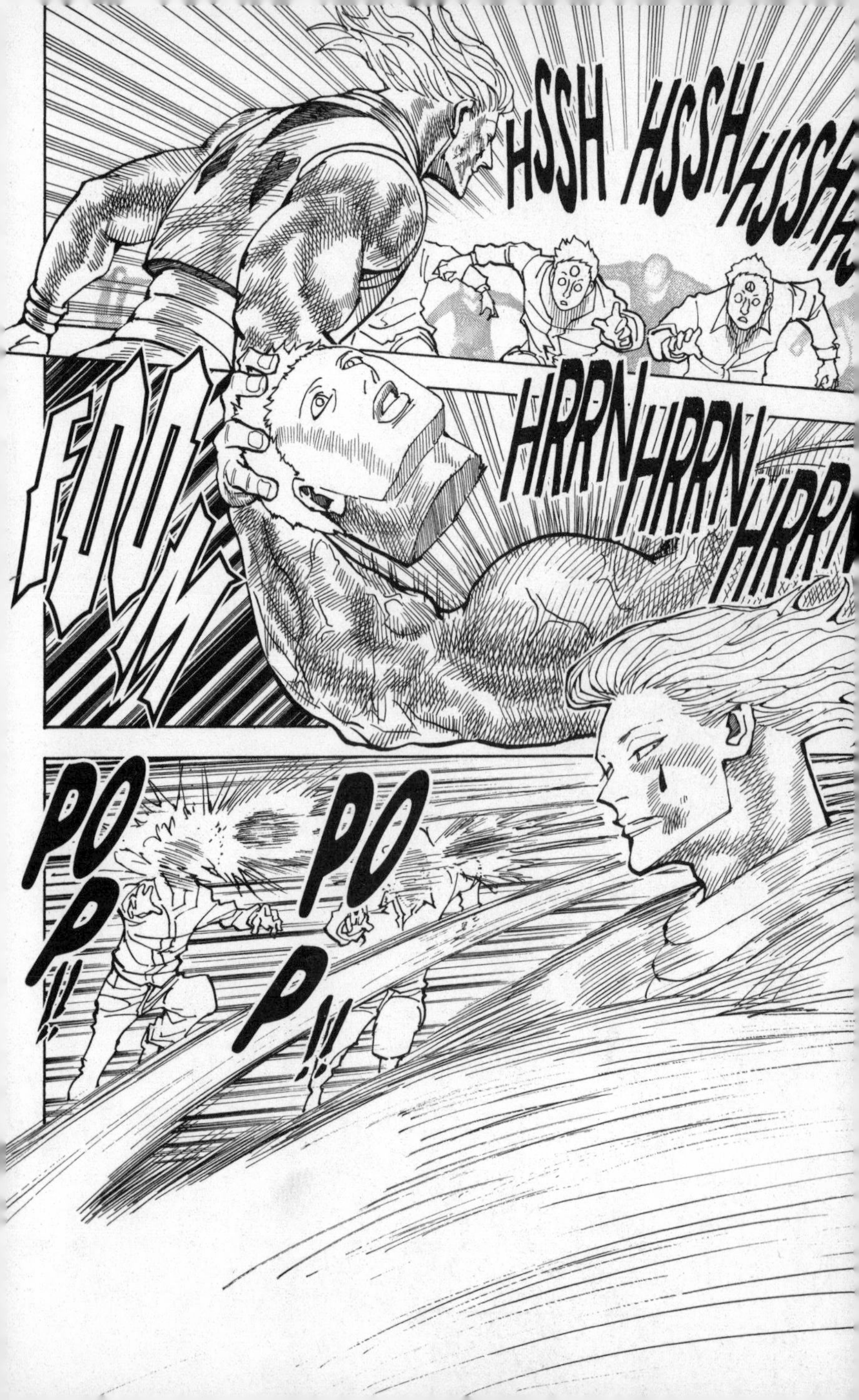
HSSH HSSH HSSH
HRRN HRRN
HRRN HRRN
HRR
FOOM
POP!!
POP!!

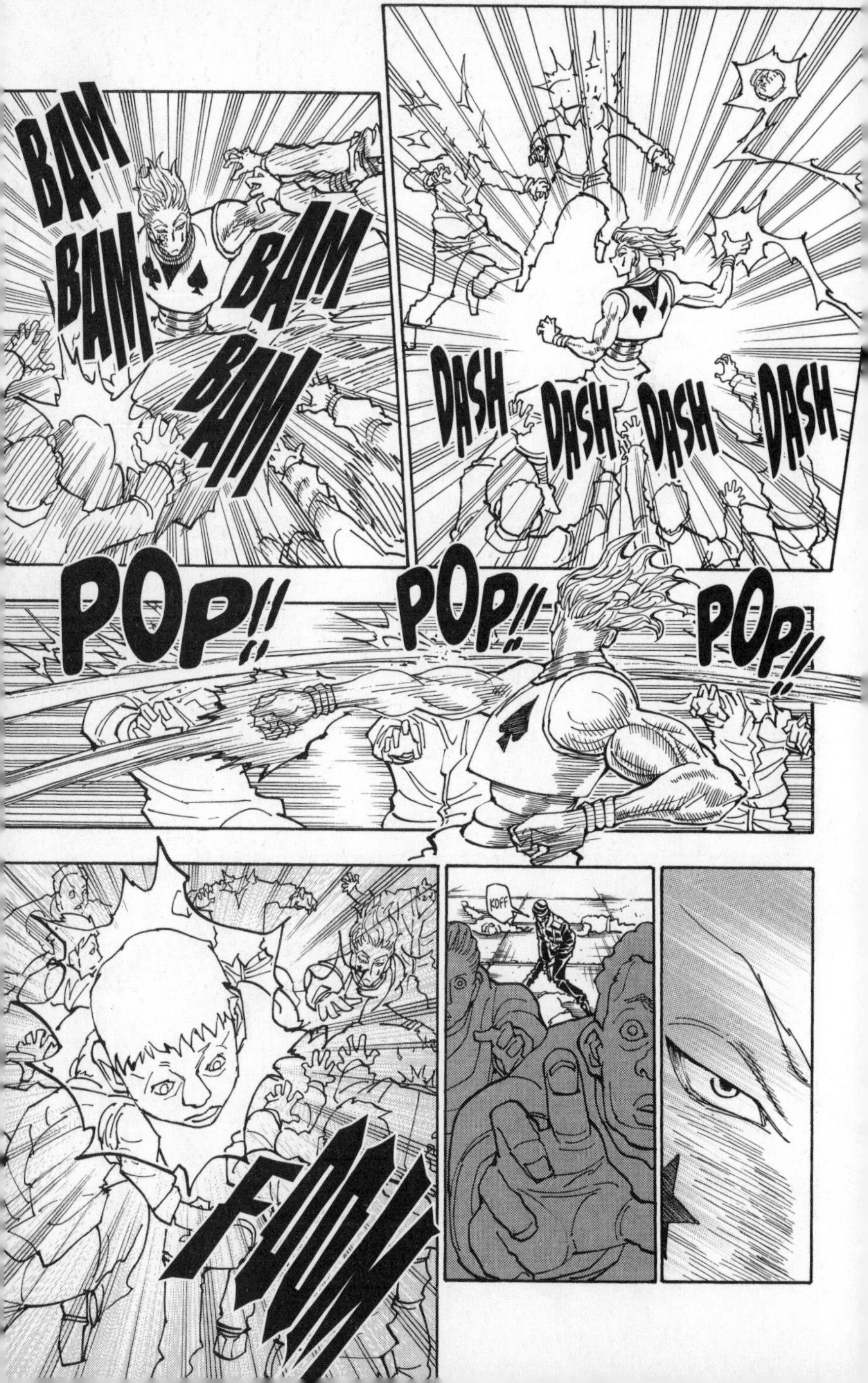
DASH
DASH
DASH
DASH
BAM
BAM
BAM
BAM
POP!!
POP!!
POP!!
KOFF

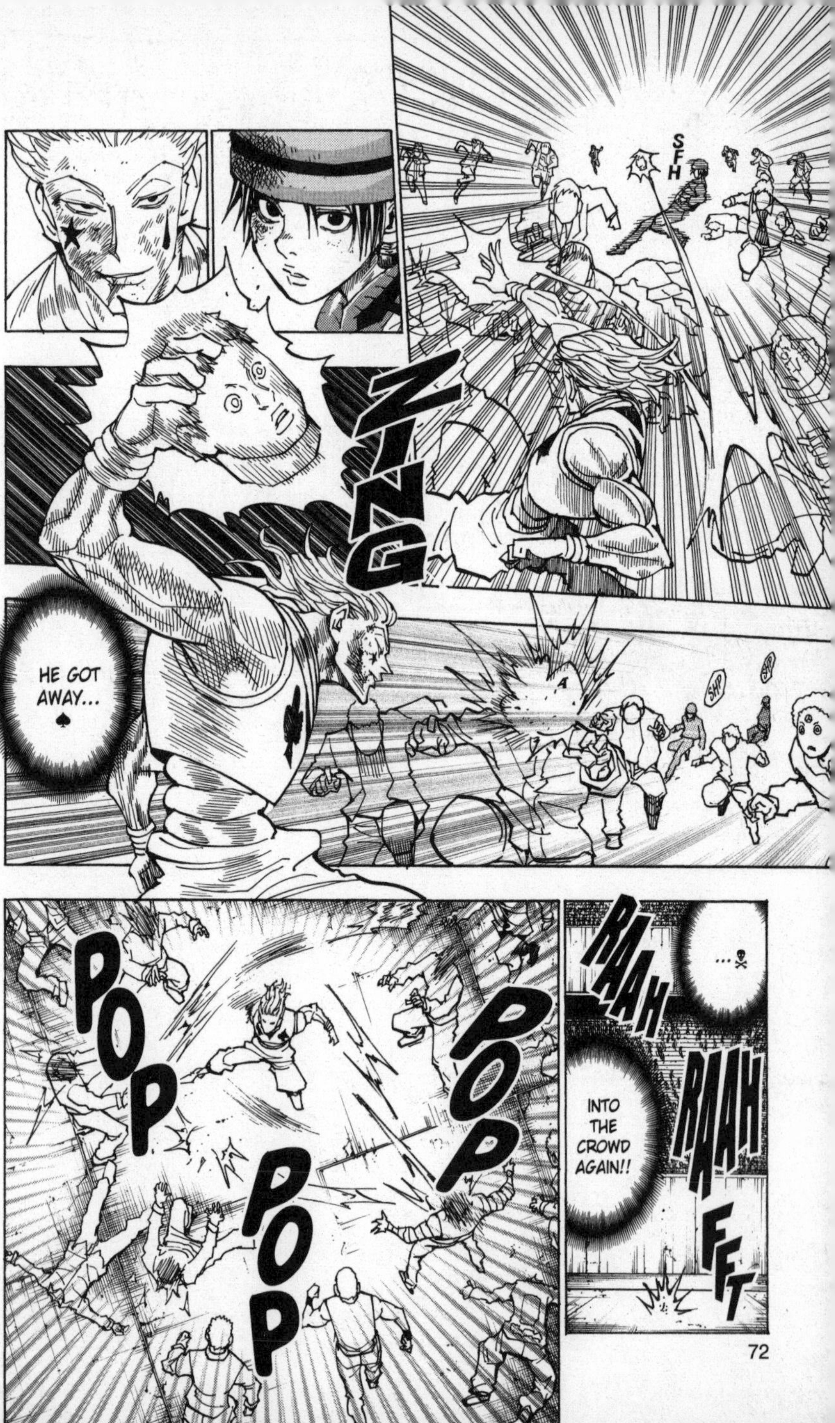
SFH
ZING
SHP
SHP
HE GOT AWAY... ♠
RAAH
...☠
RAAH
INTO THE CROWD AGAIN!!
FFFT
POP
POP
POP
POP

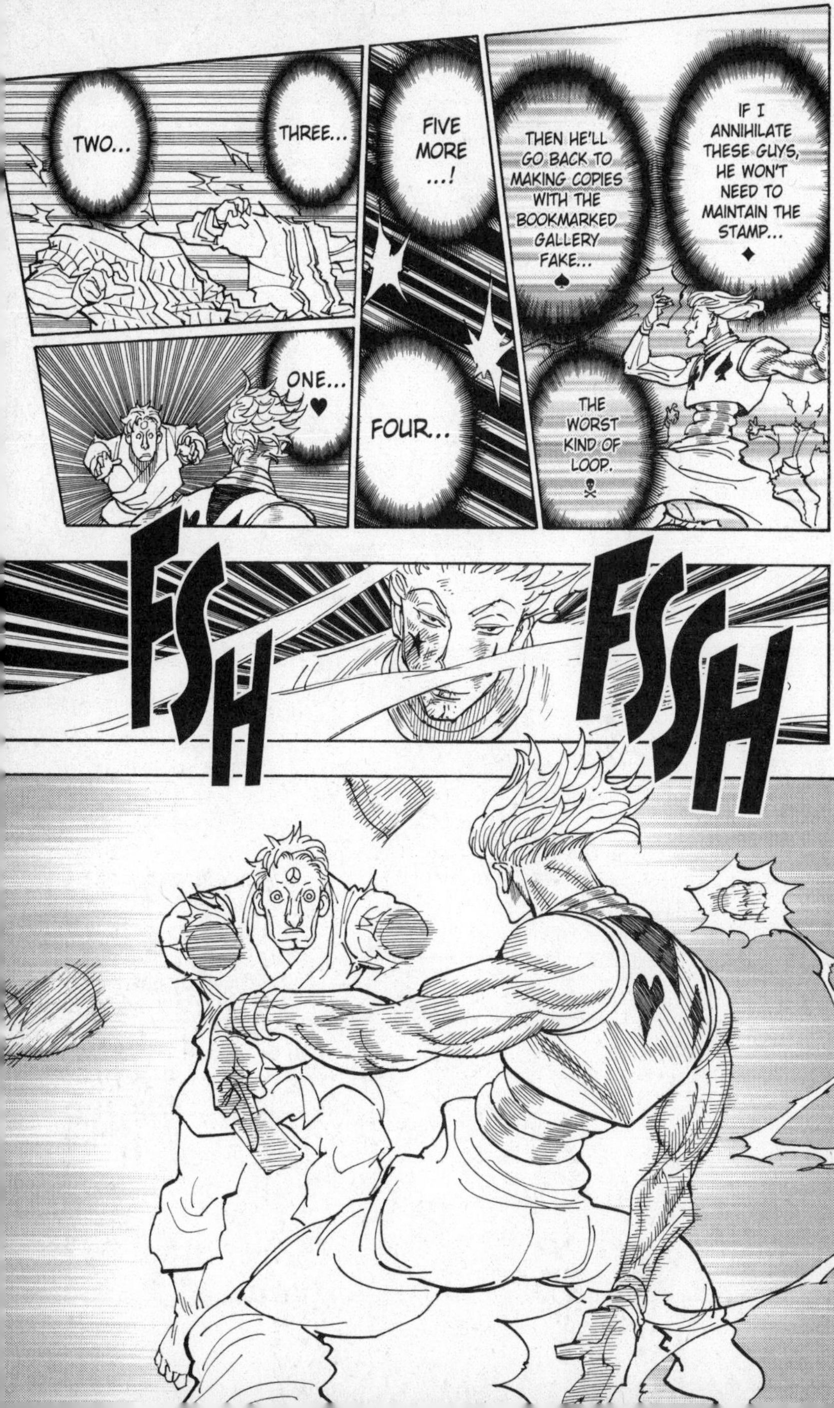
IF I ANNIHILATE THESE GUYS, HE WON'T NEED TO MAINTAIN THE STAMP... ♦
THEN HE'LL GO BACK TO MAKING COPIES WITH THE BOOKMARKED GALLERY FAKE... ♠
THE WORST KIND OF LOOP. ☠
FIVE MORE ...!
FOUR...
THREE...
TWO...
ONE... ♥
FSH
FSH

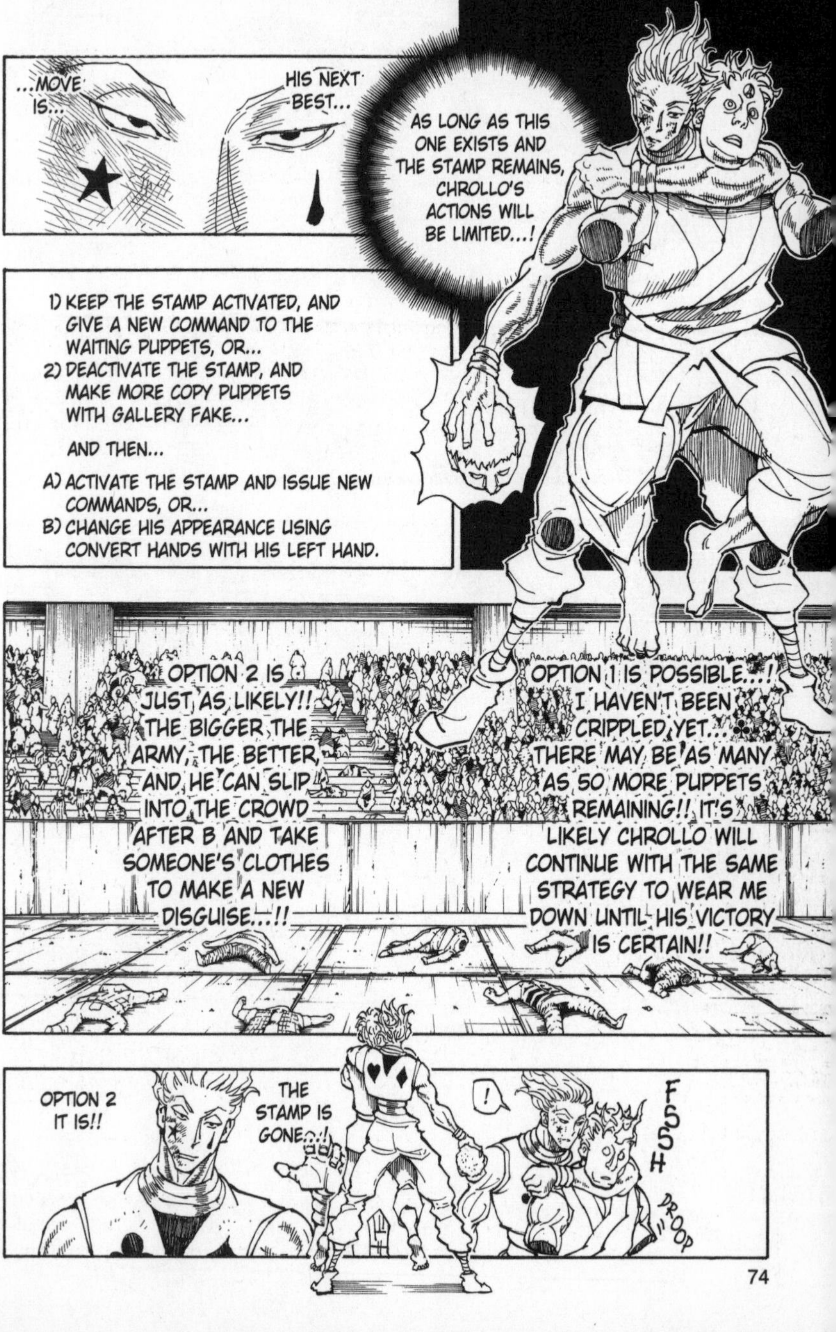
AS LONG AS THIS ONE EXISTS AND THE STAMP REMAINS, CHROLLO'S ACTIONS WILL BE LIMITED...!
HIS NEXT BEST...
...MOVE IS...
1) KEEP THE STAMP ACTIVATED, AND GIVE A NEW COMMAND TO THE WAITING PUPPETS, OR...
2) DEACTIVATE THE STAMP, AND MAKE MORE COPY PUPPETS WITH GALLERY FAKE...
AND THEN...
A) ACTIVATE THE STAMP AND ISSUE NEW COMMANDS, OR...
B) CHANGE HIS APPEARANCE USING CONVERT HANDS WITH HIS LEFT HAND.
OPTION 1 IS POSSIBLE...! I HAVEN'T BEEN CRIPPLED YET... THERE MAY BE AS MANY AS 50 MORE PUPPETS REMAINING!! IT'S LIKELY CHROLLO WILL CONTINUE WITH THE SAME STRATEGY TO WEAR ME DOWN UNTIL HIS VICTORY IS CERTAIN!!
OPTION 2 IS JUST AS LIKELY!! THE BIGGER THE ARMY, THE BETTER, AND HE CAN SLIP INTO THE CROWD AFTER B AND TAKE SOMEONE'S CLOTHES TO MAKE A NEW DISGUISE...!!
FSSH
DROOP
!
THE STAMP IS GONE...!
OPTION 2 IT IS!!

READ THIS WAY

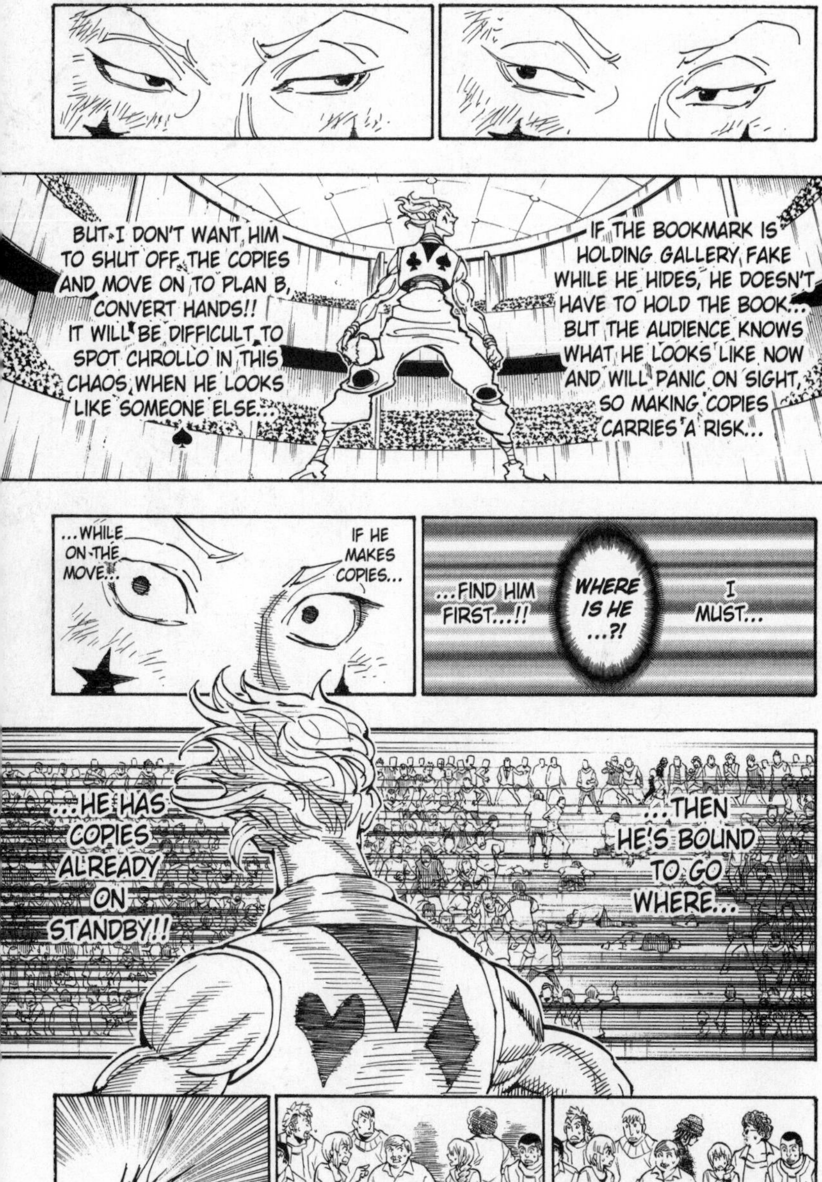
IF THE BOOKMARK IS HOLDING GALLERY FAKE WHILE HE HIDES, HE DOESN'T HAVE TO HOLD THE BOOK... BUT THE AUDIENCE KNOWS WHAT HE LOOKS LIKE NOW AND WILL PANIC ON SIGHT, SO MAKING COPIES CARRIES A RISK...
BUT I DON'T WANT HIM TO SHUT OFF THE COPIES AND MOVE ON TO PLAN B, CONVERT HANDS!! IT WILL BE DIFFICULT TO SPOT CHROLLO IN THIS CHAOS WHEN HE LOOKS LIKE SOMEONE ELSE...
I MUST...
WHERE IS HE ...?!
...FIND HIM FIRST...!!
IF HE MAKES COPIES...
...WHILE ON THE MOVE...
...THEN HE'S BOUND TO GO WHERE...
...HE HAS COPIES ALREADY ON STANDBY!!

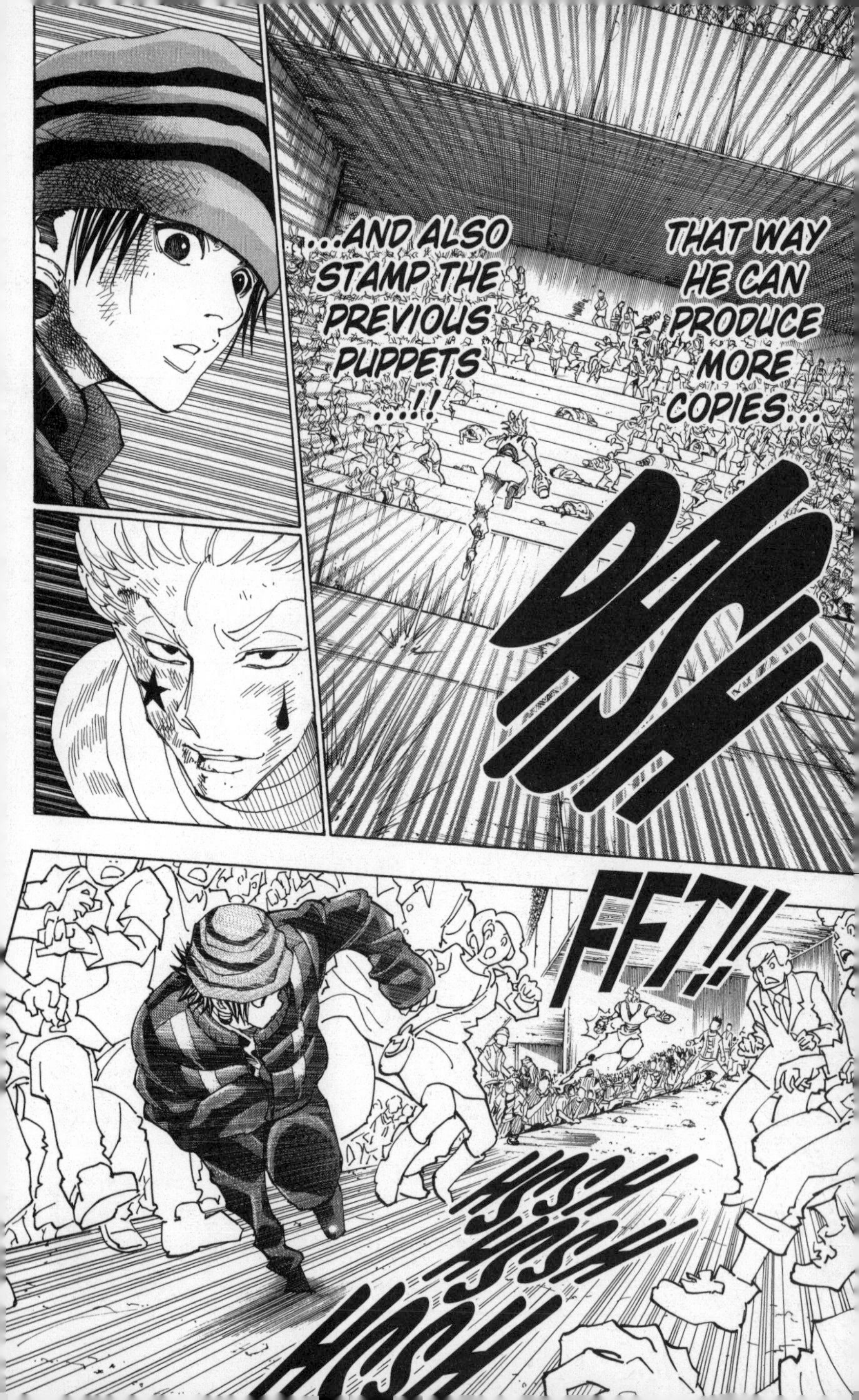
THAT WAY HE CAN PRODUCE MORE COPIES...
...AND ALSO STAMP THE PREVIOUS PUPPETS...!!
DASH
FFT!!
HUSH HUSH HUSH

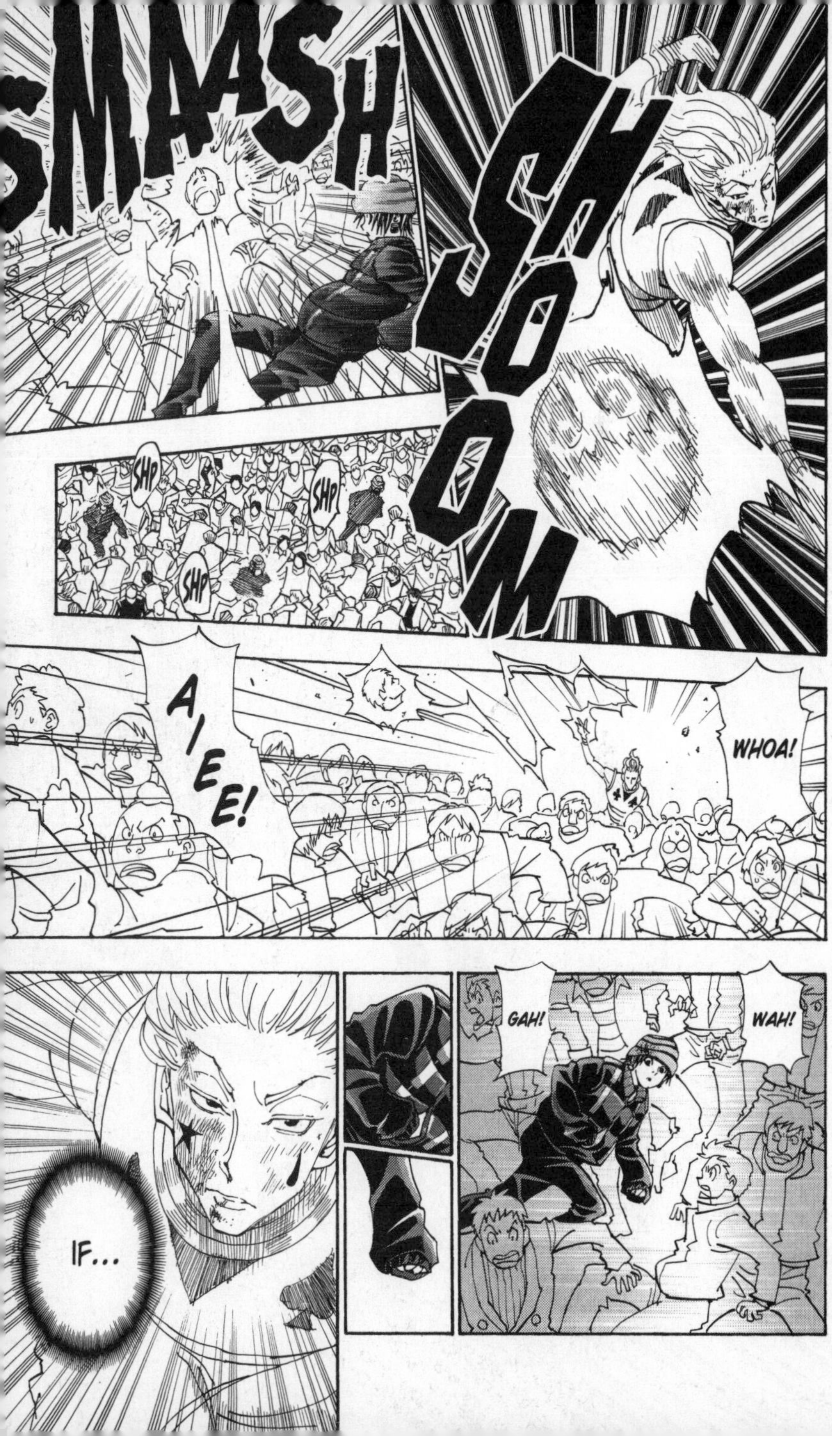
SHOOM
SMASH
SHP
SHP
SHP
WHOA!
AIEE!
WAH!
GAH!
IF...

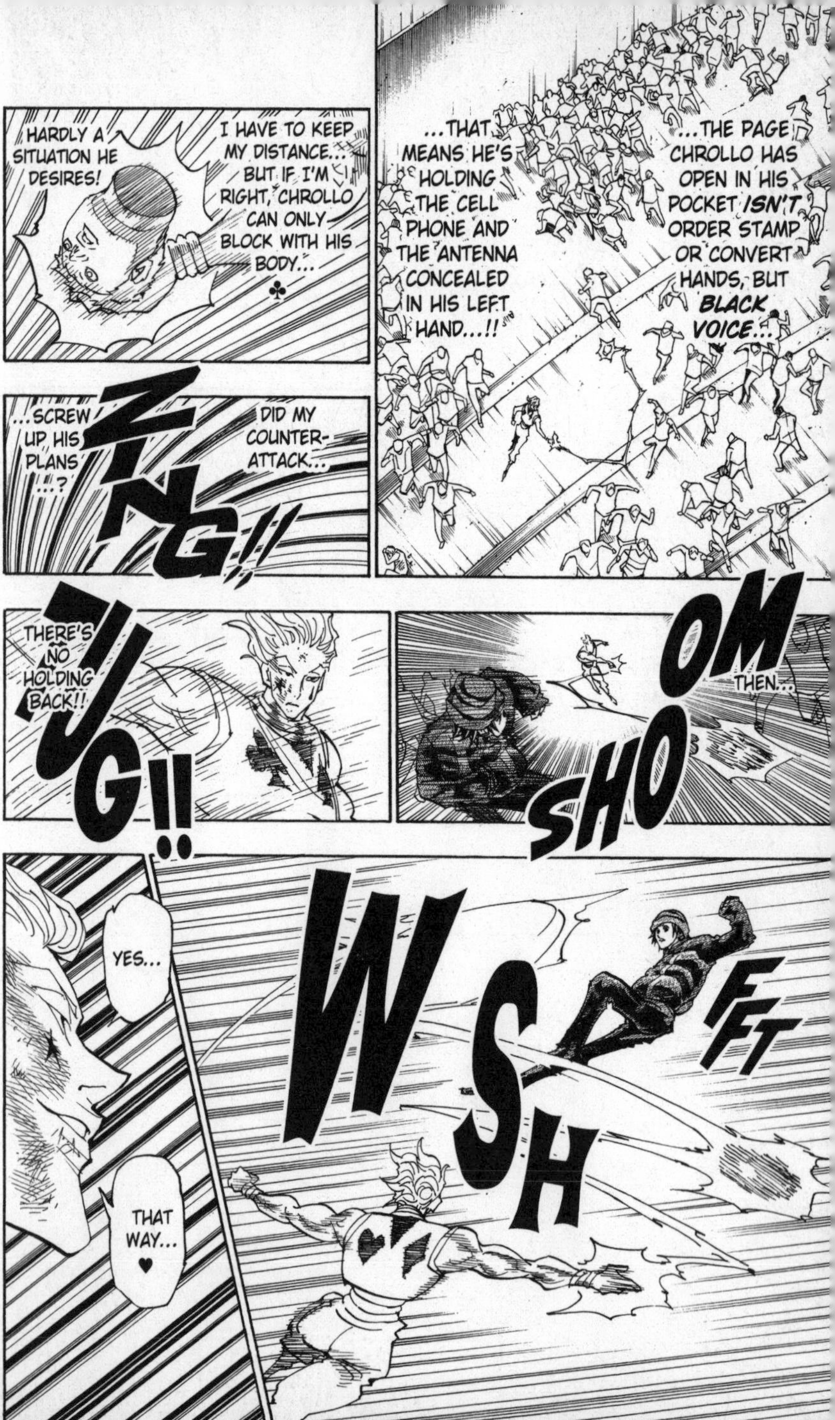
...THE PAGE CHROLLO HAS OPEN IN HIS POCKET ***ISN'T*** ORDER STAMP OR CONVERT HANDS, BUT ***BLACK VOICE***...
...THAT MEANS HE'S HOLDING THE CELL PHONE AND THE ANTENNA CONCEALED IN HIS LEFT HAND...!!
I HAVE TO KEEP MY DISTANCE... BUT IF I'M RIGHT, CHROLLO CAN ONLY BLOCK WITH HIS BODY... ♣
HARDLY A SITUATION HE DESIRES!
DID MY COUNTER-ATTACK...
ZNG!!
...SCREW UP HIS PLANS ...?
SHOOOM
THEN...
JUG!!
THERE'S NO HOLDING BACK!!
WSHFFT
YES...
THAT WAY... ♥

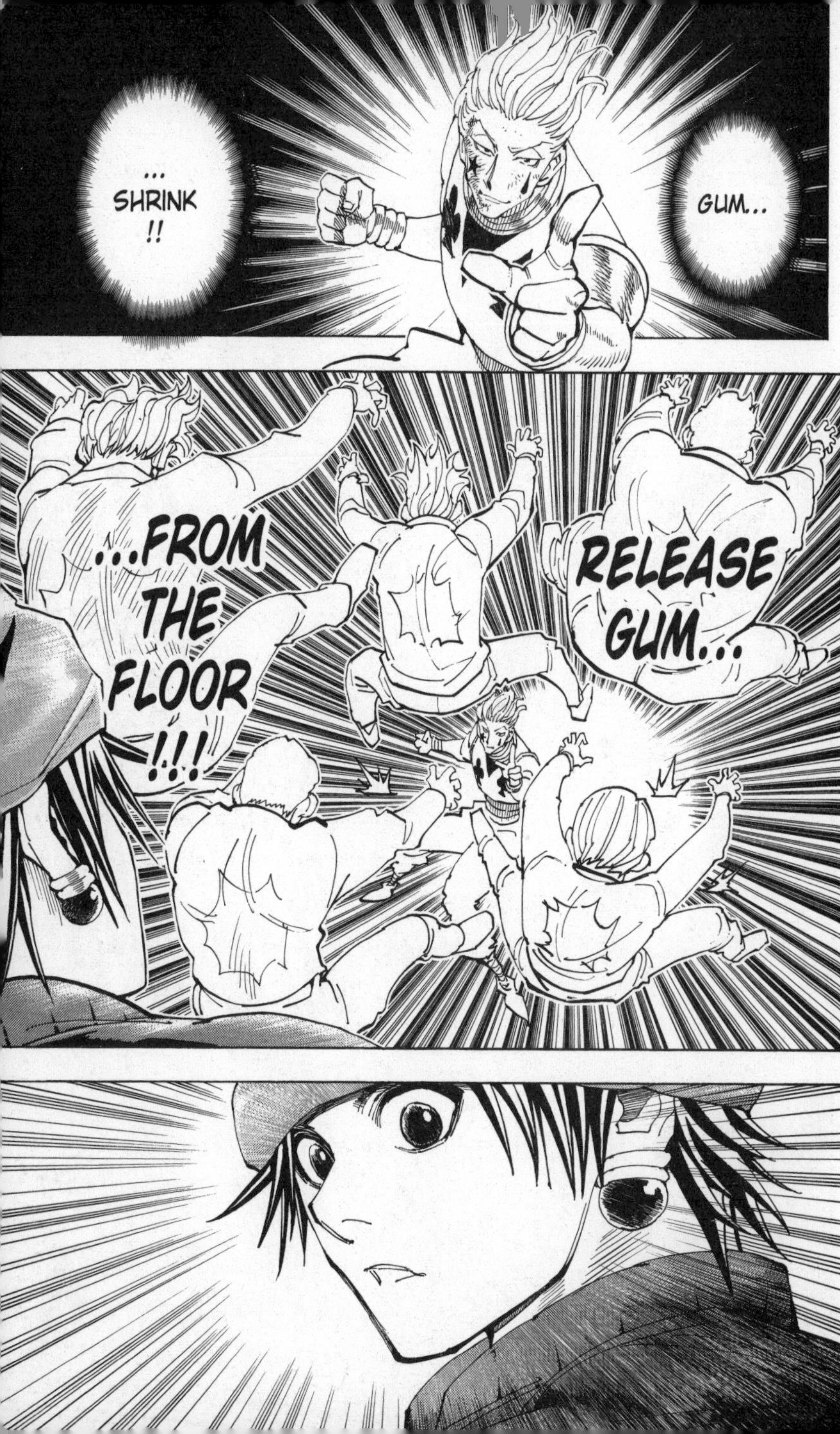
GUM...
... SHRINK !!
RELEASE GUM...
...FROM THE FLOOR !!!

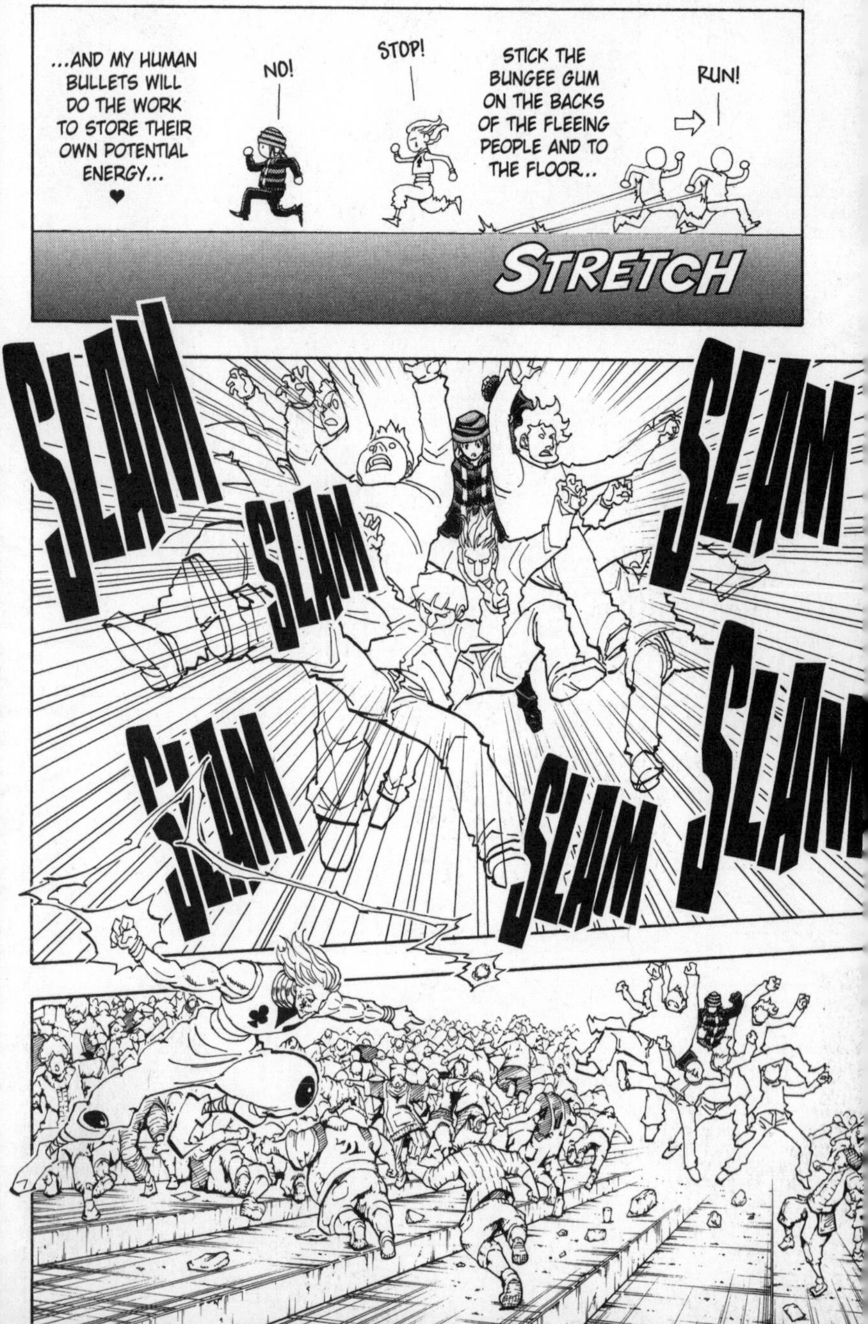
RUN!
STICK THE BUNGEE GUM ON THE BACKS OF THE FLEEING PEOPLE AND TO THE FLOOR...
STOP!
NO!
...AND MY HUMAN BULLETS WILL DO THE WORK TO STORE THEIR OWN POTENTIAL ENERGY... ♥
STRETCH
SLAM
SLAM
SLAM
SLAM
SLAM
SLAM

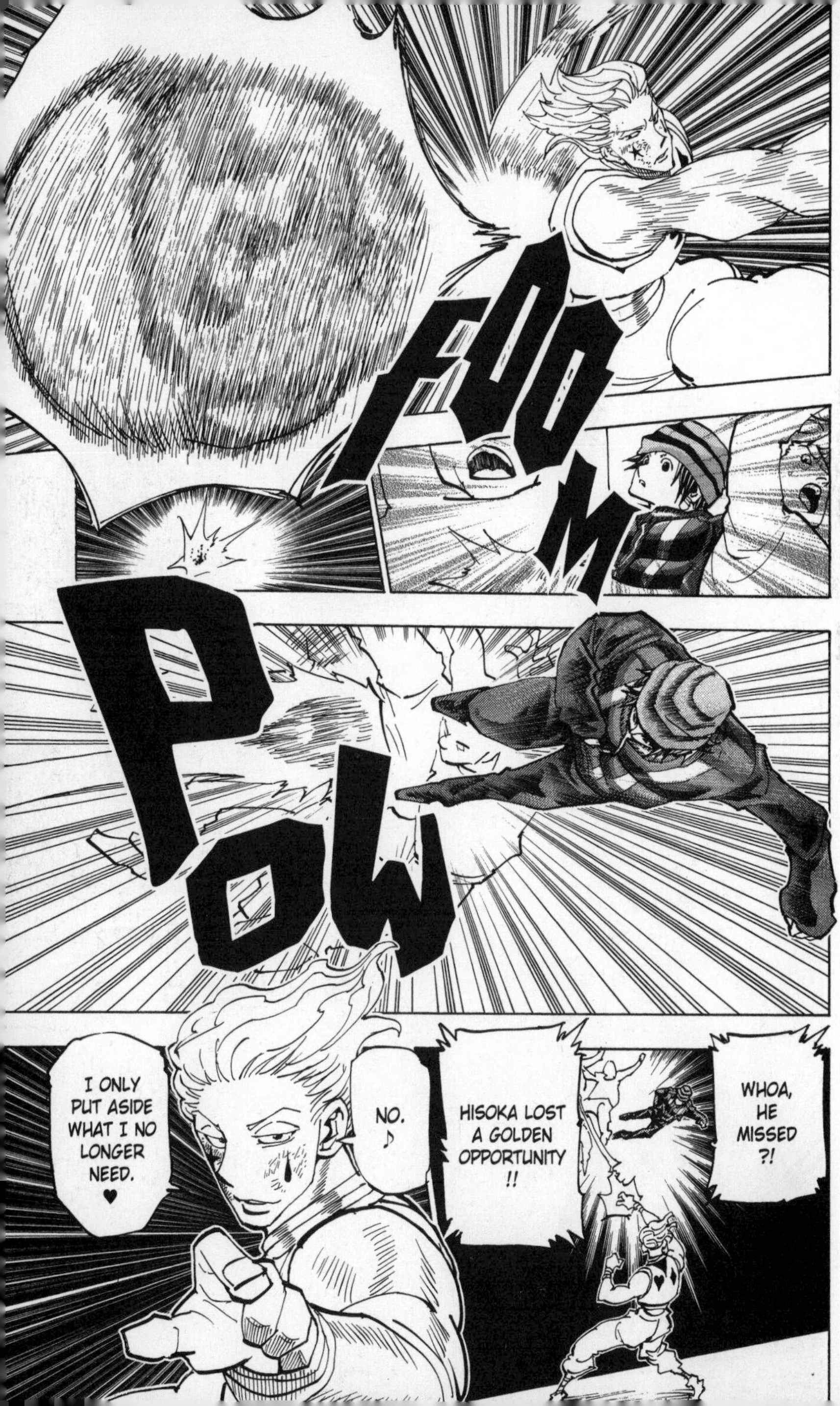
FOOM
POW
WHOA, HE MISSED ?!
HISOKA LOST A GOLDEN OPPORTUNITY !!
NO. ♪
I ONLY PUT ASIDE WHAT I NO LONGER NEED. ♥

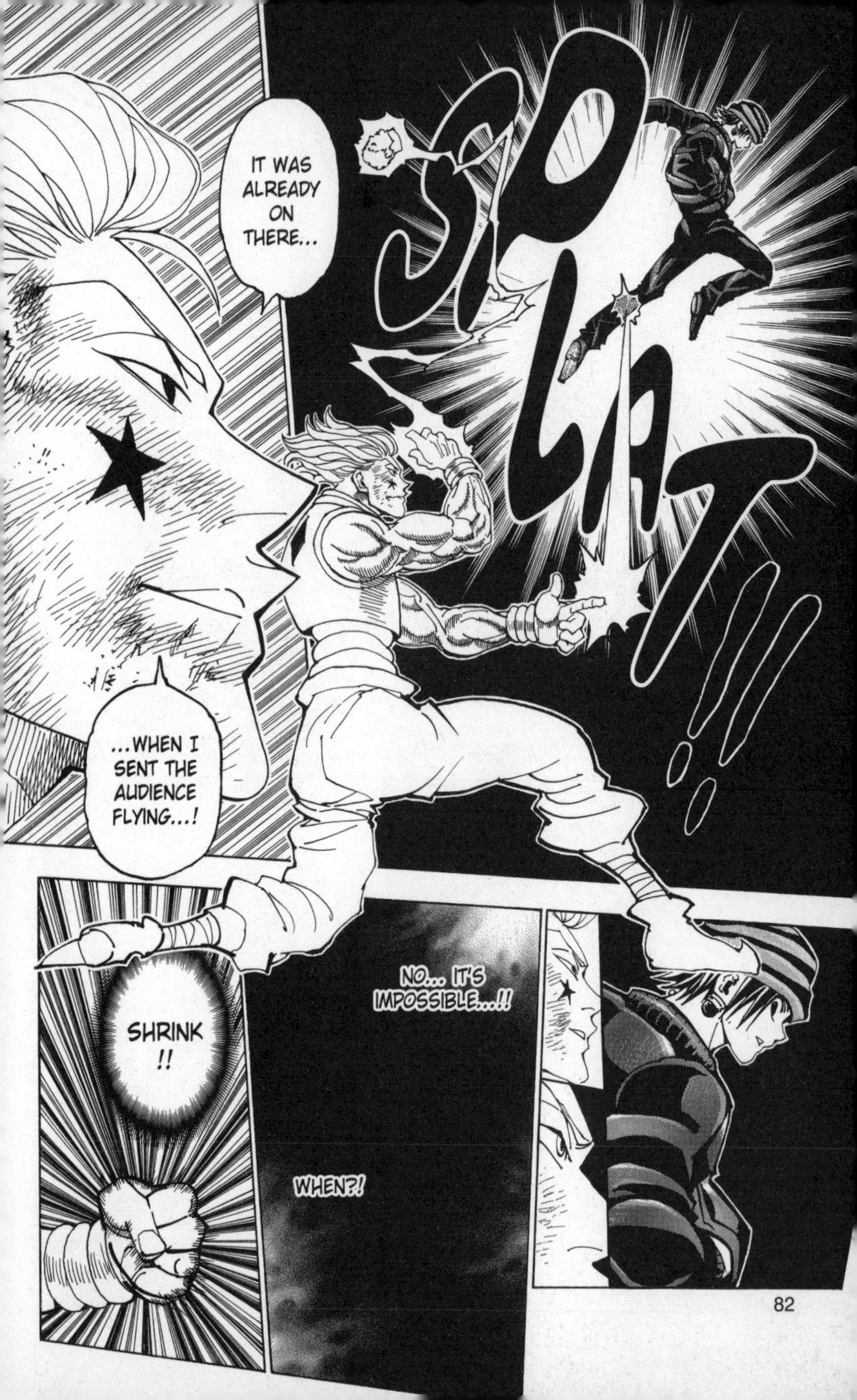
SPLAT!!
IT WAS ALREADY ON THERE...
...WHEN I SENT THE AUDIENCE FLYING...!
NO... IT'S IMPOSSIBLE...!!
WHEN?!
SHRINK!!

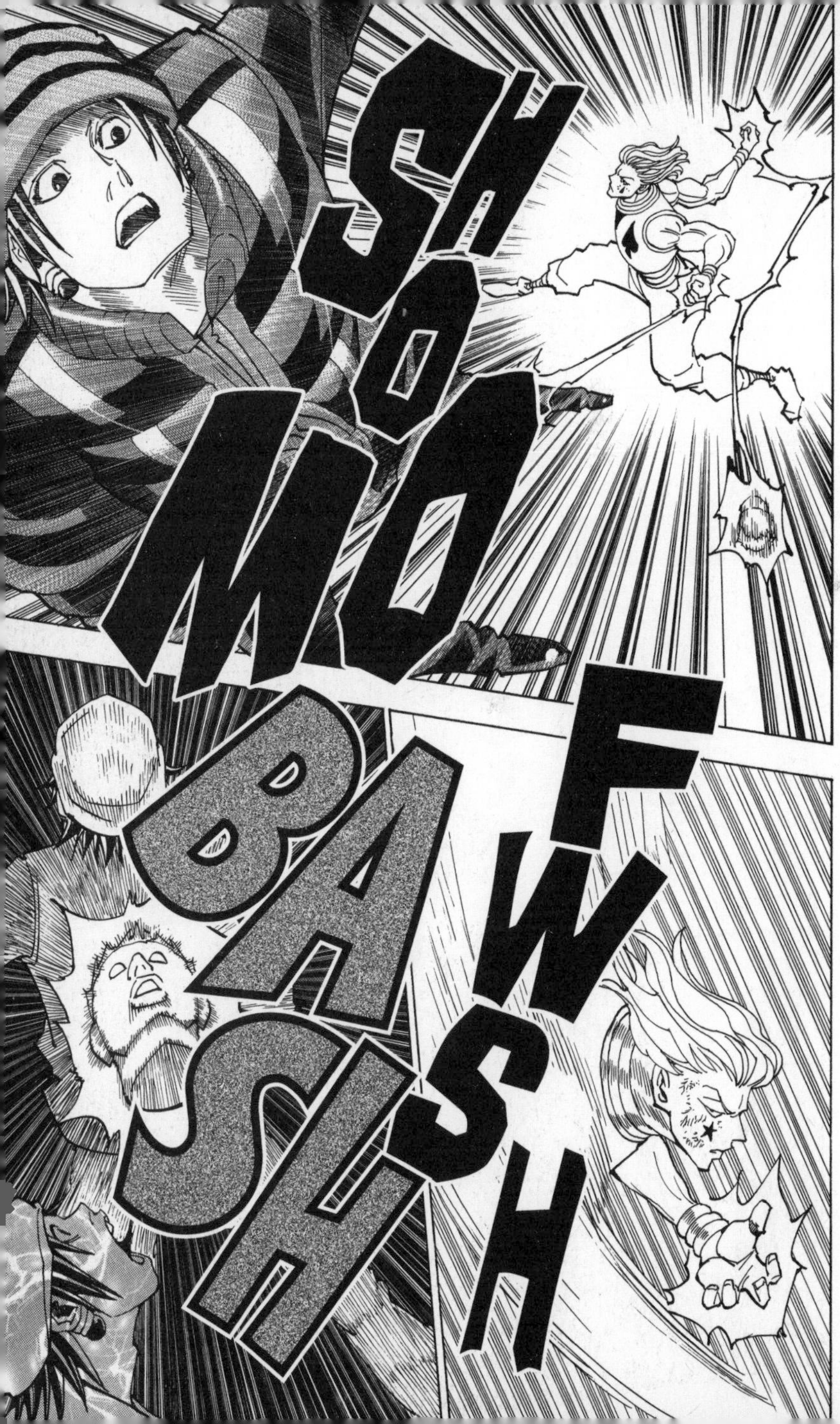

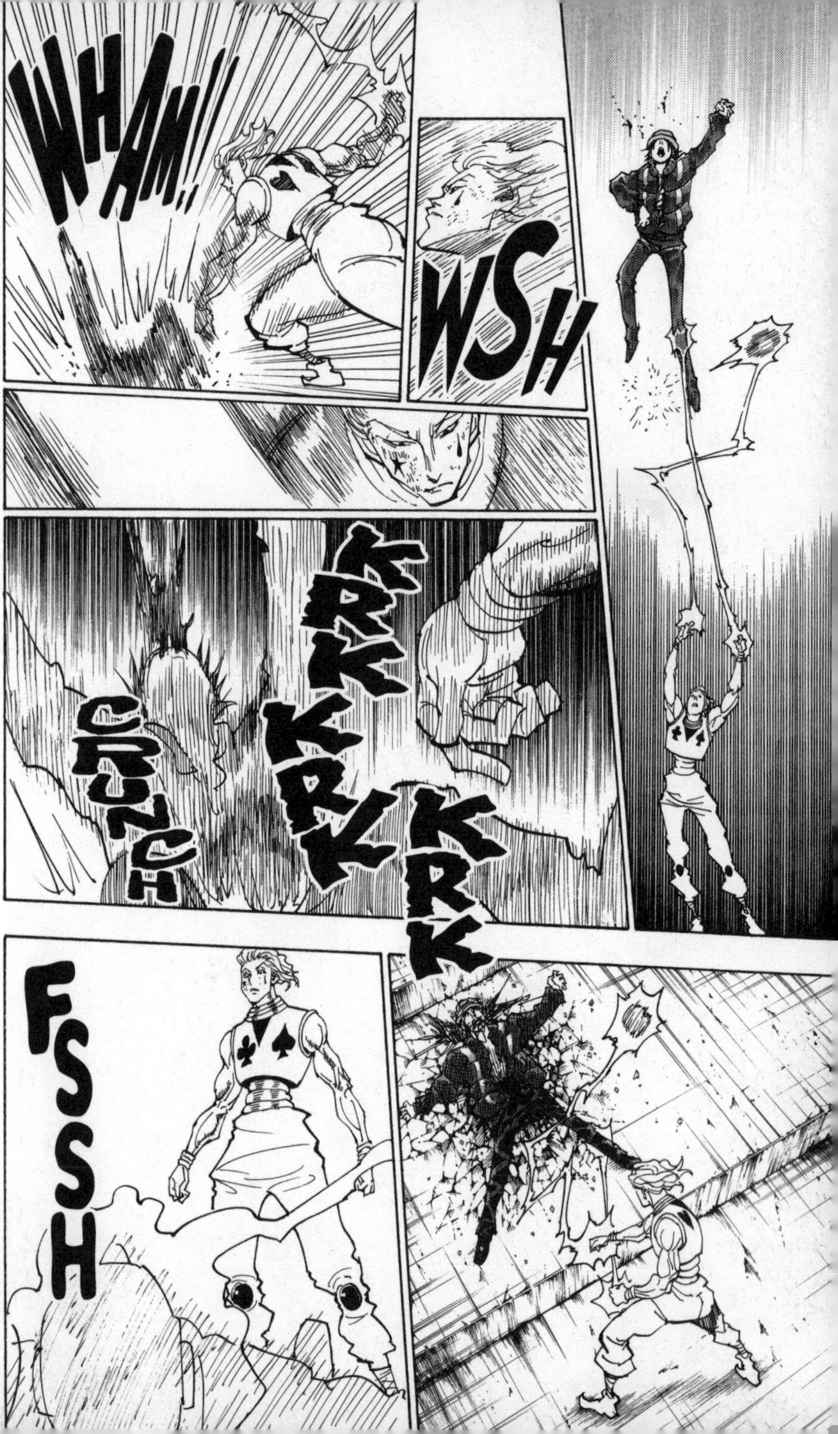
WSH
WHAM!!
KRKRKRKRKRK
CRUNCH
FSSH

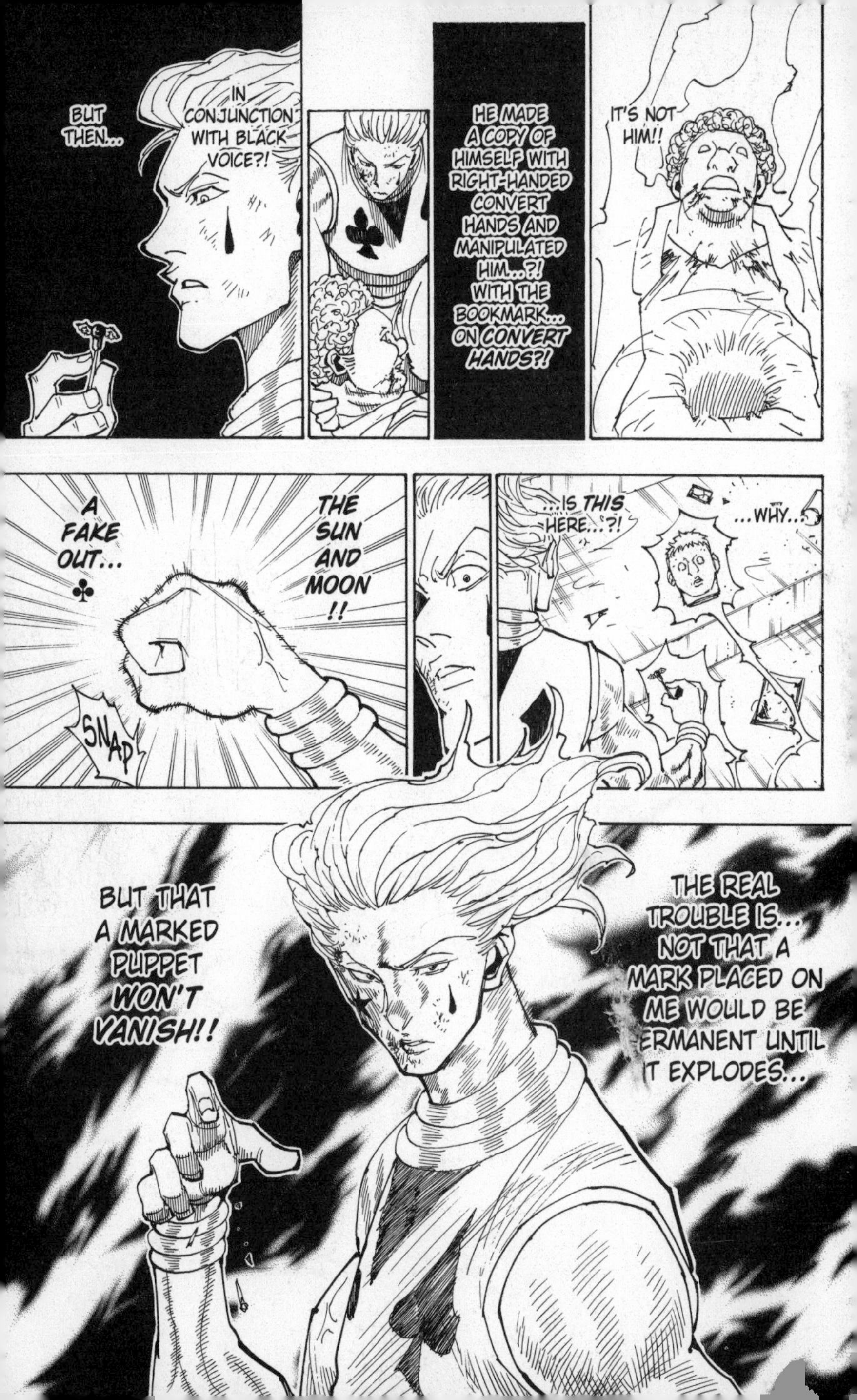
IT'S NOT HIM!!
HE MADE A COPY OF HIMSELF WITH RIGHT-HANDED CONVERT HANDS AND MANIPULATED HIM...?! WITH THE BOOKMARK... ON CONVERT HANDS?!
IN CONJUNCTION WITH BLACK VOICE?!
BUT THEN...
...WHY...
...IS THIS HERE...?!
THE SUN AND MOON!!
A FAKE OUT... ♣
SNAP
THE REAL TROUBLE IS... NOT THAT A MARK PLACED ON ME WOULD BE ERMANENT UNTIL IT EXPLODES...
BUT THAT A MARKED PUPPET WON'T VANISH!!

MY YEARLY AVERAGE
USED TO BE 190...
I REMEMBER I USED TO
AIM FOR A BROOKLYN ON
PURPOSE WHEN I HAD TOO
MANY TEN PINS LEFT...

HIYAH!

IN SINGLE LANE... I DON'T THINK I'D HIT 170 IN DOUBLE LANE.

2/3

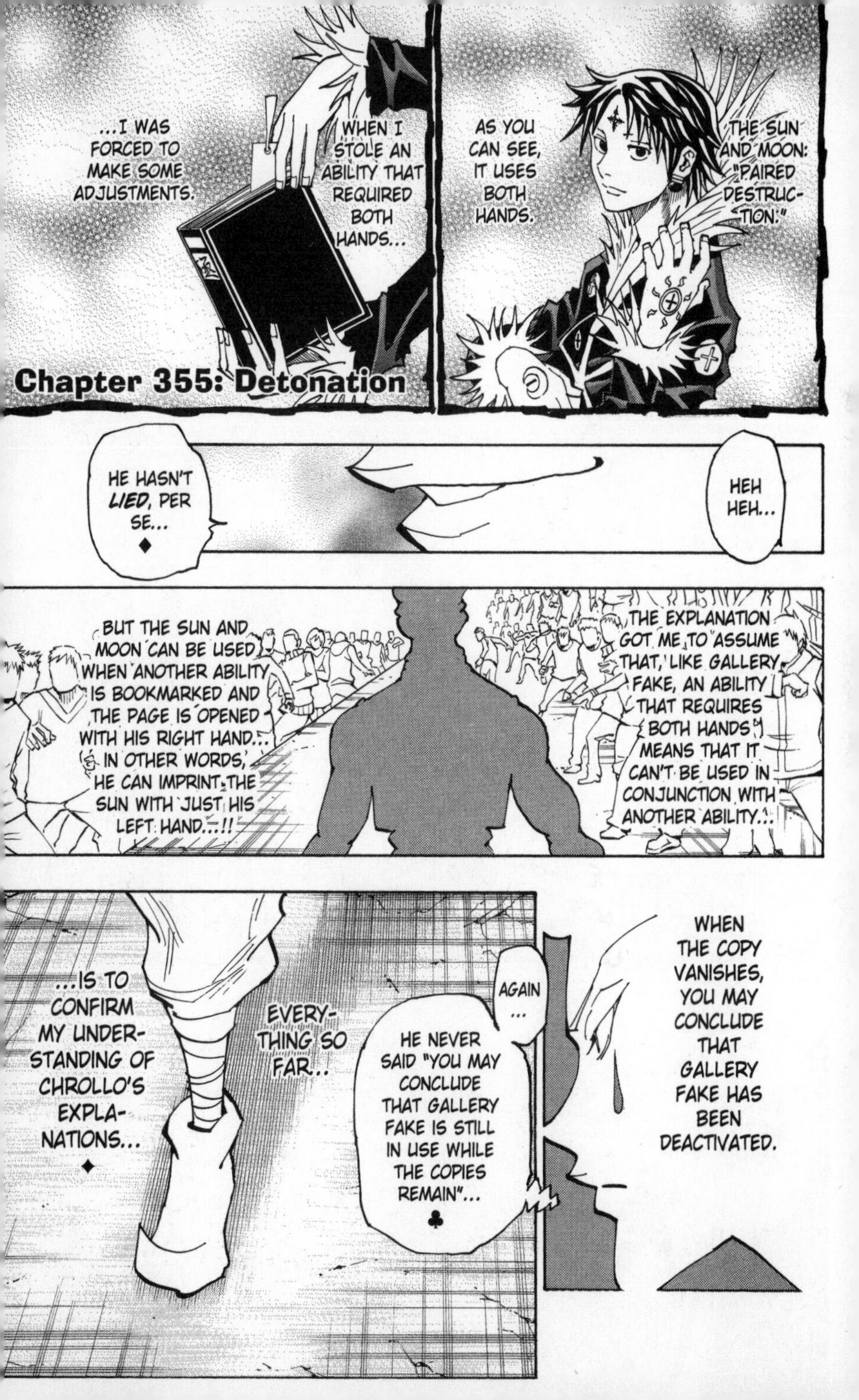
THE SUN AND MOON: "PAIRED DESTRUCTION."
AS YOU CAN SEE, IT USES BOTH HANDS.
WHEN I STOLE AN ABILITY THAT REQUIRED BOTH HANDS...
...I WAS FORCED TO MAKE SOME ADJUSTMENTS.
Chapter 355: Detonation
HEH HEH...
HE HASN'T *LIED*, PER SE... ♦
THE EXPLANATION GOT ME TO ASSUME THAT, LIKE GALLERY FAKE, AN ABILITY THAT REQUIRES BOTH HANDS MEANS THAT IT CAN'T BE USED IN CONJUNCTION WITH ANOTHER ABILITY...
BUT THE SUN AND MOON CAN BE USED WHEN ANOTHER ABILITY IS BOOKMARKED AND THE PAGE IS OPENED WITH HIS RIGHT HAND... IN OTHER WORDS, HE CAN IMPRINT THE SUN WITH JUST HIS LEFT HAND...!!
WHEN THE COPY VANISHES, YOU MAY CONCLUDE THAT GALLERY FAKE HAS BEEN DEACTIVATED.
AGAIN...
HE NEVER SAID "YOU MAY CONCLUDE THAT GALLERY FAKE IS STILL IN USE WHILE THE COPIES REMAIN"... ♣
EVERYTHING SO FAR...
...IS TO CONFIRM MY UNDERSTANDING OF CHROLLO'S EXPLANATIONS... ♦

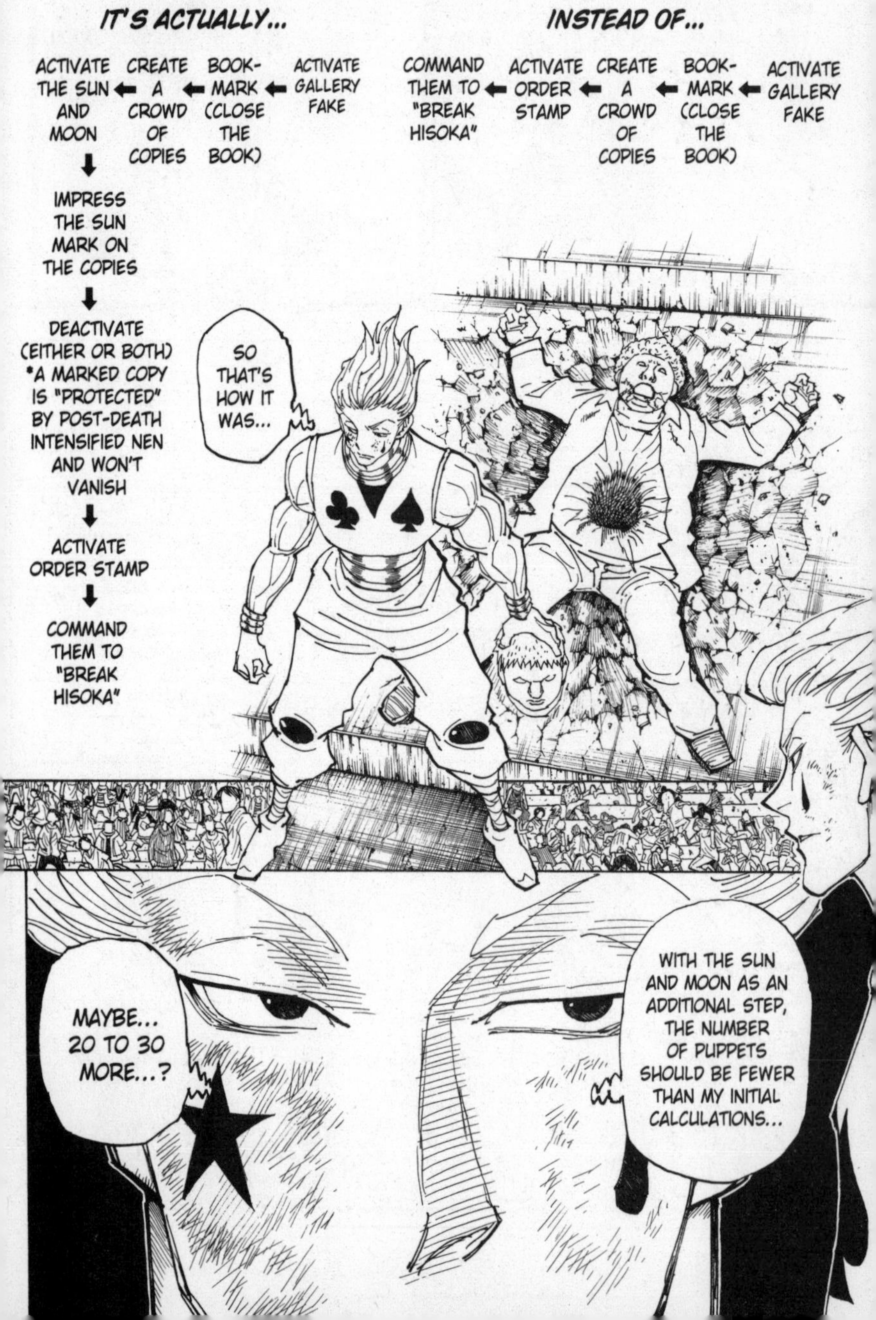
INSTEAD OF...
ACTIVATE GALLERY FAKE
BOOK-MARK (CLOSE THE BOOK)
CREATE A CROWD OF COPIES
ACTIVATE ORDER STAMP
COMMAND THEM TO "BREAK HISOKA"
IT'S ACTUALLY...
ACTIVATE GALLERY FAKE
BOOK-MARK (CLOSE THE BOOK)
CREATE A CROWD OF COPIES
ACTIVATE THE SUN AND MOON
IMPRESS THE SUN MARK ON THE COPIES
DEACTIVATE (EITHER OR BOTH) *A MARKED COPY IS "PROTECTED" BY POST-DEATH INTENSIFIED NEN AND WON'T VANISH
ACTIVATE ORDER STAMP
COMMAND THEM TO "BREAK HISOKA"
SO THAT'S HOW IT WAS...
WITH THE SUN AND MOON AS AN ADDITIONAL STEP, THE NUMBER OF PUPPETS SHOULD BE FEWER THAN MY INITIAL CALCULATIONS...
MAYBE... 20 TO 30 MORE...?

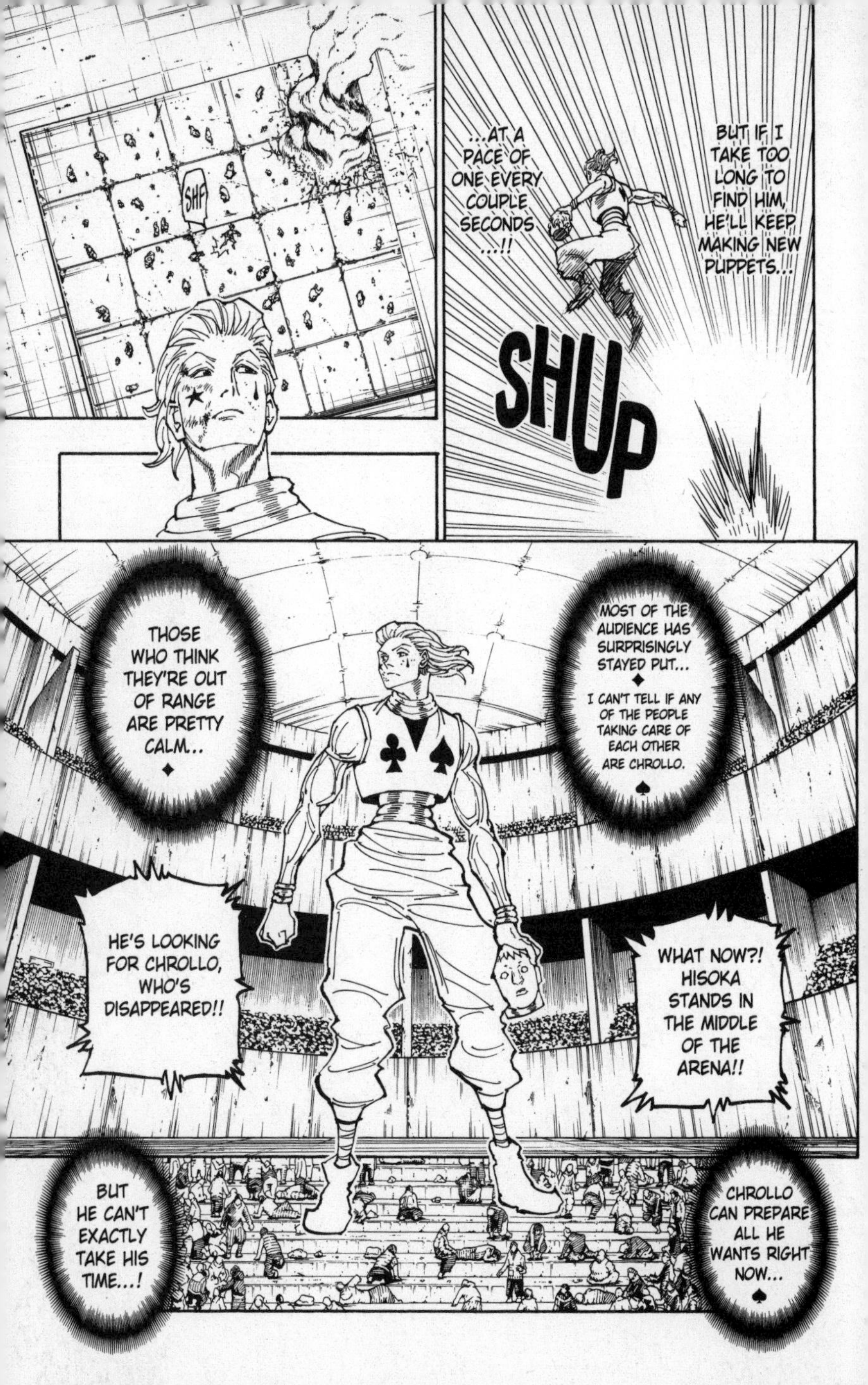
BUT IF I TAKE TOO LONG TO FIND HIM, HE'LL KEEP MAKING NEW PUPPETS...
...AT A PACE OF ONE EVERY COUPLE SECONDS...!!
SHUP
SHF
MOST OF THE AUDIENCE HAS SURPRISINGLY STAYED PUT... ♦ I CAN'T TELL IF ANY OF THE PEOPLE TAKING CARE OF EACH OTHER ARE CHROLLO. ♠
THOSE WHO THINK THEY'RE OUT OF RANGE ARE PRETTY CALM... ♦
WHAT NOW?! HISOKA STANDS IN THE MIDDLE OF THE ARENA!!
HE'S LOOKING FOR CHROLLO, WHO'S DISAPPEARED!!
CHROLLO CAN PREPARE ALL HE WANTS RIGHT NOW... ♠
BUT HE CAN'T EXACTLY TAKE HIS TIME...!

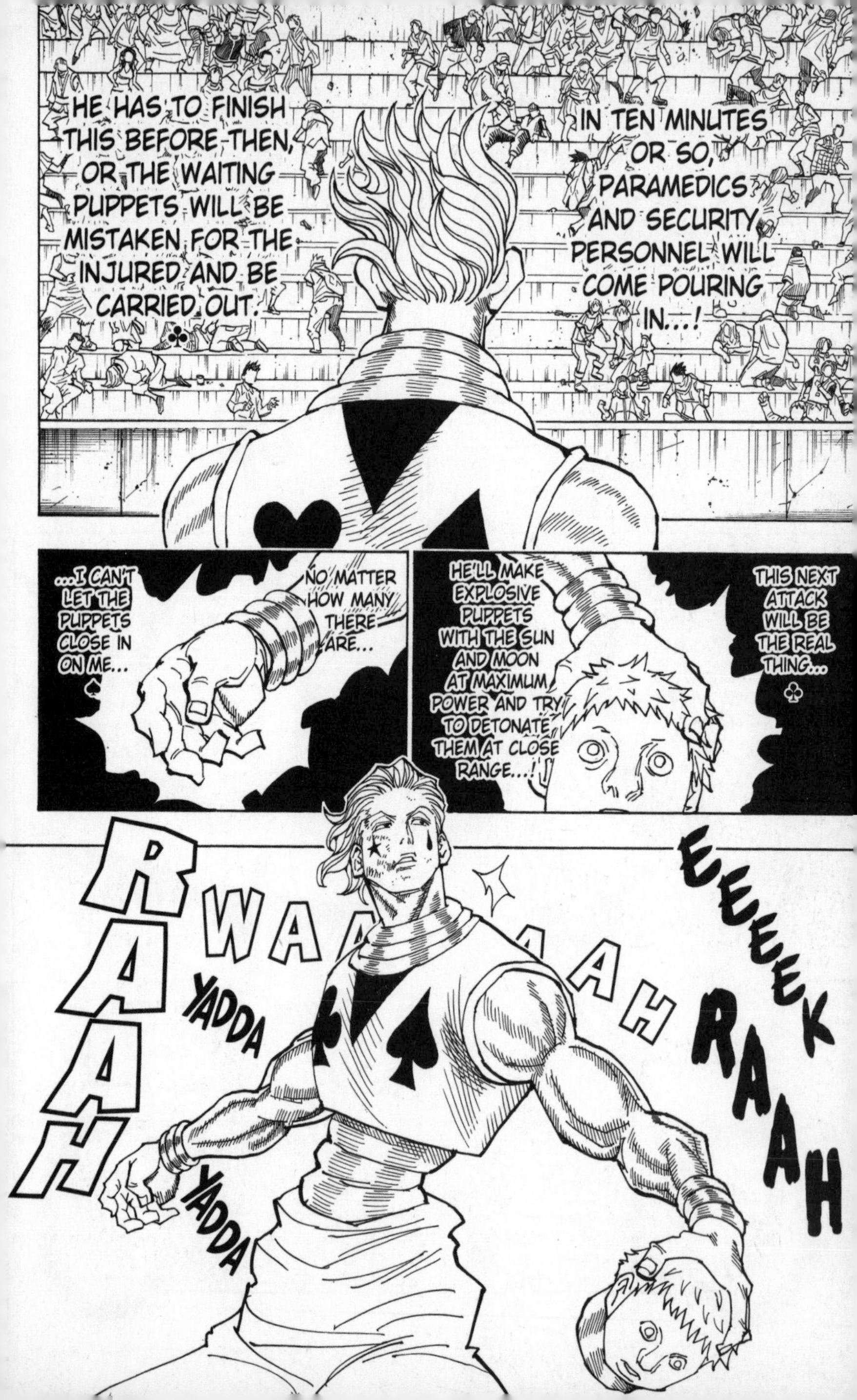
IN TEN MINUTES OR SO, PARAMEDICS AND SECURITY PERSONNEL WILL COME POURING IN...!
HE HAS TO FINISH THIS BEFORE THEN, OR THE WAITING PUPPETS WILL BE MISTAKEN FOR THE INJURED AND BE CARRIED OUT. ♣
THIS NEXT ATTACK WILL BE THE REAL THING... ♣
HE'LL MAKE EXPLOSIVE PUPPETS WITH THE SUN AND MOON AT MAXIMUM POWER AND TRY TO DETONATE THEM AT CLOSE RANGE...!
NO MATTER HOW MANY THERE ARE...
...I CAN'T LET THE PUPPETS CLOSE IN ON ME... ♠
EEEEEK
RAAAH
WAAAAH
YADDA
YADDA
RAAH

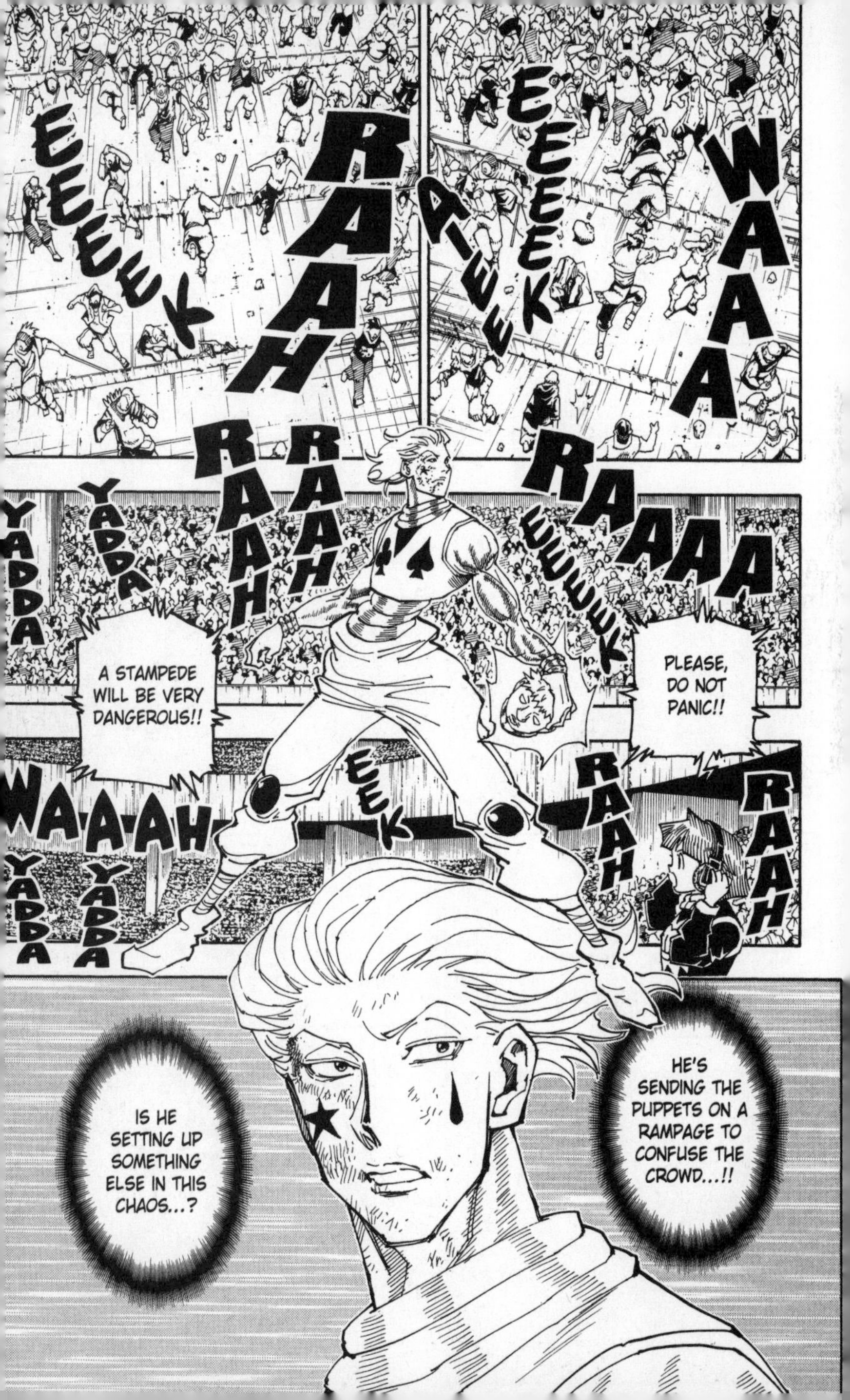
WAAAA
EEEEEK
AIEEEK
RAAAH
EEEEEK
RAAAAA
EEEEEEK
PLEASE, DO NOT PANIC!!
RAAAH
RAAAH
YADDA YADDA
YADDA YADDA
A STAMPEDE WILL BE VERY DANGEROUS!!
RAAAH
RAAAH
EEEK
WA-A-AH
YADDA YADDA
YADDA YADDA
HE'S SENDING THE PUPPETS ON A RAMPAGE TO CONFUSE THE CROWD...!!
IS HE SETTING UP SOMETHING ELSE IN THIS CHAOS...?

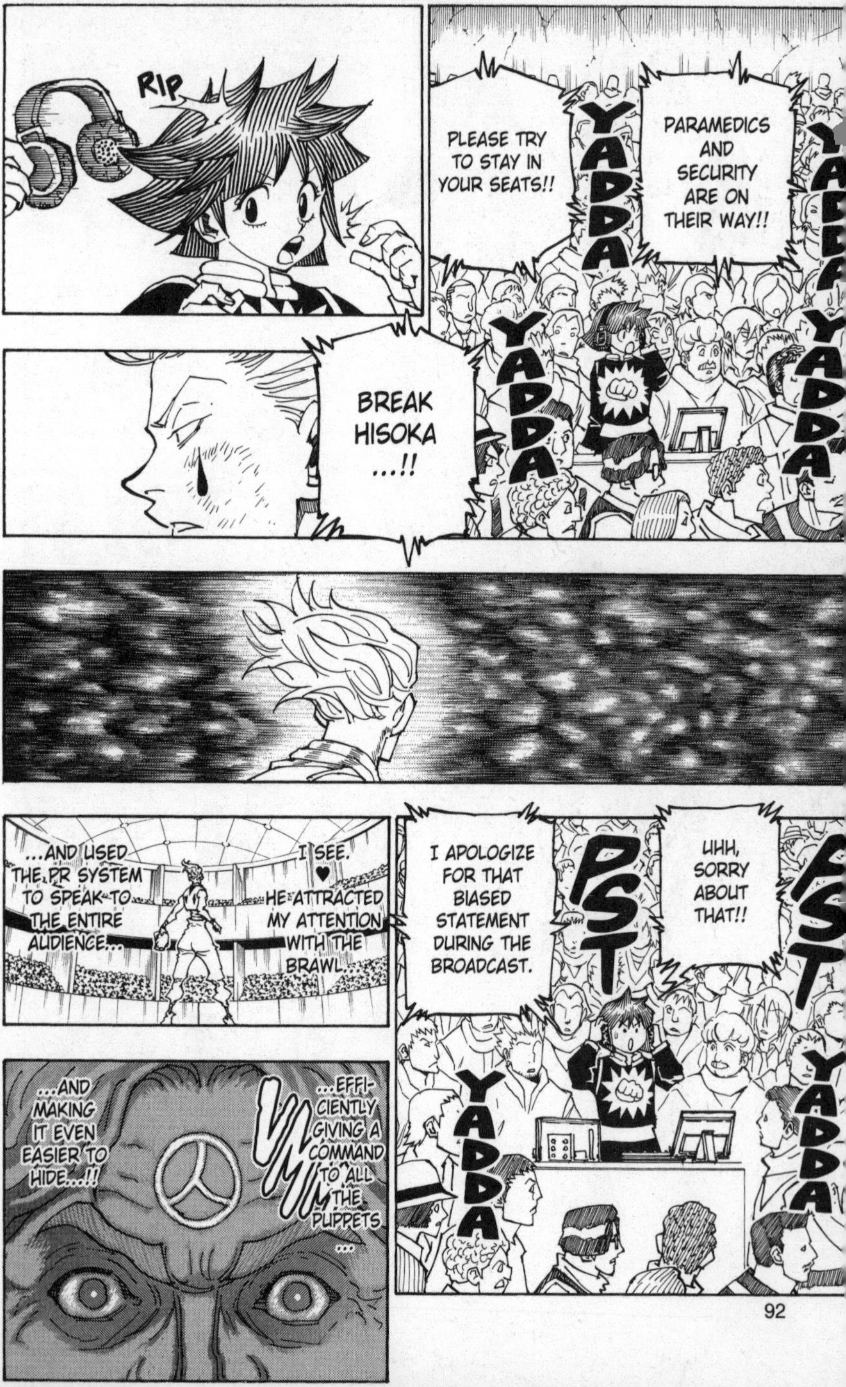
PARAMEDICS AND SECURITY ARE ON THEIR WAY!!
YADDA
PLEASE TRY TO STAY IN YOUR SEATS!!
YADDA
YADDA
RIP
BREAK HISOKA ...!!
UHH, SORRY ABOUT THAT!!
PST
I APOLOGIZE FOR THAT BIASED STATEMENT DURING THE BROADCAST.
PST
YADDA
YADDA
I SEE. ♥ HE ATTRACTED MY ATTENTION WITH THE BRAWL...
...AND USED THE PR SYSTEM TO SPEAK TO THE ENTIRE AUDIENCE...
...EFFICIENTLY GIVING A COMMAND TO ALL THE PUPPETS...
...AND MAKING IT EVEN EASIER TO HIDE...!!

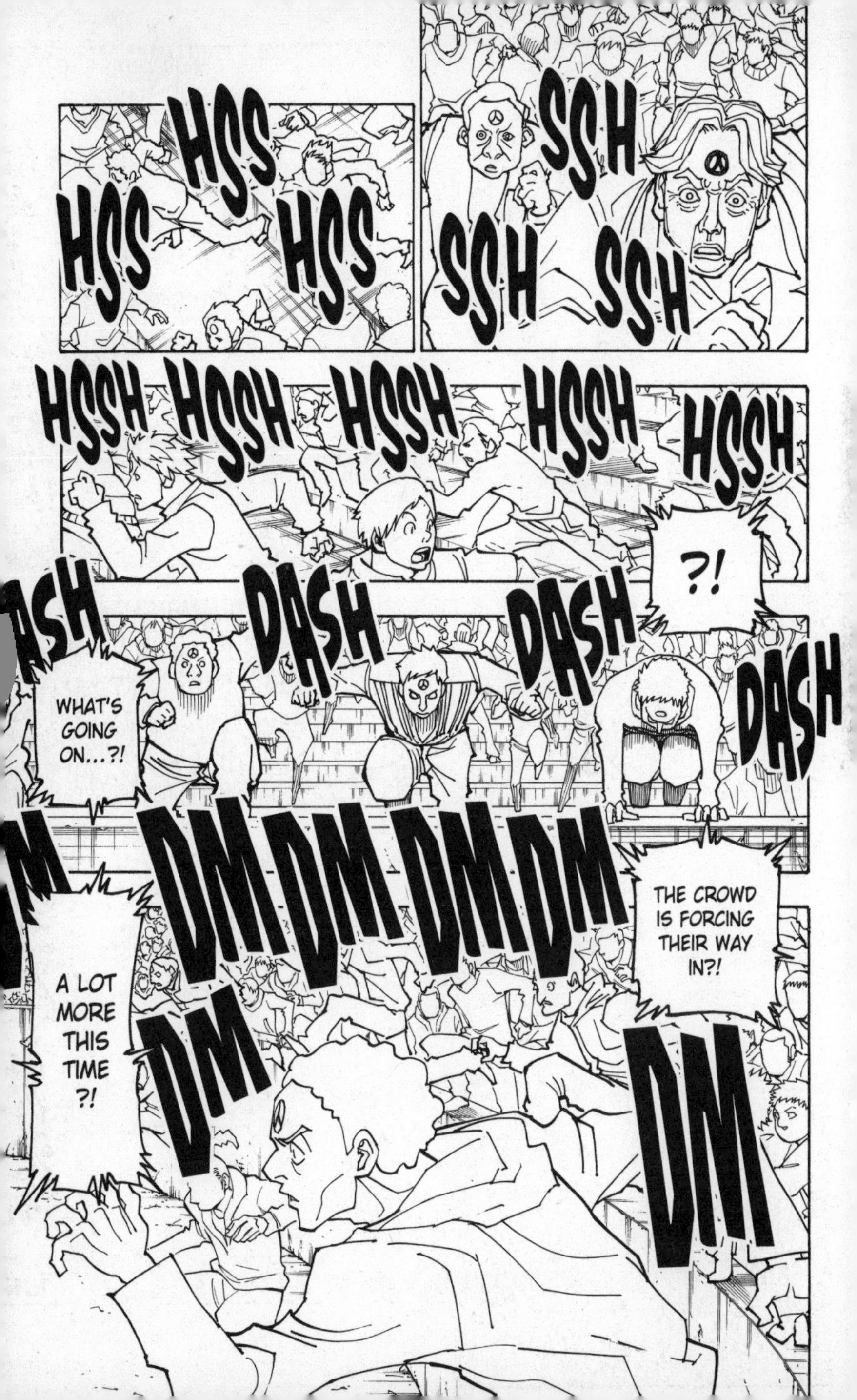
SSH
SSH
SSH
SSH
HSS
HSS
HSS
HSS
HSSH
HSSH
HSSH
HSSH
HSSH
?!
DASH
DASH
DASH
WHAT'S GOING ON...?!
THE CROWD IS FORCING THEIR WAY IN?!
DM
DM
DM
DM
DM
DM
DM
A LOT MORE THIS TIME?!

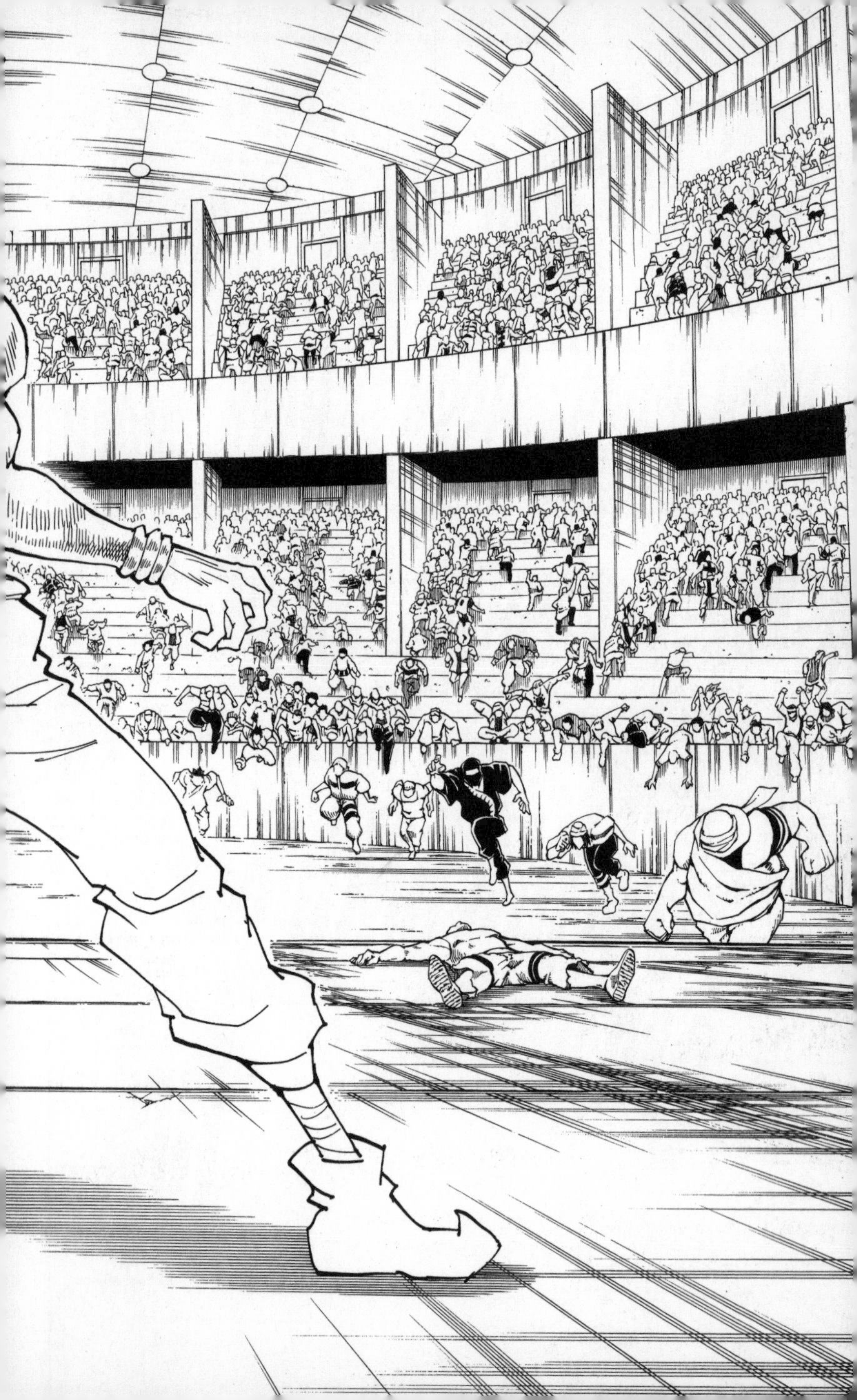

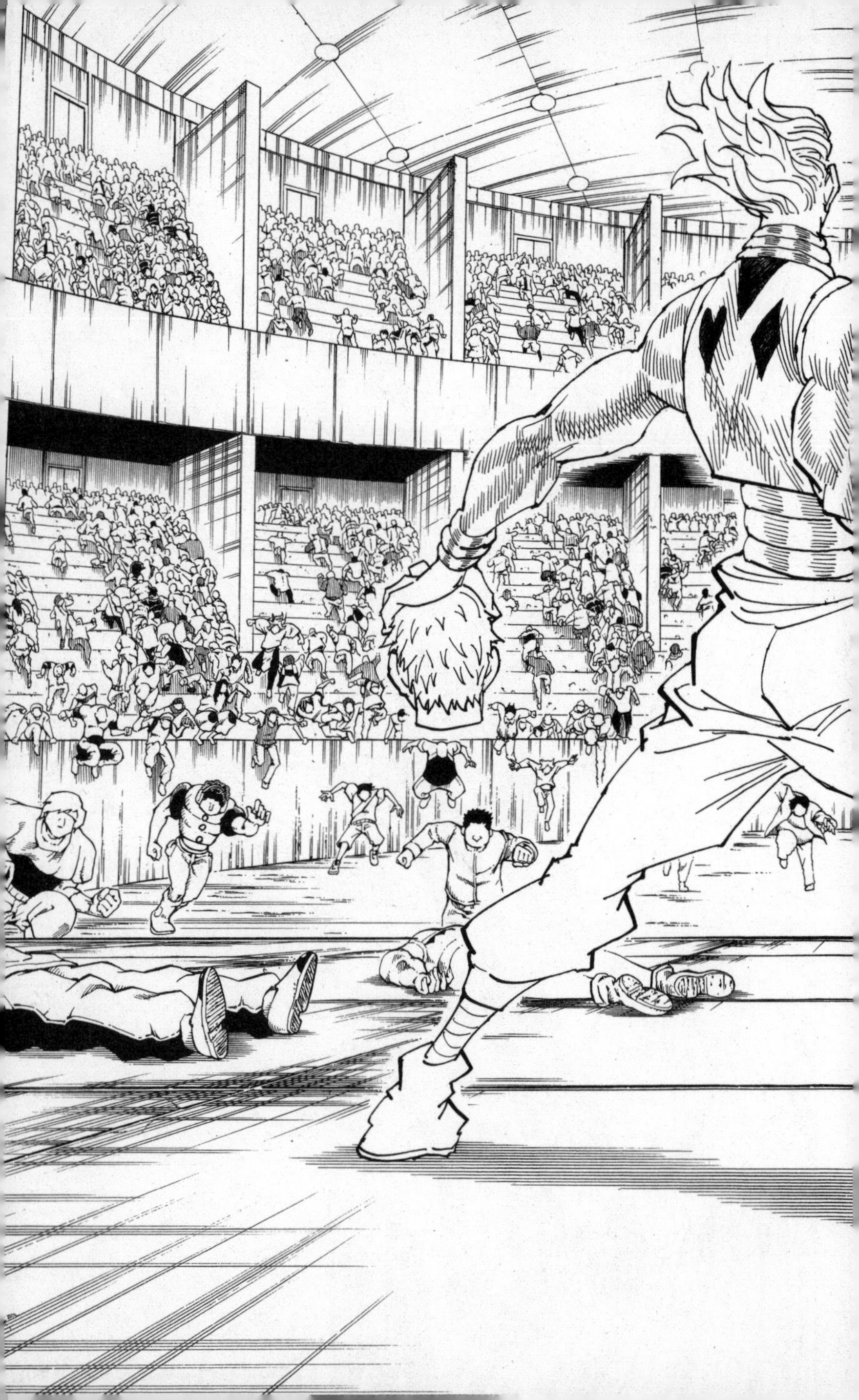

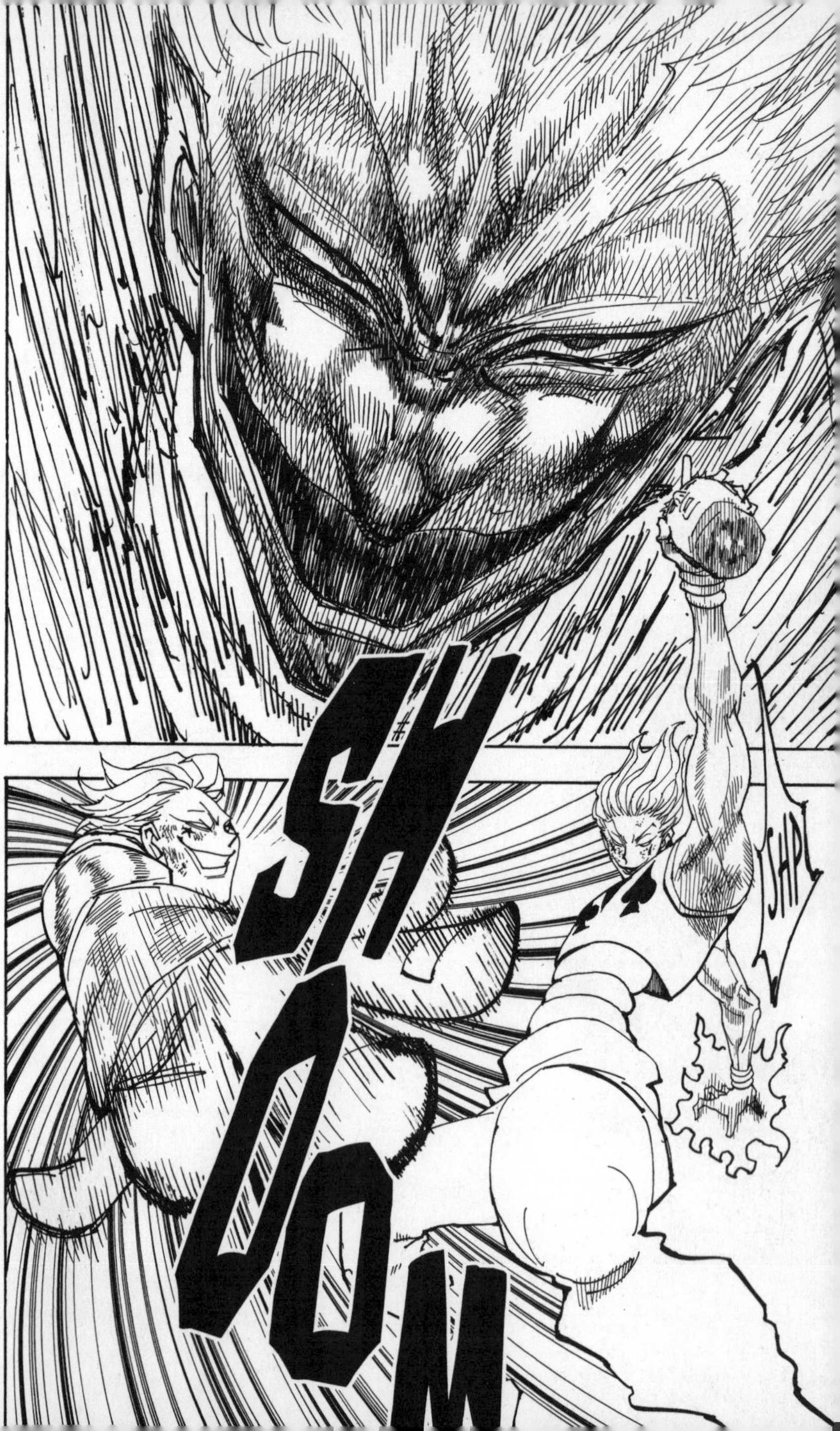
SHP!
SHOOM

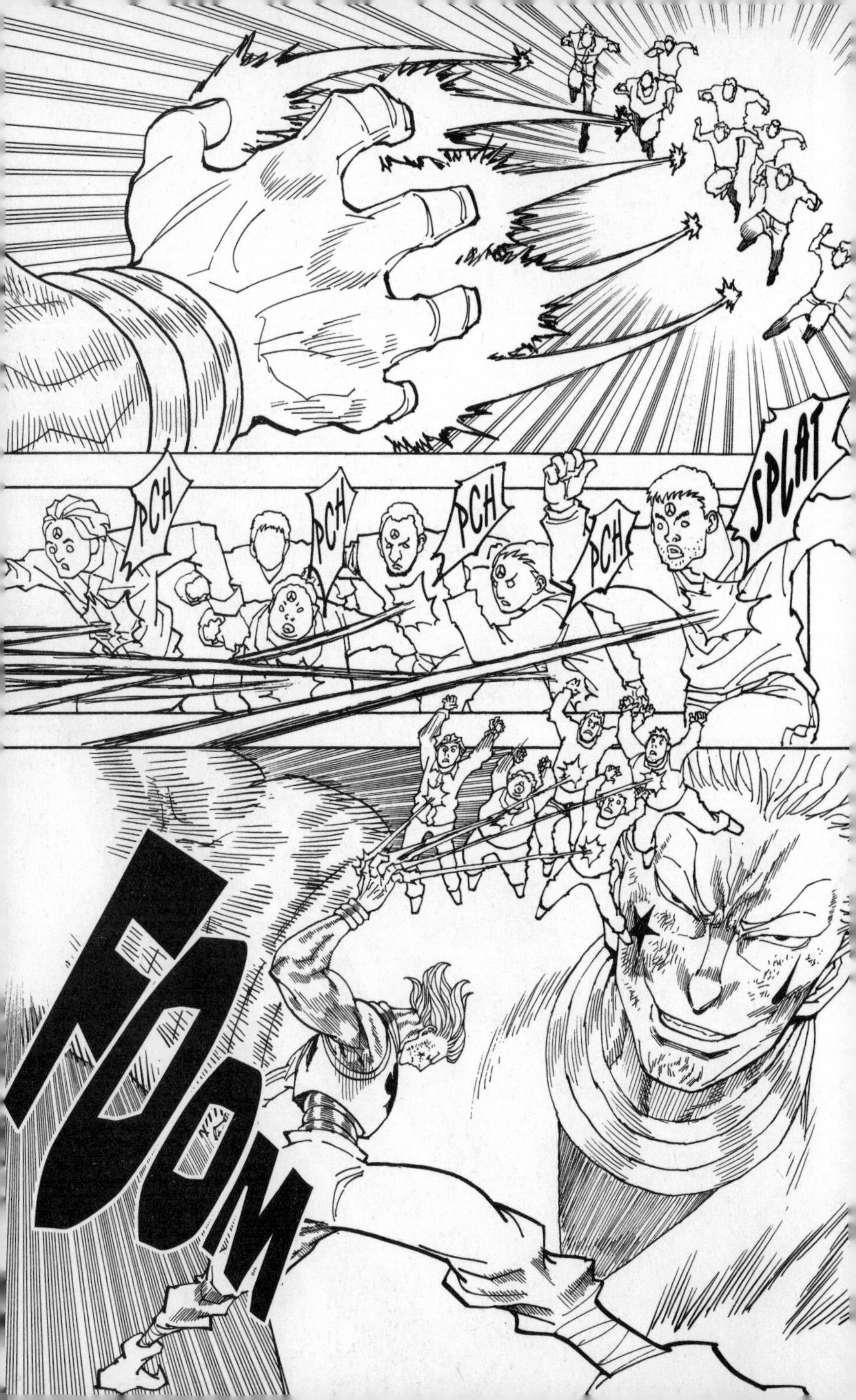
SPLAT
PCH
PCH
PCH
PCH
FOOM

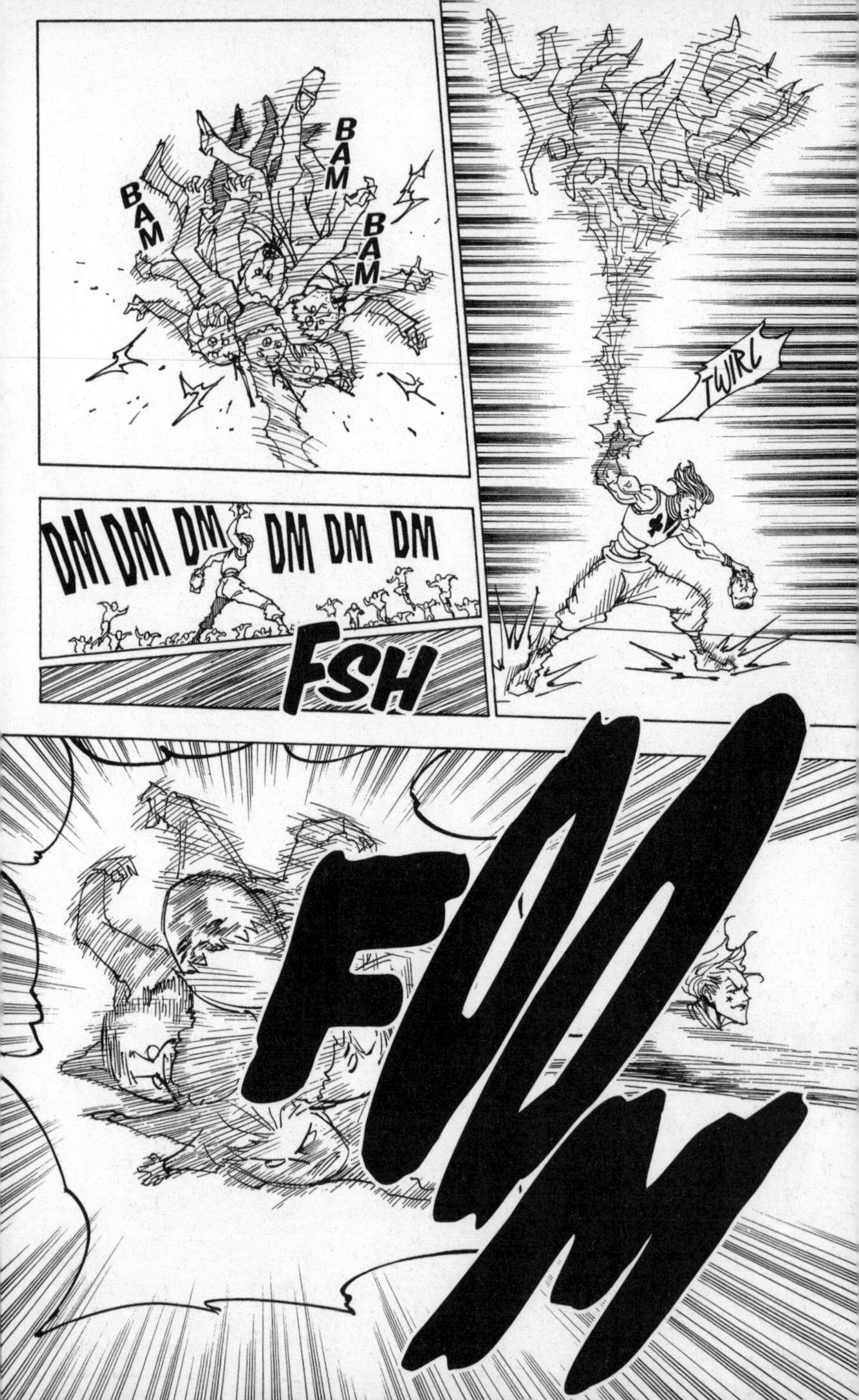
TWIRL
BAM
BAM
BAM
BAM
DM DM DM
DM DM DM
FSH
FWM

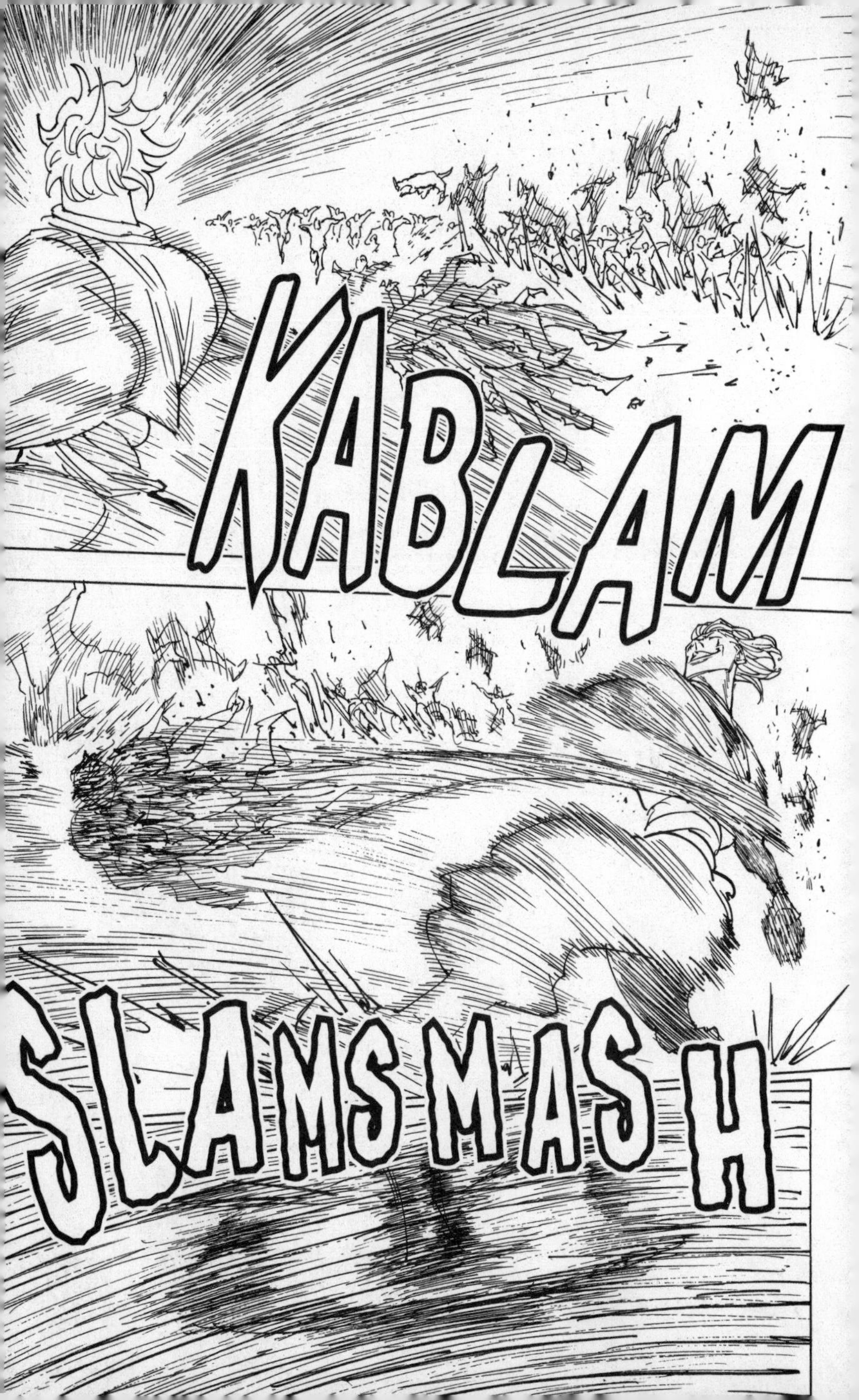
KABLAM
SLAMSMASH

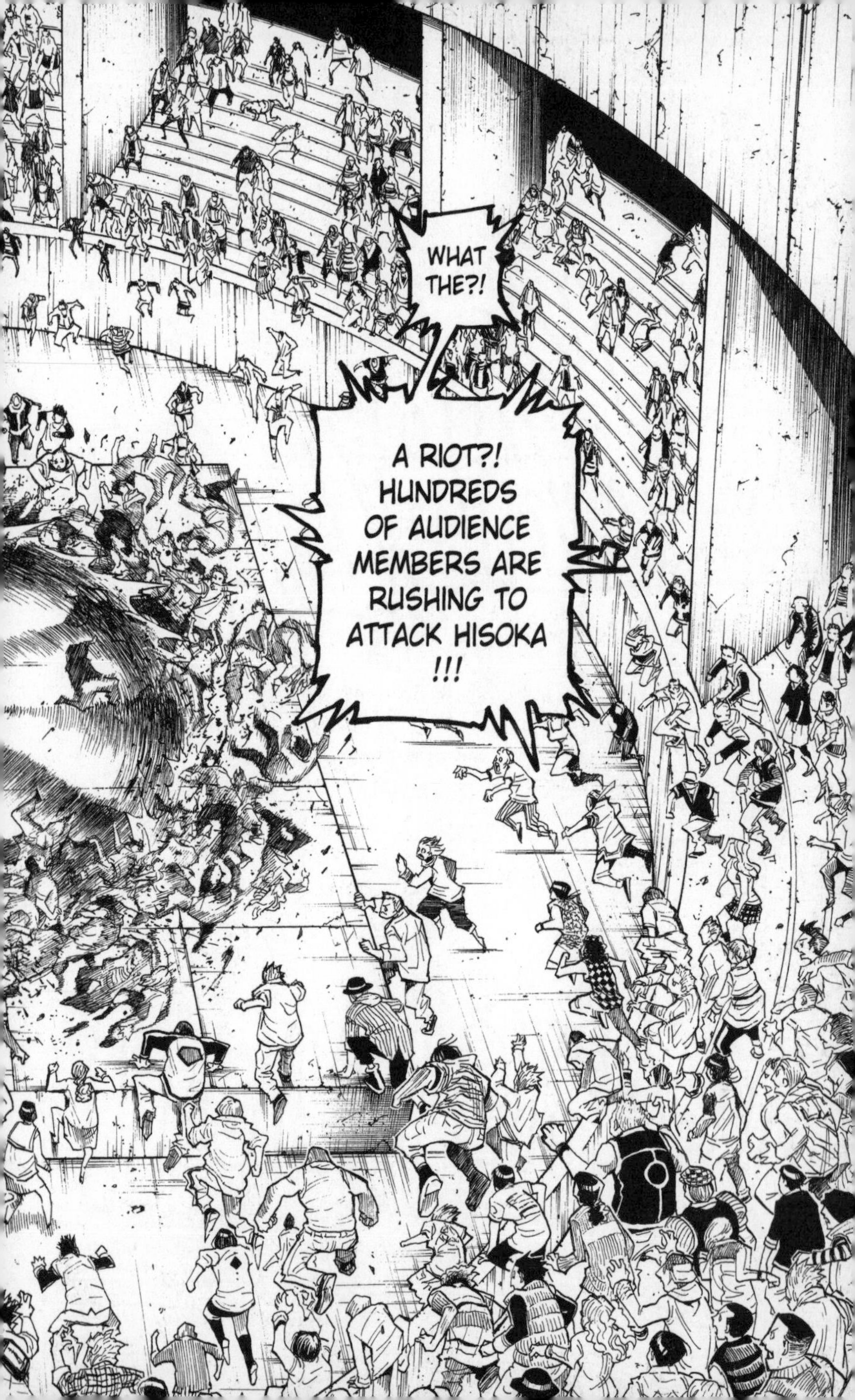
WHAT THE?!
A RIOT?! HUNDREDS OF AUDIENCE MEMBERS ARE RUSHING TO ATTACK HISOKA !!!

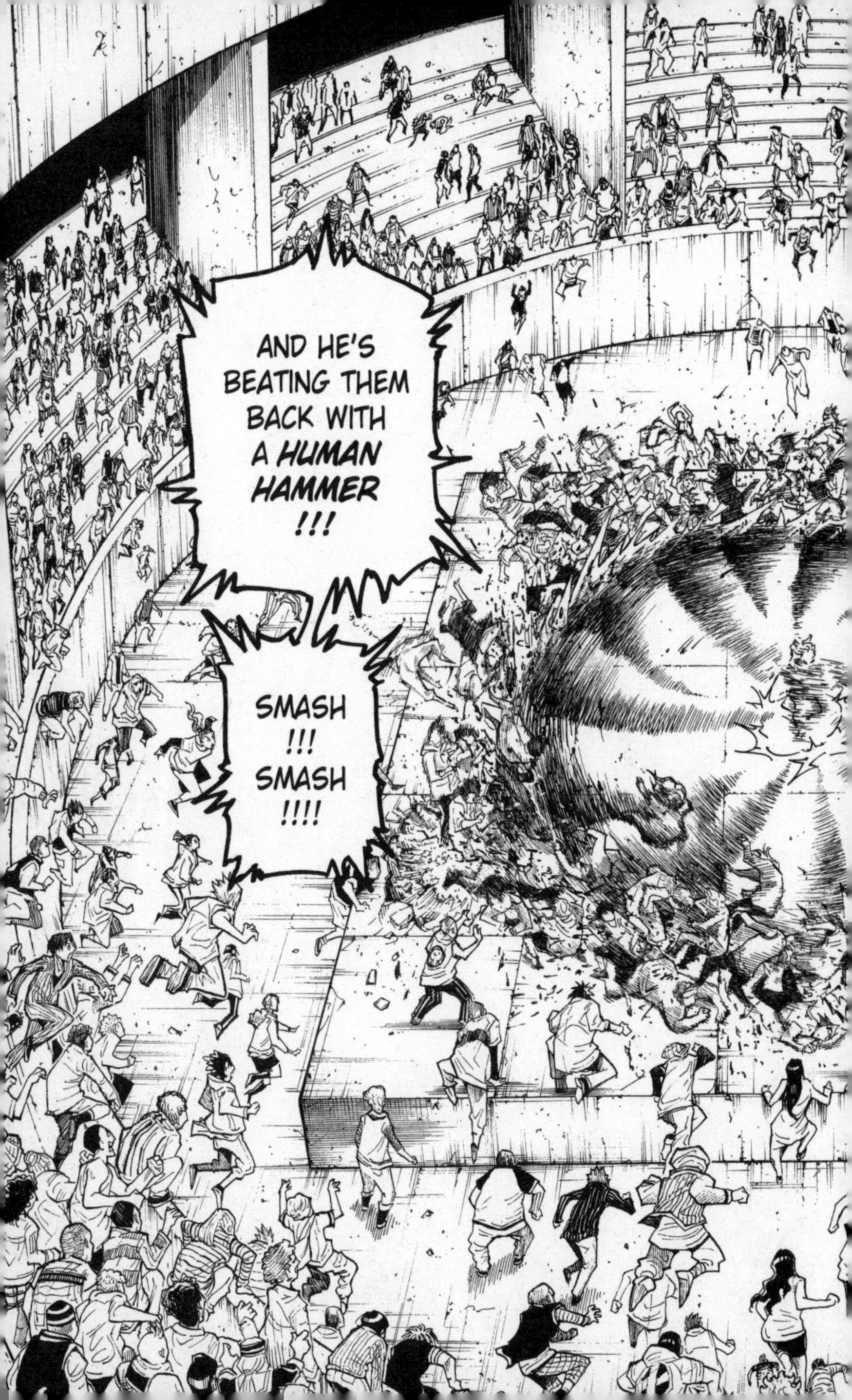
AND HE'S BEATING THEM BACK WITH A *HUMAN HAMMER* !!!
SMASH !!! SMASH !!!!

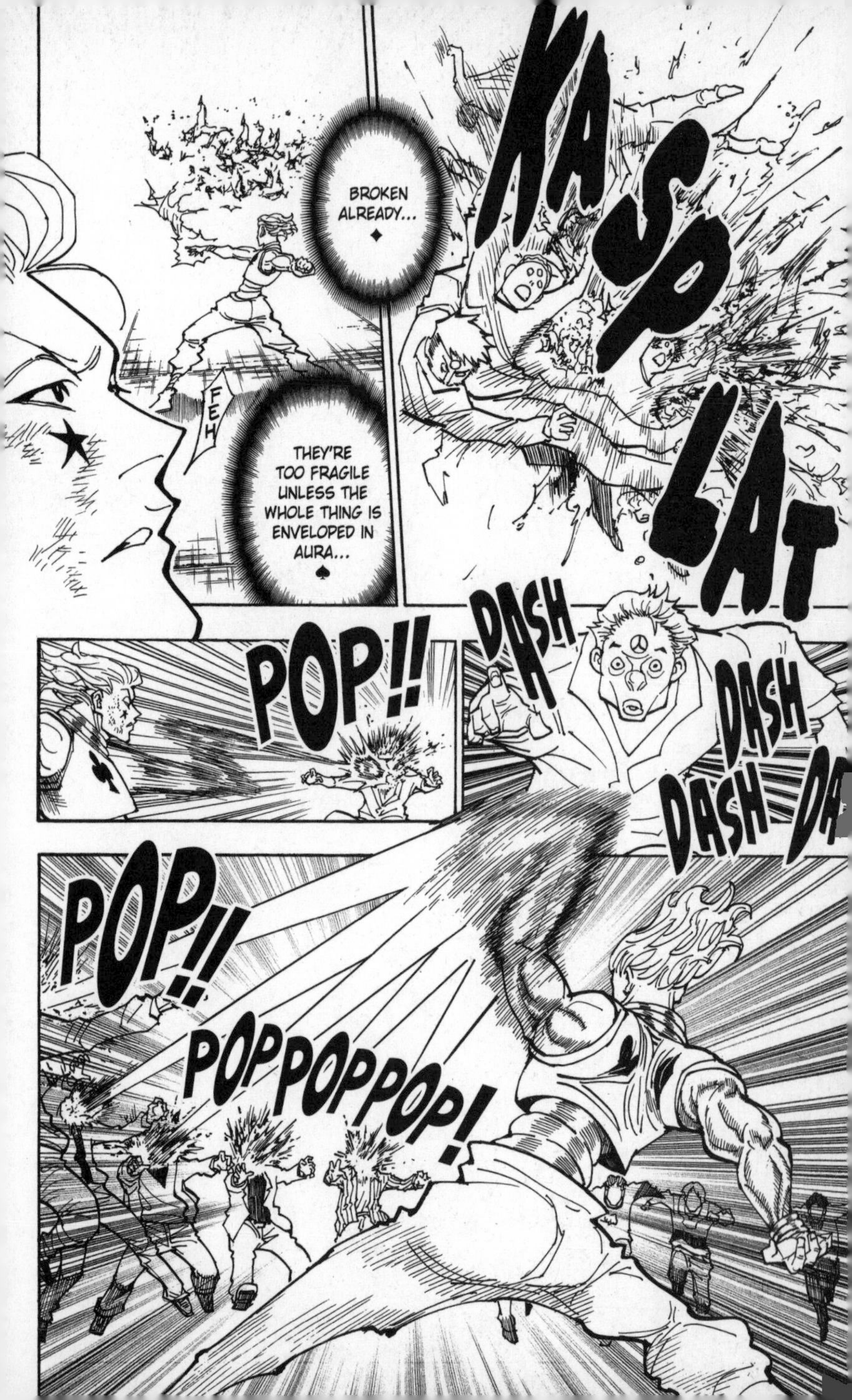
KASPLAT
BROKEN ALREADY... ♦
FEH
THEY'RE TOO FRAGILE UNLESS THE WHOLE THING IS ENVELOPED IN AURA... ♠
DASH
DASH
DASH
DA
POP!!
POP!!
POPPOPPOP!

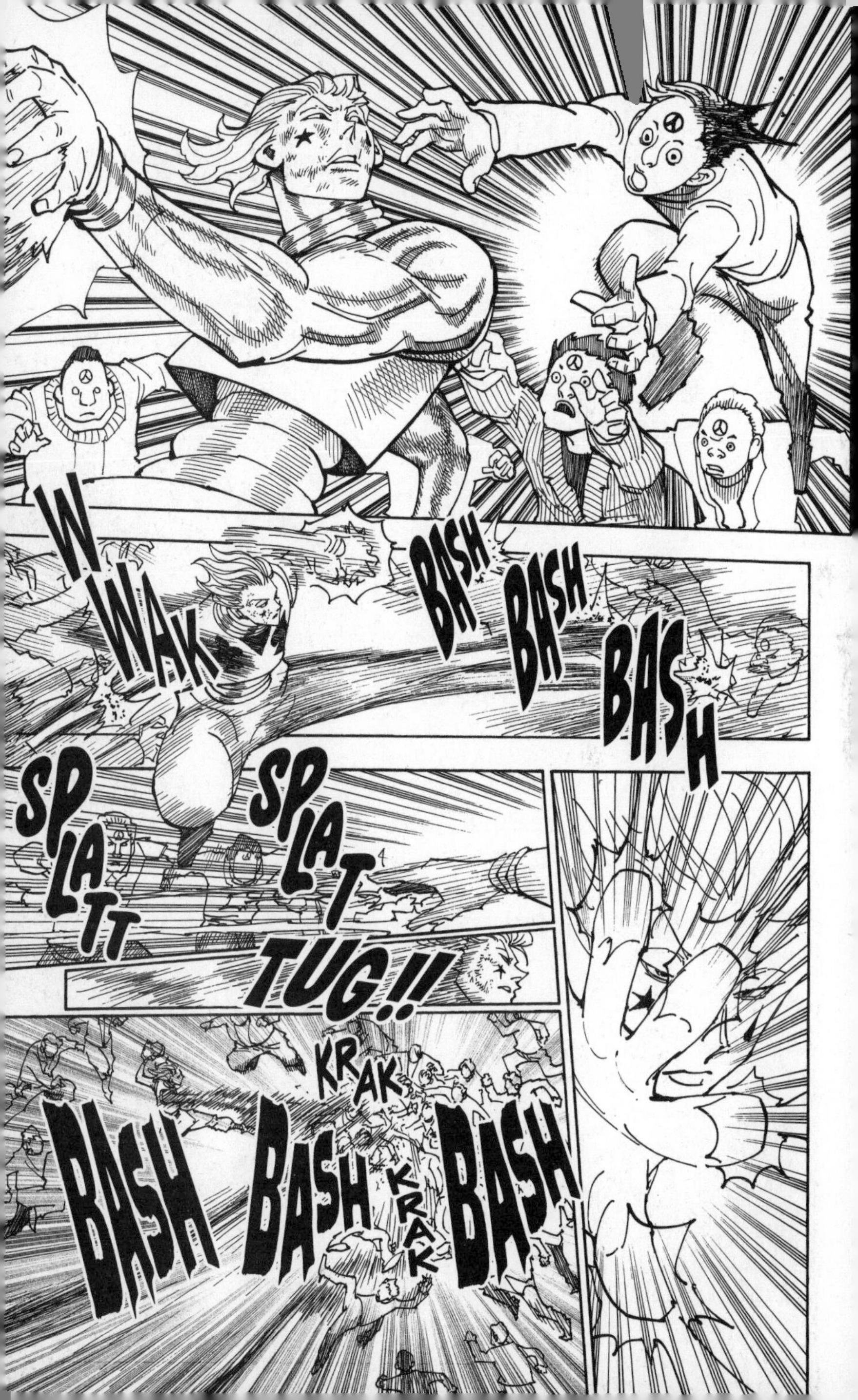
BASH
BASH
BASH
WWAK
SPLAT
SPLATT
TUG!!
BASH
KRAK
KRAK
BASH
BASH

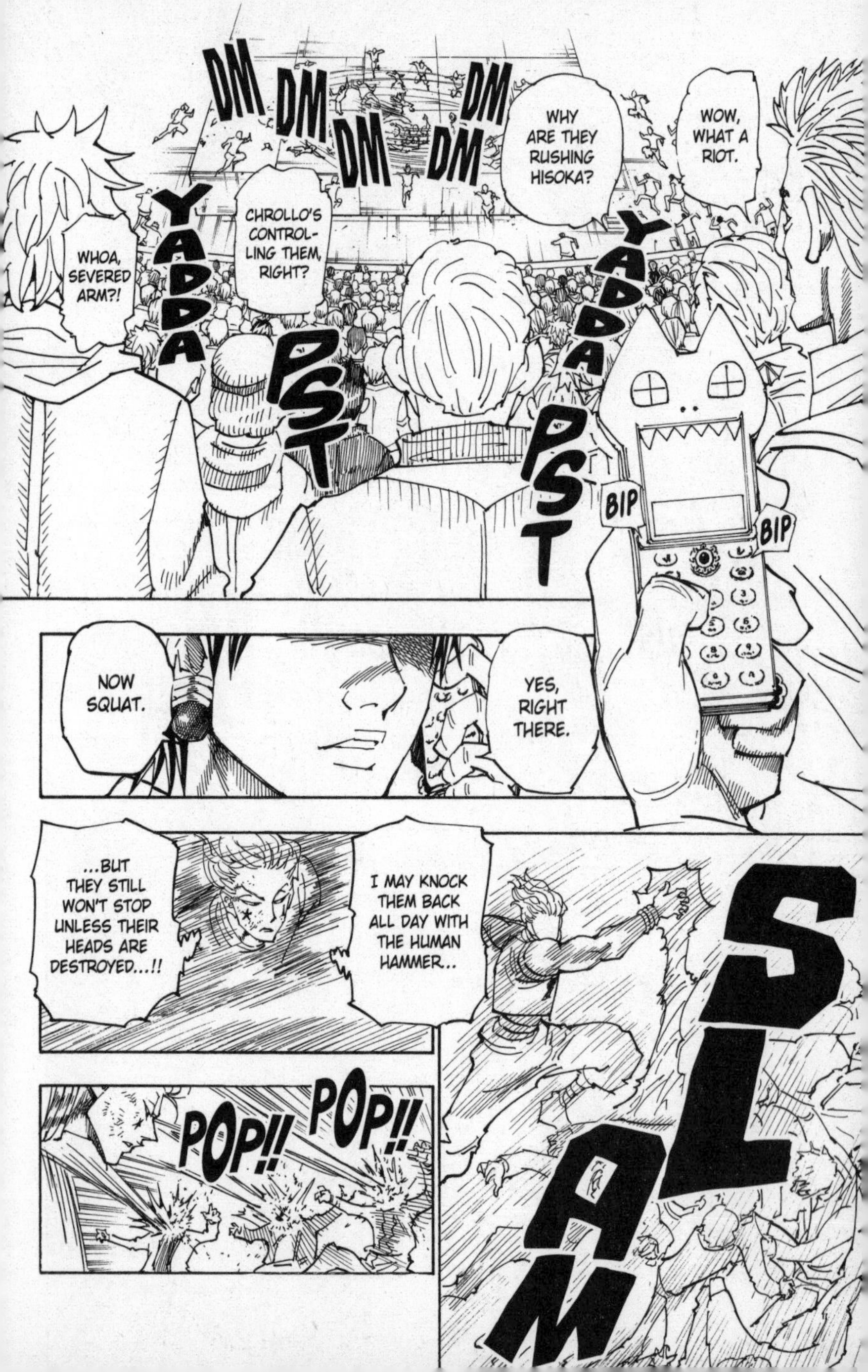

DM DM DM DM DM DM
WOW, WHAT A RIOT.
WHY ARE THEY RUSHING HISOKA?
YADDA YADDA
CHROLLO'S CONTROL-LING THEM, RIGHT?
WHOA, SEVERED ARM?!
PST PST
BIP BIP
YES, RIGHT THERE.
NOW SQUAT.
SLAM
I MAY KNOCK THEM BACK ALL DAY WITH THE HUMAN HAMMER...
...BUT THEY STILL WON'T STOP UNLESS THEIR HEADS ARE DESTROYED...!!
POP!! POP!!

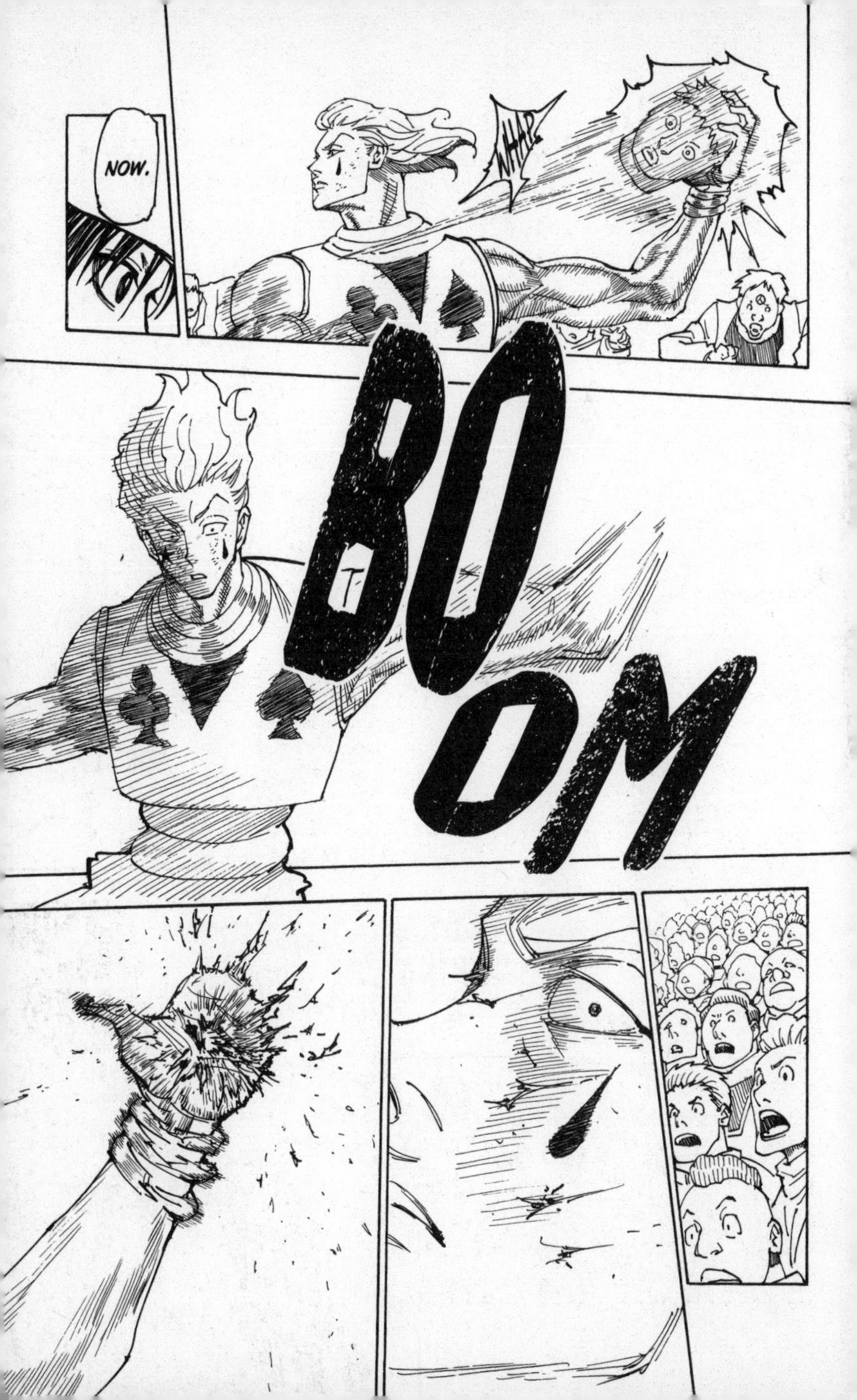
WHAP!
NOW.
BOOM

NOW I JUST WATCH THE P-LEAGUE, THE WOMEN'S TOURNAMENT. I ESPECIALLY LIKE PROFESSIONAL PLAYERS TERASHITA AND TSURUI.

YESSS, STRIKE !!

MATSUNAGA'S POSE AND HER SMILE WHEN SHE HITS A STRIKE MAKE MY DAY.

3/3

Chapter 356: Unfortunate: Part 1

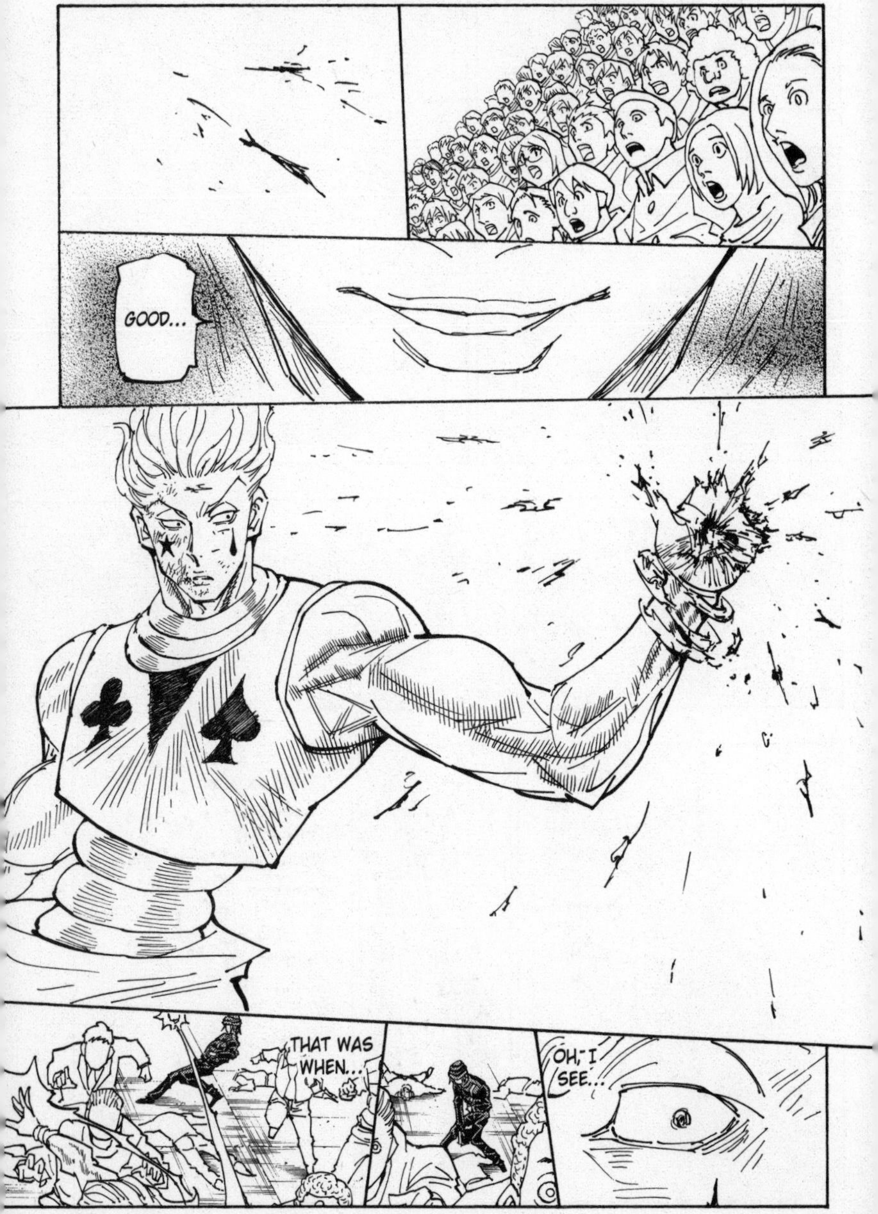

GOOD...
OH, I SEE...
THAT WAS WHEN...

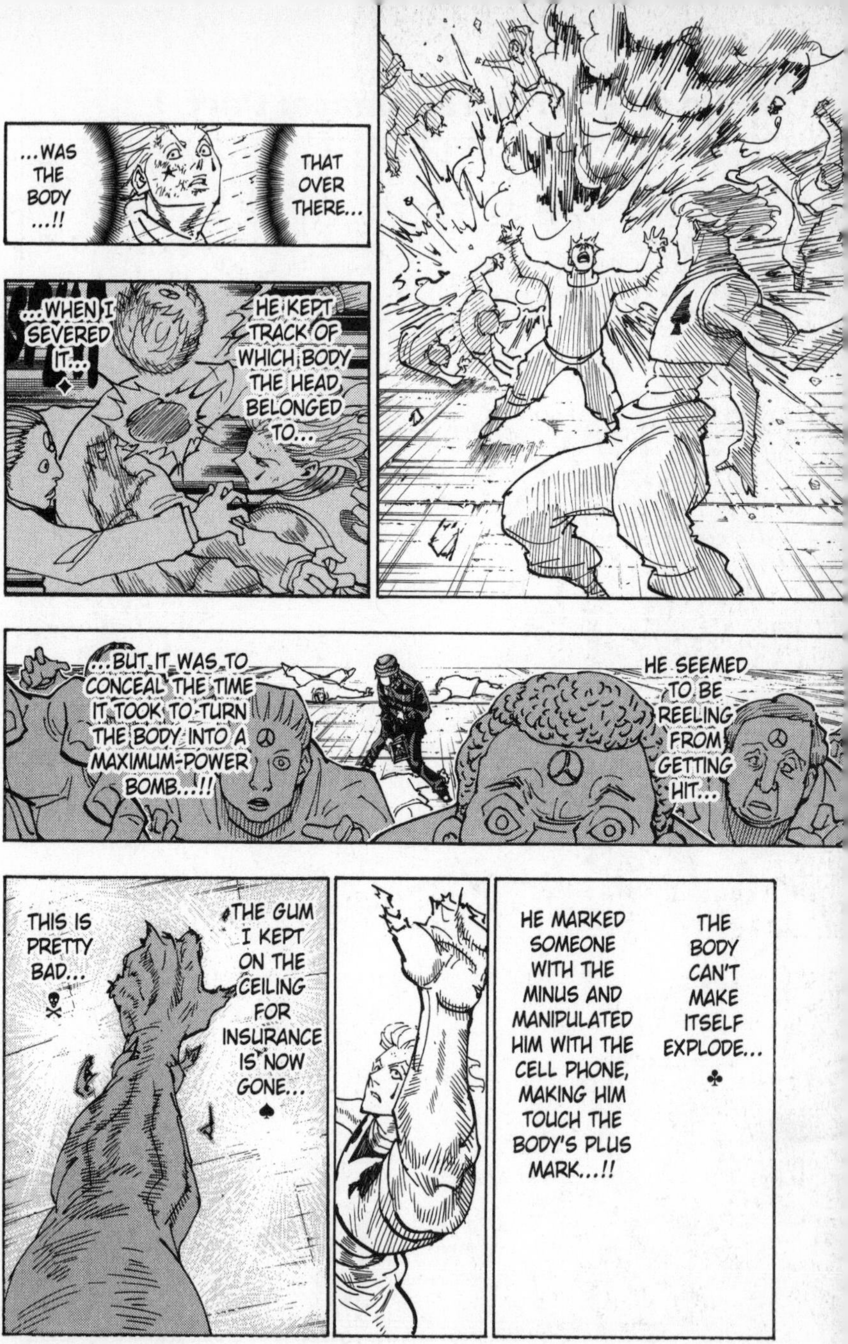
THAT OVER THERE...
...WAS THE BODY ...!!
HE KEPT TRACK OF WHICH BODY THE HEAD BELONGED TO...
...WHEN I SEVERED IT...
HE SEEMED TO BE REELING FROM GETTING HIT...
...BUT IT WAS TO CONCEAL THE TIME IT TOOK TO TURN THE BODY INTO A MAXIMUM-POWER BOMB...!!
THE BODY CAN'T MAKE ITSELF EXPLODE...
HE MARKED SOMEONE WITH THE MINUS AND MANIPULATED HIM WITH THE CELL PHONE, MAKING HIM TOUCH THE BODY'S PLUS MARK...!!
THE GUM I KEPT ON THE CEILING FOR INSURANCE IS NOW GONE...
THIS IS PRETTY BAD...

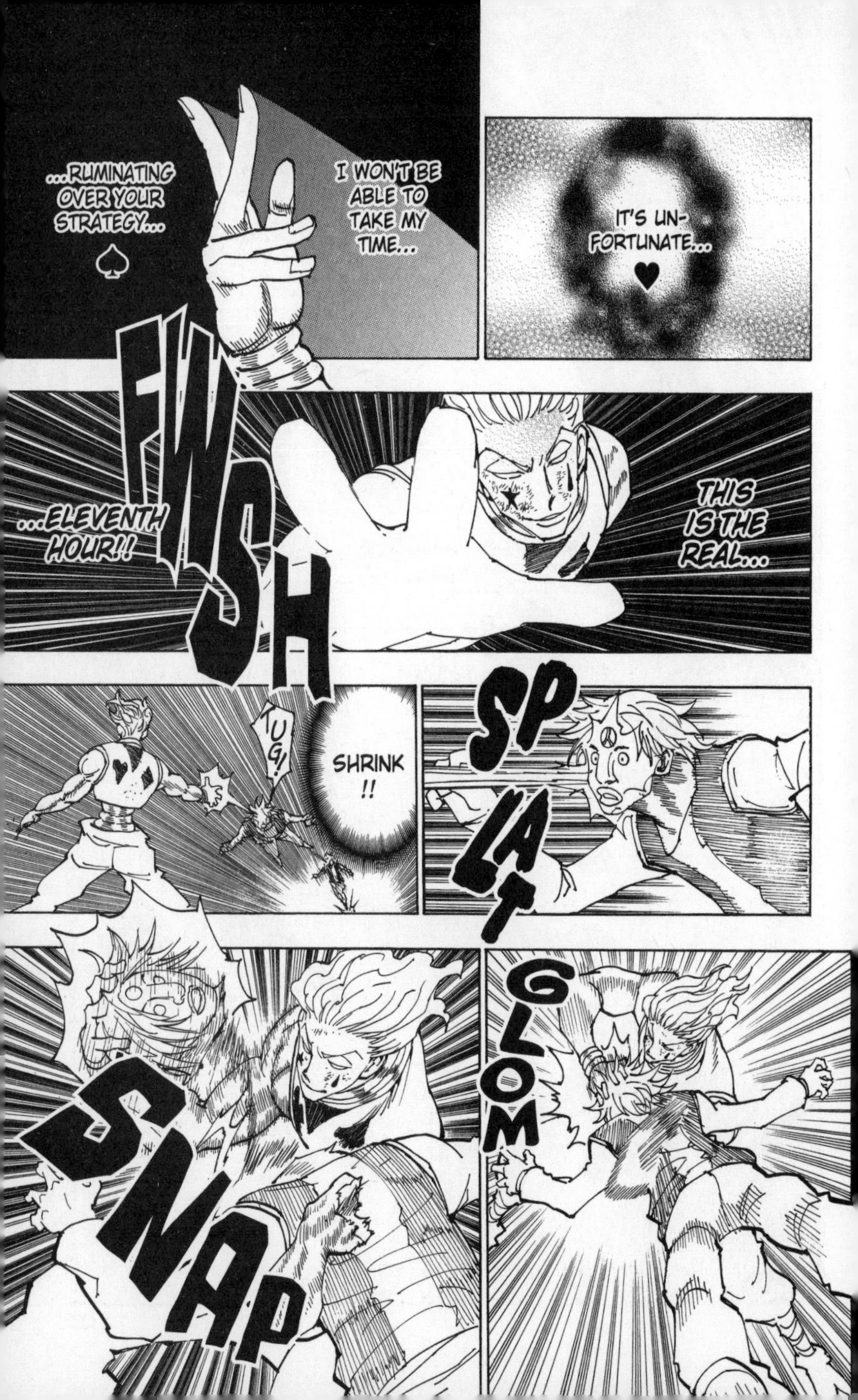
IT'S UN-FORTUNATE... ♥
I WON'T BE ABLE TO TAKE MY TIME...
...RUMINATING OVER YOUR STRATEGY... ♠
FWSH
THIS IS THE REAL...
...ELEVENTH HOUR!!
SPLAT
TUG!
SHRINK !!
GLOM
SNAP

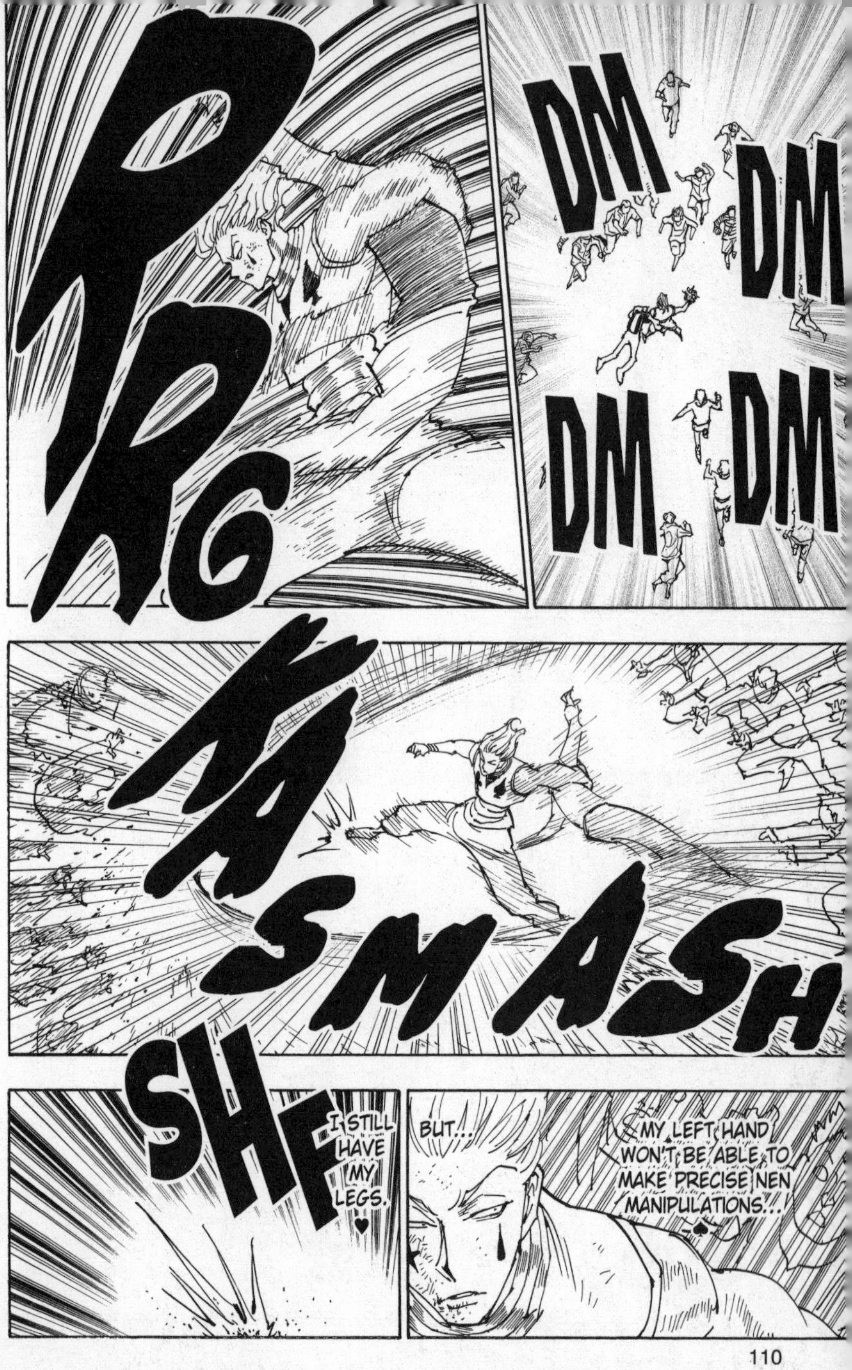
DM
DM
DM
DM
SMASH
SHF
I STILL HAVE MY LEGS. ♥
BUT...
MY LEFT HAND WON'T BE ABLE TO MAKE PRECISE NEN MANIPULATIONS... ♠

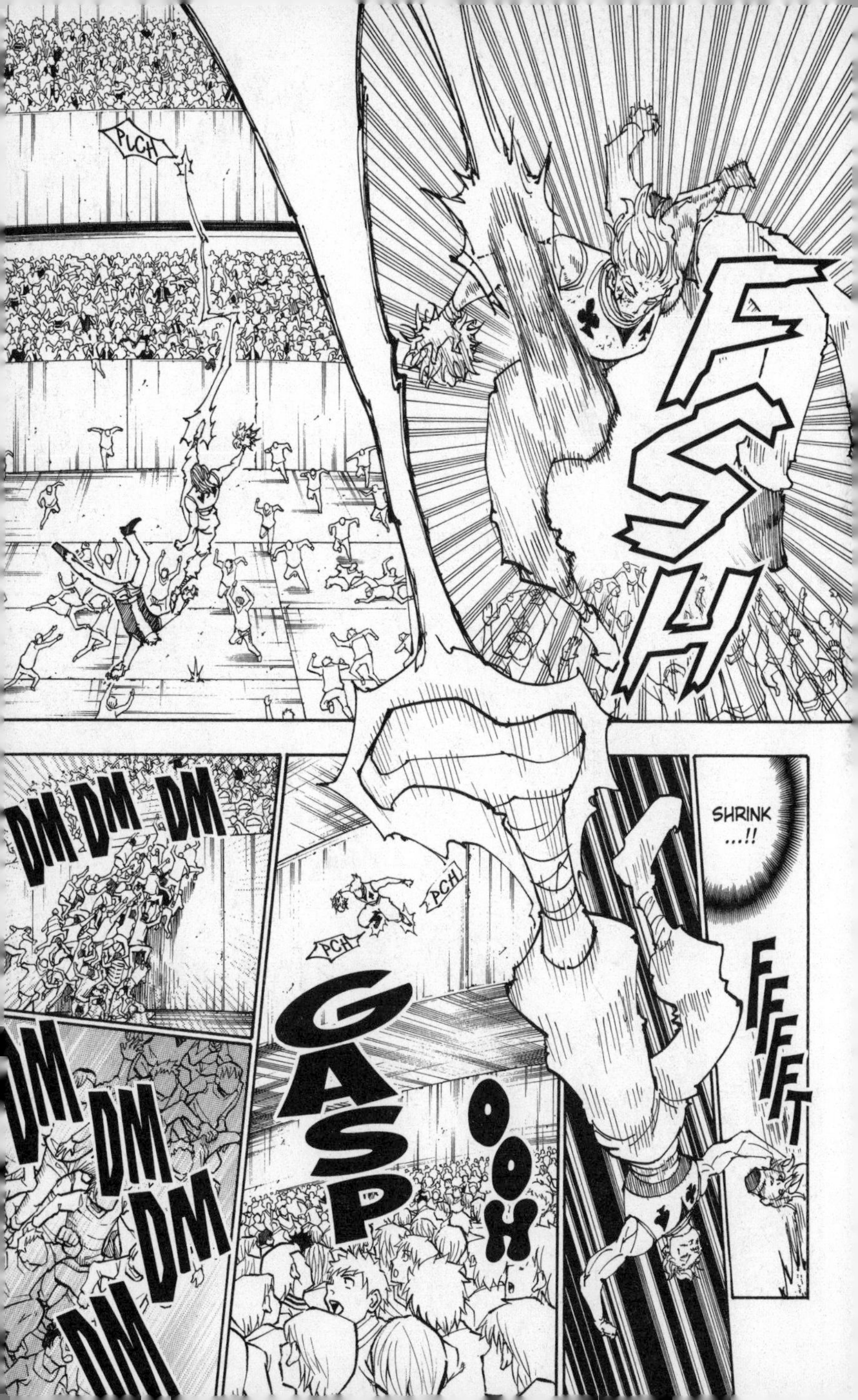
FSSH
PLCH
SHRINK ...!!
FFFFFT
PCH
PCH
GASP
OOOH
DM DM DM
DM DM DM DM

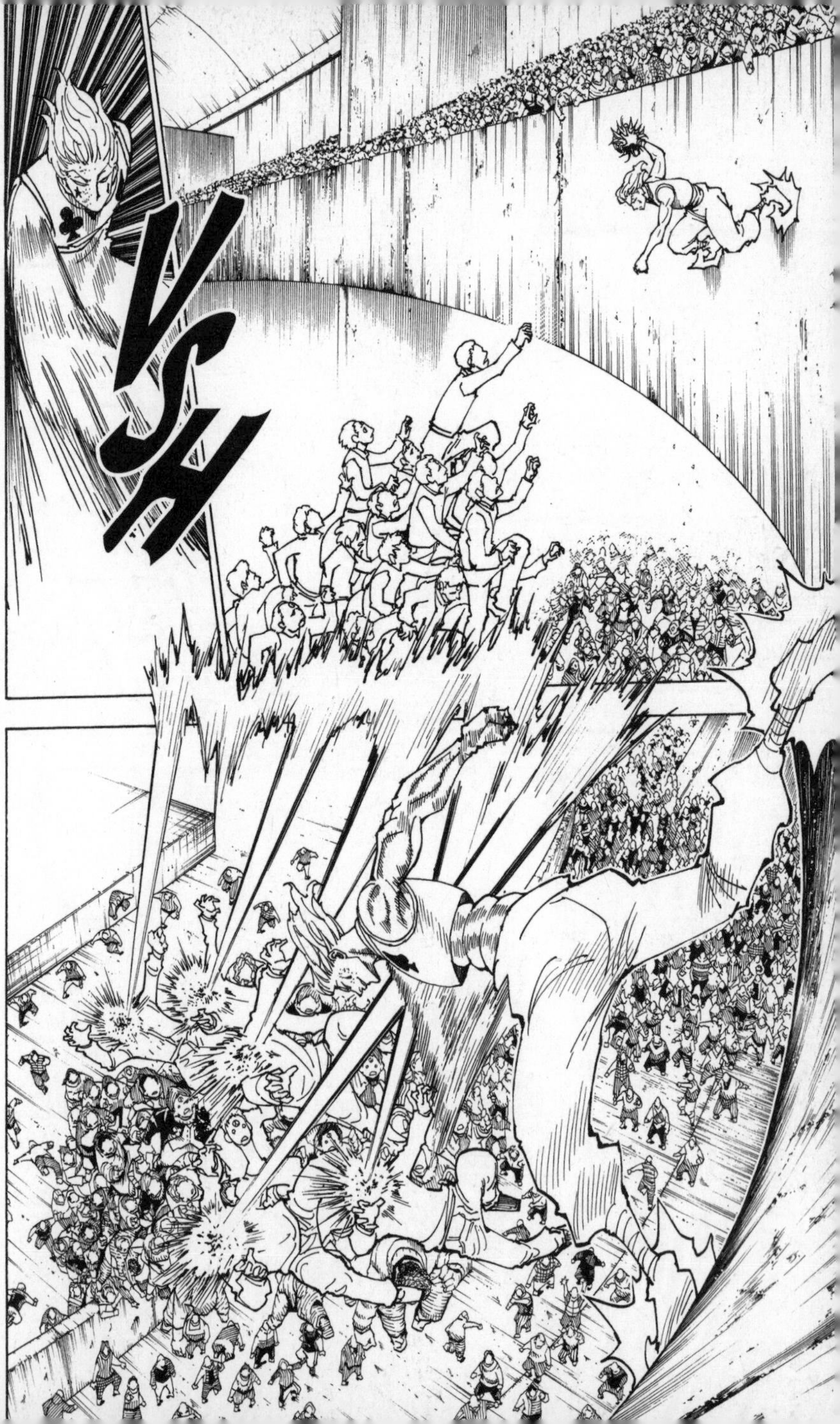
VSH

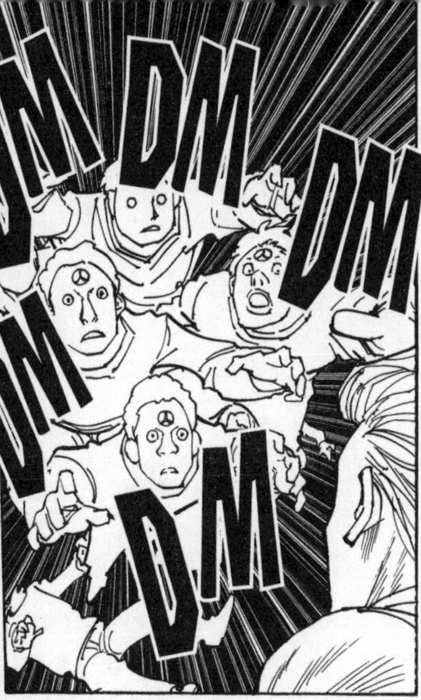
DM
DM
DM
DM
DM
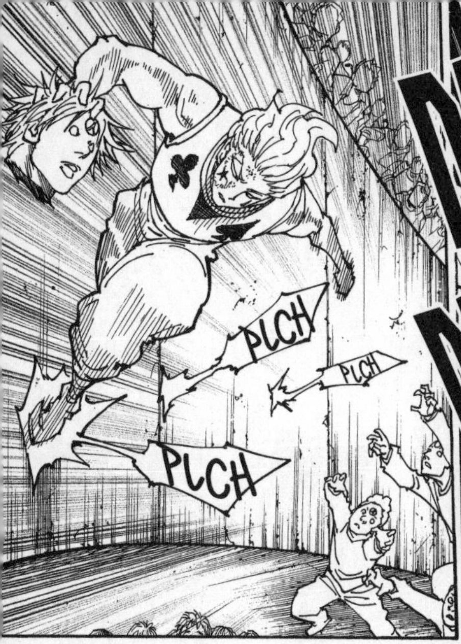
PLCH
PLCH
PLCH
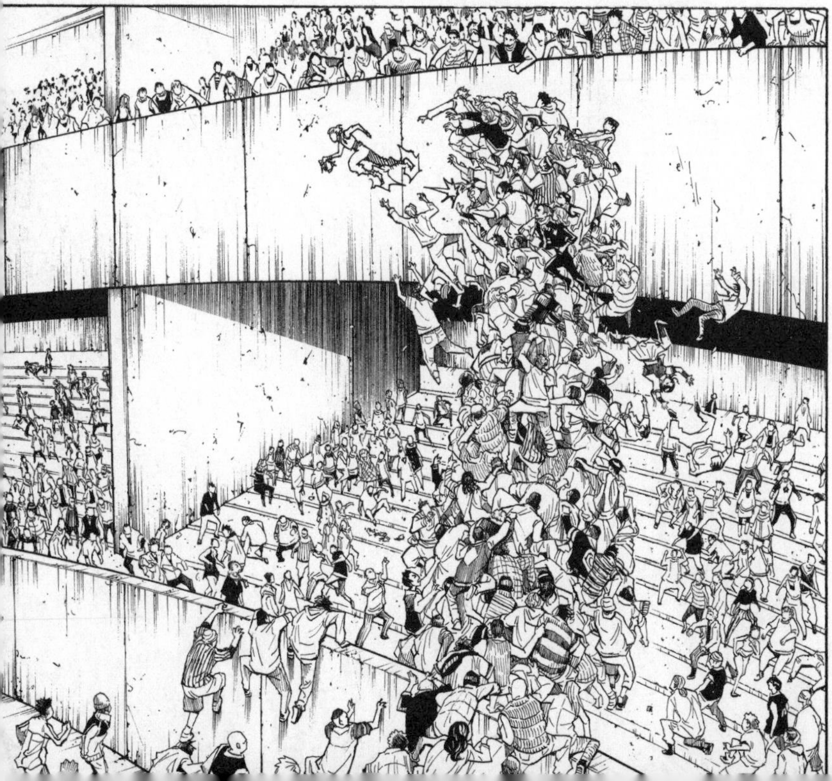

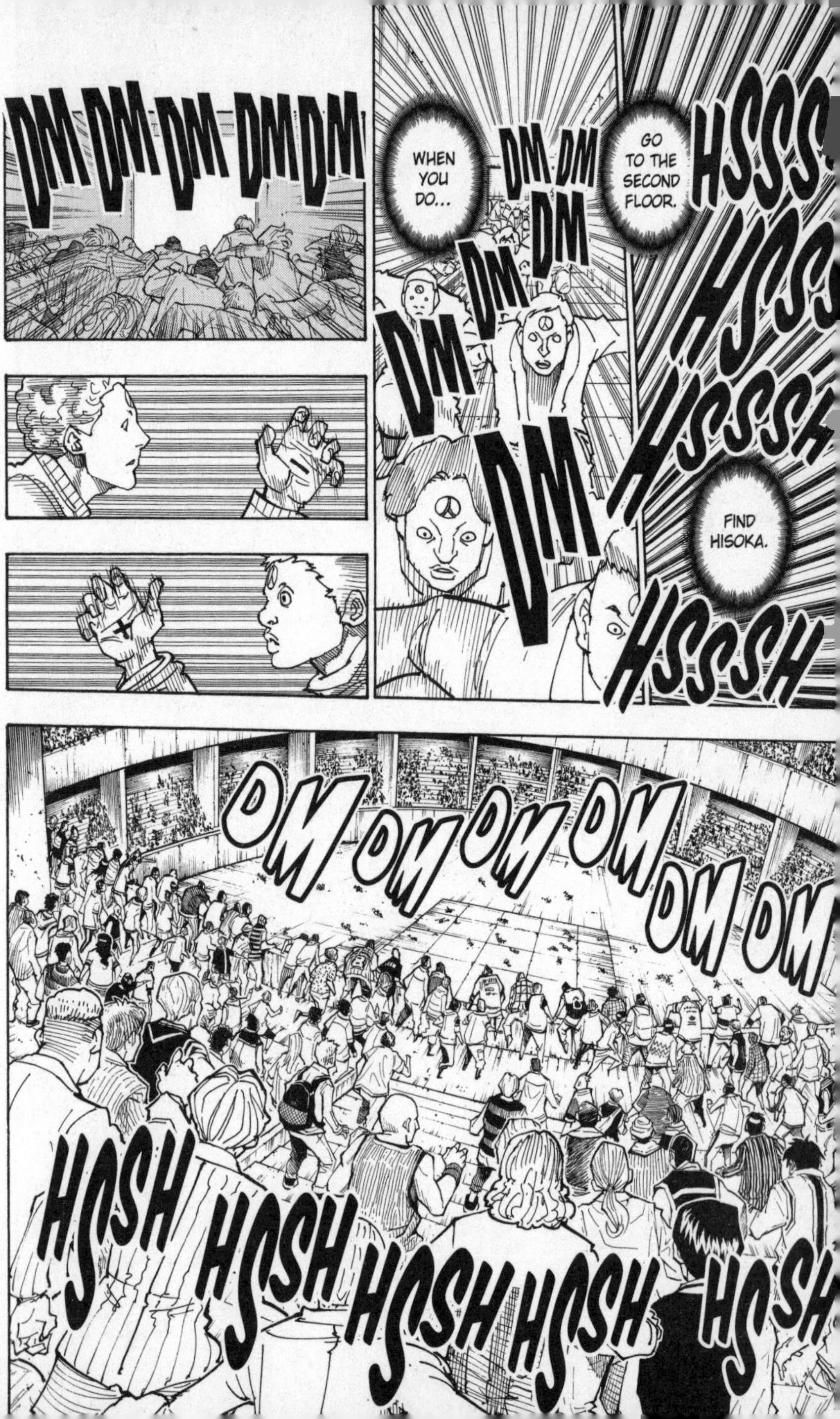
HSSS
GO TO THE SECOND FLOOR.
HSSSH
FIND HISOKA.
HSSSH
WHEN YOU DO...
DM DM DM
DM DM DM
DM DM DM DM DM
DM DM DM DM DM DM DM DM

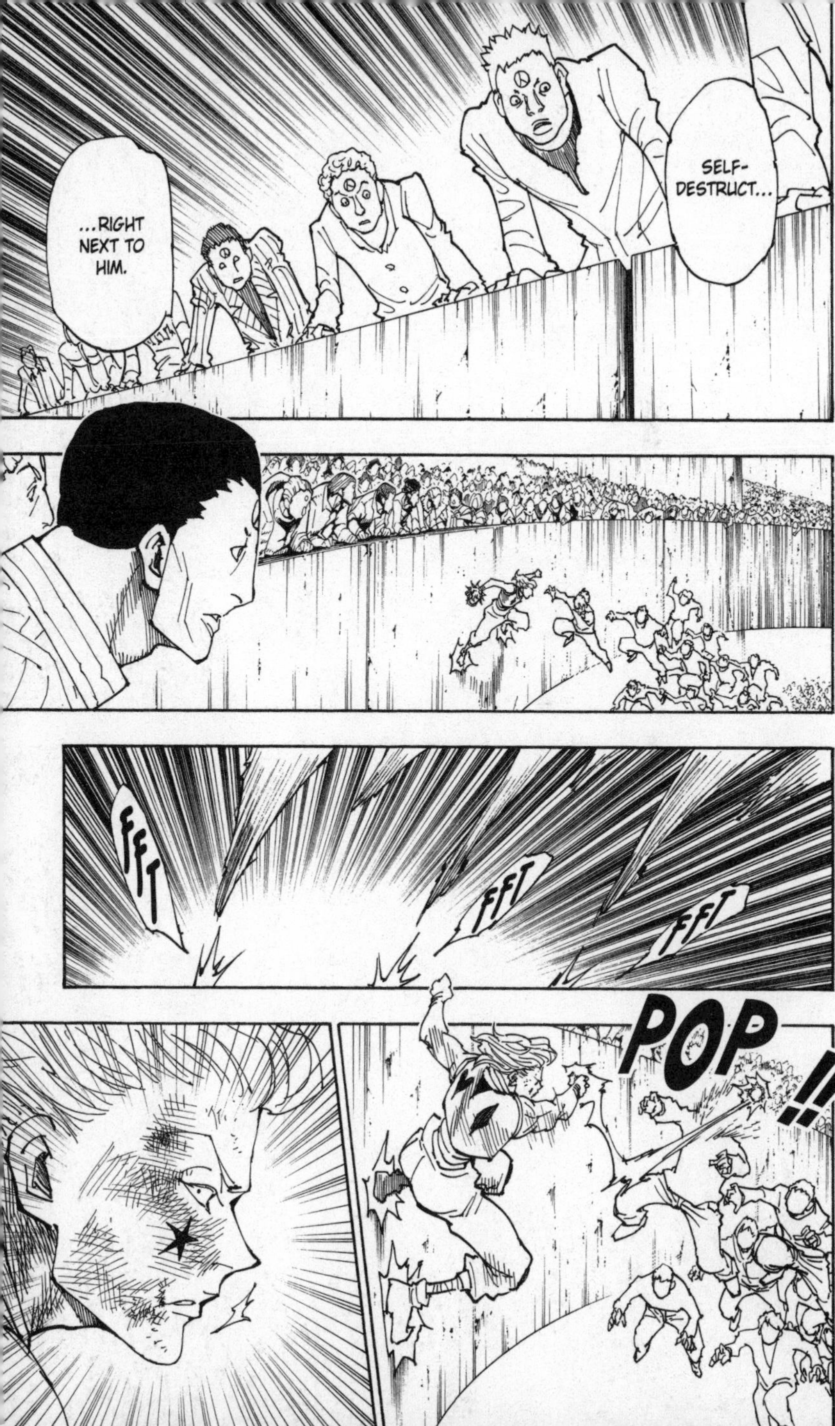
SELF-DESTRUCT...
...RIGHT NEXT TO HIM.
FFT
FFT
FFT
POP!!

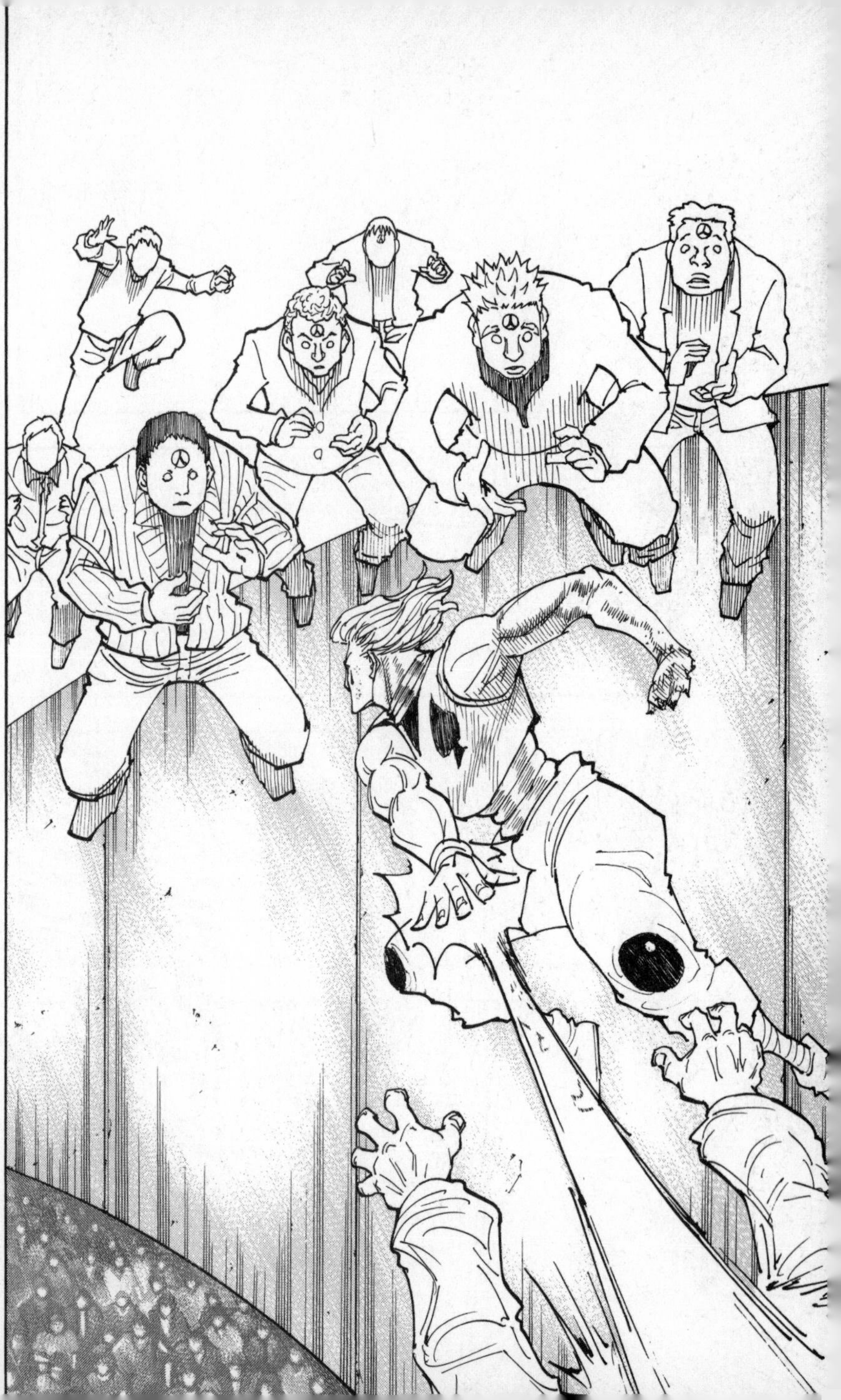

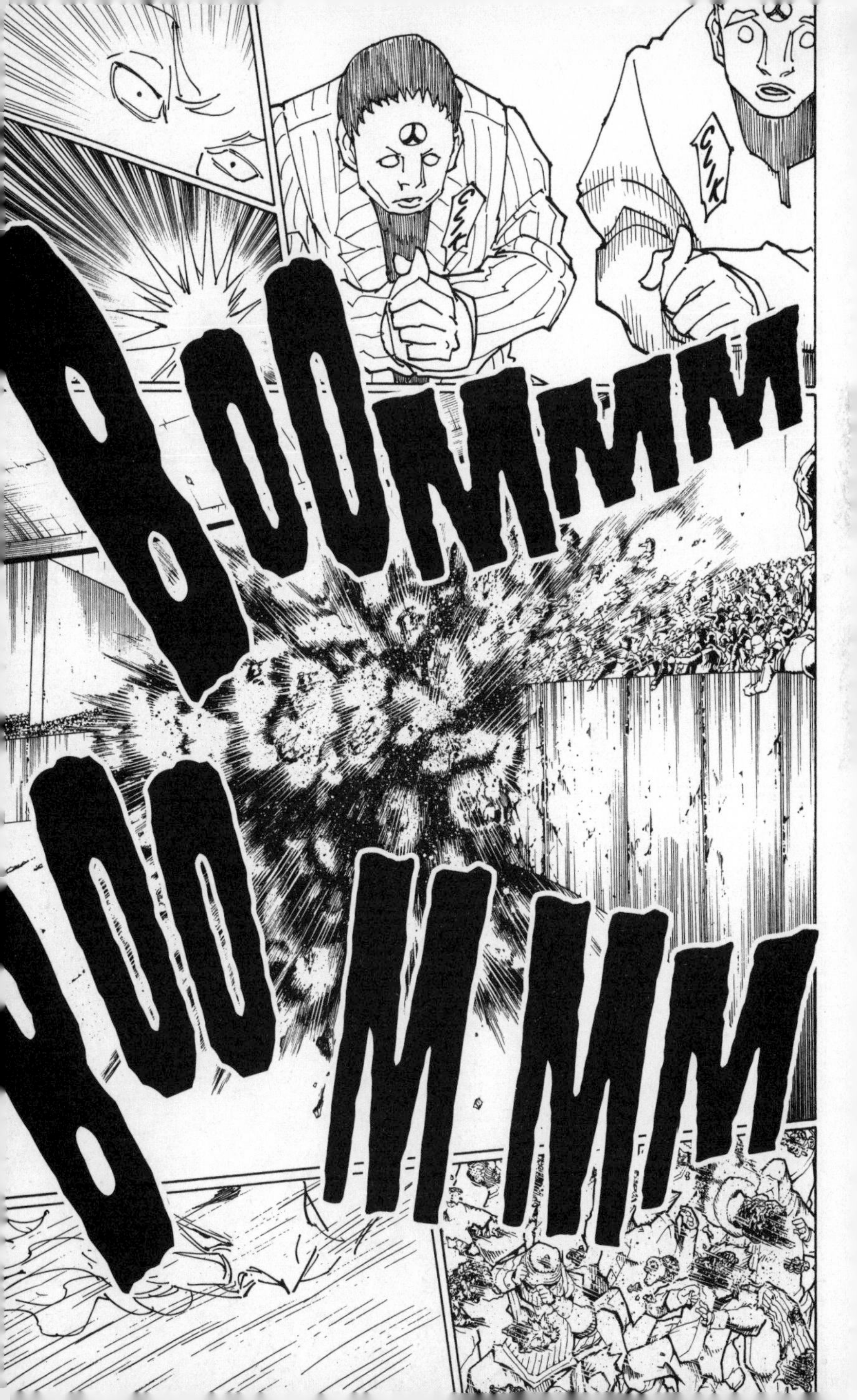
CLIK
CLIK
BOOMMM
BOOMMMM

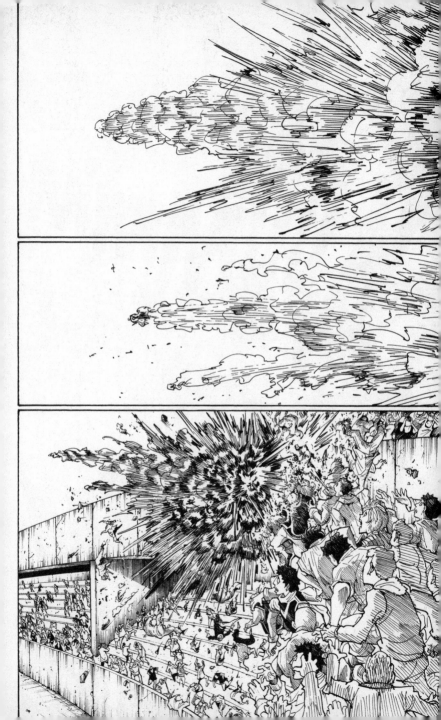

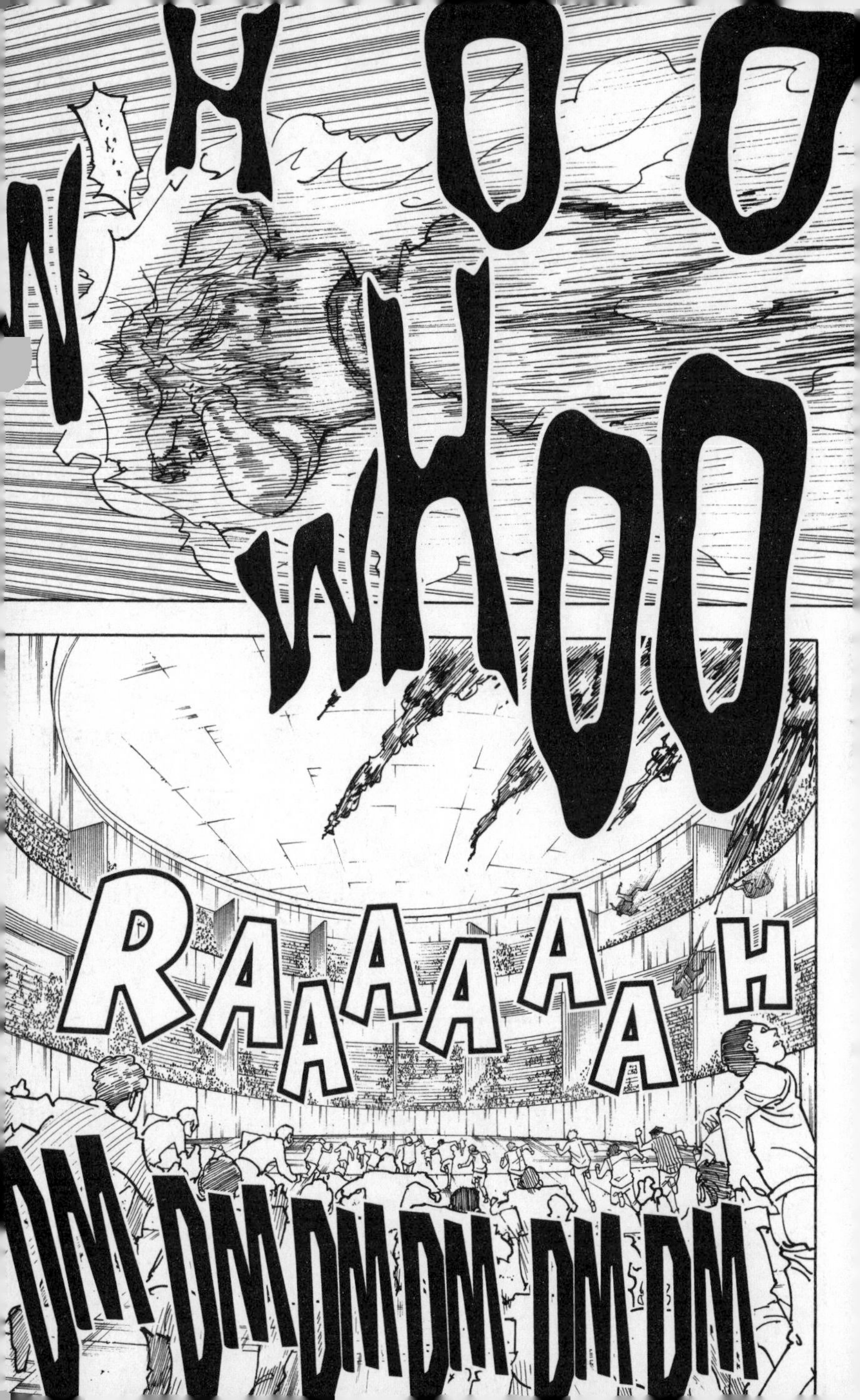
WHOO
WHOO
RAAAAAAH
DM DM DM DM DM DM

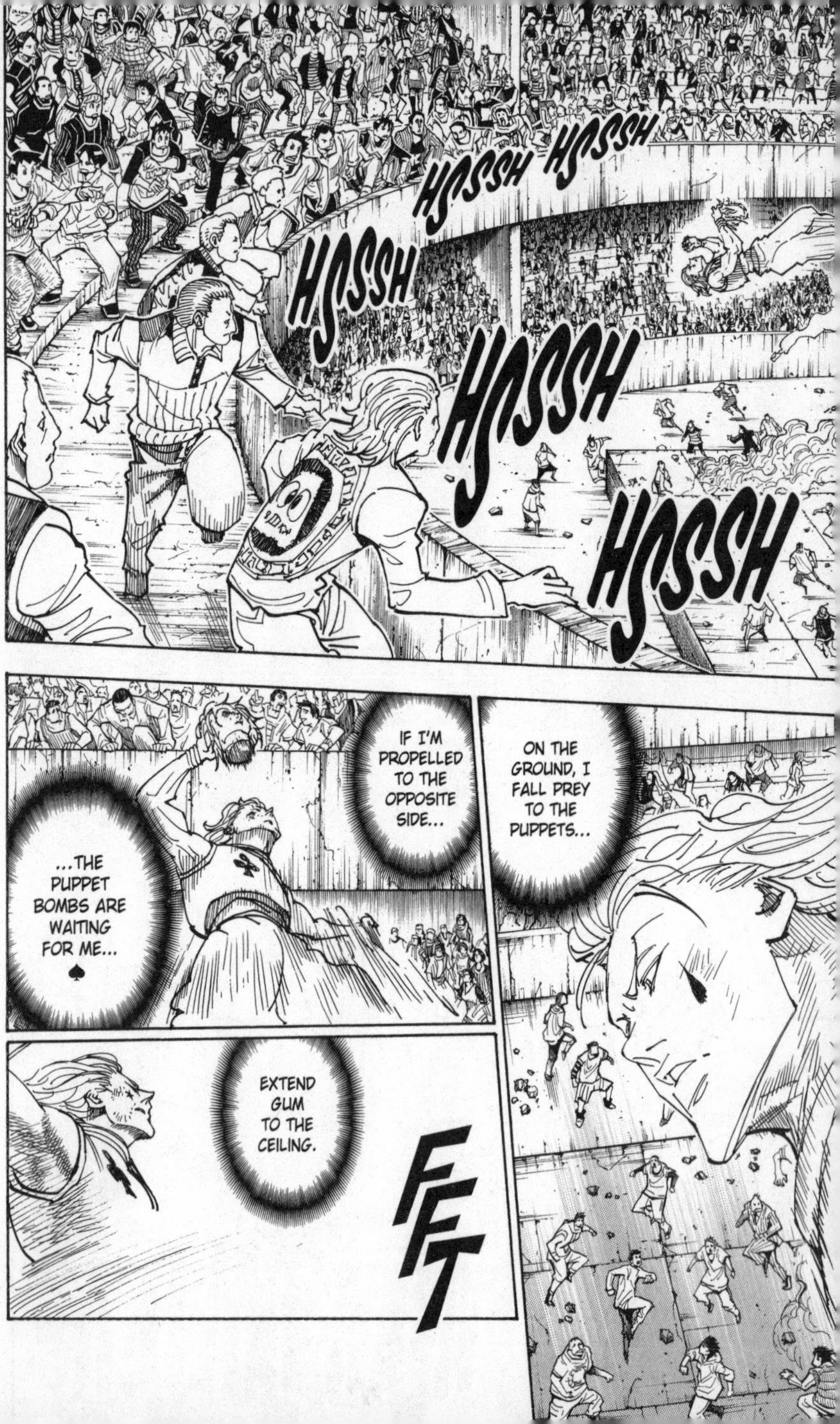
HOSSH
HOSSH
HOSSH
HOSSH
HOSSH
ON THE GROUND, I FALL PREY TO THE PUPPETS...
IF I'M PROPELLED TO THE OPPOSITE SIDE...
...THE PUPPET BOMBS ARE WAITING FOR ME... ♠
EXTEND GUM TO THE CEILING.
FFT

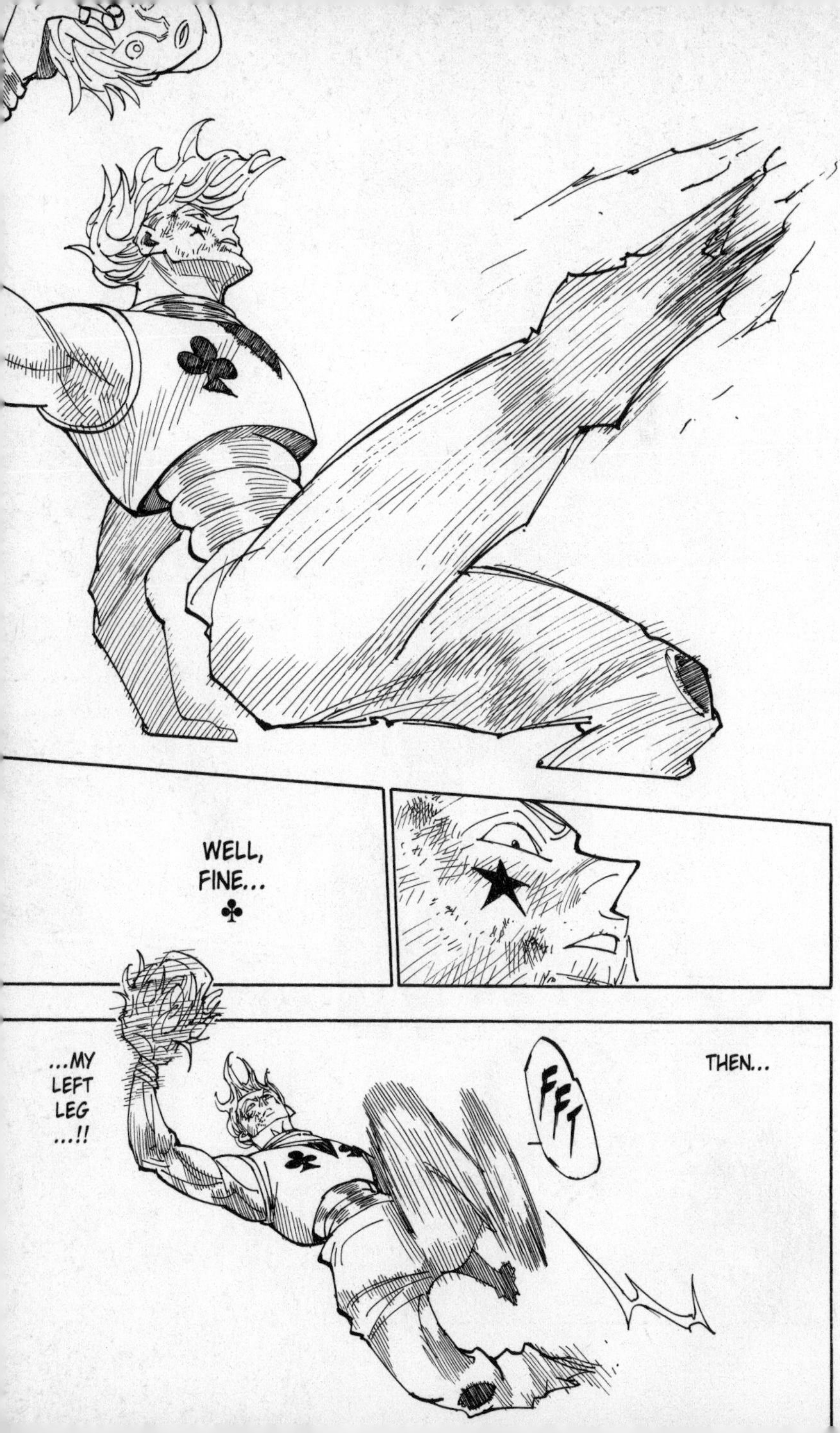
WELL, FINE... ♣
THEN...
FFT
...MY LEFT LEG ...!!

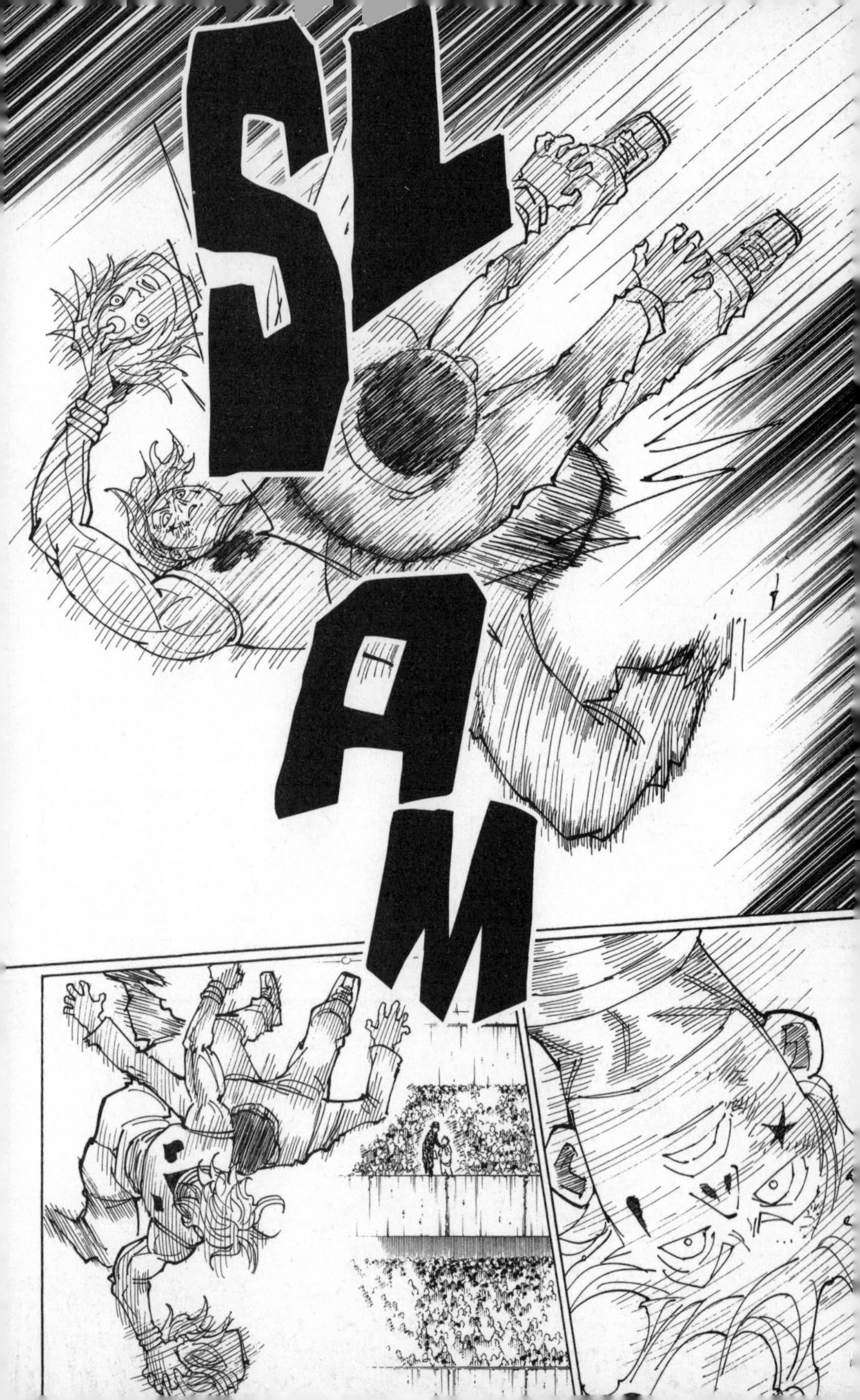
SLAM

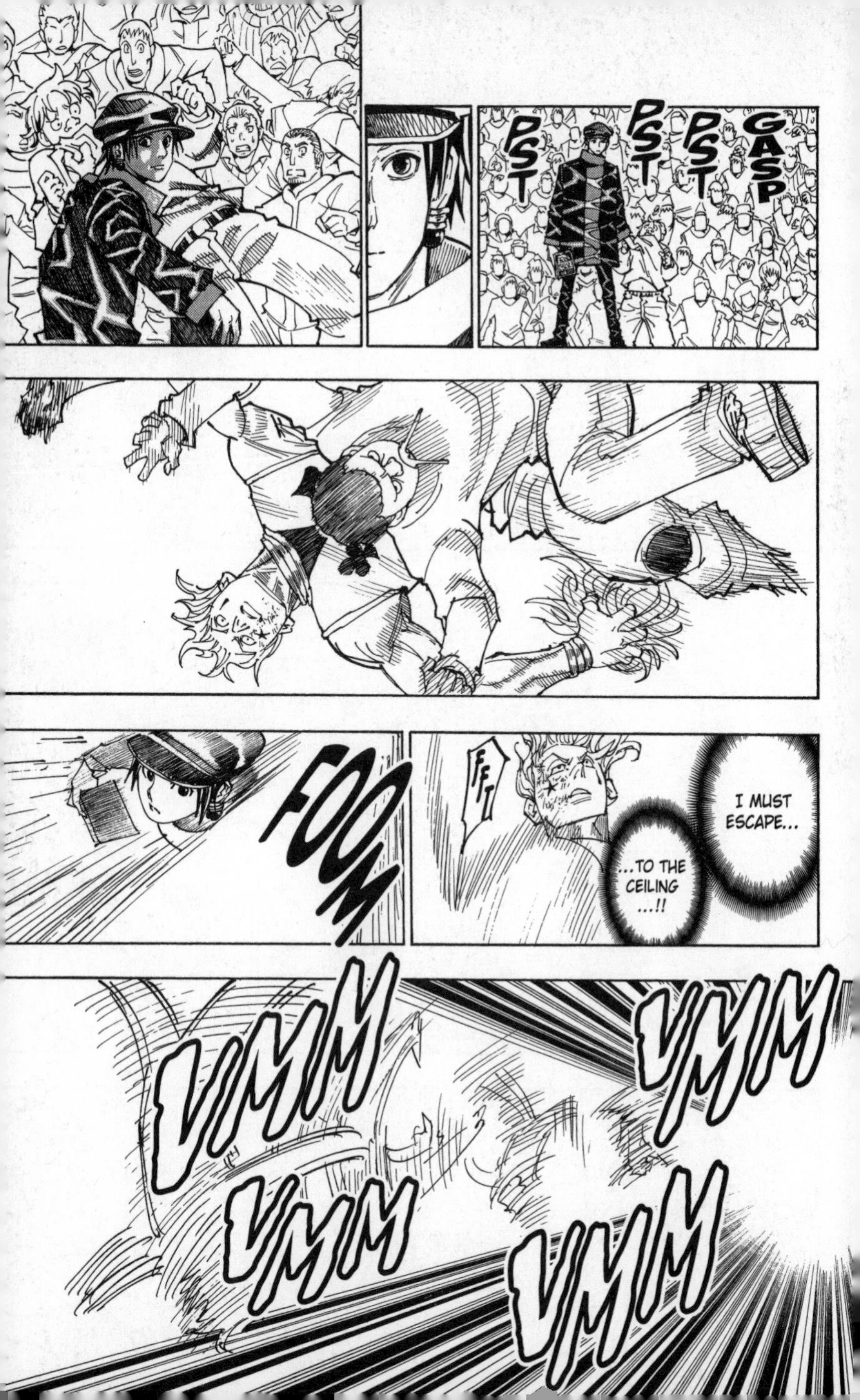
GASP
PST
PST
PST
FFT
I MUST ESCAPE...
...TO THE CEILING...!!
FOOM
VMM
VMM
VMM
VMM

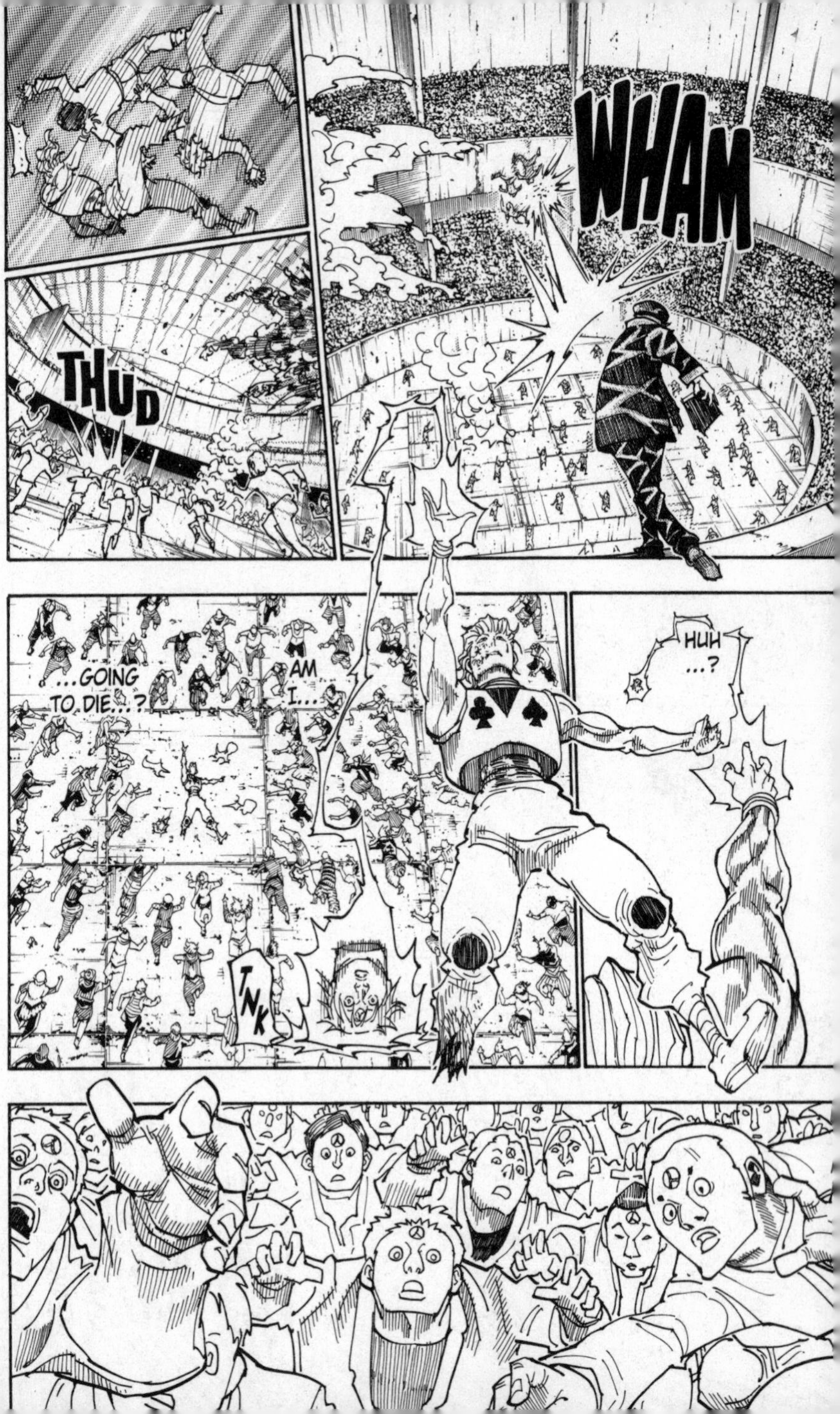
WHAM
THUD
HUH ...?
AM I...
...GOING TO DIE...?
TNK

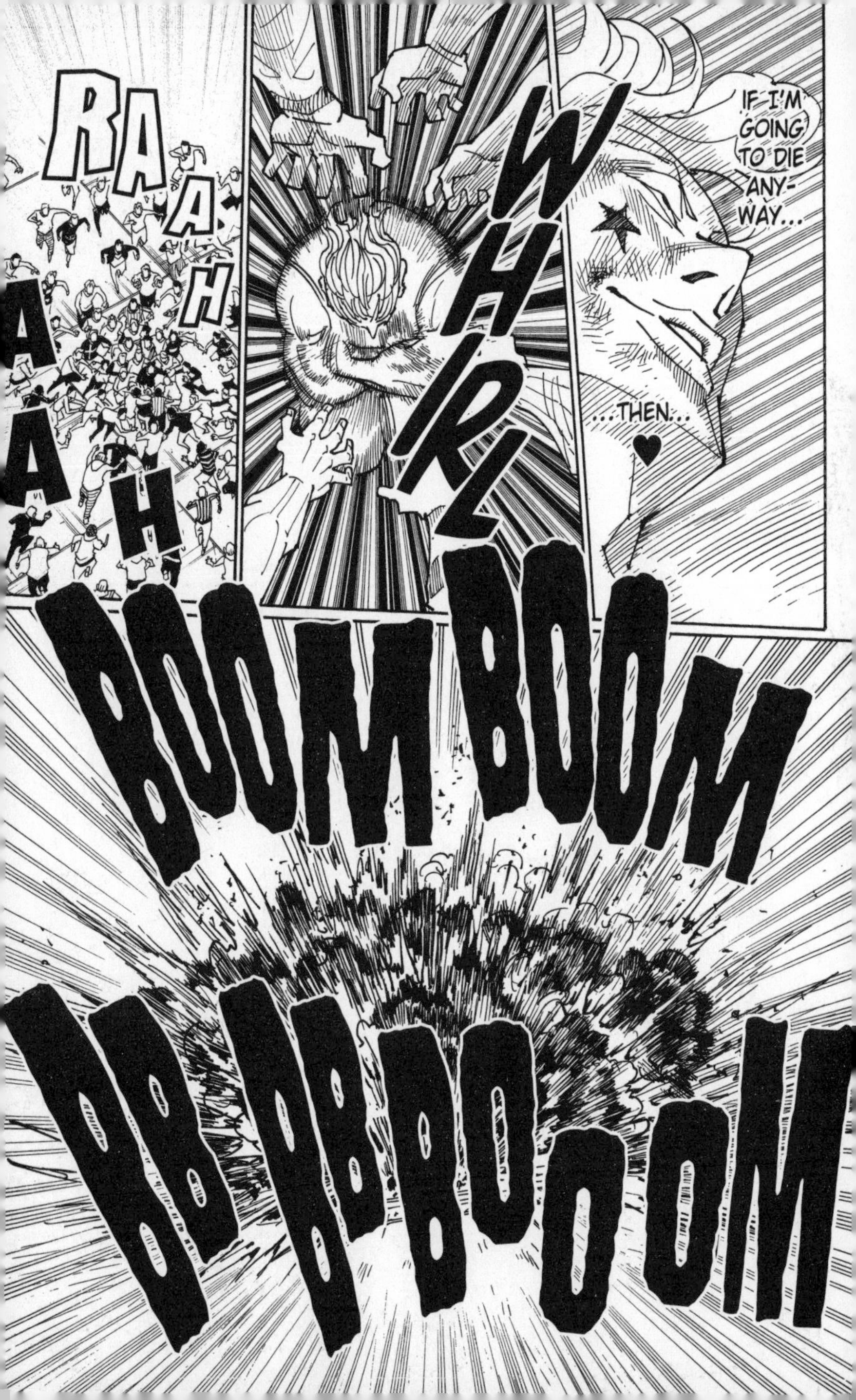
IF I'M GOING TO DIE ANYWAY...
...THEN... ♥
WHIRL
RAAH
AAH
BOOM BOOM
BBBBBOOOM

MATIY

KOHMATIYNEIT

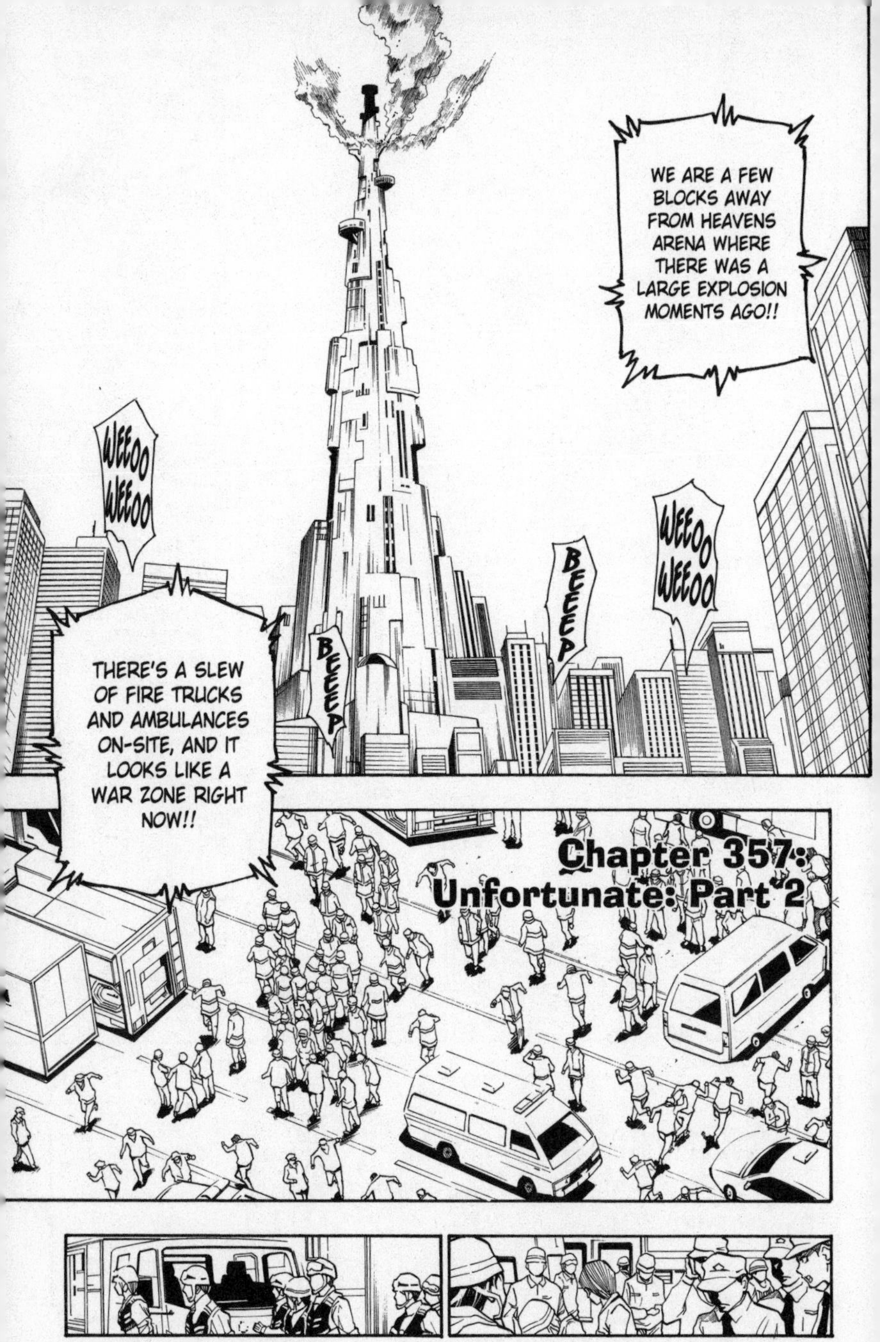
WE ARE A FEW BLOCKS AWAY FROM HEAVENS ARENA WHERE THERE WAS A LARGE EXPLOSION MOMENTS AGO!!
WEEOO WEEOO
BEEEP
BEEEP
WEEOO WEEOO
THERE'S A SLEW OF FIRE TRUCKS AND AMBULANCES ON-SITE, AND IT LOOKS LIKE A WAR ZONE RIGHT NOW!!
Chapter 357: Unfortunate: Part 2

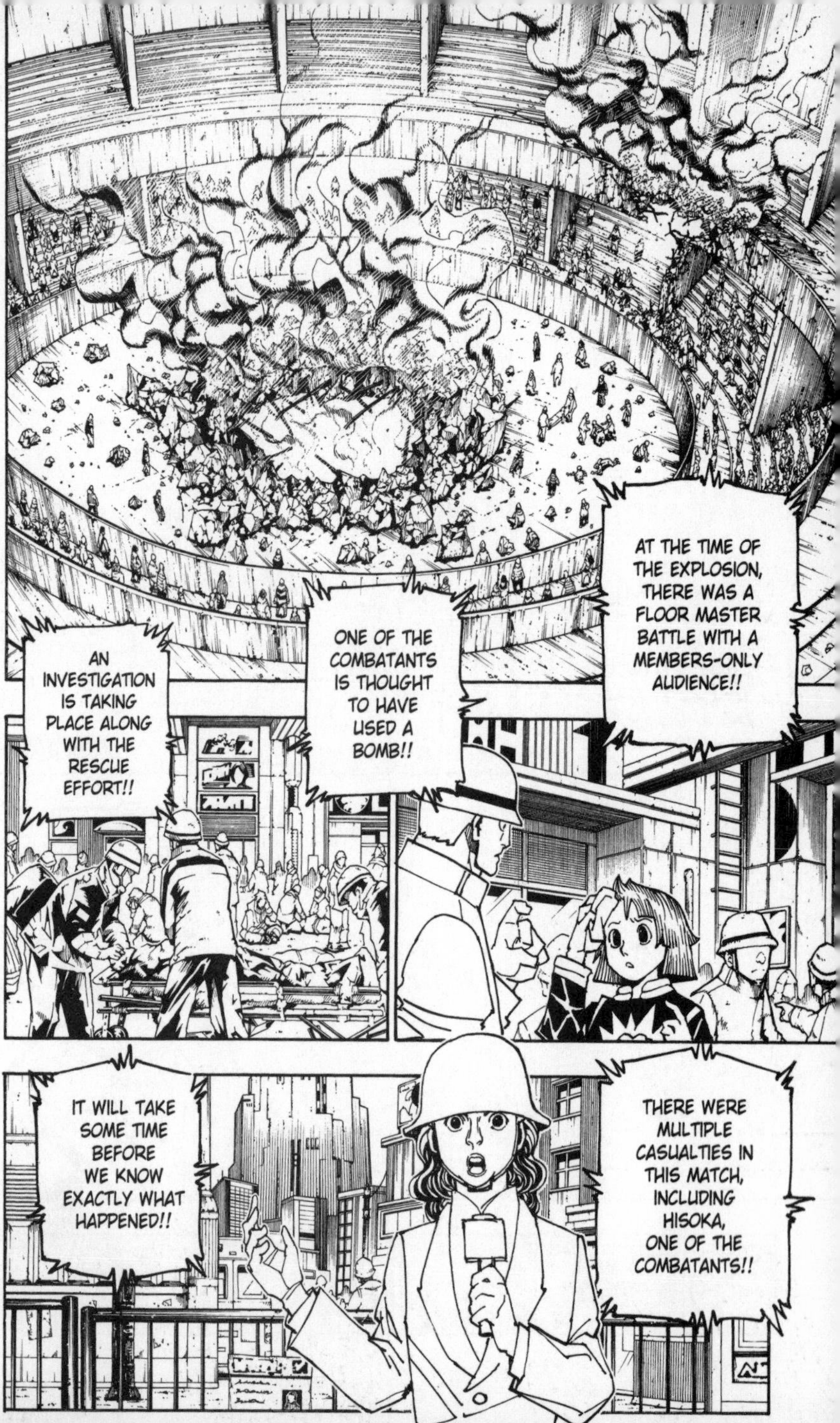
AT THE TIME OF THE EXPLOSION, THERE WAS A FLOOR MASTER BATTLE WITH A MEMBERS-ONLY AUDIENCE!!
ONE OF THE COMBATANTS IS THOUGHT TO HAVE USED A BOMB!!
AN INVESTIGATION IS TAKING PLACE ALONG WITH THE RESCUE EFFORT!!
THERE WERE MULTIPLE CASUALTIES IN THIS MATCH, INCLUDING HISOKA, ONE OF THE COMBATANTS!!
IT WILL TAKE SOME TIME BEFORE WE KNOW EXACTLY WHAT HAPPENED!!

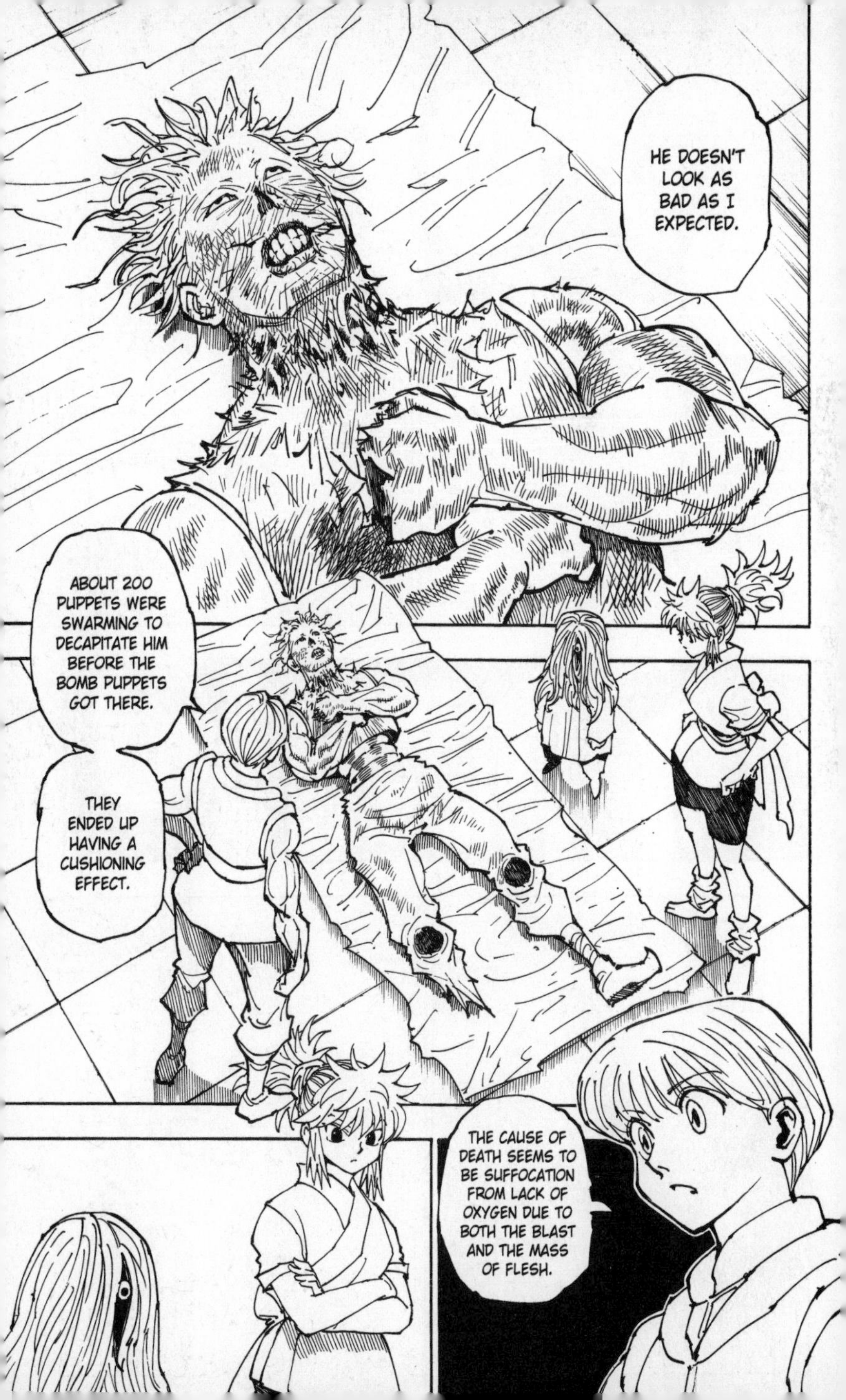
HE DOESN'T LOOK AS BAD AS I EXPECTED.
ABOUT 200 PUPPETS WERE SWARMING TO DECAPITATE HIM BEFORE THE BOMB PUPPETS GOT THERE.
THEY ENDED UP HAVING A CUSHIONING EFFECT.
THE CAUSE OF DEATH SEEMS TO BE SUFFOCATION FROM LACK OF OXYGEN DUE TO BOTH THE BLAST AND THE MASS OF FLESH.

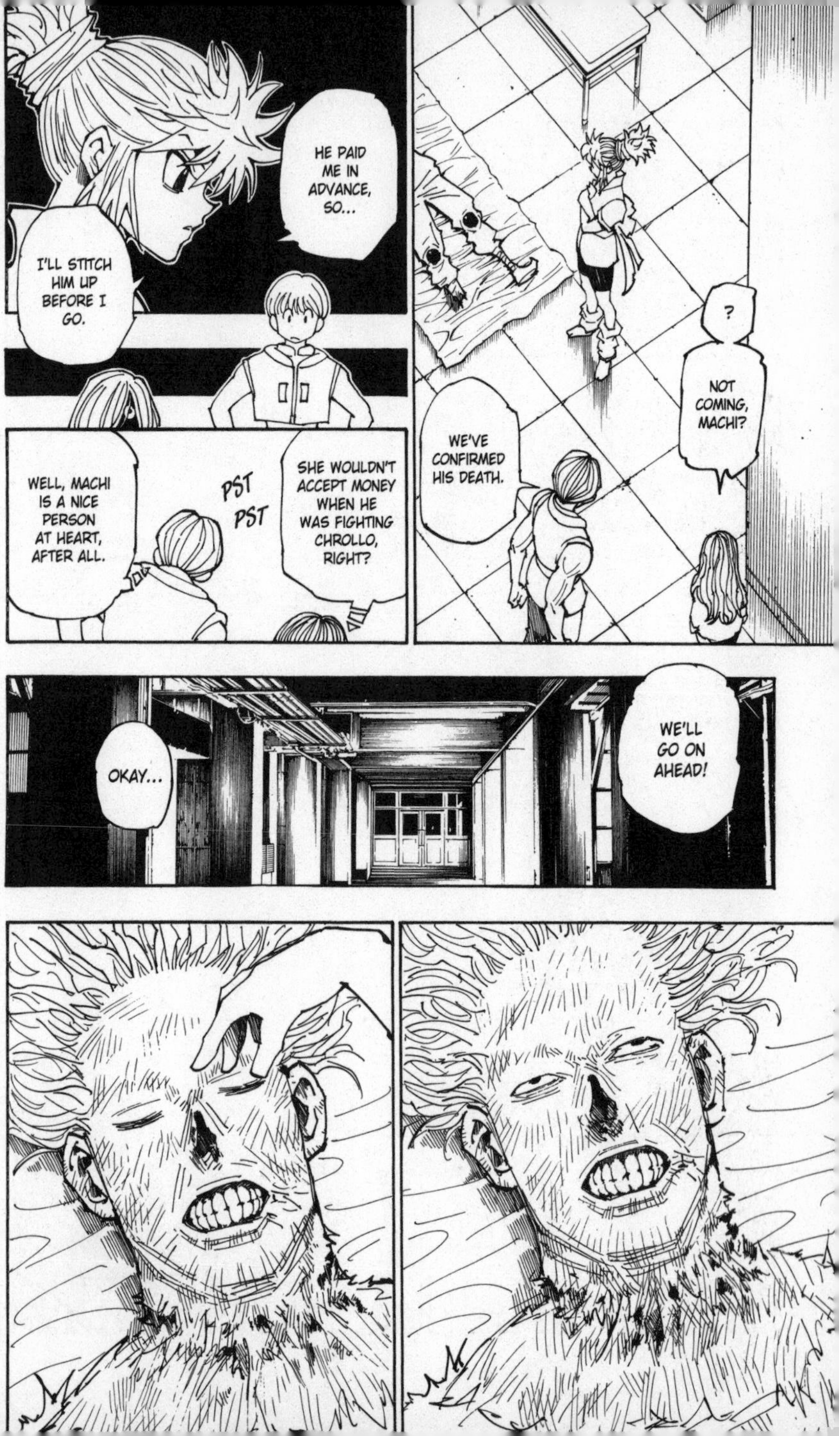
?
NOT COMING, MACHI?
WE'VE CONFIRMED HIS DEATH.
HE PAID ME IN ADVANCE, SO...
I'LL STITCH HIM UP BEFORE I GO.
SHE WOULDN'T ACCEPT MONEY WHEN HE WAS FIGHTING CHROLLO, RIGHT?
PST PST
WELL, MACHI IS A NICE PERSON AT HEART, AFTER ALL.
WE'LL GO ON AHEAD!
OKAY...

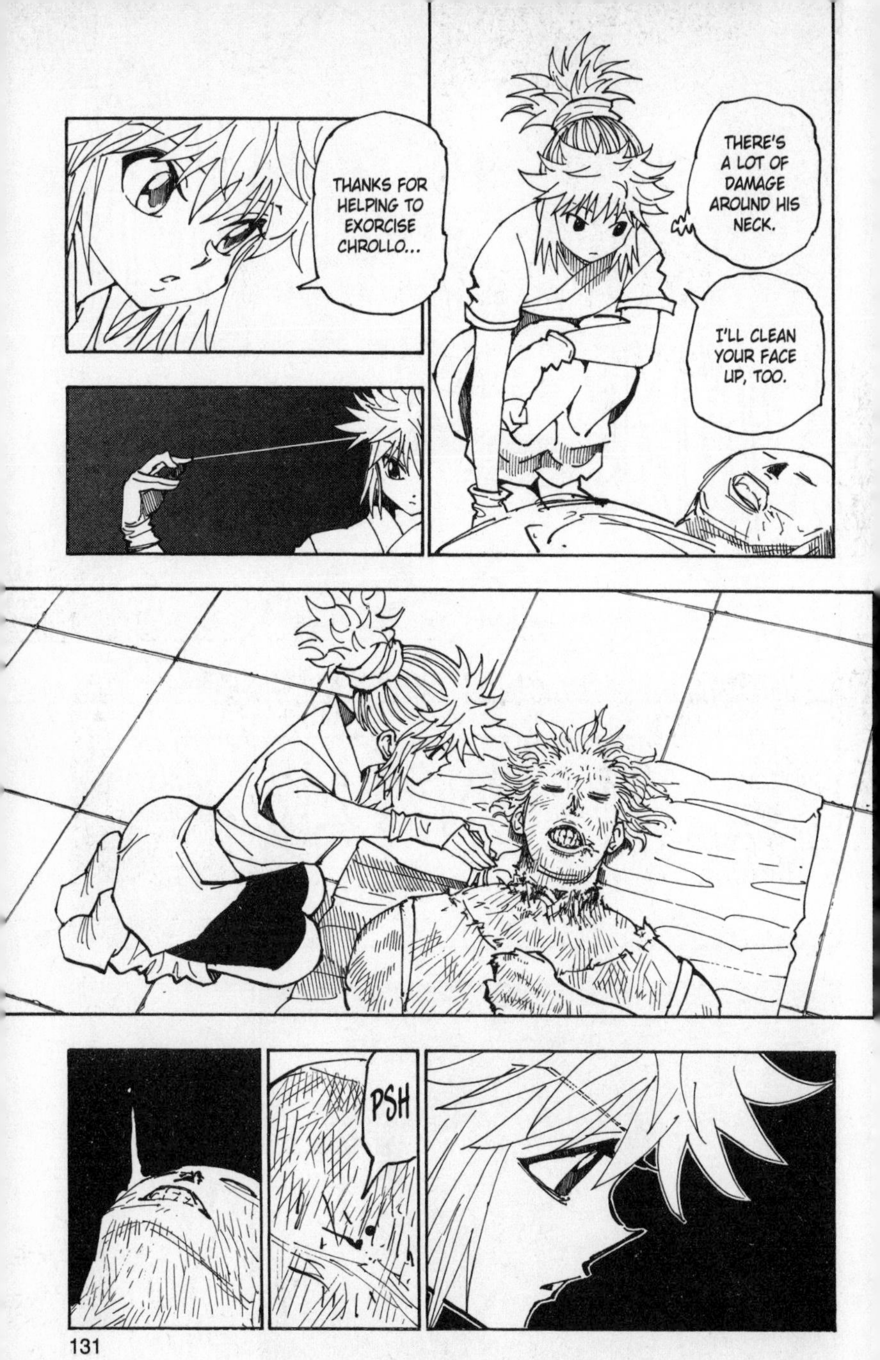
THERE'S A LOT OF DAMAGE AROUND HIS NECK.
I'LL CLEAN YOUR FACE UP, TOO.
THANKS FOR HELPING TO EXORCISE CHROLLO...
PSH

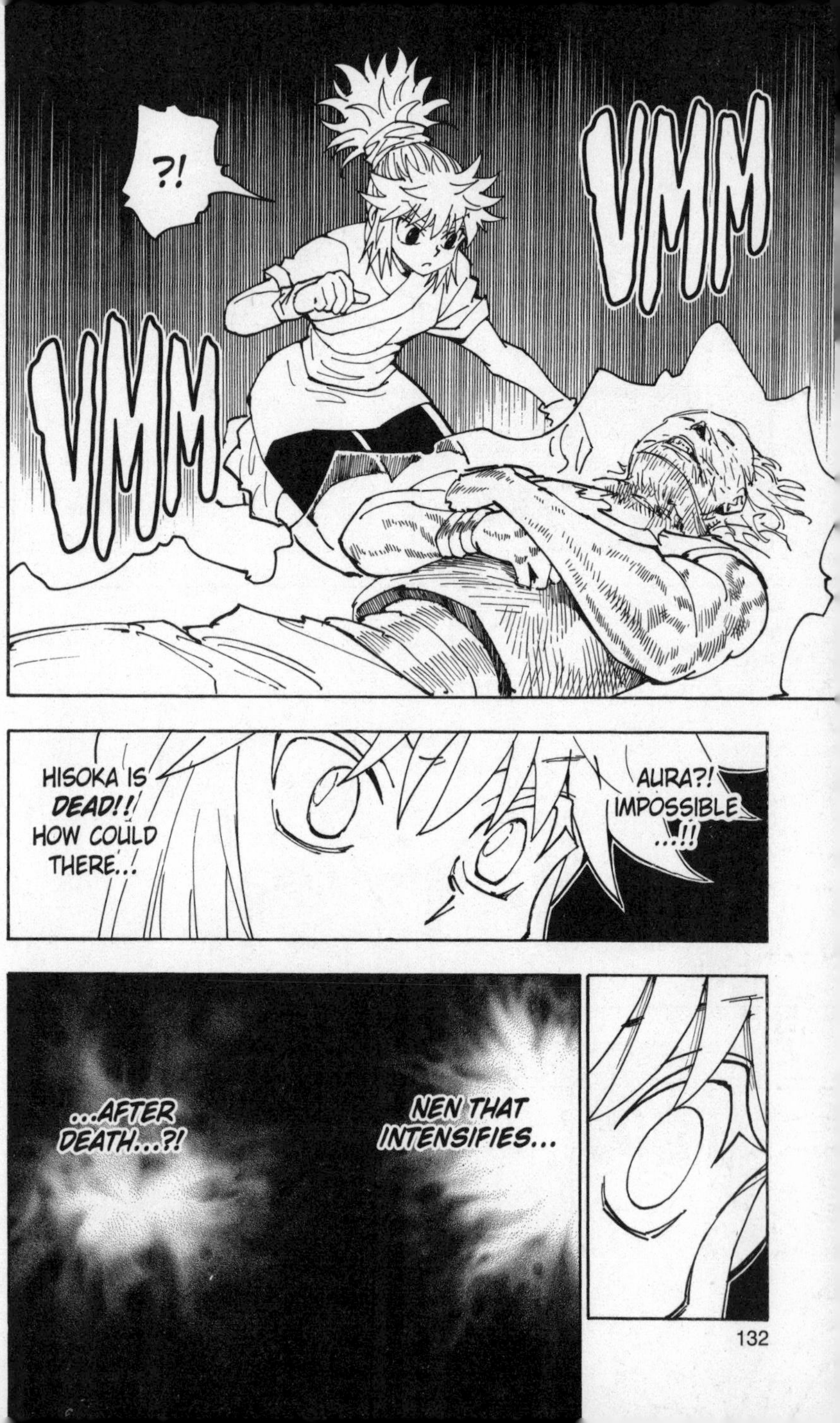
?!
VMM
VMM
AURA?! IMPOSSIBLE ...!!
HISOKA IS DEAD!! HOW COULD THERE...
NEN THAT INTENSIFIES...
...AFTER DEATH...?!

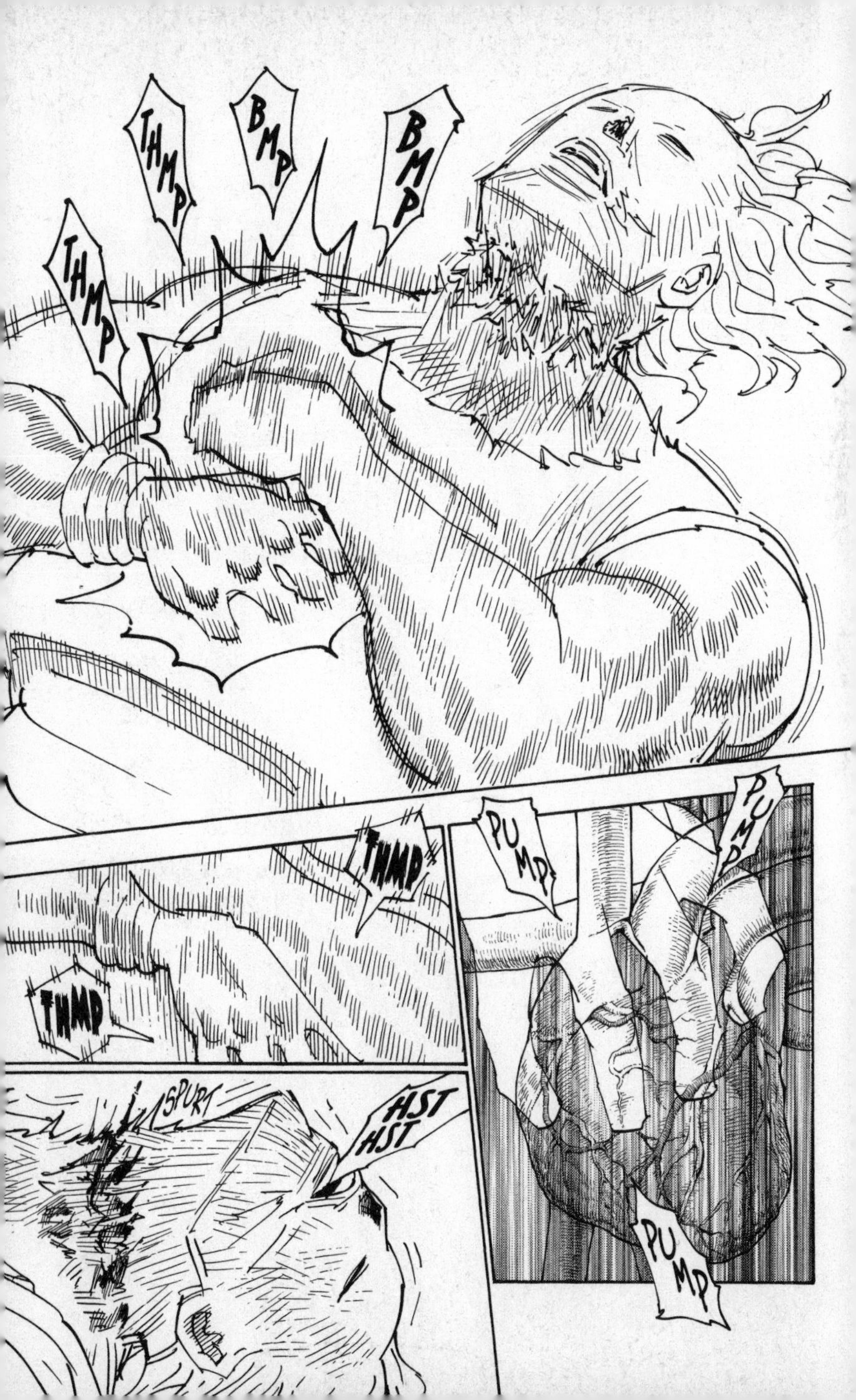
BMP
BMP
THMP
THMP
PUMP
PUMP
PUMP
THMP
THMP
HST HST
SPURT

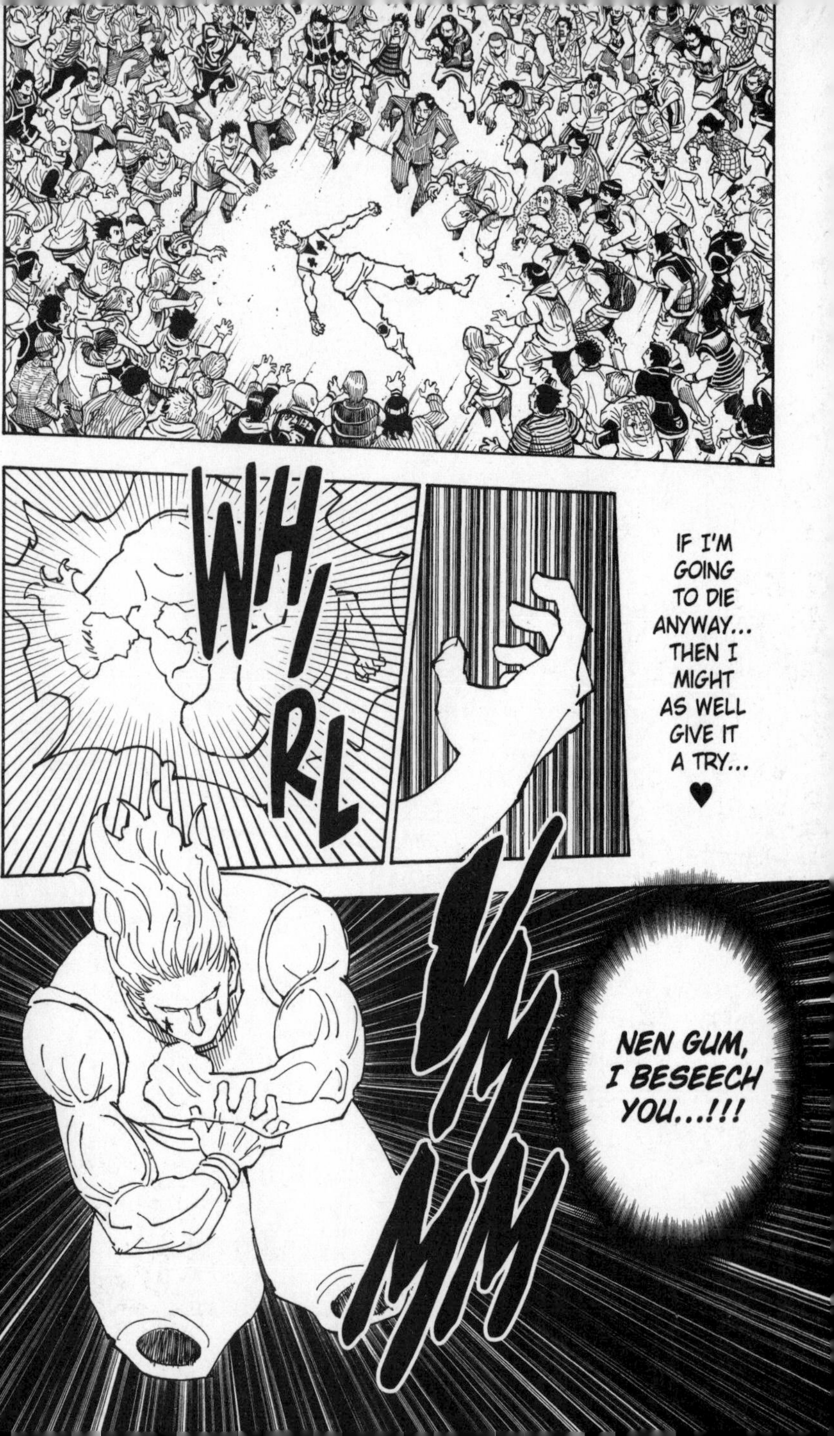
IF I'M GOING TO DIE ANYWAY... THEN I MIGHT AS WELL GIVE IT A TRY... ♥
WHIRL
NEN GUM, I BESEECH YOU...!!!

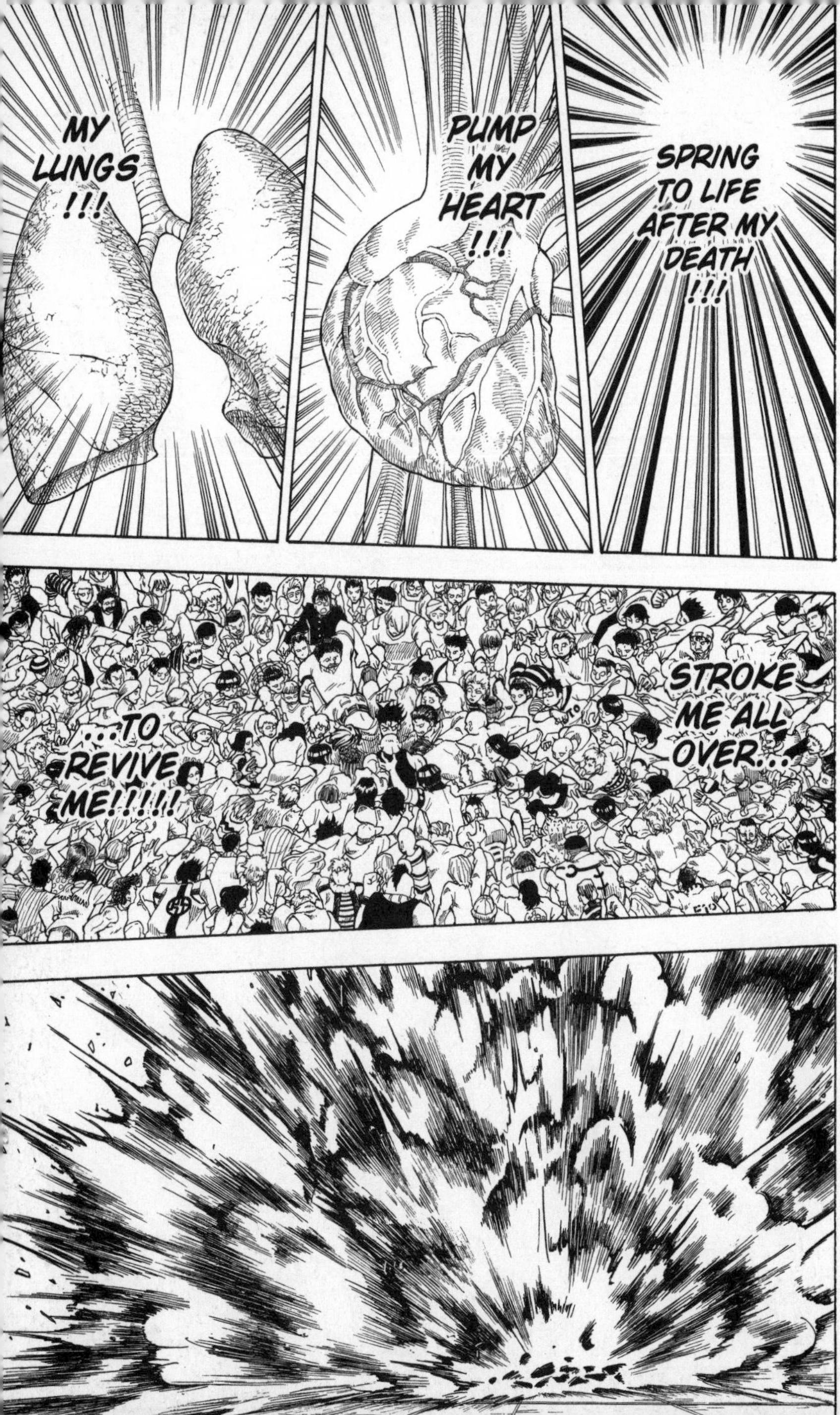
SPRING TO LIFE AFTER MY DEATH!!!
PUMP MY HEART!!!
MY LUNGS!!!
STROKE ME ALL OVER...
...TO REVIVE ME!!!!!

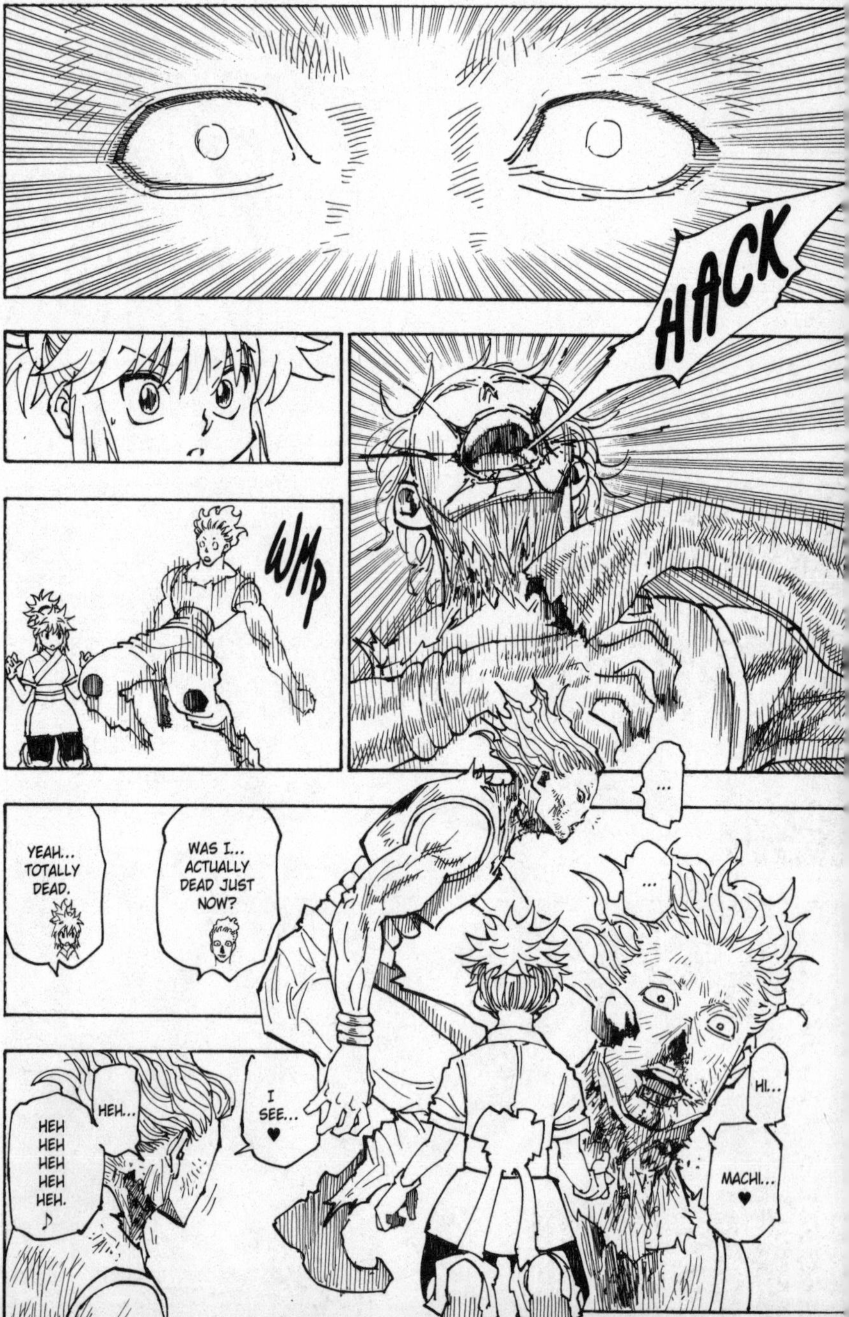
HACK
WMP
...
...
WAS I... ACTUALLY DEAD JUST NOW?
YEAH... TOTALLY DEAD.
HI...
MACHI... ♥
I SEE... ♥
HEH...
HEH HEH HEH HEH HEH. ♪

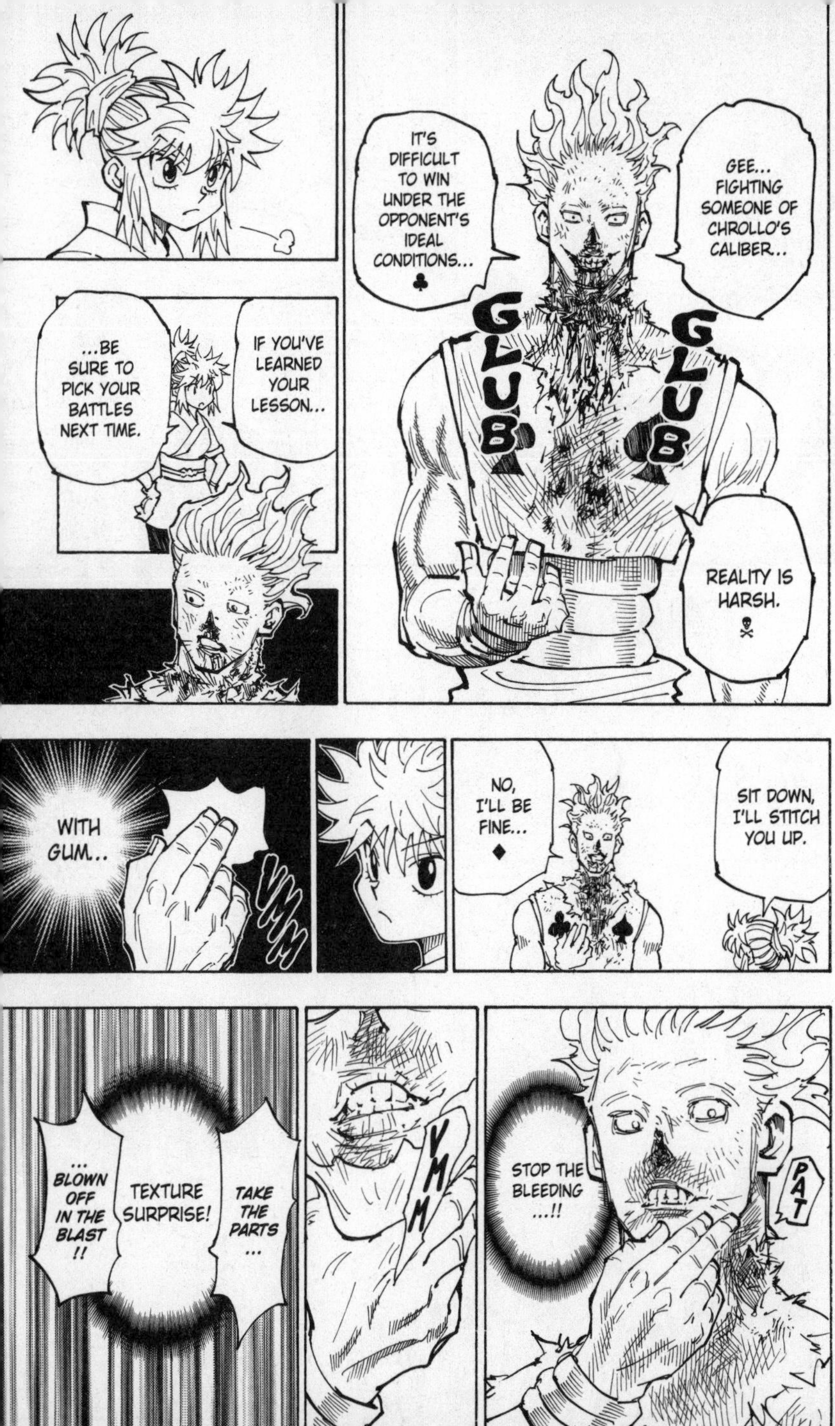
GEE... FIGHTING SOMEONE OF CHROLLO'S CALIBER...
IT'S DIFFICULT TO WIN UNDER THE OPPONENT'S IDEAL CONDITIONS... ♣
GLUB ♠
GLUB ♠
REALITY IS HARSH. ☠
IF YOU'VE LEARNED YOUR LESSON...
...BE SURE TO PICK YOUR BATTLES NEXT TIME.
SIT DOWN, I'LL STITCH YOU UP.
NO, I'LL BE FINE... ♦
VMMM
WITH GUM...
PAT
STOP THE BLEEDING ...!!
VMM
TAKE THE PARTS ...
TEXTURE SURPRISE!
...BLOWN OFF IN THE BLAST !!

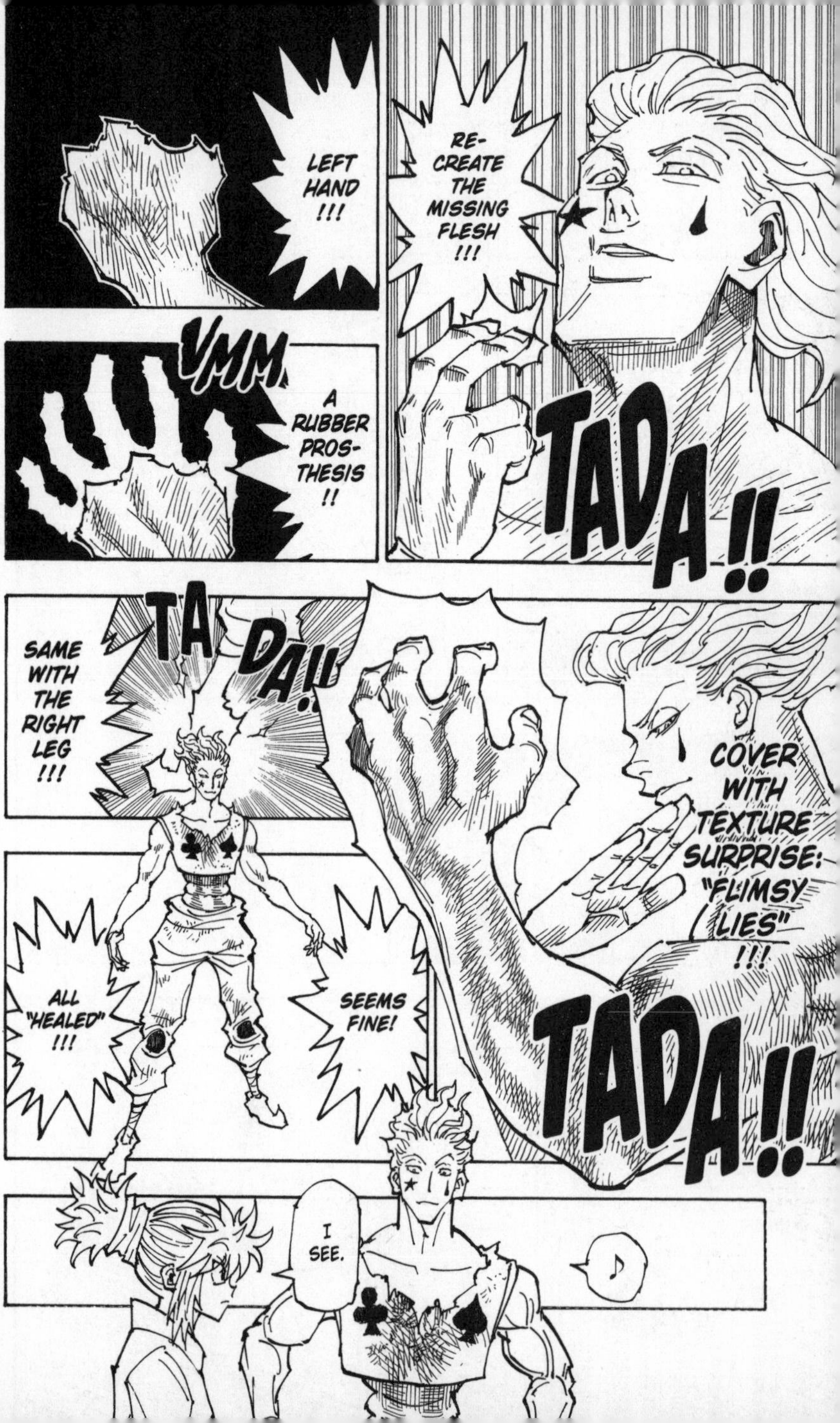
RE-CREATE THE MISSING FLESH!!!
TADA!!
LEFT HAND!!!
VMM.
A RUBBER PROSTHESIS!!
COVER WITH TEXTURE SURPRISE: "FLIMSY LIES"!!!
TADA!!
TA DA!!
SAME WITH THE RIGHT LEG!!!
SEEMS FINE!
ALL "HEALED"!!!
♪
I SEE.

READ THIS WAY

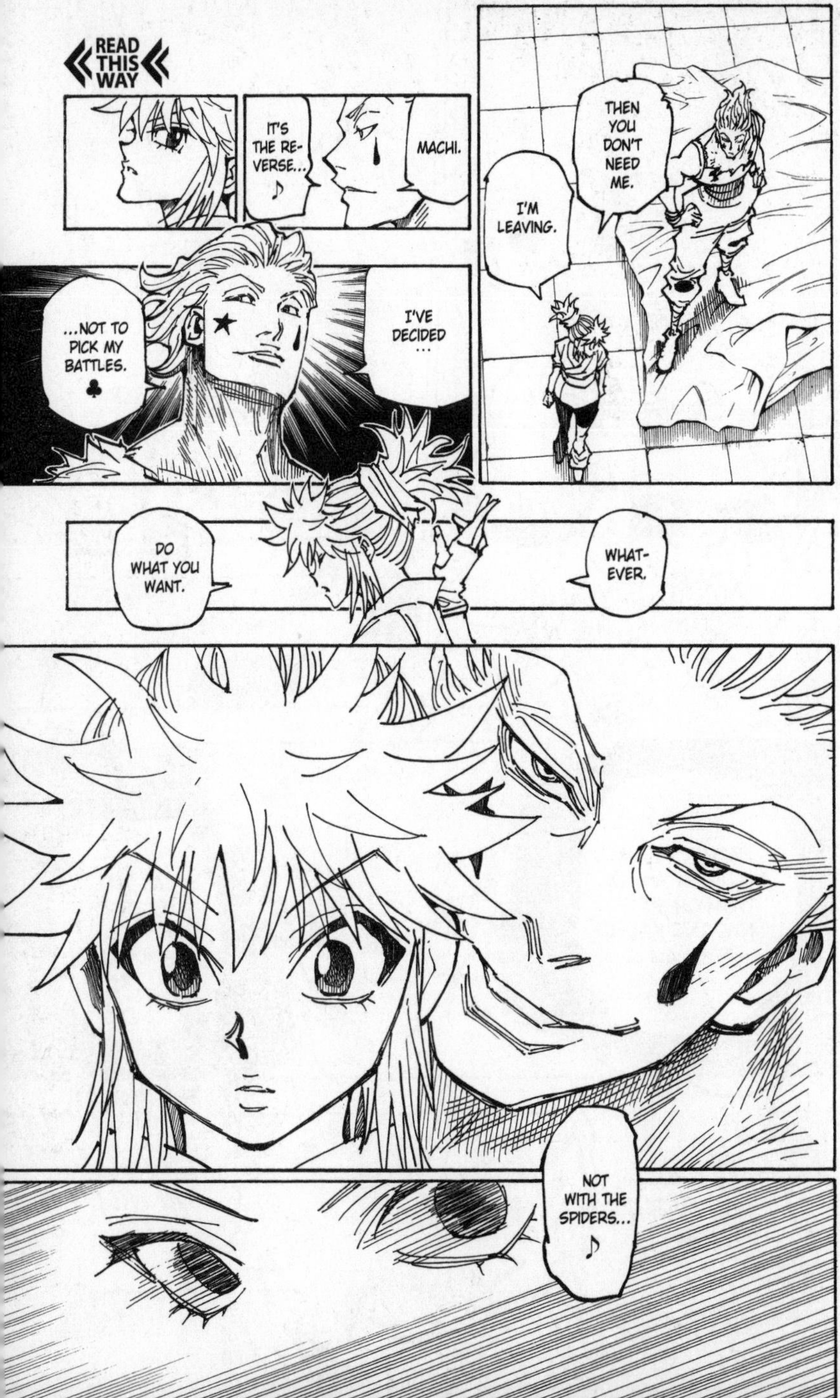
THEN YOU DON'T NEED ME.
I'M LEAVING.
MACHI.
IT'S THE RE-VERSE... ♪
I'VE DECIDED ...
...NOT TO PICK MY BATTLES. ♣
WHAT-EVER.
DO WHAT YOU WANT.
NOT WITH THE SPIDERS... ♪

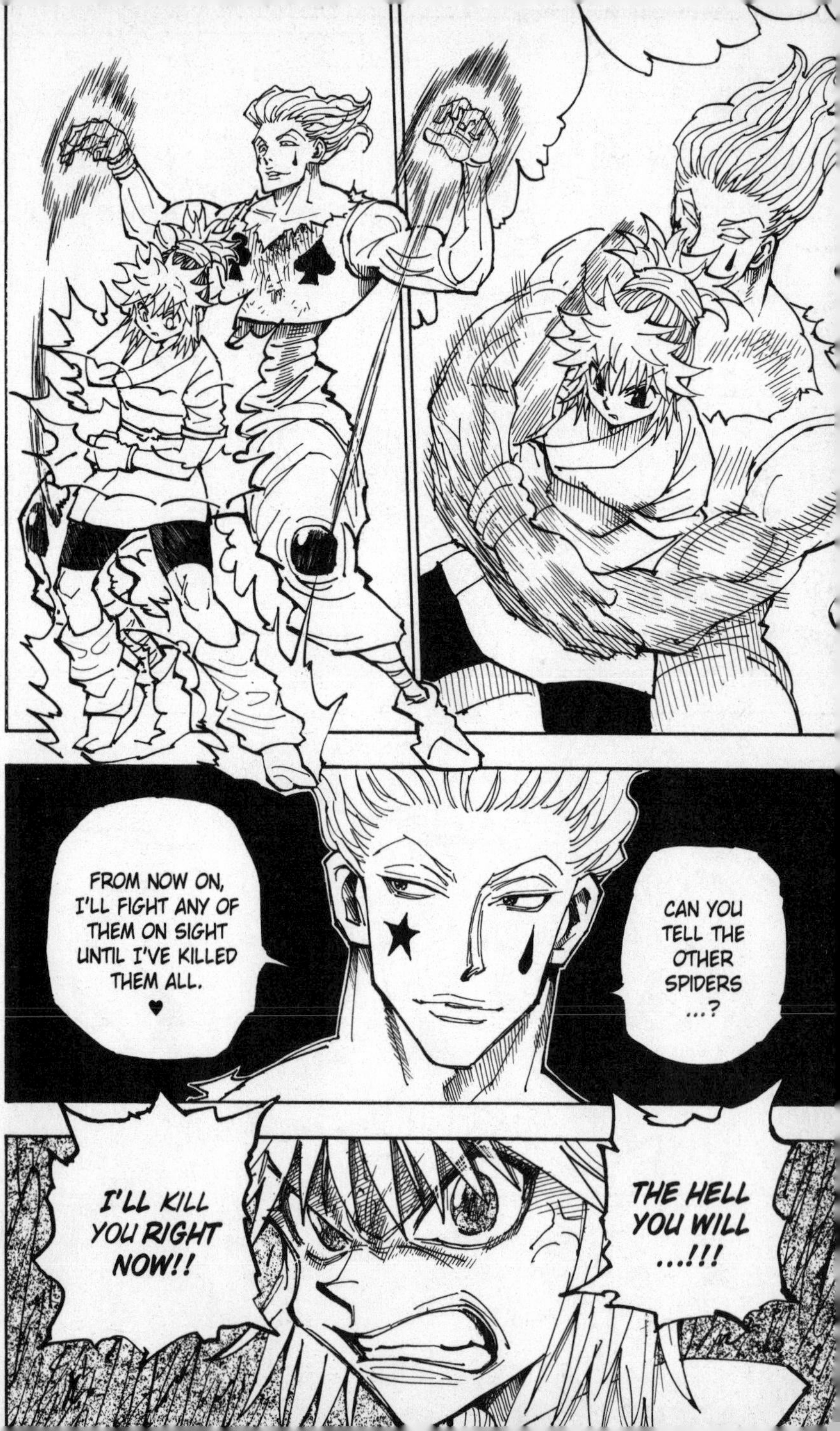
CAN YOU TELL THE OTHER SPIDERS ...?
FROM NOW ON, I'LL FIGHT ANY OF THEM ON SIGHT UNTIL I'VE KILLED THEM ALL. ♥
THE HELL YOU WILL ...!!!
I'LL KILL YOU RIGHT NOW!!

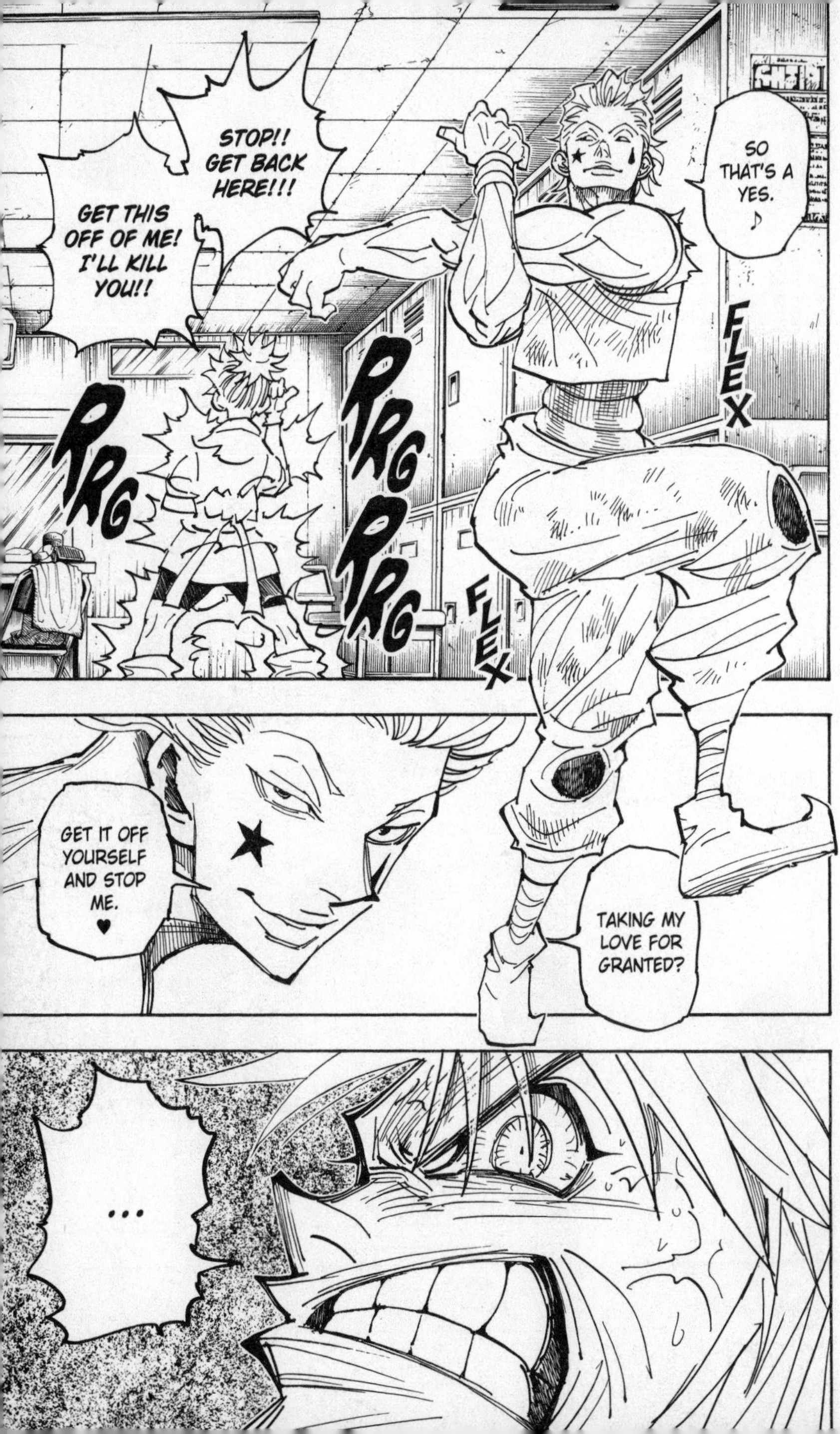
SO THAT'S A YES. ♪
FLEX
STOP!! GET BACK HERE!!!
GET THIS OFF OF ME! I'LL KILL YOU!!
RRG RRG
RRG
FLEX
RRG
TAKING MY LOVE FOR GRANTED?
GET IT OFF YOURSELF AND STOP ME. ♥
...

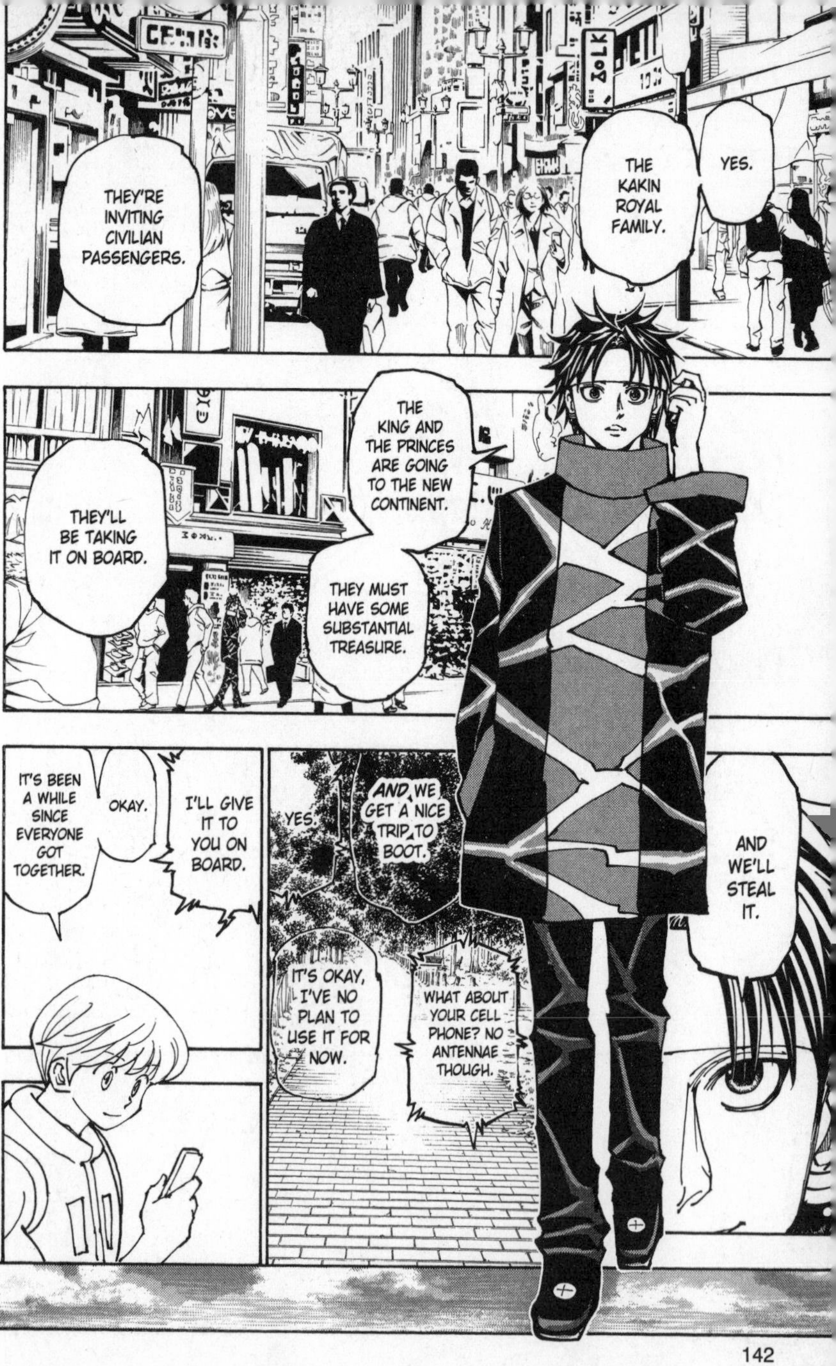
YES.
THE KAKIN ROYAL FAMILY.
THEY'RE INVITING CIVILIAN PASSENGERS.
THE KING AND THE PRINCES ARE GOING TO THE NEW CONTINENT.
THEY MUST HAVE SOME SUBSTANTIAL TREASURE.
THEY'LL BE TAKING IT ON BOARD.
AND WE'LL STEAL IT.
AND WE GET A NICE TRIP TO BOOT.
YES.
WHAT ABOUT YOUR CELL PHONE? NO ANTENNAE THOUGH.
IT'S OKAY, I'VE NO PLAN TO USE IT FOR NOW.
I'LL GIVE IT TO YOU ON BOARD.
OKAY.
IT'S BEEN A WHILE SINCE EVERYONE GOT TOGETHER.

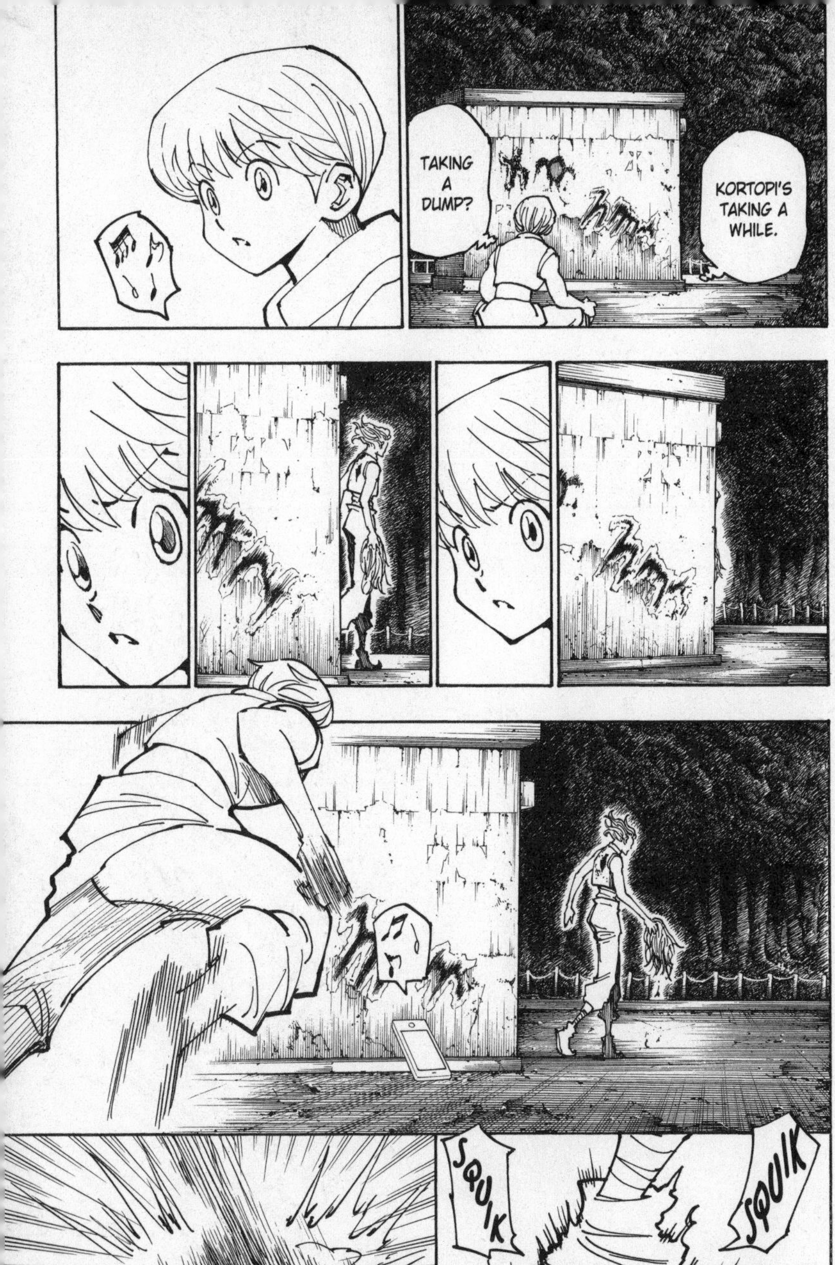
KORTOPI'S TAKING A WHILE.
TAKING A DUMP?
SQUIK
SQUIK

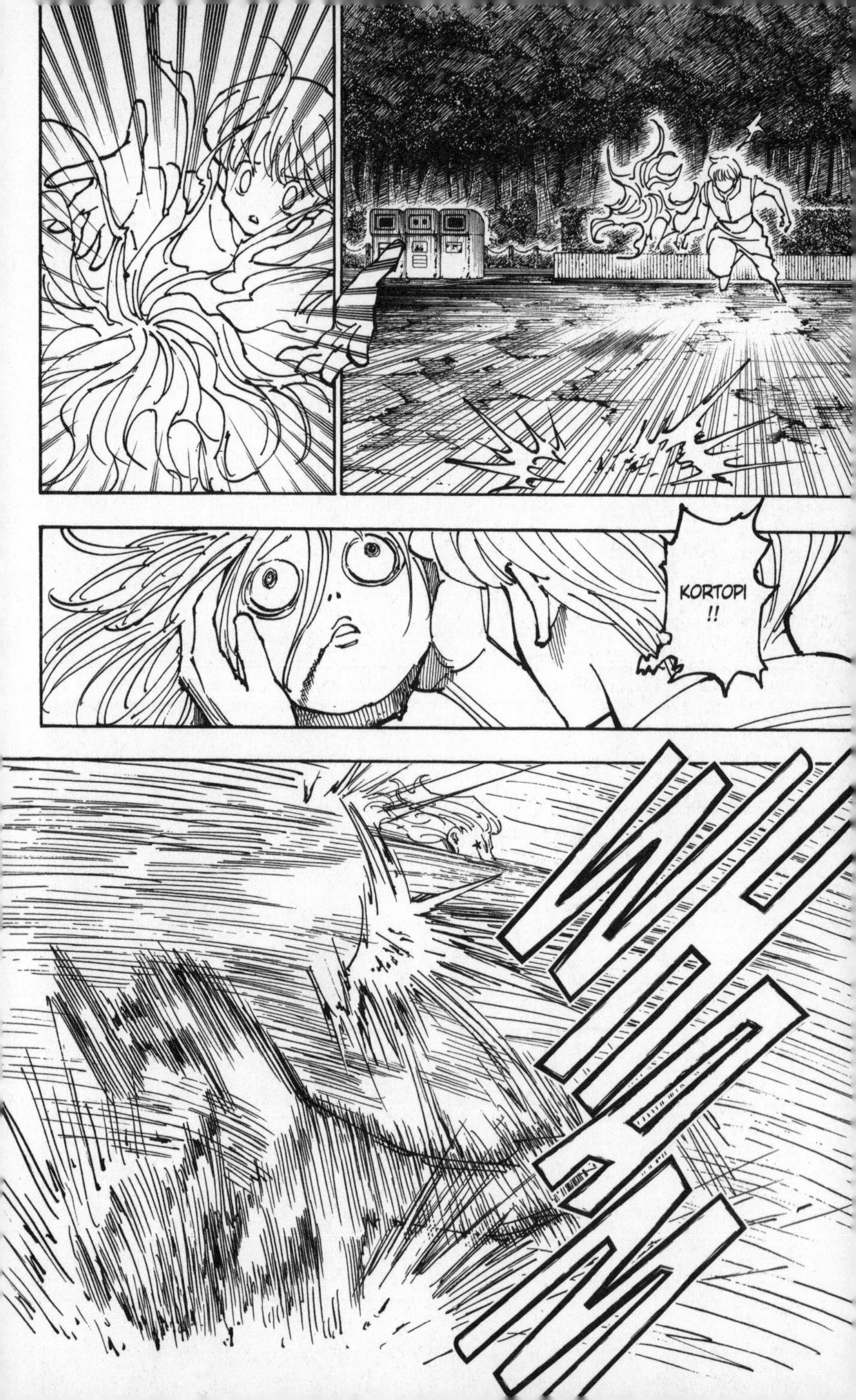
KORTOPI
!!

KRI...
KRI...
KRI...
KRI...
TWO DOWN...
TEN TO GO... ♪

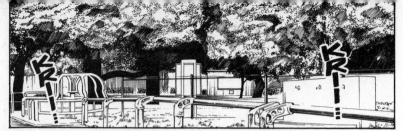

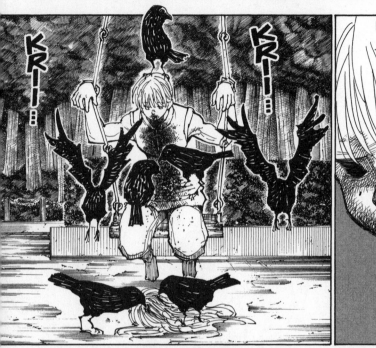

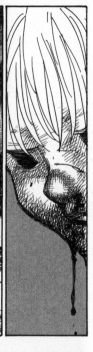

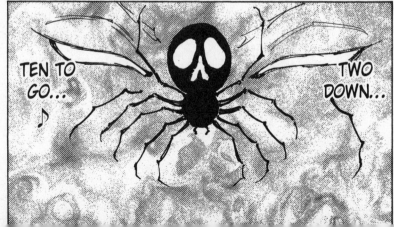

SYARNORKE
RYUSEIH

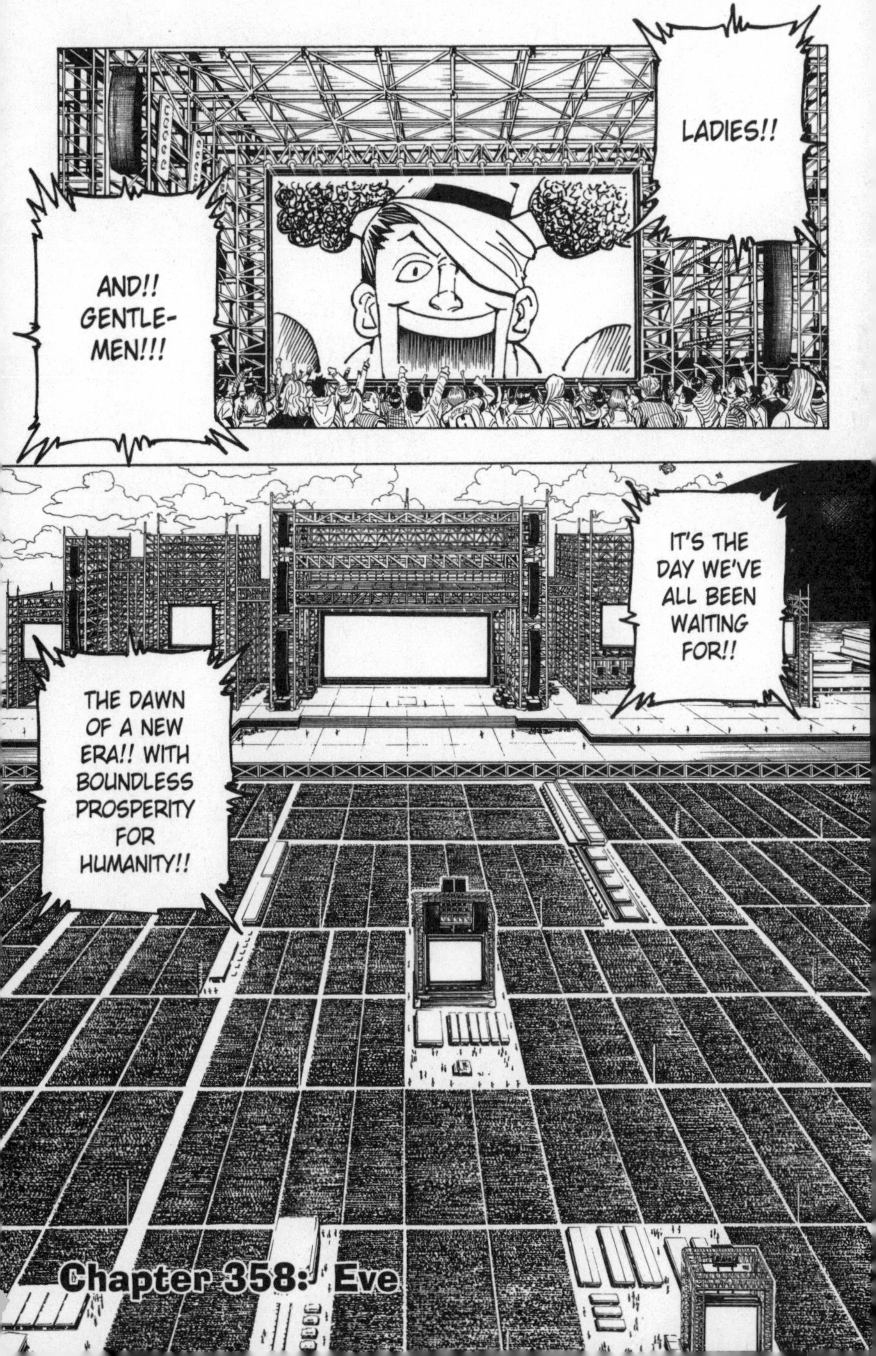
LADIES!!
AND!! GENTLE-MEN!!!
IT'S THE DAY WE'VE ALL BEEN WAITING FOR!!
THE DAWN OF A NEW ERA!! WITH BOUNDLESS PROSPERITY FOR HUMANITY!!
Chapter 358: Eve

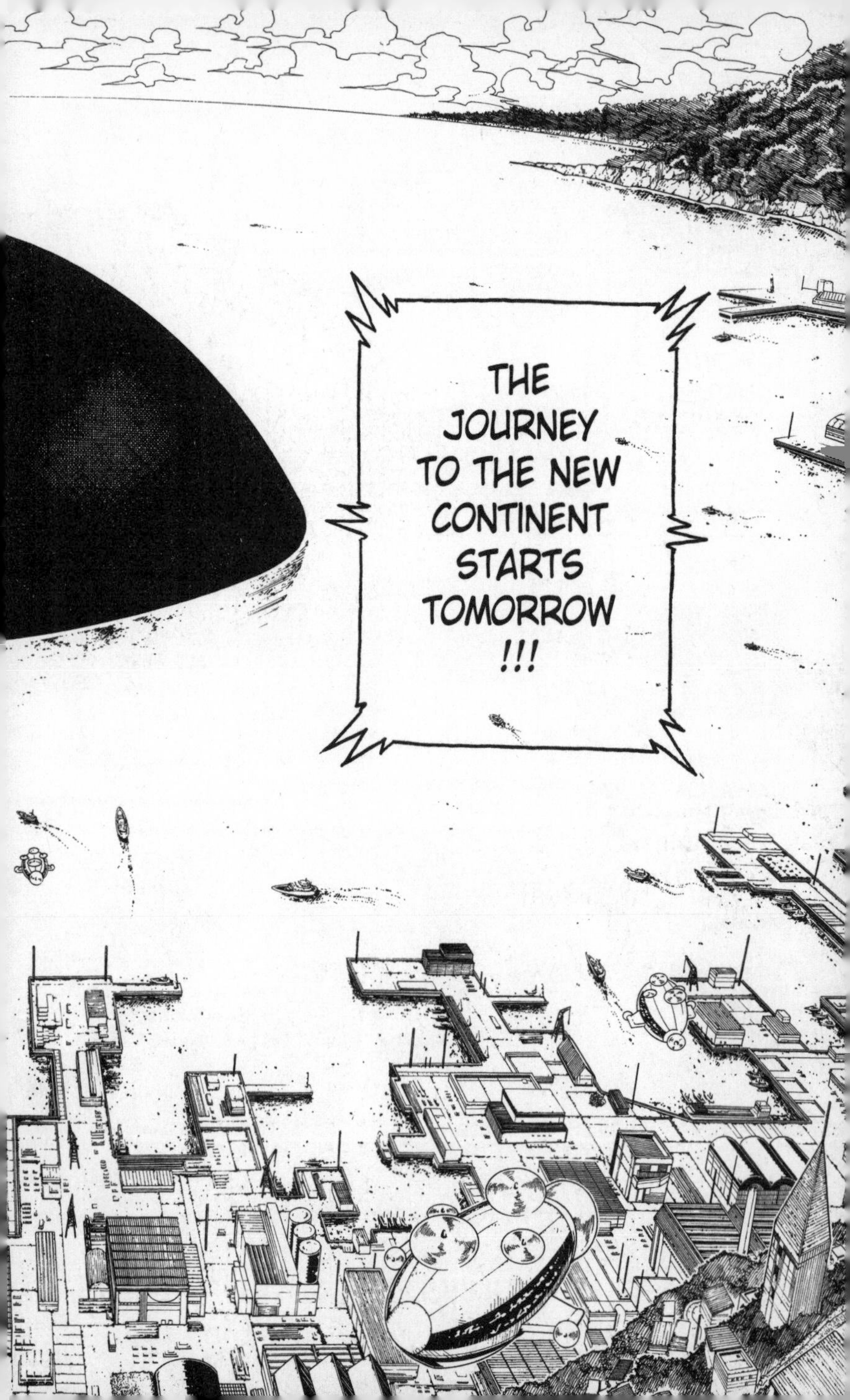
THE JOURNEY TO THE NEW CONTINENT STARTS TOMORROW !!!

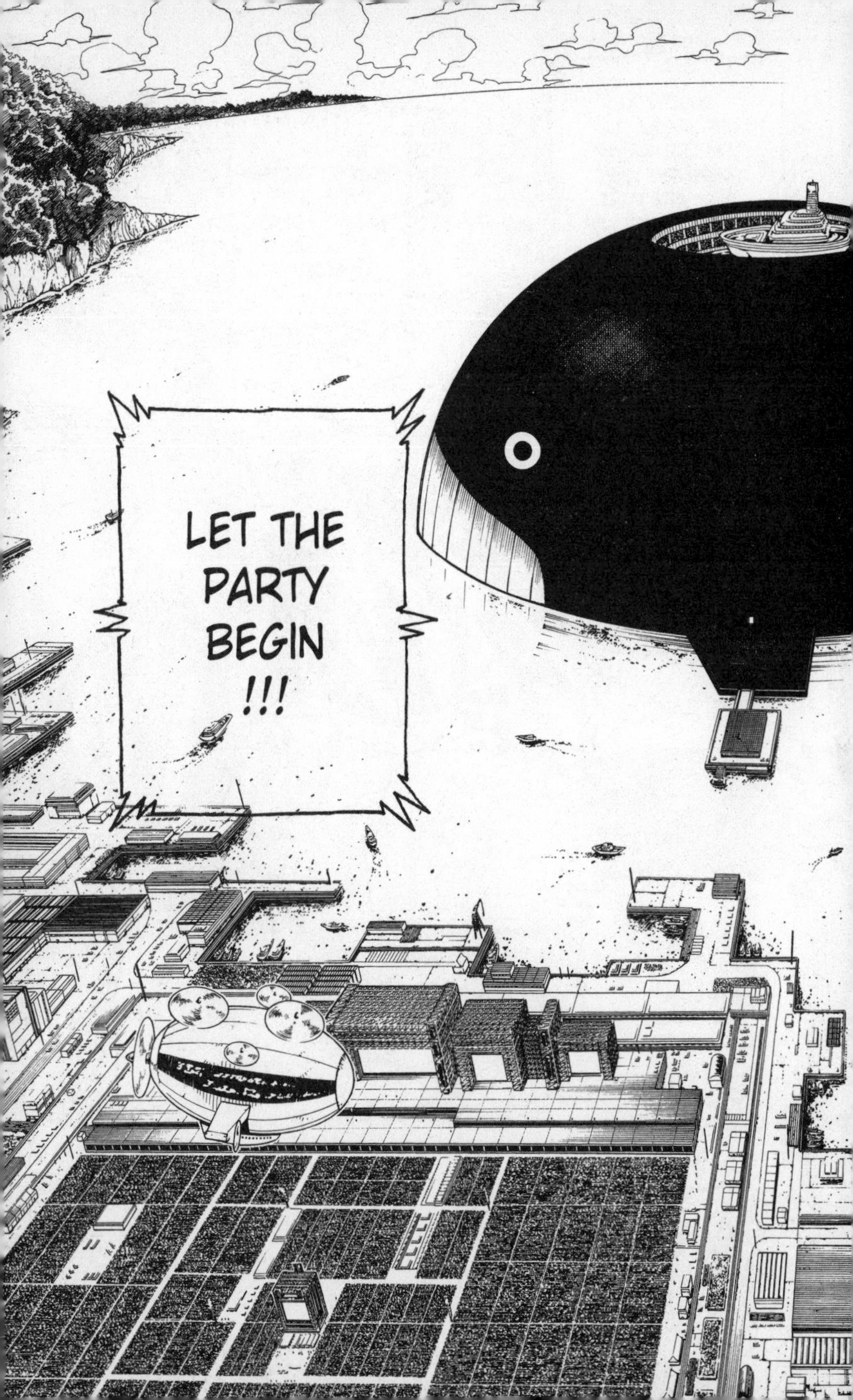
LET THE PARTY BEGIN !!!

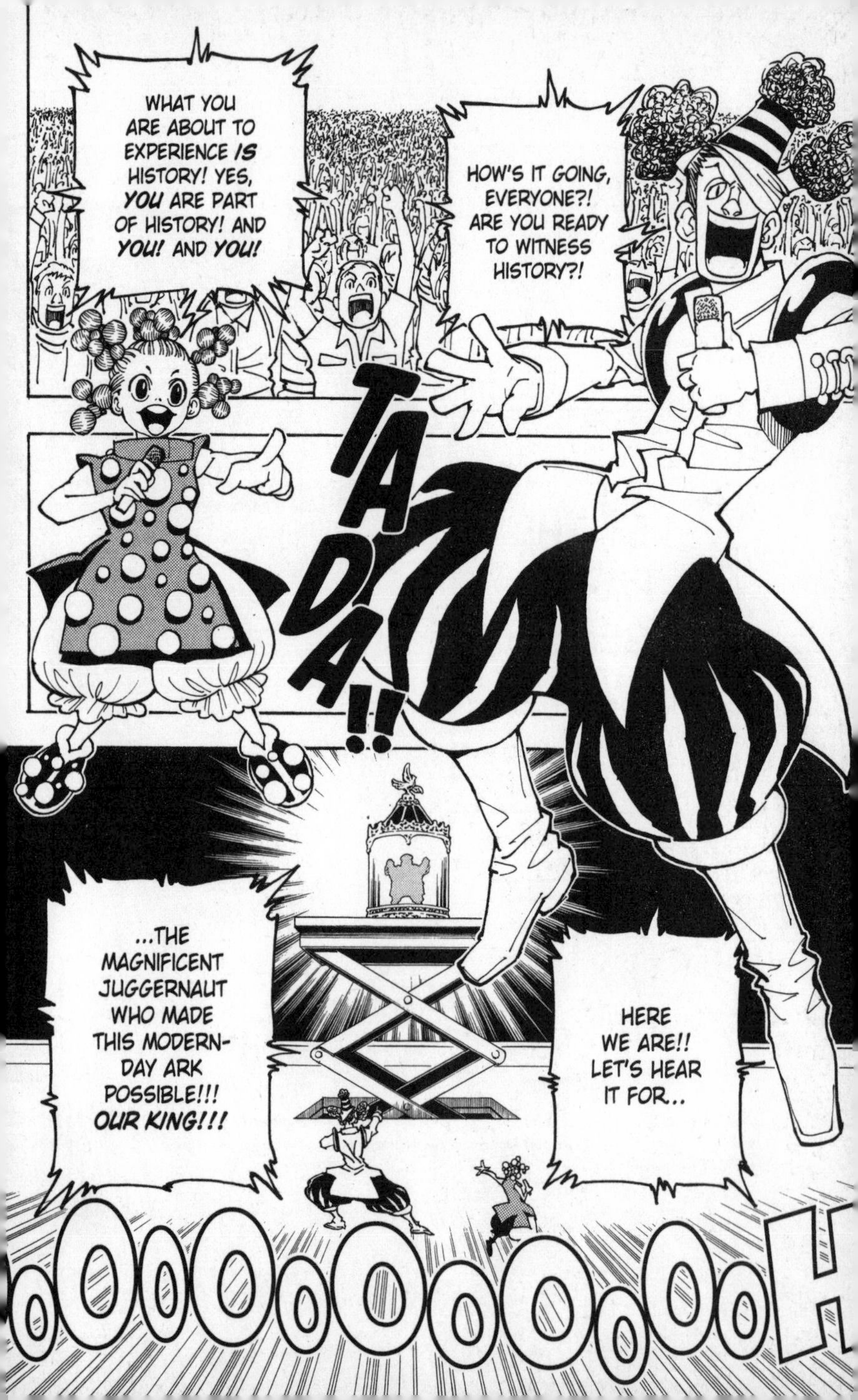
HOW'S IT GOING, EVERYONE?! ARE YOU READY TO WITNESS HISTORY?!
WHAT YOU ARE ABOUT TO EXPERIENCE *IS* HISTORY! YES, ***YOU*** ARE PART OF HISTORY! AND ***YOU!*** AND ***YOU!***
TA DA!!
HERE WE ARE!! LET'S HEAR IT FOR...
...THE MAGNIFICENT JUGGERNAUT WHO MADE THIS MODERN-DAY ARK POSSIBLE!!! ***OUR KING!!!***
OOOOOOOOOOOOOH

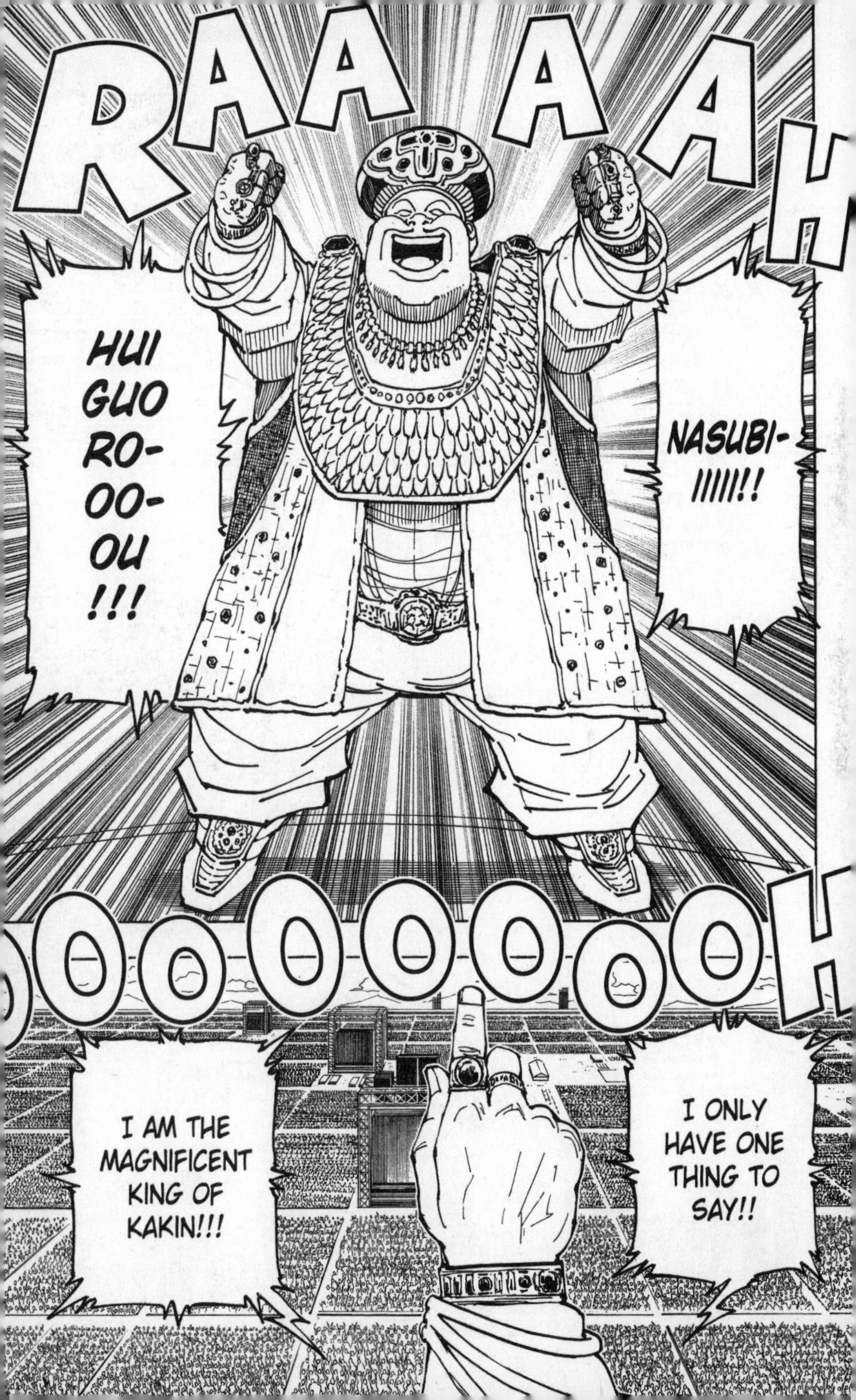
RAAAAH
NASUBI-IIIIII!!
HUI GUO RO-OO-OU!!!
OOOOOOOOH
I ONLY HAVE ONE THING TO SAY!!
I AM THE MAGNIFICENT KING OF KAKIN!!!

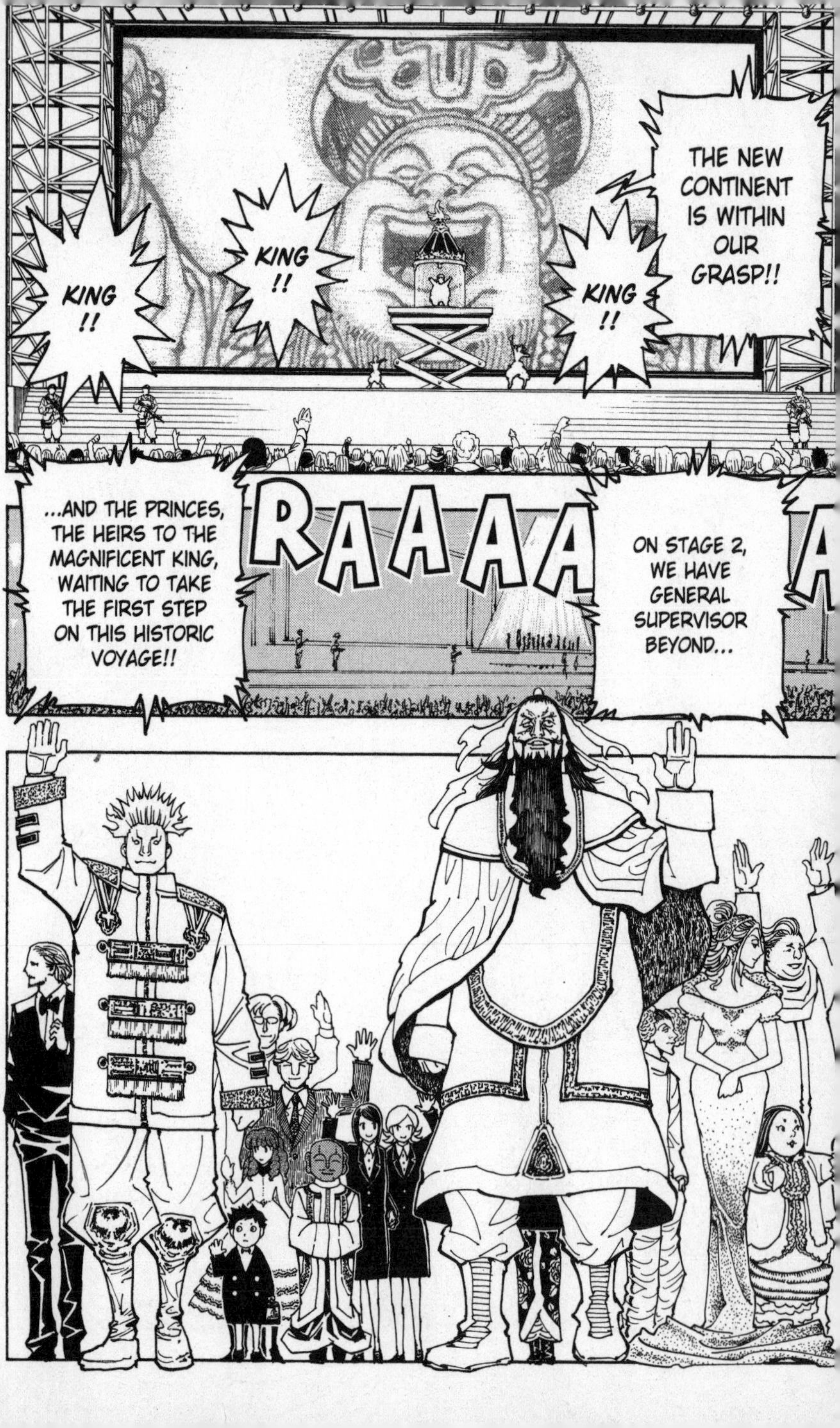
THE NEW CONTINENT IS WITHIN OUR GRASP!!
KING !!
KING !!
KING !!
ON STAGE 2, WE HAVE GENERAL SUPERVISOR BEYOND...
RAAAAA
...AND THE PRINCES, THE HEIRS TO THE MAGNIFICENT KING, WAITING TO TAKE THE FIRST STEP ON THIS HISTORIC VOYAGE!!

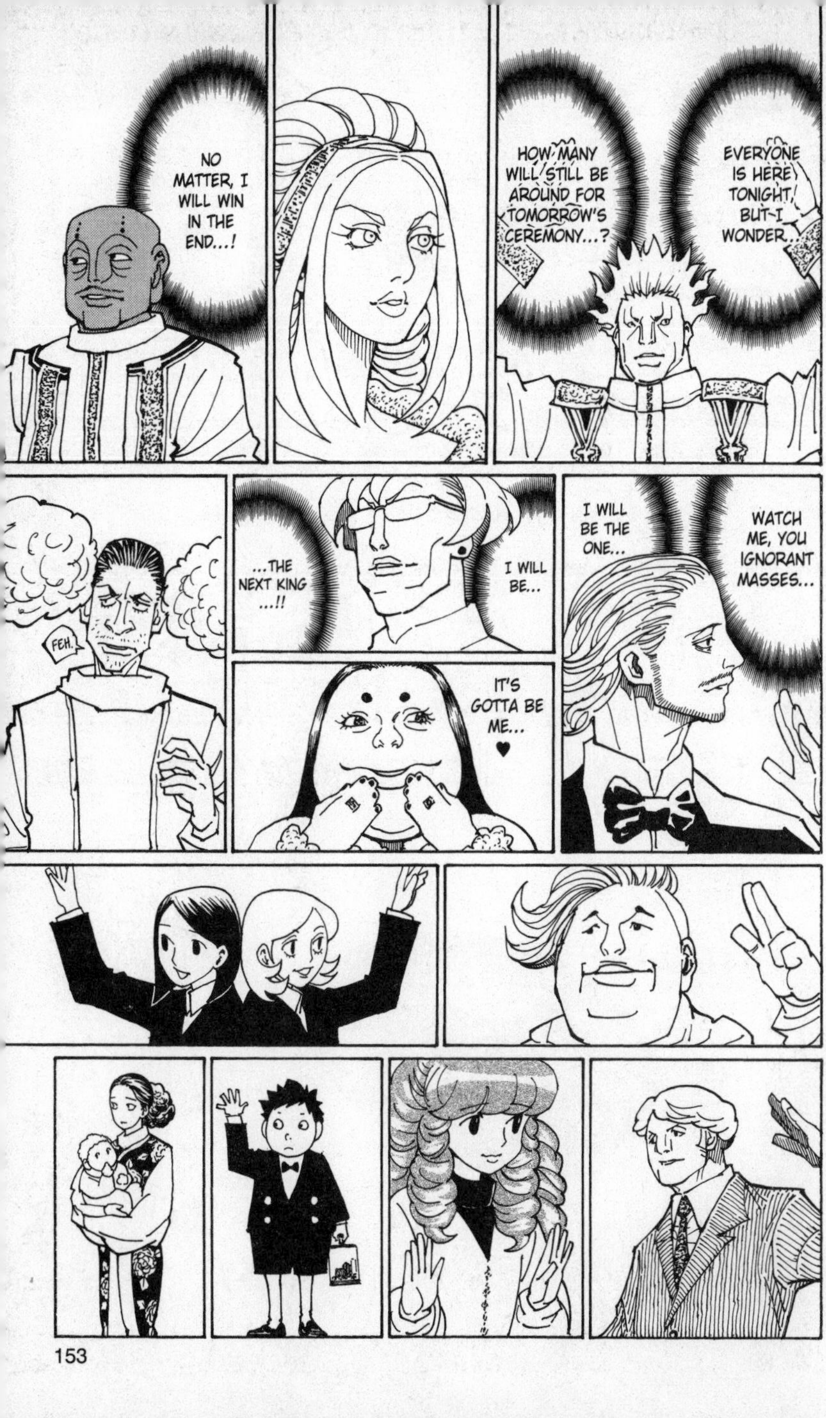
EVERYONE IS HERE TONIGHT, BUT I WONDER...
HOW MANY WILL STILL BE AROUND FOR TOMORROW'S CEREMONY...?
NO MATTER, I WILL WIN IN THE END...!
WATCH ME, YOU IGNORANT MASSES...
I WILL BE THE ONE...
I WILL BE...
...THE NEXT KING...!!
IT'S GOTTA BE ME... ♥
FEH.

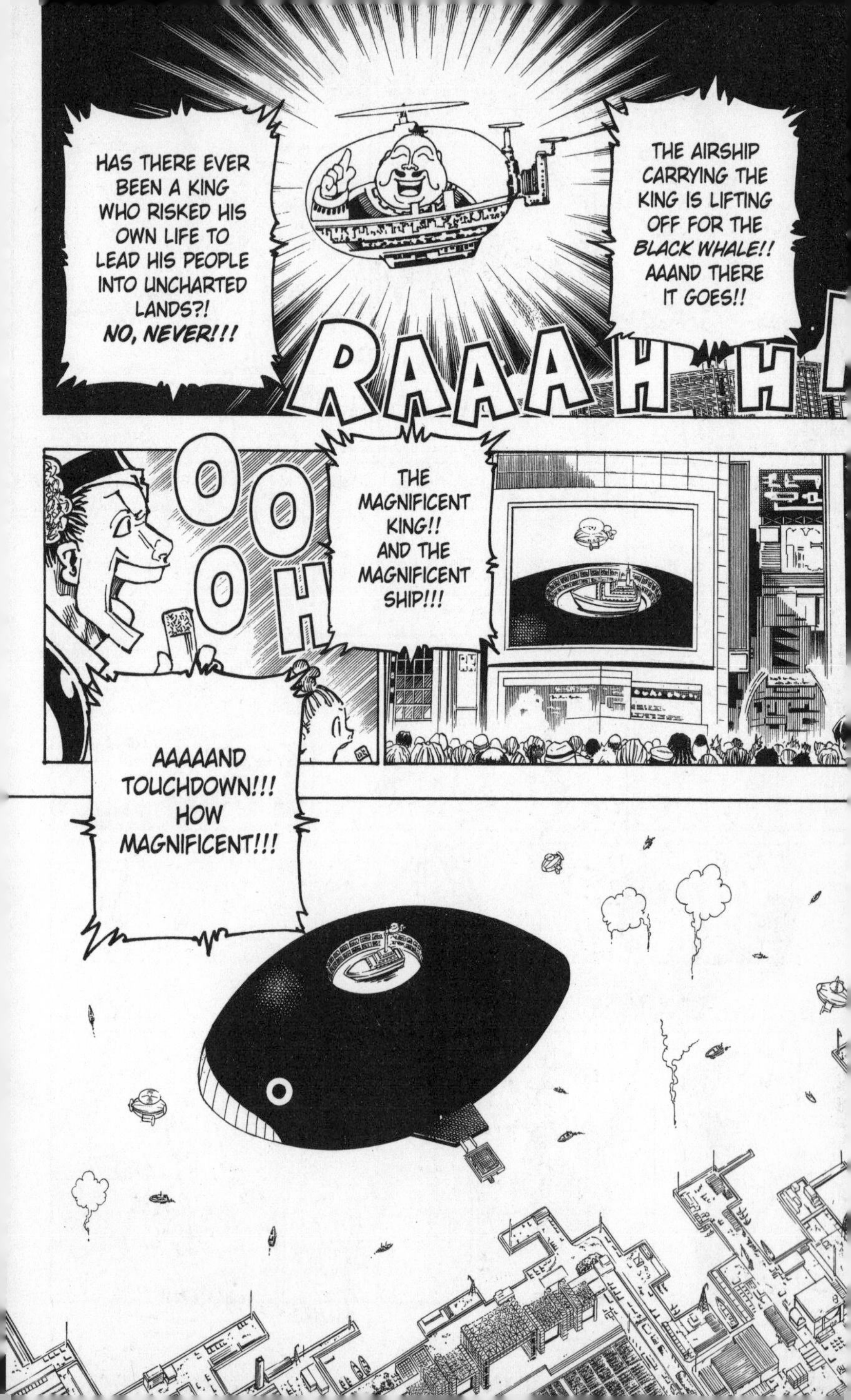
THE AIRSHIP CARRYING THE KING IS LIFTING OFF FOR THE *BLACK WHALE!!* AAAND THERE IT GOES!!
HAS THERE EVER BEEN A KING WHO RISKED HIS OWN LIFE TO LEAD HIS PEOPLE INTO UNCHARTED LANDS?! *NO, NEVER!!!*
RAAAHHH
THE MAGNIFICENT KING!! AND THE MAGNIFICENT SHIP!!!
OOOH
AAAAAND TOUCHDOWN!!! HOW MAGNIFICENT!!!

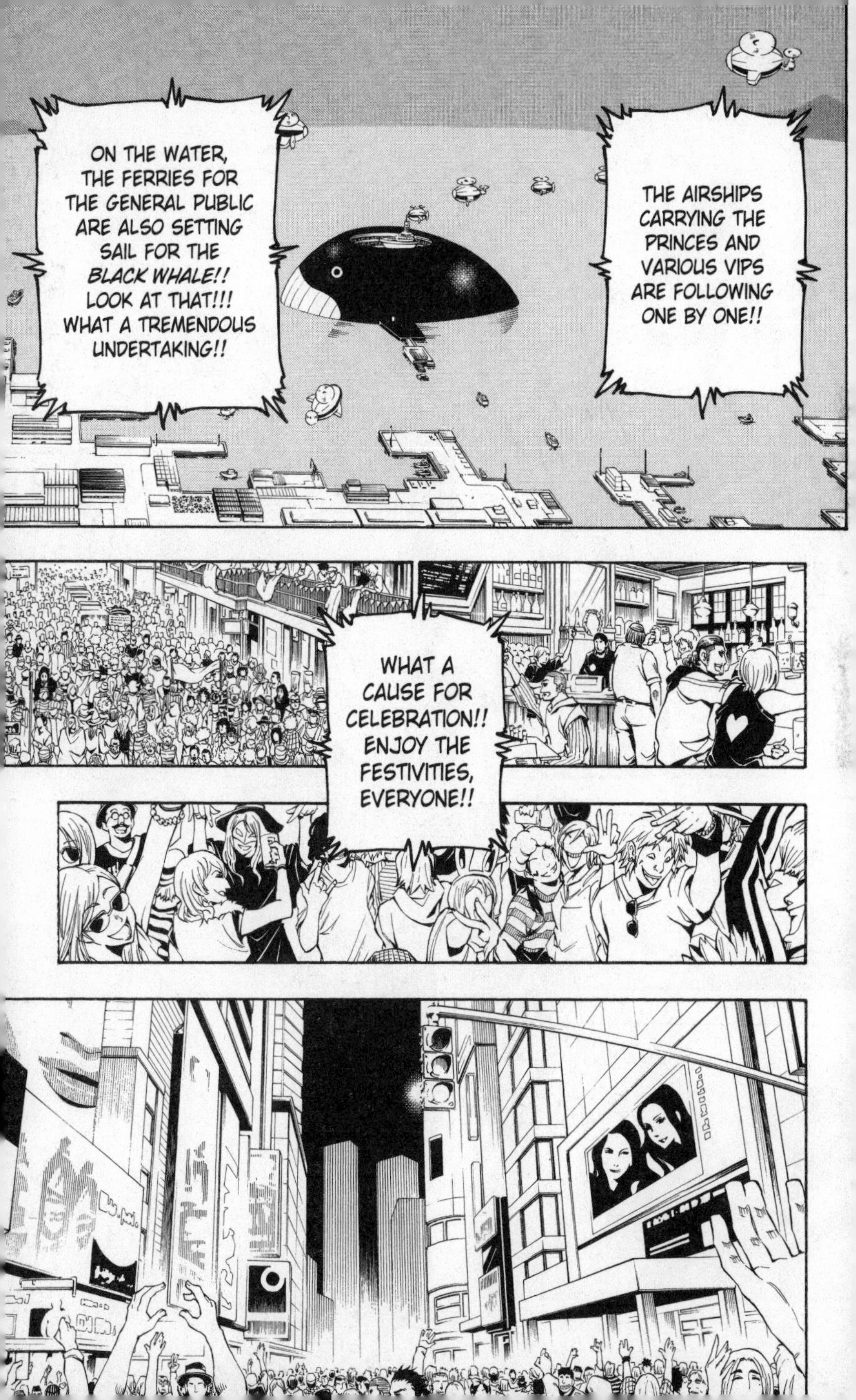
THE AIRSHIPS CARRYING THE PRINCES AND VARIOUS VIPS ARE FOLLOWING ONE BY ONE!!
ON THE WATER, THE FERRIES FOR THE GENERAL PUBLIC ARE ALSO SETTING SAIL FOR THE *BLACK WHALE*!! LOOK AT THAT!!! WHAT A TREMENDOUS UNDERTAKING!!
WHAT A CAUSE FOR CELEBRATION!! ENJOY THE FESTIVITIES, EVERYONE!!

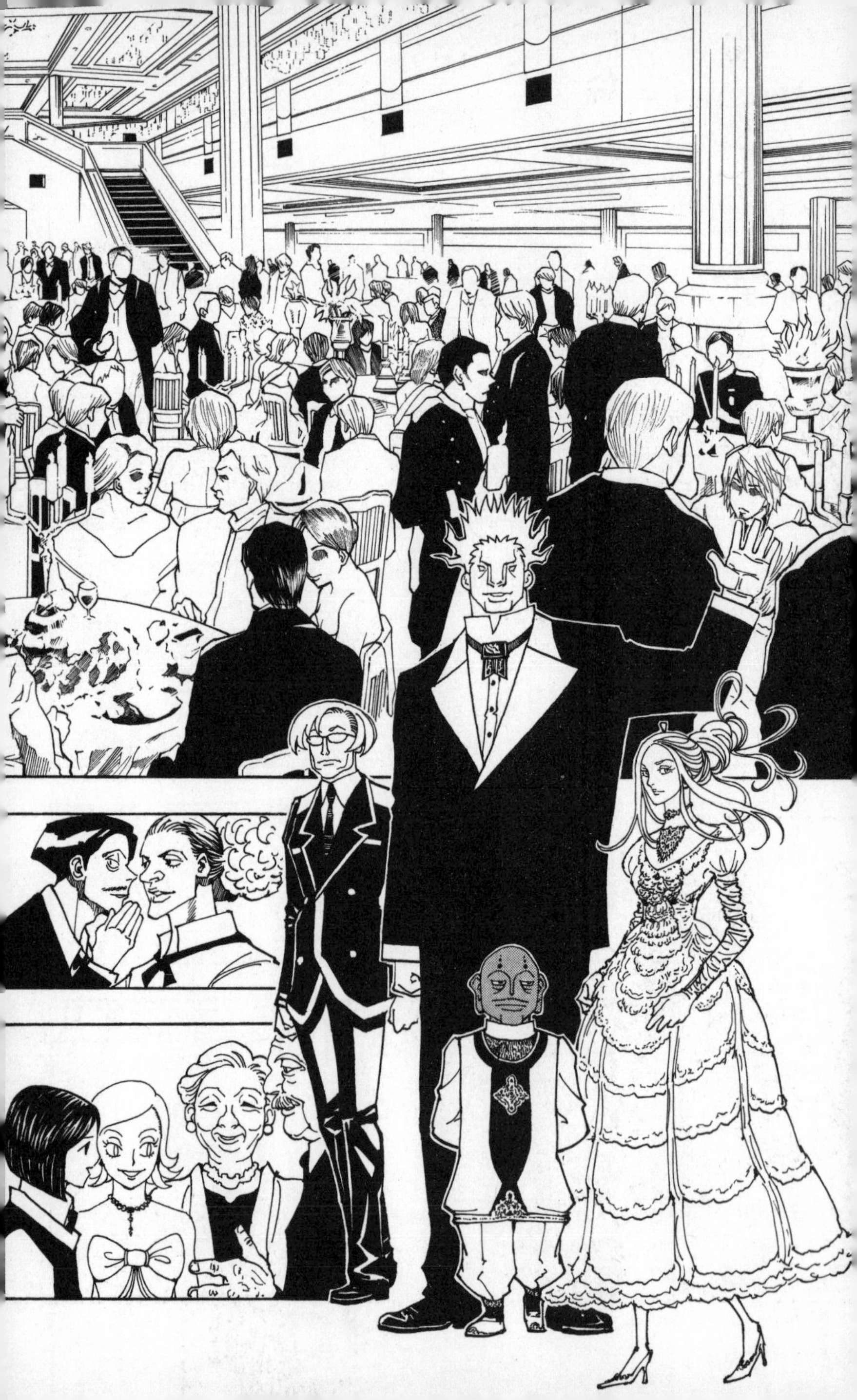

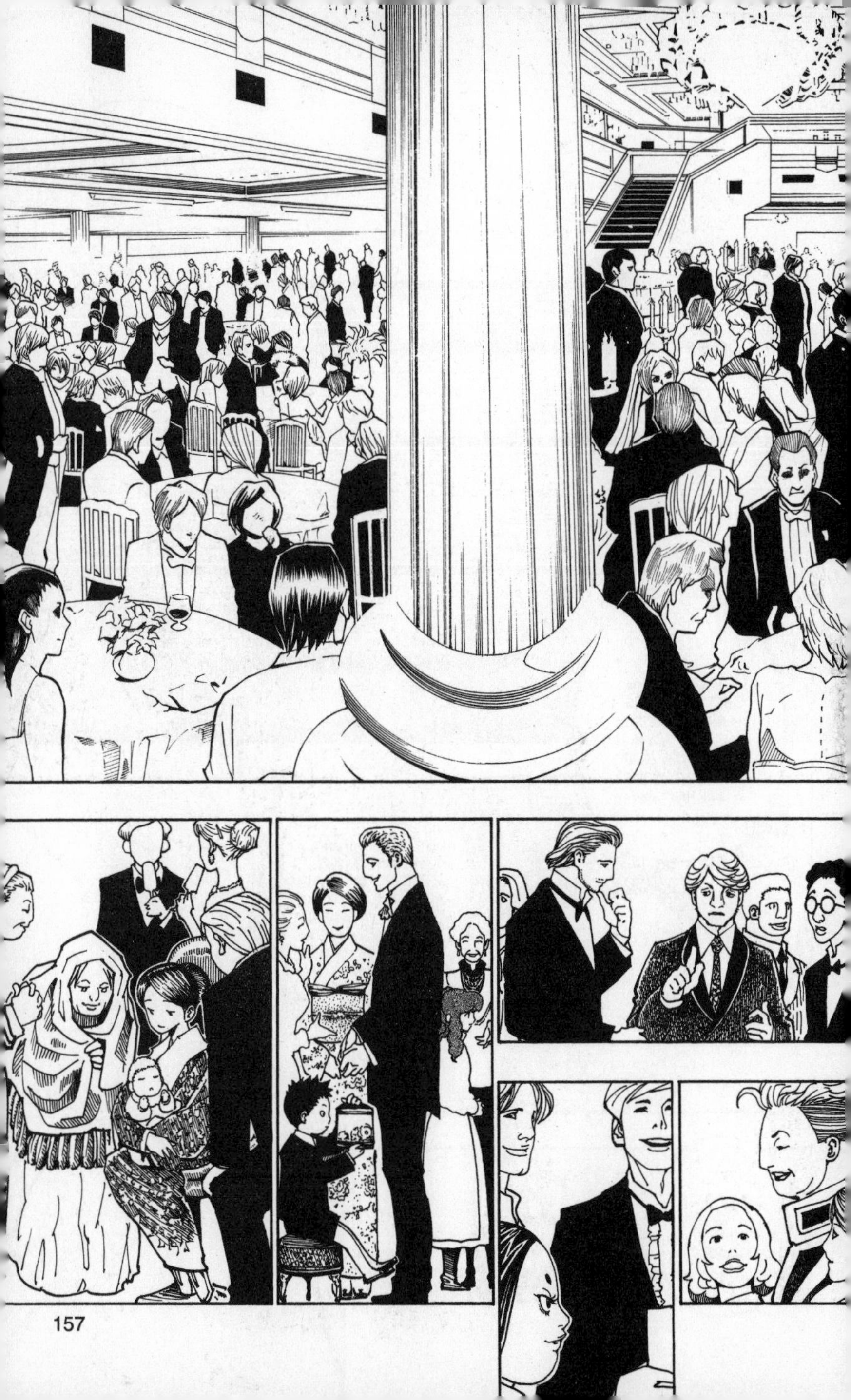

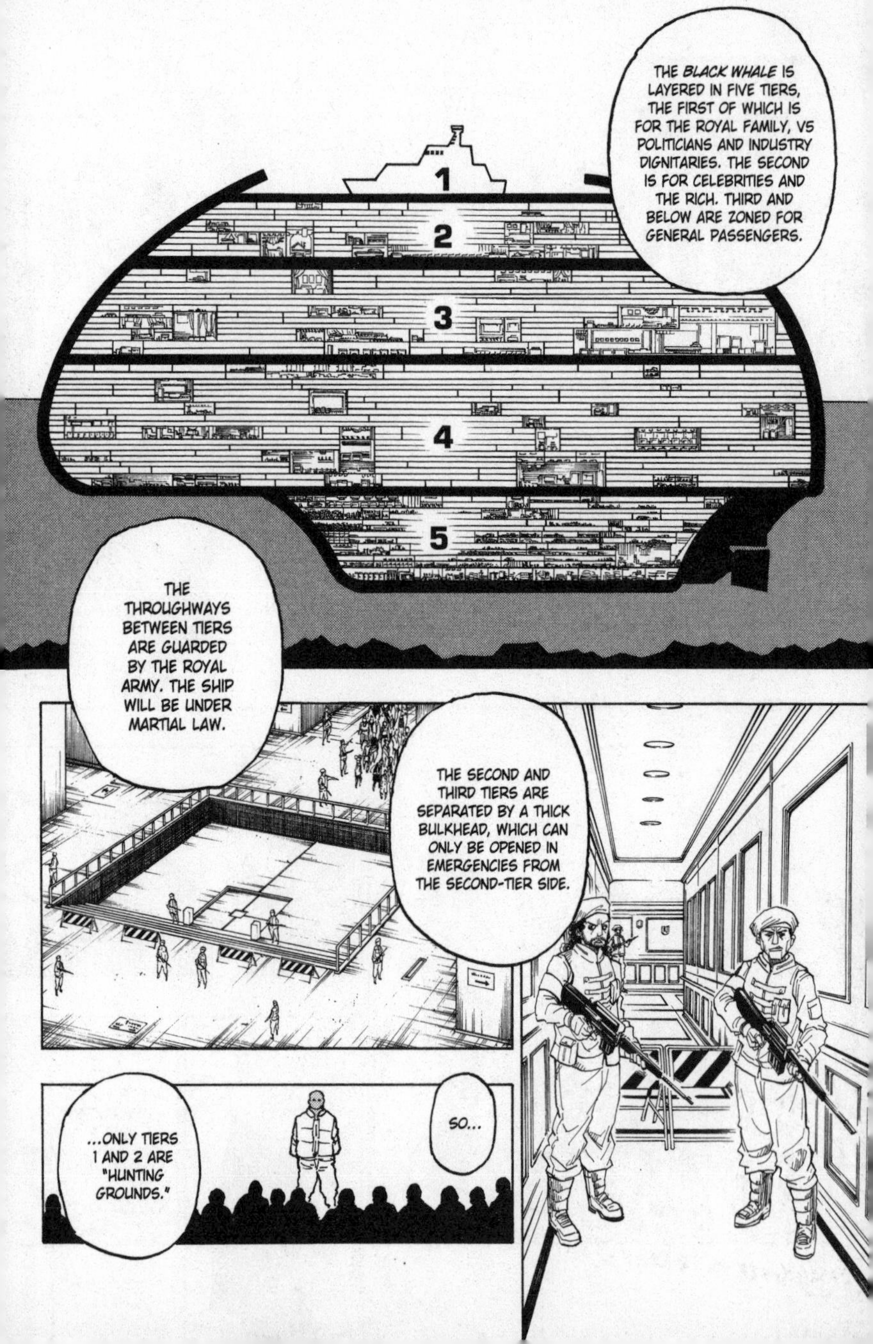
THE *BLACK WHALE* IS LAYERED IN FIVE TIERS, THE FIRST OF WHICH IS FOR THE ROYAL FAMILY, V5 POLITICIANS AND INDUSTRY DIGNITARIES. THE SECOND IS FOR CELEBRITIES AND THE RICH. THIRD AND BELOW ARE ZONED FOR GENERAL PASSENGERS.
1
2
3
4
5
THE THROUGHWAYS BETWEEN TIERS ARE GUARDED BY THE ROYAL ARMY. THE SHIP WILL BE UNDER MARTIAL LAW.
THE SECOND AND THIRD TIERS ARE SEPARATED BY A THICK BULKHEAD, WHICH CAN ONLY BE OPENED IN EMERGENCIES FROM THE SECOND-TIER SIDE.
SO...
...ONLY TIERS 1 AND 2 ARE "HUNTING GROUNDS."

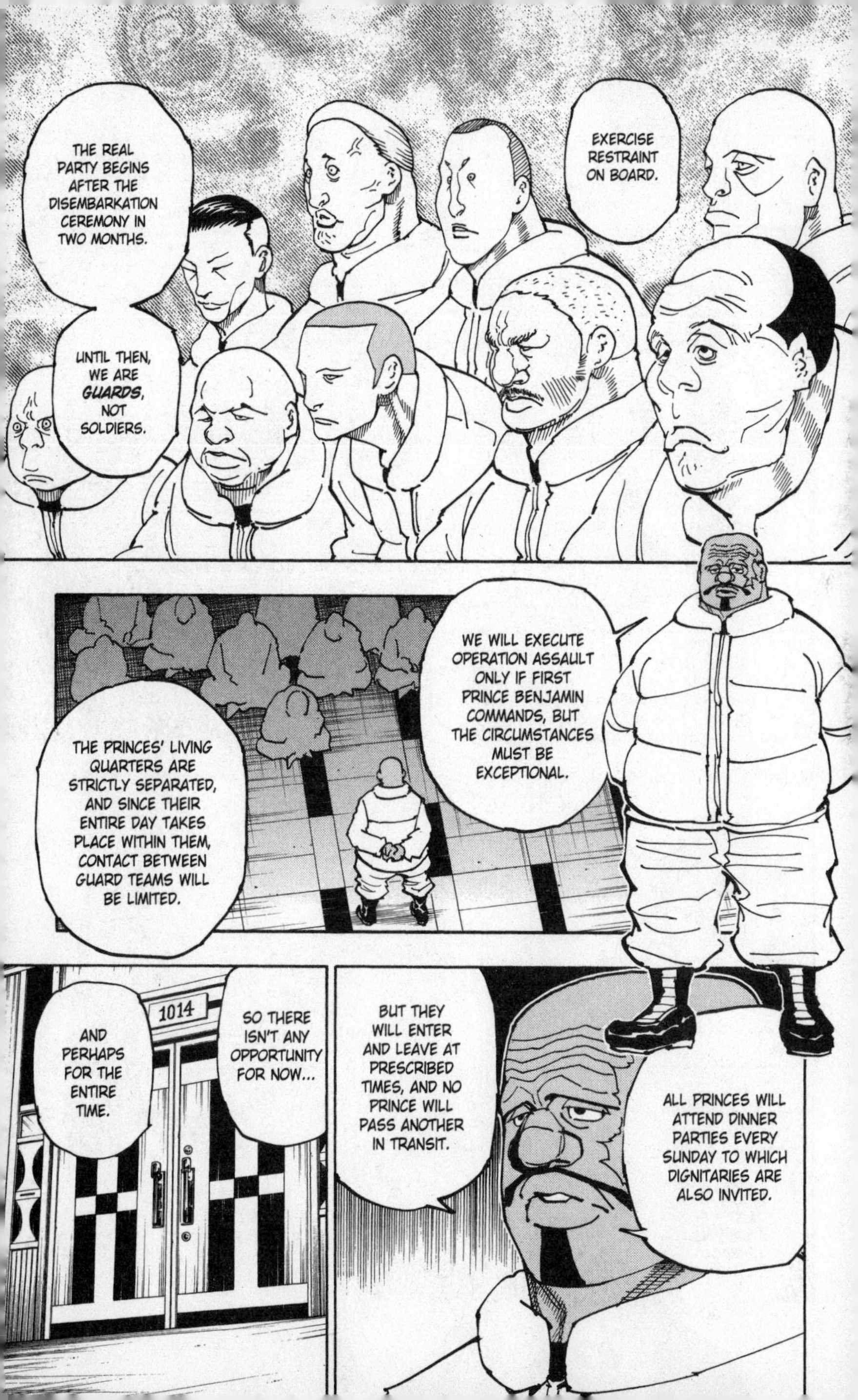
EXERCISE RESTRAINT ON BOARD.
THE REAL PARTY BEGINS AFTER THE DISEMBARKATION CEREMONY IN TWO MONTHS.
UNTIL THEN, WE ARE ***GUARDS***, NOT SOLDIERS.
WE WILL EXECUTE OPERATION ASSAULT ONLY IF FIRST PRINCE BENJAMIN COMMANDS, BUT THE CIRCUMSTANCES MUST BE EXCEPTIONAL.
THE PRINCES' LIVING QUARTERS ARE STRICTLY SEPARATED, AND SINCE THEIR ENTIRE DAY TAKES PLACE WITHIN THEM, CONTACT BETWEEN GUARD TEAMS WILL BE LIMITED.
ALL PRINCES WILL ATTEND DINNER PARTIES EVERY SUNDAY TO WHICH DIGNITARIES ARE ALSO INVITED.
BUT THEY WILL ENTER AND LEAVE AT PRESCRIBED TIMES, AND NO PRINCE WILL PASS ANOTHER IN TRANSIT.
1014
SO THERE ISN'T ANY OPPORTUNITY FOR NOW...
AND PERHAPS FOR THE ENTIRE TIME.

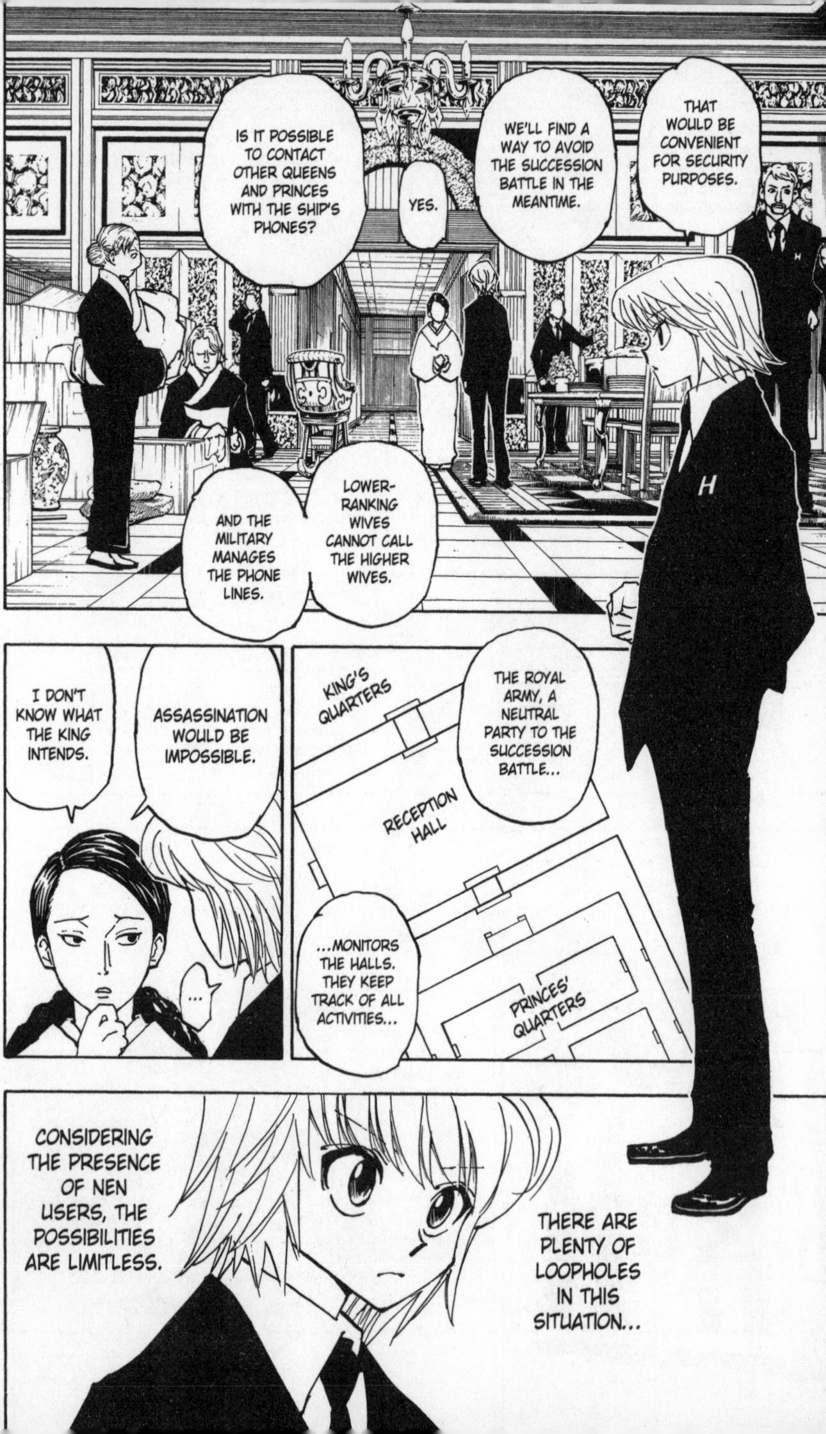
THAT WOULD BE CONVENIENT FOR SECURITY PURPOSES.
WE'LL FIND A WAY TO AVOID THE SUCCESSION BATTLE IN THE MEANTIME.
YES.
IS IT POSSIBLE TO CONTACT OTHER QUEENS AND PRINCES WITH THE SHIP'S PHONES?
LOWER-RANKING WIVES CANNOT CALL THE HIGHER WIVES.
AND THE MILITARY MANAGES THE PHONE LINES.
THE ROYAL ARMY, A NEUTRAL PARTY TO THE SUCCESSION BATTLE...
KING'S QUARTERS
RECEPTION HALL
PRINCES' QUARTERS
...MONITORS THE HALLS. THEY KEEP TRACK OF ALL ACTIVITIES...
ASSASSINATION WOULD BE IMPOSSIBLE.
I DON'T KNOW WHAT THE KING INTENDS.
...
THERE ARE PLENTY OF LOOPHOLES IN THIS SITUATION...
CONSIDERING THE PRESENCE OF NEN USERS, THE POSSIBILITIES ARE LIMITLESS.

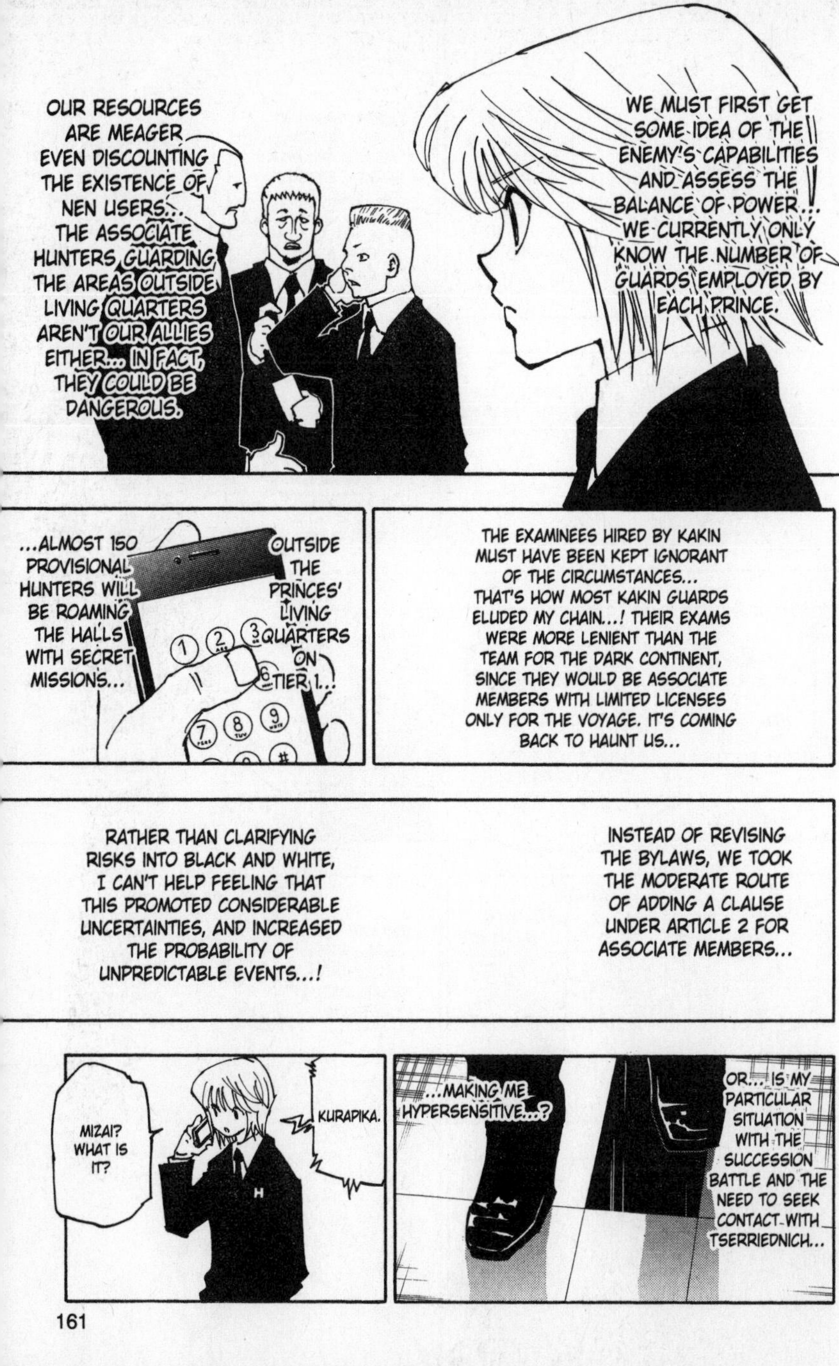
WE MUST FIRST GET SOME IDEA OF THE ENEMY'S CAPABILITIES AND ASSESS THE BALANCE OF POWER... WE CURRENTLY ONLY KNOW THE NUMBER OF GUARDS EMPLOYED BY EACH PRINCE.
OUR RESOURCES ARE MEAGER EVEN DISCOUNTING THE EXISTENCE OF NEN USERS... THE ASSOCIATE HUNTERS GUARDING THE AREAS OUTSIDE LIVING QUARTERS AREN'T OUR ALLIES EITHER... IN FACT, THEY COULD BE DANGEROUS.
THE EXAMINEES HIRED BY KAKIN MUST HAVE BEEN KEPT IGNORANT OF THE CIRCUMSTANCES... THAT'S HOW MOST KAKIN GUARDS ELUDED MY CHAIN...! THEIR EXAMS WERE MORE LENIENT THAN THE TEAM FOR THE DARK CONTINENT, SINCE THEY WOULD BE ASSOCIATE MEMBERS WITH LIMITED LICENSES ONLY FOR THE VOYAGE. IT'S COMING BACK TO HAUNT US...
OUTSIDE THE PRINCES' LIVING QUARTERS ON TIER 1...
...ALMOST 150 PROVISIONAL HUNTERS WILL BE ROAMING THE HALLS WITH SECRET MISSIONS...
INSTEAD OF REVISING THE BYLAWS, WE TOOK THE MODERATE ROUTE OF ADDING A CLAUSE UNDER ARTICLE 2 FOR ASSOCIATE MEMBERS...
RATHER THAN CLARIFYING RISKS INTO BLACK AND WHITE, I CAN'T HELP FEELING THAT THIS PROMOTED CONSIDERABLE UNCERTAINTIES, AND INCREASED THE PROBABILITY OF UNPREDICTABLE EVENTS...!
OR... IS MY PARTICULAR SITUATION WITH THE SUCCESSION BATTLE AND THE NEED TO SEEK CONTACT WITH TSERRIEDNICH...
...MAKING ME HYPERSENSITIVE...?
KURAPIKA.
MIZAI? WHAT IS IT?

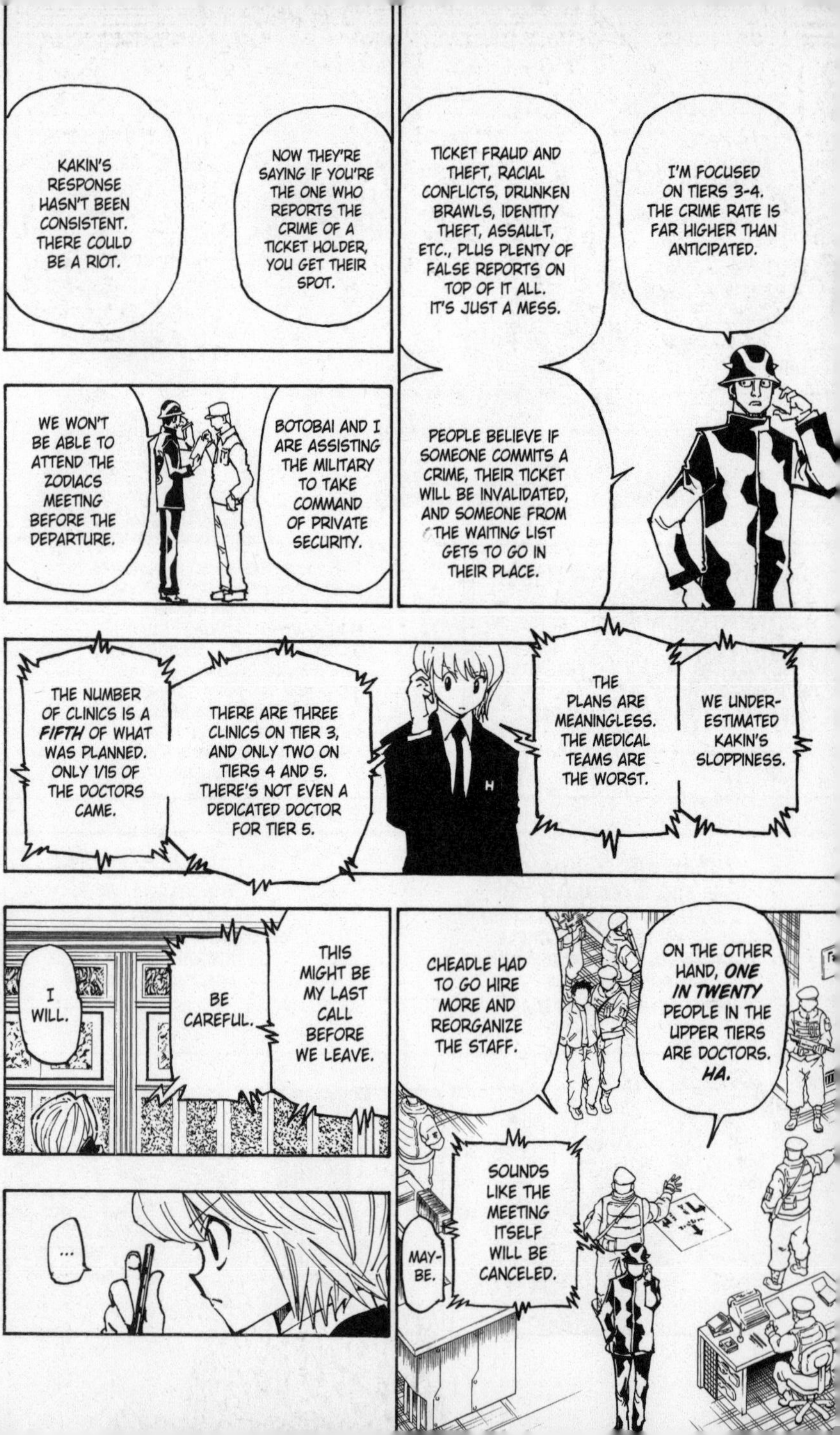
I'M FOCUSED ON TIERS 3-4. THE CRIME RATE IS FAR HIGHER THAN ANTICIPATED.
TICKET FRAUD AND THEFT, RACIAL CONFLICTS, DRUNKEN BRAWLS, IDENTITY THEFT, ASSAULT, ETC., PLUS PLENTY OF FALSE REPORTS ON TOP OF IT ALL. IT'S JUST A MESS.
PEOPLE BELIEVE IF SOMEONE COMMITS A CRIME, THEIR TICKET WILL BE INVALIDATED, AND SOMEONE FROM THE WAITING LIST GETS TO GO IN THEIR PLACE.
NOW THEY'RE SAYING IF YOU'RE THE ONE WHO REPORTS THE CRIME OF A TICKET HOLDER, YOU GET THEIR SPOT.
KAKIN'S RESPONSE HASN'T BEEN CONSISTENT. THERE COULD BE A RIOT.
BOTOBAI AND I ARE ASSISTING THE MILITARY TO TAKE COMMAND OF PRIVATE SECURITY.
WE WON'T BE ABLE TO ATTEND THE ZODIACS MEETING BEFORE THE DEPARTURE.
WE UNDER-ESTIMATED KAKIN'S SLOPPINESS.
THE PLANS ARE MEANINGLESS. THE MEDICAL TEAMS ARE THE WORST.
THERE ARE THREE CLINICS ON TIER 3, AND ONLY TWO ON TIERS 4 AND 5. THERE'S NOT EVEN A DEDICATED DOCTOR FOR TIER 5.
THE NUMBER OF CLINICS IS A *FIFTH* OF WHAT WAS PLANNED. ONLY 1/15 OF THE DOCTORS CAME.
ON THE OTHER HAND, ***ONE IN TWENTY*** PEOPLE IN THE UPPER TIERS ARE DOCTORS. ***HA.***
CHEADLE HAD TO GO HIRE MORE AND REORGANIZE THE STAFF.
SOUNDS LIKE THE MEETING ITSELF WILL BE CANCELED.
MAY-BE.
THIS MIGHT BE MY LAST CALL BEFORE WE LEAVE.
BE CAREFUL.
I WILL.
...

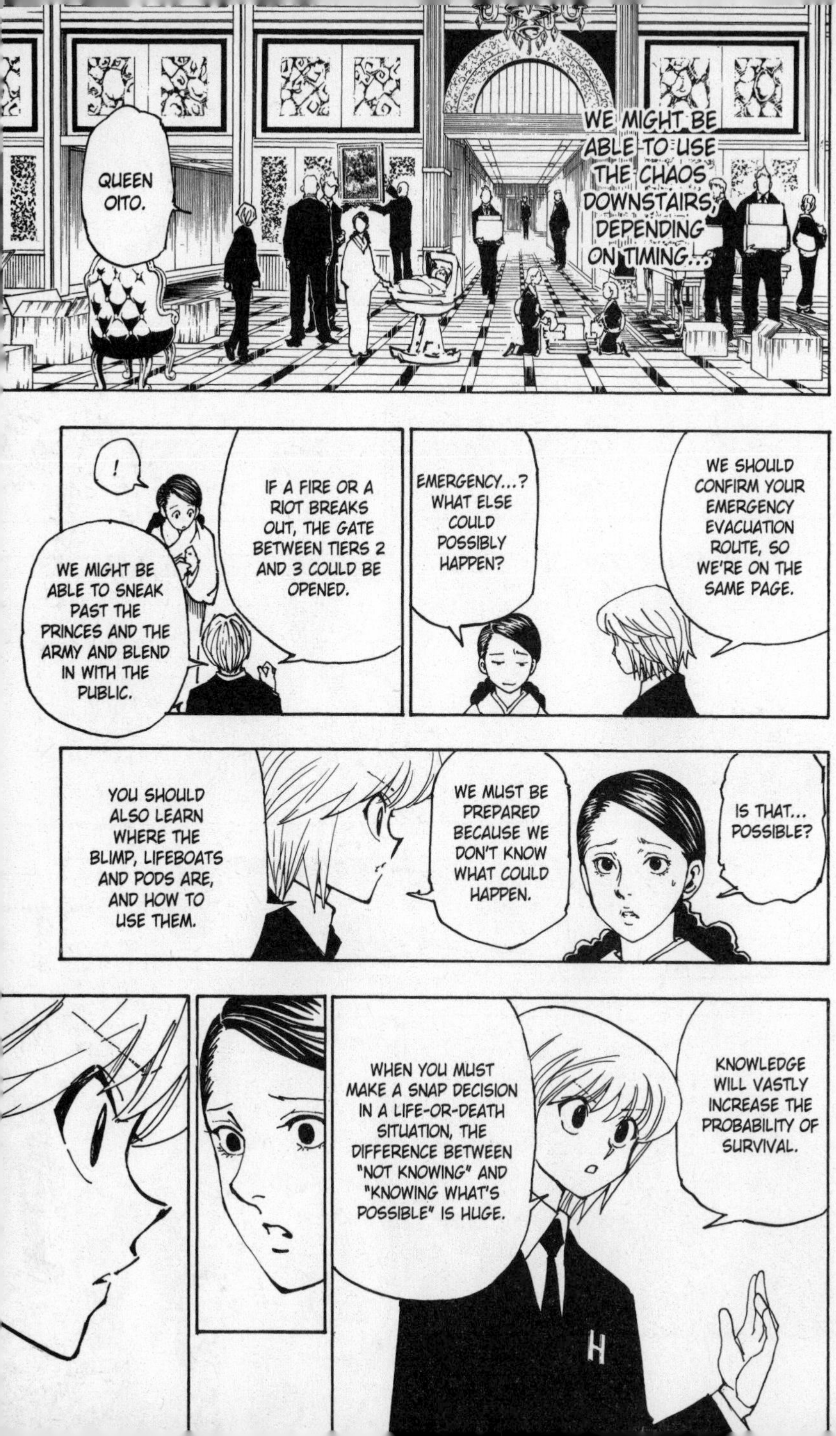

WE MIGHT BE ABLE TO USE THE CHAOS DOWNSTAIRS, DEPENDING ON TIMING...
QUEEN OITO.
WE SHOULD CONFIRM YOUR EMERGENCY EVACUATION ROUTE, SO WE'RE ON THE SAME PAGE.
EMERGENCY...? WHAT ELSE COULD POSSIBLY HAPPEN?
IF A FIRE OR A RIOT BREAKS OUT, THE GATE BETWEEN TIERS 2 AND 3 COULD BE OPENED.
!
WE MIGHT BE ABLE TO SNEAK PAST THE PRINCES AND THE ARMY AND BLEND IN WITH THE PUBLIC.
IS THAT... POSSIBLE?
WE MUST BE PREPARED BECAUSE WE DON'T KNOW WHAT COULD HAPPEN.
YOU SHOULD ALSO LEARN WHERE THE BLIMP, LIFEBOATS AND PODS ARE, AND HOW TO USE THEM.
KNOWLEDGE WILL VASTLY INCREASE THE PROBABILITY OF SURVIVAL.
WHEN YOU MUST MAKE A SNAP DECISION IN A LIFE-OR-DEATH SITUATION, THE DIFFERENCE BETWEEN "NOT KNOWING" AND "KNOWING WHAT'S POSSIBLE" IS HUGE.

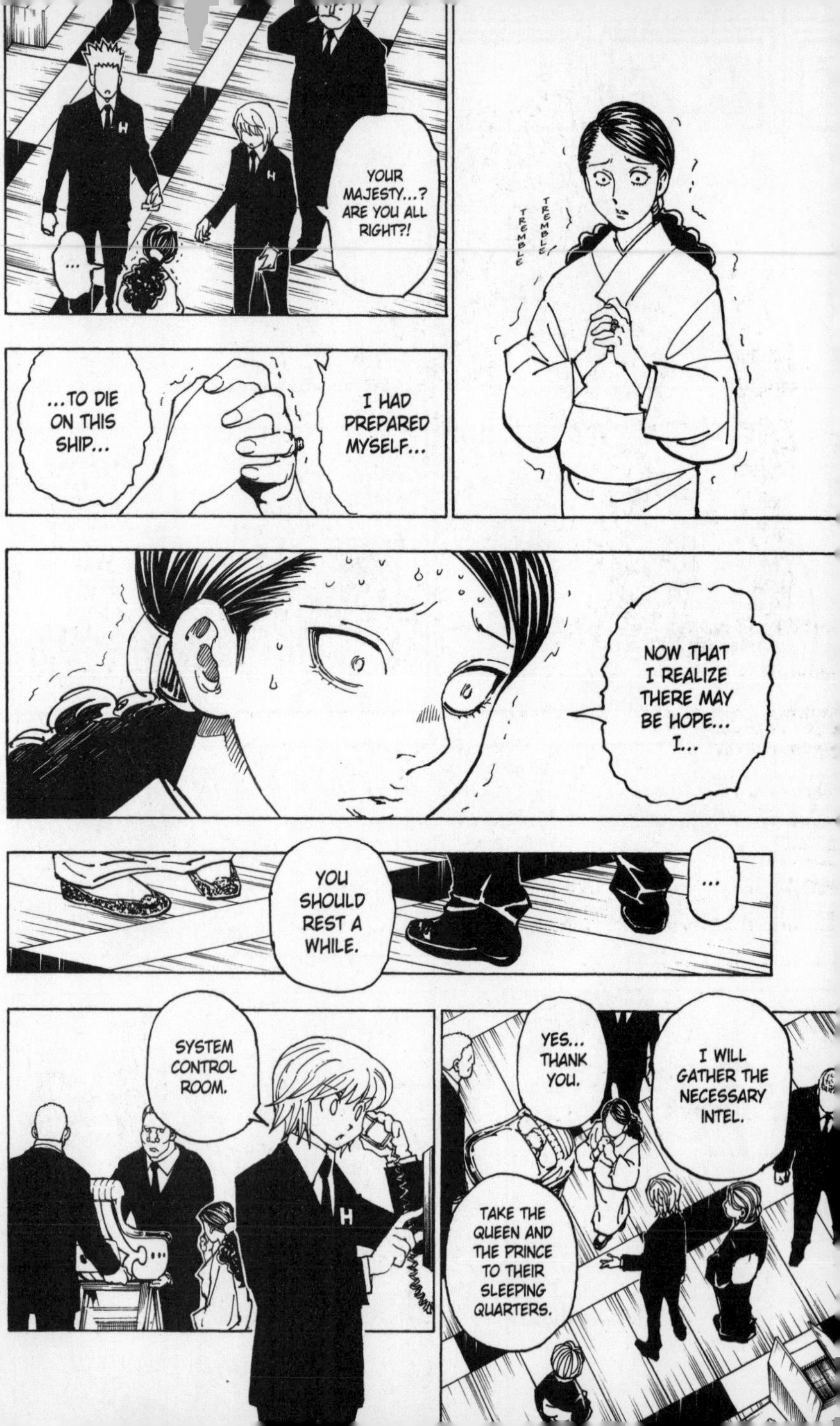
TREMBLE TREMBLE
YOUR MAJESTY...? ARE YOU ALL RIGHT?!
...
I HAD PREPARED MYSELF...
...TO DIE ON THIS SHIP...
NOW THAT I REALIZE THERE MAY BE HOPE... I...
...
YOU SHOULD REST A WHILE.
I WILL GATHER THE NECESSARY INTEL.
YES... THANK YOU.
TAKE THE QUEEN AND THE PRINCE TO THEIR SLEEPING QUARTERS.
SYSTEM CONTROL ROOM.

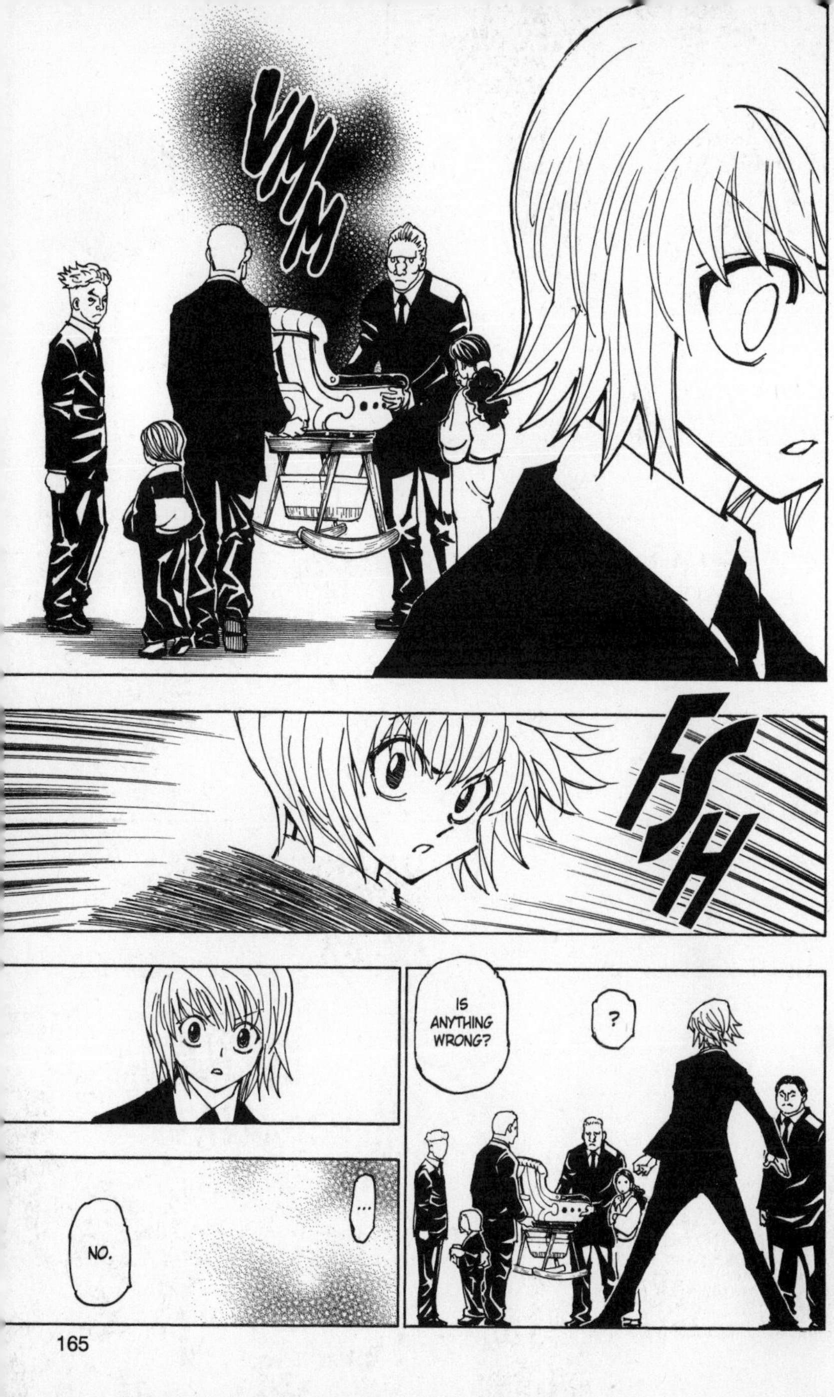
VMM
FSH
?
IS ANYTHING WRONG?
...
NO.

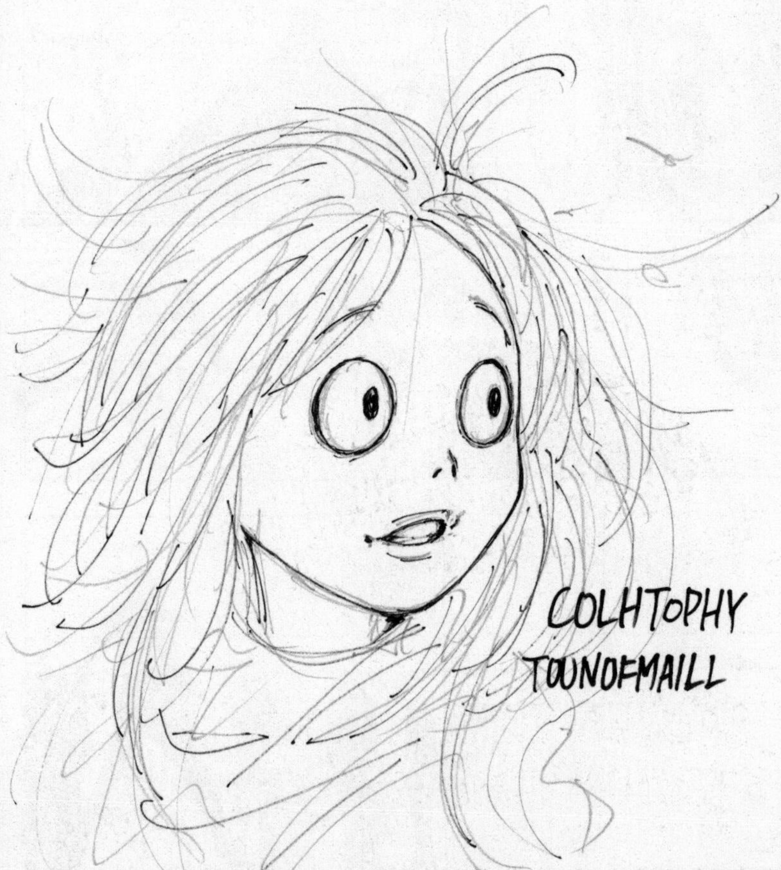
COLHTOPHY
TOUNOFMAILL

Chapter 359: Departure

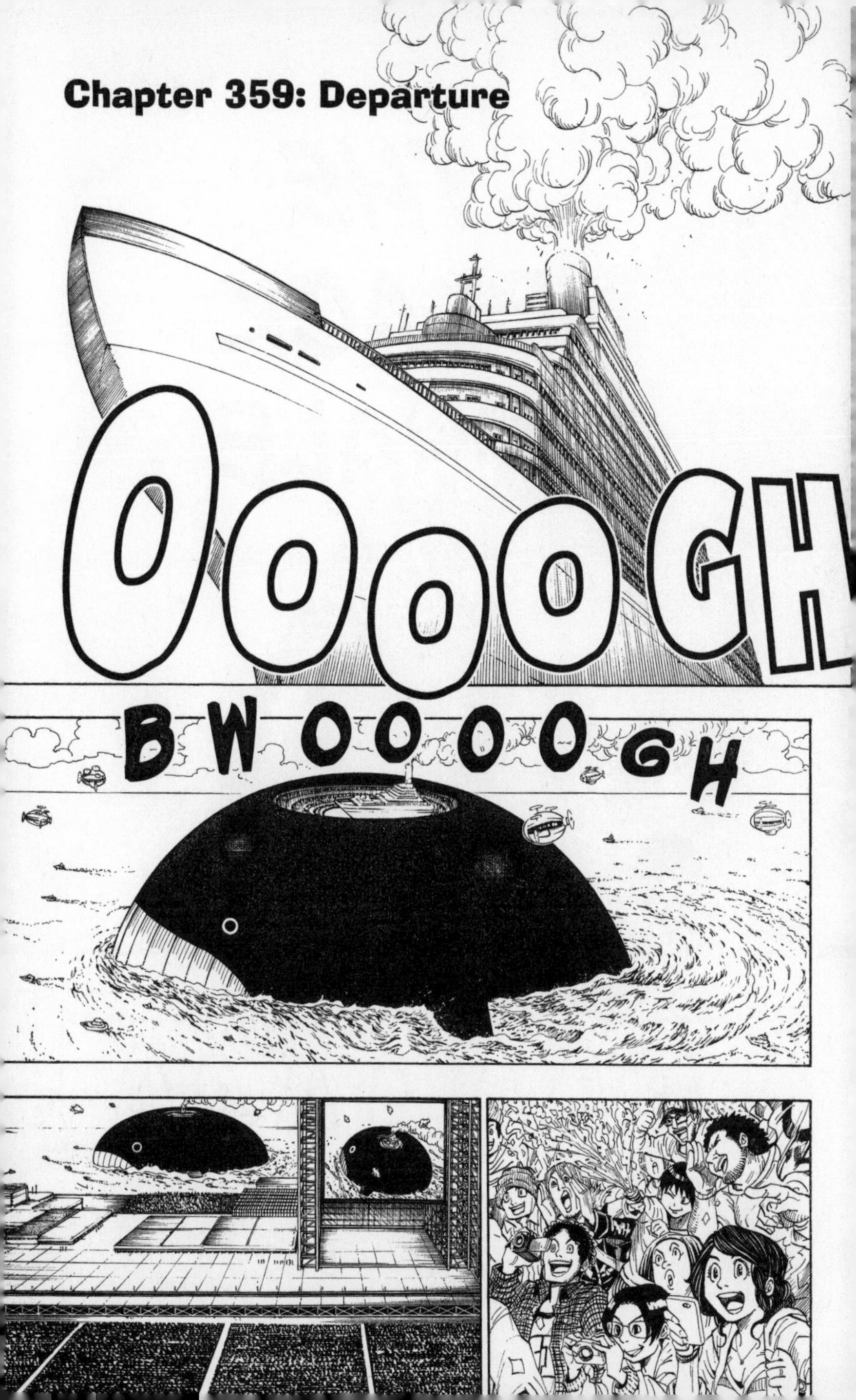
OOOOGH
BWOOOOGH

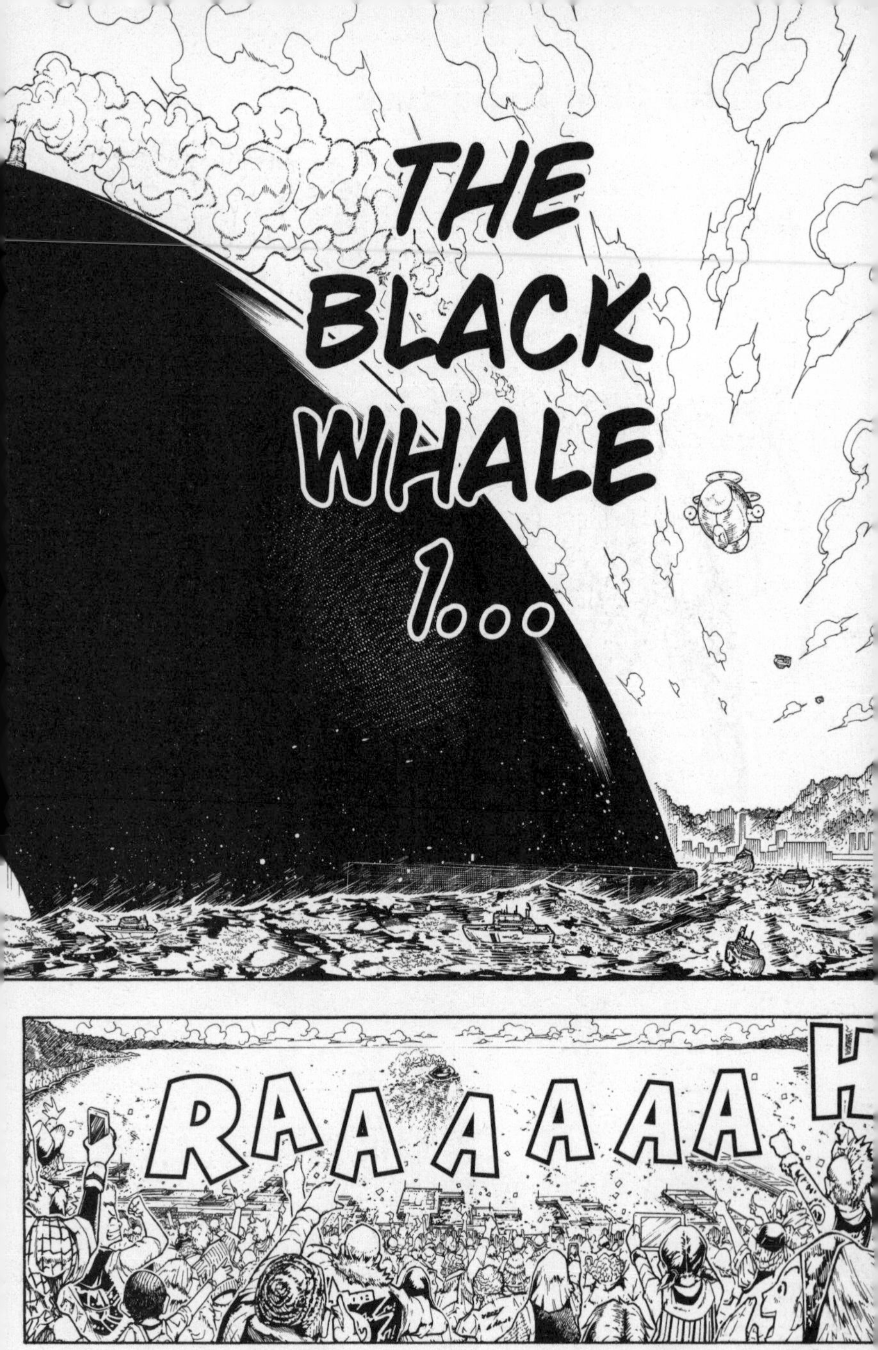
THE BLACK WHALE 1...
RAAAAAH

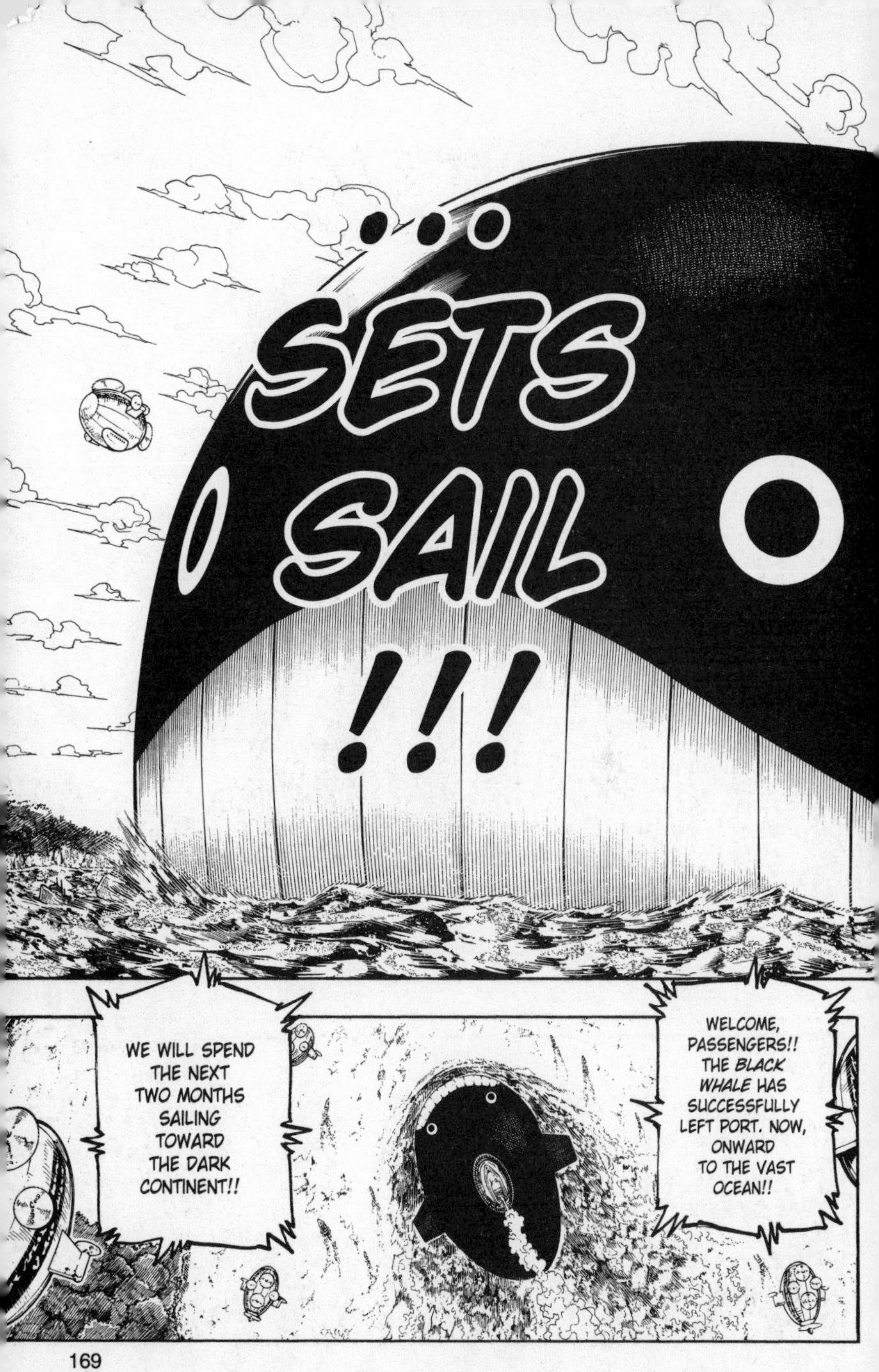
...SETS SAIL!!!
WELCOME, PASSENGERS!! THE *BLACK WHALE* HAS SUCCESSFULLY LEFT PORT. NOW, ONWARD TO THE VAST OCEAN!!
WE WILL SPEND THE NEXT TWO MONTHS SAILING TOWARD THE DARK CONTINENT!!

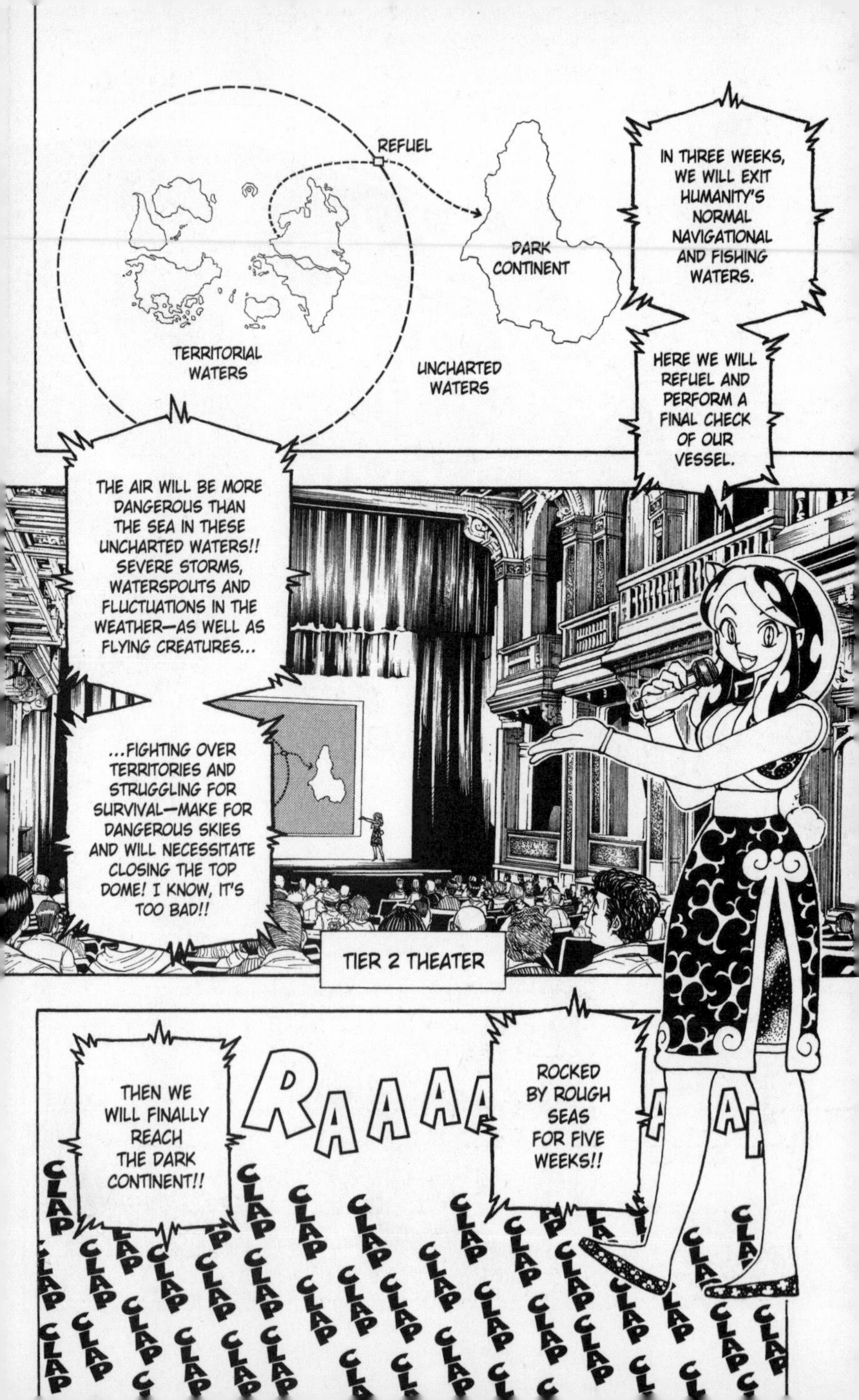
IN THREE WEEKS, WE WILL EXIT HUMANITY'S NORMAL NAVIGATIONAL AND FISHING WATERS.
HERE WE WILL REFUEL AND PERFORM A FINAL CHECK OF OUR VESSEL.
DARK CONTINENT
REFUEL
UNCHARTED WATERS
TERRITORIAL WATERS
THE AIR WILL BE MORE DANGEROUS THAN THE SEA IN THESE UNCHARTED WATERS!! SEVERE STORMS, WATERSPOUTS AND FLUCTUATIONS IN THE WEATHER—AS WELL AS FLYING CREATURES...
...FIGHTING OVER TERRITORIES AND STRUGGLING FOR SURVIVAL—MAKE FOR DANGEROUS SKIES AND WILL NECESSITATE CLOSING THE TOP DOME! I KNOW, IT'S TOO BAD!!
TIER 2 THEATER
ROCKED BY ROUGH SEAS FOR FIVE WEEKS!!
THEN WE WILL FINALLY REACH THE DARK CONTINENT!!
RAAAA
CLAP CLAP CLAP CLAP CLAP CLAP CLAP CLAP

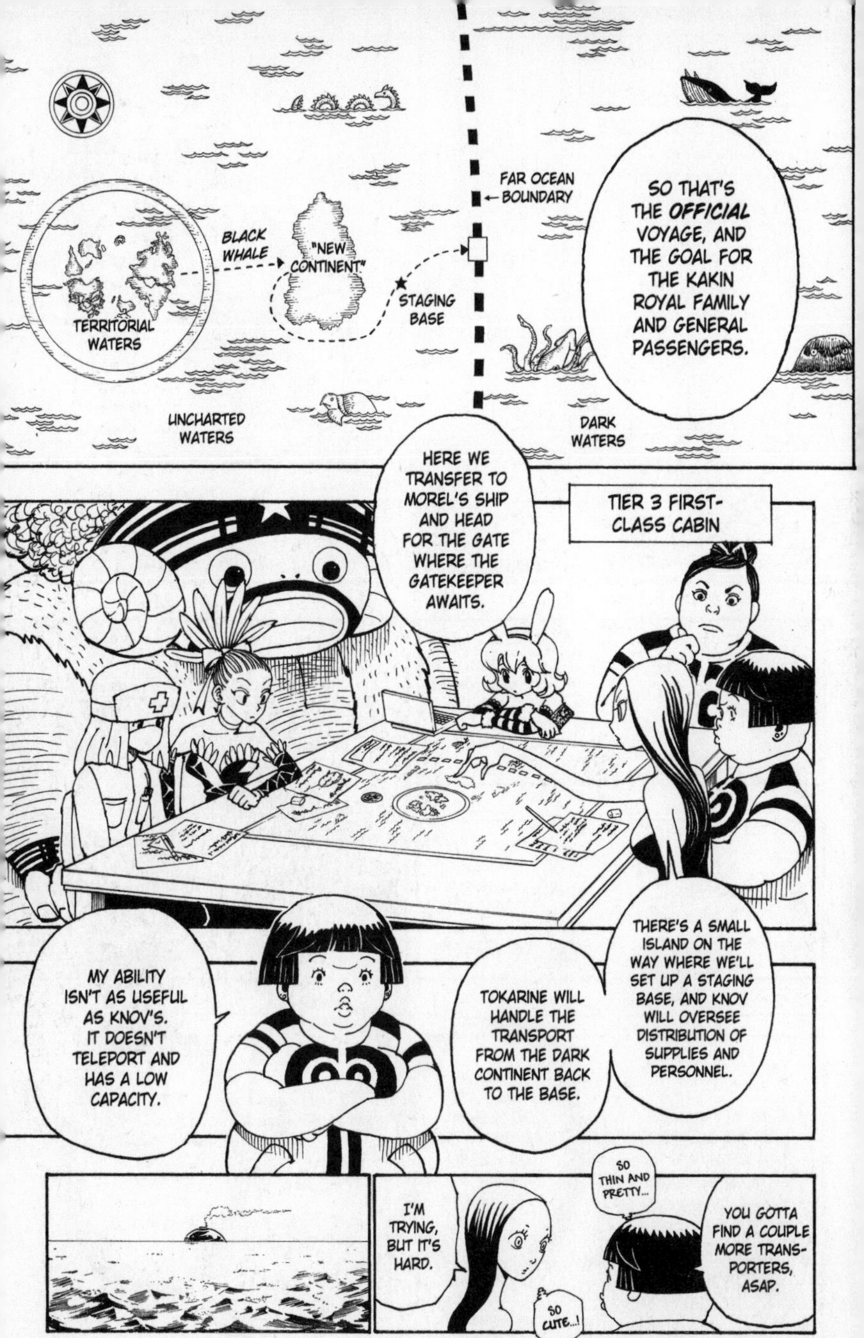
SO THAT'S THE *OFFICIAL* VOYAGE, AND THE GOAL FOR THE KAKIN ROYAL FAMILY AND GENERAL PASSENGERS.
FAR OCEAN BOUNDARY
"NEW CONTINENT"
BLACK WHALE
STAGING BASE
TERRITORIAL WATERS
DARK WATERS
UNCHARTED WATERS
TIER 3 FIRST-CLASS CABIN
HERE WE TRANSFER TO MOREL'S SHIP AND HEAD FOR THE GATE WHERE THE GATEKEEPER AWAITS.
THERE'S A SMALL ISLAND ON THE WAY WHERE WE'LL SET UP A STAGING BASE, AND KNOV WILL OVERSEE DISTRIBUTION OF SUPPLIES AND PERSONNEL.
TOKARINE WILL HANDLE THE TRANSPORT FROM THE DARK CONTINENT BACK TO THE BASE.
MY ABILITY ISN'T AS USEFUL AS KNOV'S. IT DOESN'T TELEPORT AND HAS A LOW CAPACITY.
YOU GOTTA FIND A COUPLE MORE TRANS-PORTERS, ASAP.
SO THIN AND PRETTY...
I'M TRYING, BUT IT'S HARD.
SO CUTE...!

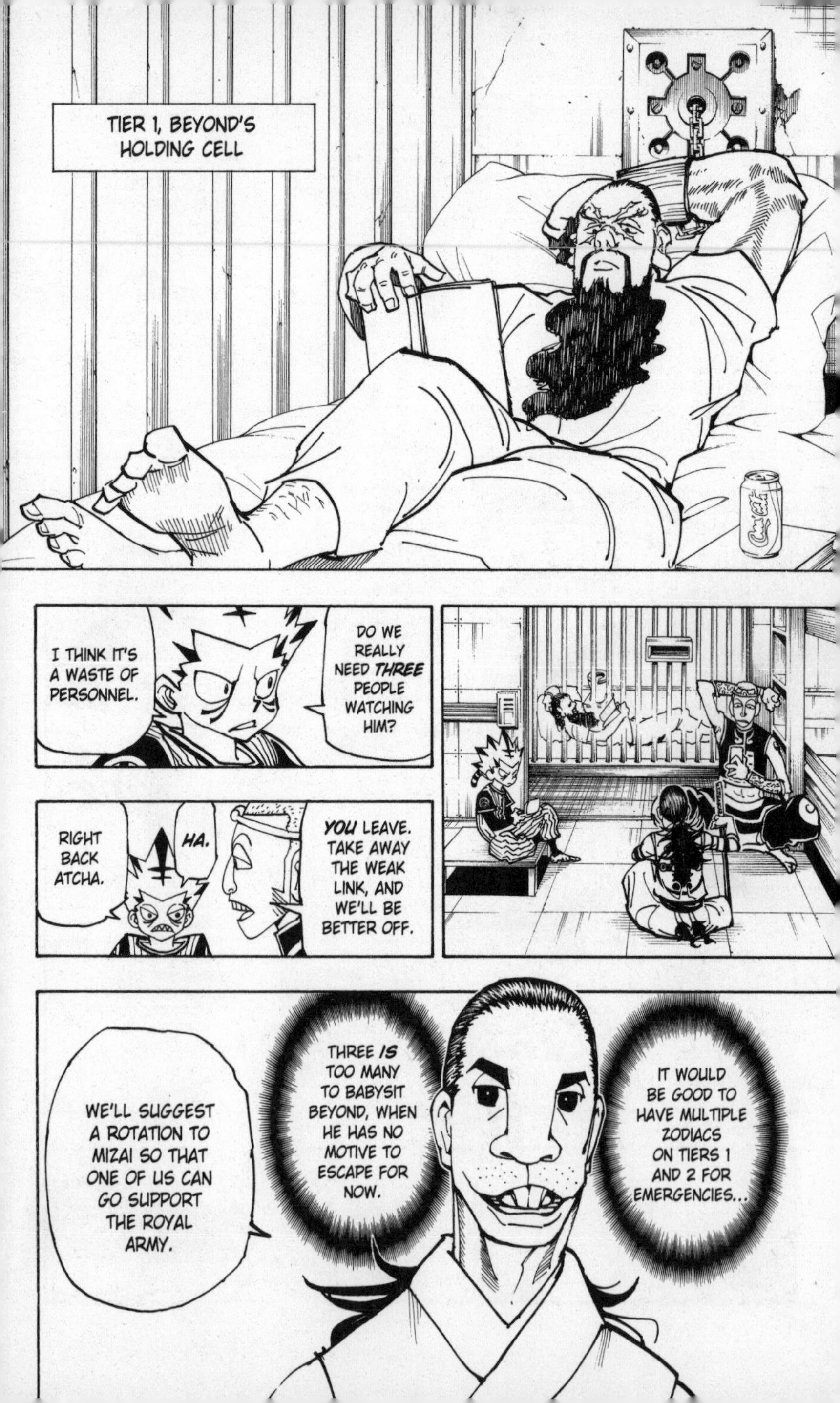
TIER 1, BEYOND'S HOLDING CELL
DO WE REALLY NEED *THREE* PEOPLE WATCHING HIM?
I THINK IT'S A WASTE OF PERSONNEL.
YOU LEAVE. TAKE AWAY THE WEAK LINK, AND WE'LL BE BETTER OFF.
HA.
RIGHT BACK ATCHA.
IT WOULD BE GOOD TO HAVE MULTIPLE ZODIACS ON TIERS 1 AND 2 FOR EMERGENCIES...
THREE *IS* TOO MANY TO BABYSIT BEYOND, WHEN HE HAS NO MOTIVE TO ESCAPE FOR NOW.
WE'LL SUGGEST A ROTATION TO MIZAI SO THAT ONE OF US CAN GO SUPPORT THE ROYAL ARMY.

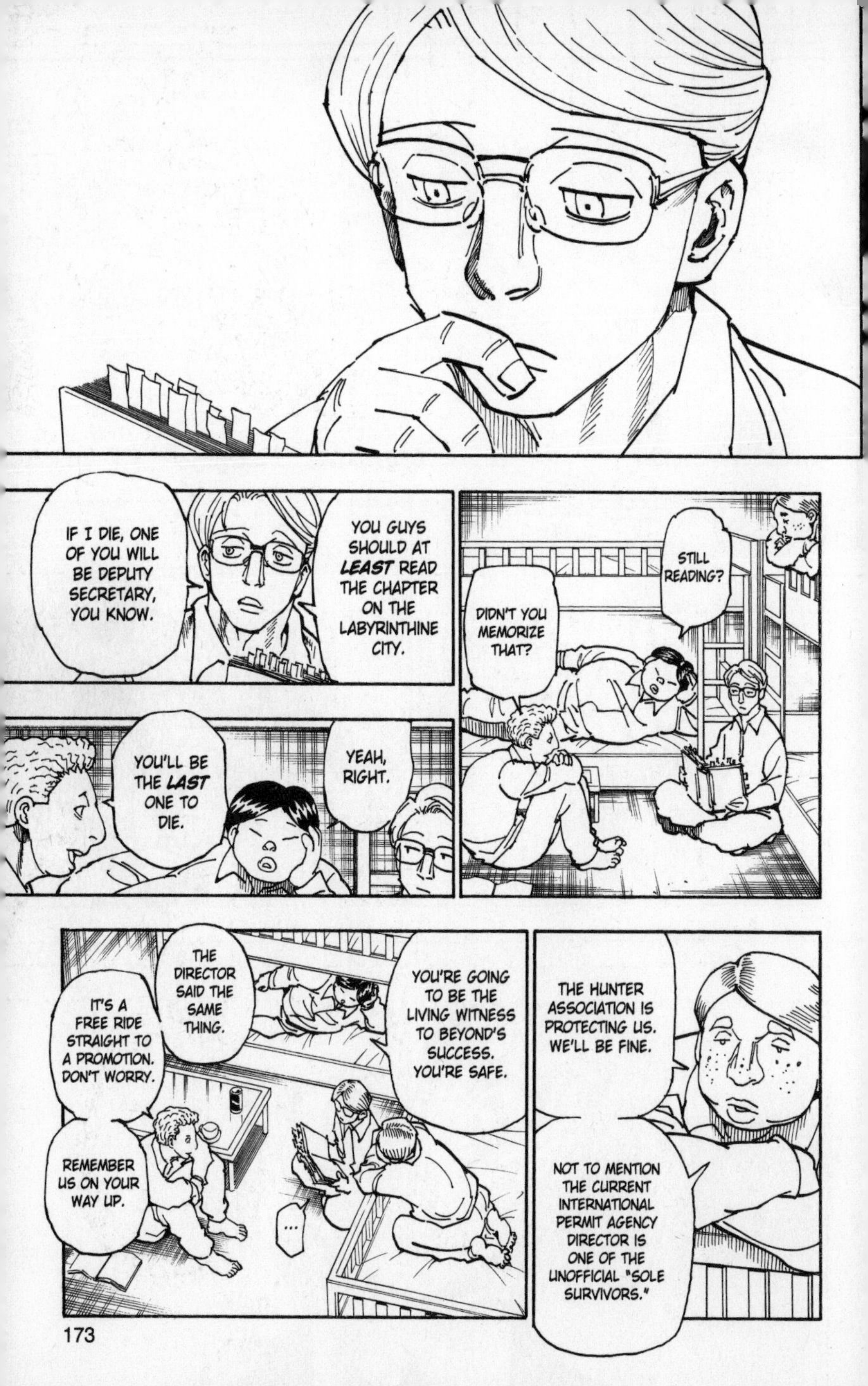
STILL READING?
DIDN'T YOU MEMORIZE THAT?
YOU GUYS SHOULD AT *LEAST* READ THE CHAPTER ON THE LABYRINTHINE CITY.
IF I DIE, ONE OF YOU WILL BE DEPUTY SECRETARY, YOU KNOW.
YEAH, RIGHT.
YOU'LL BE THE *LAST* ONE TO DIE.
THE HUNTER ASSOCIATION IS PROTECTING US. WE'LL BE FINE.
NOT TO MENTION THE CURRENT INTERNATIONAL PERMIT AGENCY DIRECTOR IS ONE OF THE UNOFFICIAL "SOLE SURVIVORS."
YOU'RE GOING TO BE THE LIVING WITNESS TO BEYOND'S SUCCESS. YOU'RE SAFE.
THE DIRECTOR SAID THE SAME THING.
IT'S A FREE RIDE STRAIGHT TO A PROMOTION. DON'T WORRY.
REMEMBER US ON YOUR WAY UP.
...

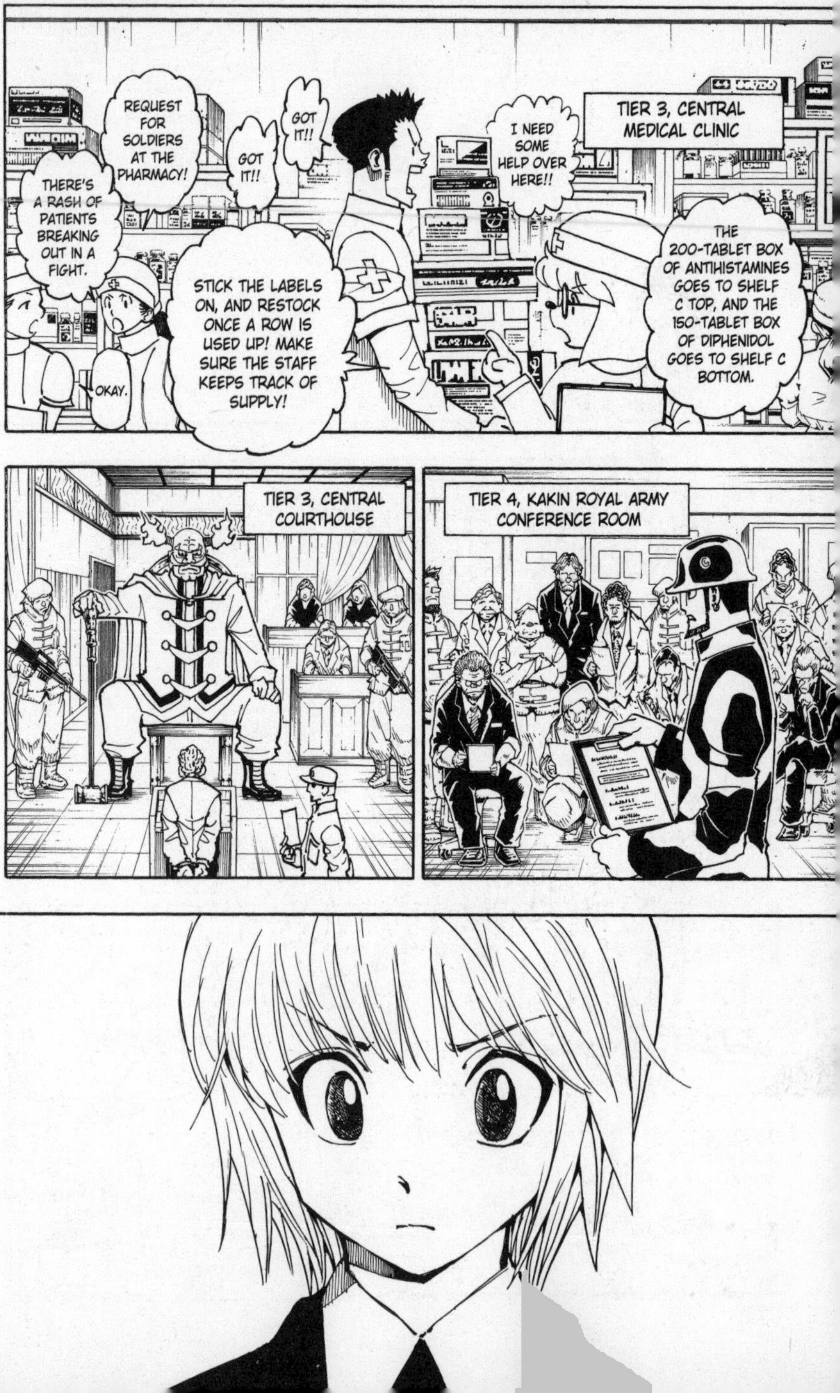
TIER 3, CENTRAL MEDICAL CLINIC
THE 200-TABLET BOX OF ANTIHISTAMINES GOES TO SHELF C TOP, AND THE 150-TABLET BOX OF DIPHENIDOL GOES TO SHELF C BOTTOM.
I NEED SOME HELP OVER HERE!!
GOT IT!!
GOT IT!!
STICK THE LABELS ON, AND RESTOCK ONCE A ROW IS USED UP! MAKE SURE THE STAFF KEEPS TRACK OF SUPPLY!
REQUEST FOR SOLDIERS AT THE PHARMACY!
THERE'S A RASH OF PATIENTS BREAKING OUT IN A FIGHT.
OKAY.
TIER 4, KAKIN ROYAL ARMY CONFERENCE ROOM
TIER 3, CENTRAL COURTHOUSE

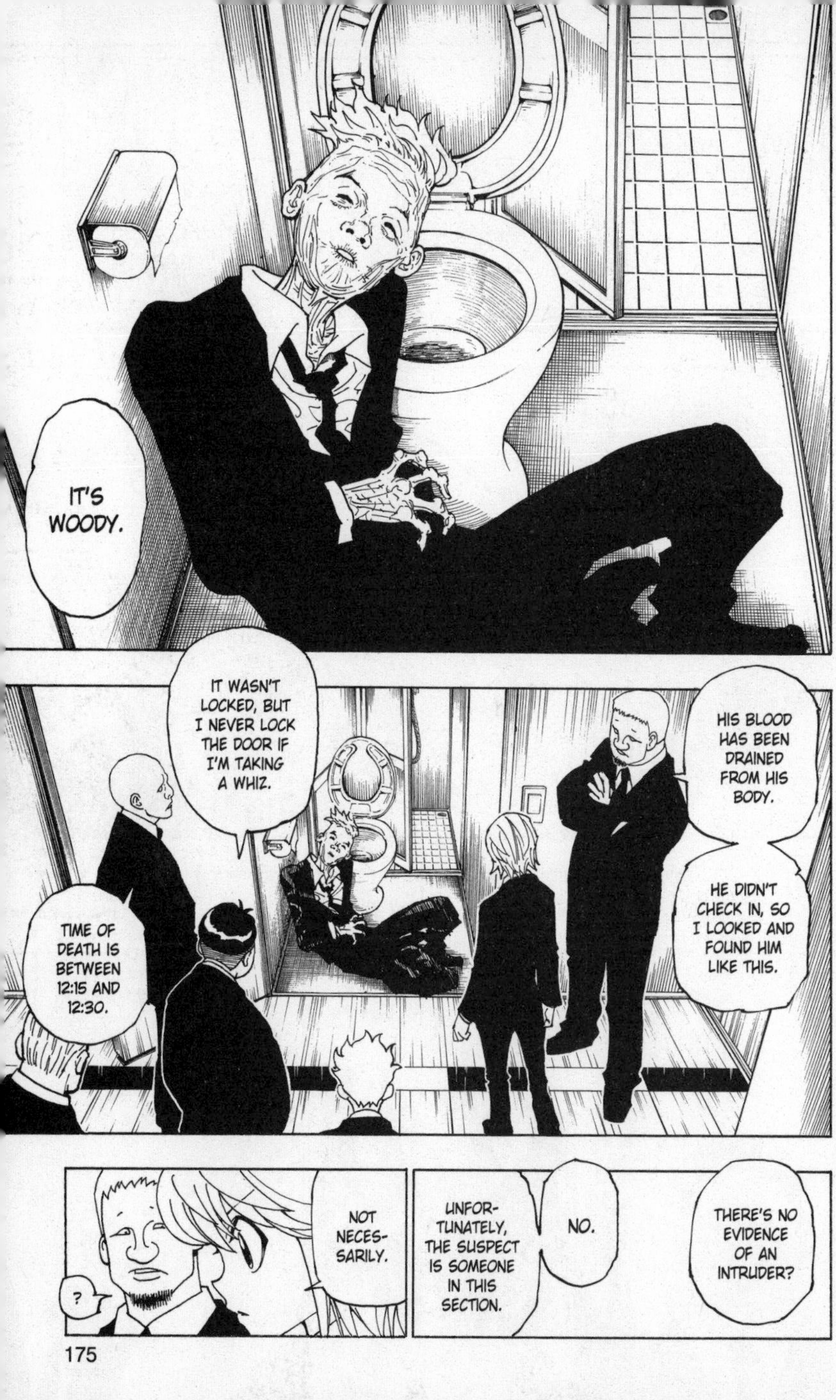
IT'S WOODY.
HIS BLOOD HAS BEEN DRAINED FROM HIS BODY.
HE DIDN'T CHECK IN, SO I LOOKED AND FOUND HIM LIKE THIS.
IT WASN'T LOCKED, BUT I NEVER LOCK THE DOOR IF I'M TAKING A WHIZ.
TIME OF DEATH IS BETWEEN 12:15 AND 12:30.
THERE'S NO EVIDENCE OF AN INTRUDER?
NO.
UNFOR-TUNATELY, THE SUSPECT IS SOMEONE IN THIS SECTION.
NOT NECES-SARILY.
?

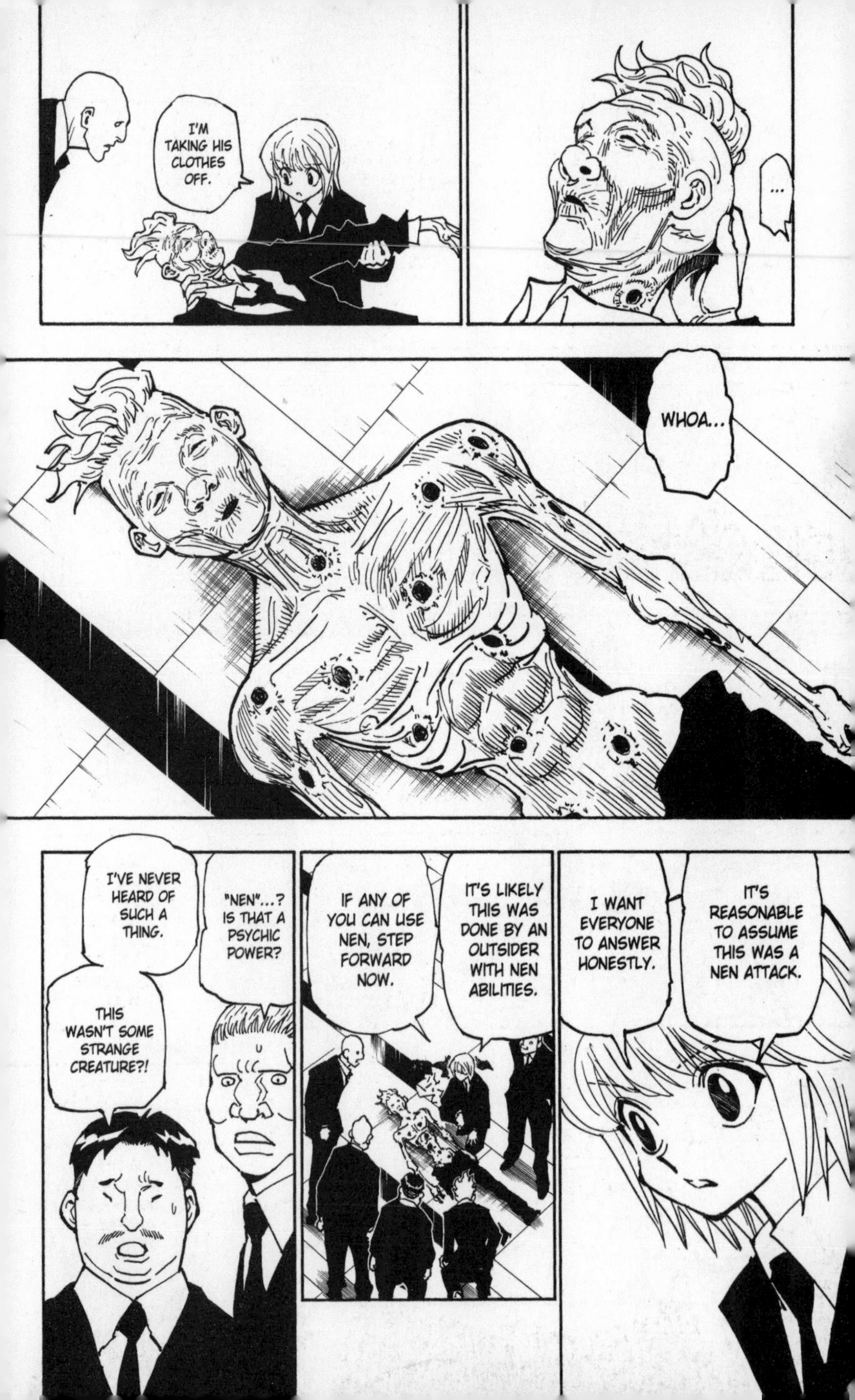
...
I'M TAKING HIS CLOTHES OFF.
WHOA...
IT'S REASONABLE TO ASSUME THIS WAS A NEN ATTACK.
I WANT EVERYONE TO ANSWER HONESTLY.
IT'S LIKELY THIS WAS DONE BY AN OUTSIDER WITH NEN ABILITIES.
IF ANY OF YOU CAN USE NEN, STEP FORWARD NOW.
"NEN"...? IS THAT A PSYCHIC POWER?
I'VE NEVER HEARD OF SUCH A THING.
THIS WASN'T SOME STRANGE CREATURE?!

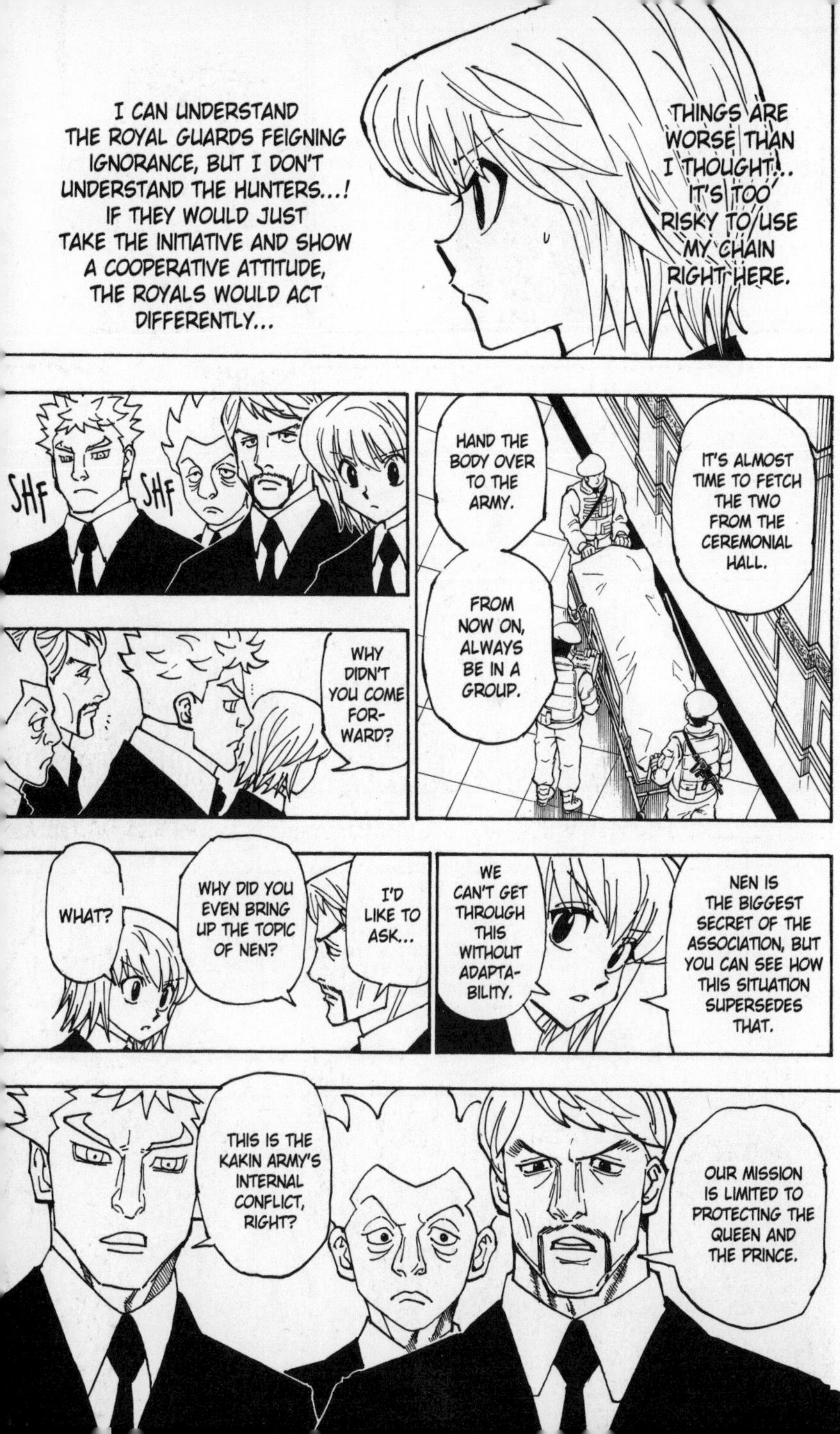
THINGS ARE WORSE THAN I THOUGHT... IT'S TOO RISKY TO USE MY CHAIN RIGHT HERE.
I CAN UNDERSTAND THE ROYAL GUARDS FEIGNING IGNORANCE, BUT I DON'T UNDERSTAND THE HUNTERS...! IF THEY WOULD JUST TAKE THE INITIATIVE AND SHOW A COOPERATIVE ATTITUDE, THE ROYALS WOULD ACT DIFFERENTLY...
IT'S ALMOST TIME TO FETCH THE TWO FROM THE CEREMONIAL HALL.
HAND THE BODY OVER TO THE ARMY.
FROM NOW ON, ALWAYS BE IN A GROUP.
SHF
SHF
WHY DIDN'T YOU COME FOR-WARD?
NEN IS THE BIGGEST SECRET OF THE ASSOCIATION, BUT YOU CAN SEE HOW THIS SITUATION SUPERSEDES THAT.
WE CAN'T GET THROUGH THIS WITHOUT ADAPTA-BILITY.
I'D LIKE TO ASK...
WHY DID YOU EVEN BRING UP THE TOPIC OF NEN?
WHAT?
OUR MISSION IS LIMITED TO PROTECTING THE QUEEN AND THE PRINCE.
THIS IS THE KAKIN ARMY'S INTERNAL CONFLICT, RIGHT?

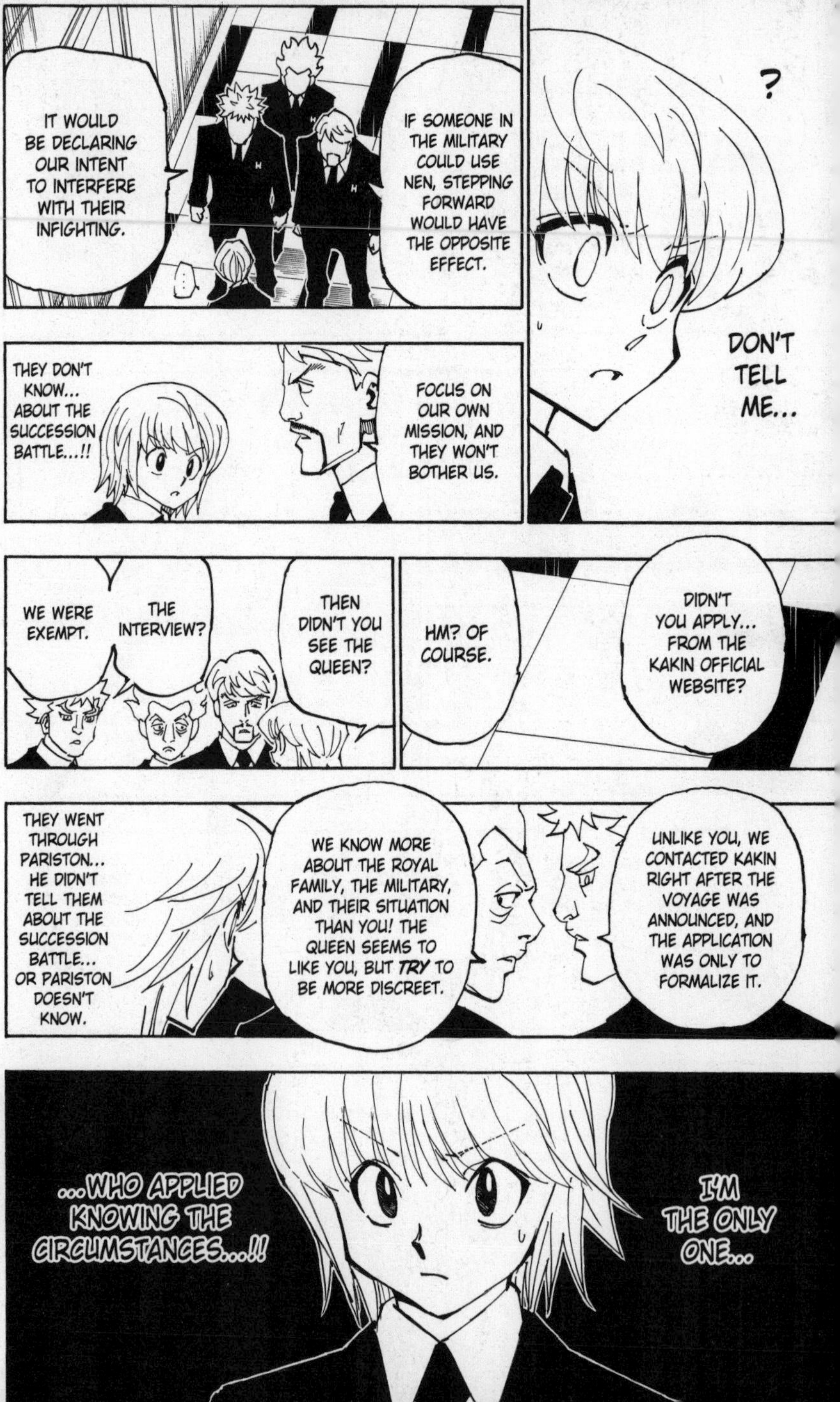
?
DON'T TELL ME...
IF SOMEONE IN THE MILITARY COULD USE NEN, STEPPING FORWARD WOULD HAVE THE OPPOSITE EFFECT.
IT WOULD BE DECLARING OUR INTENT TO INTERFERE WITH THEIR INFIGHTING.
...
FOCUS ON OUR OWN MISSION, AND THEY WON'T BOTHER US.
THEY DON'T KNOW... ABOUT THE SUCCESSION BATTLE...!!
DIDN'T YOU APPLY... FROM THE KAKIN OFFICIAL WEBSITE?
HM? OF COURSE.
THEN DIDN'T YOU SEE THE QUEEN?
THE INTERVIEW?
WE WERE EXEMPT.
UNLIKE YOU, WE CONTACTED KAKIN RIGHT AFTER THE VOYAGE WAS ANNOUNCED, AND THE APPLICATION WAS ONLY TO FORMALIZE IT.
WE KNOW MORE ABOUT THE ROYAL FAMILY, THE MILITARY, AND THEIR SITUATION THAN YOU! THE QUEEN SEEMS TO LIKE YOU, BUT TRY TO BE MORE DISCREET.
THEY WENT THROUGH PARISTON... HE DIDN'T TELL THEM ABOUT THE SUCCESSION BATTLE... OR PARISTON DOESN'T KNOW.
I'M THE ONLY ONE...
...WHO APPLIED KNOWING THE CIRCUMSTANCES...!!

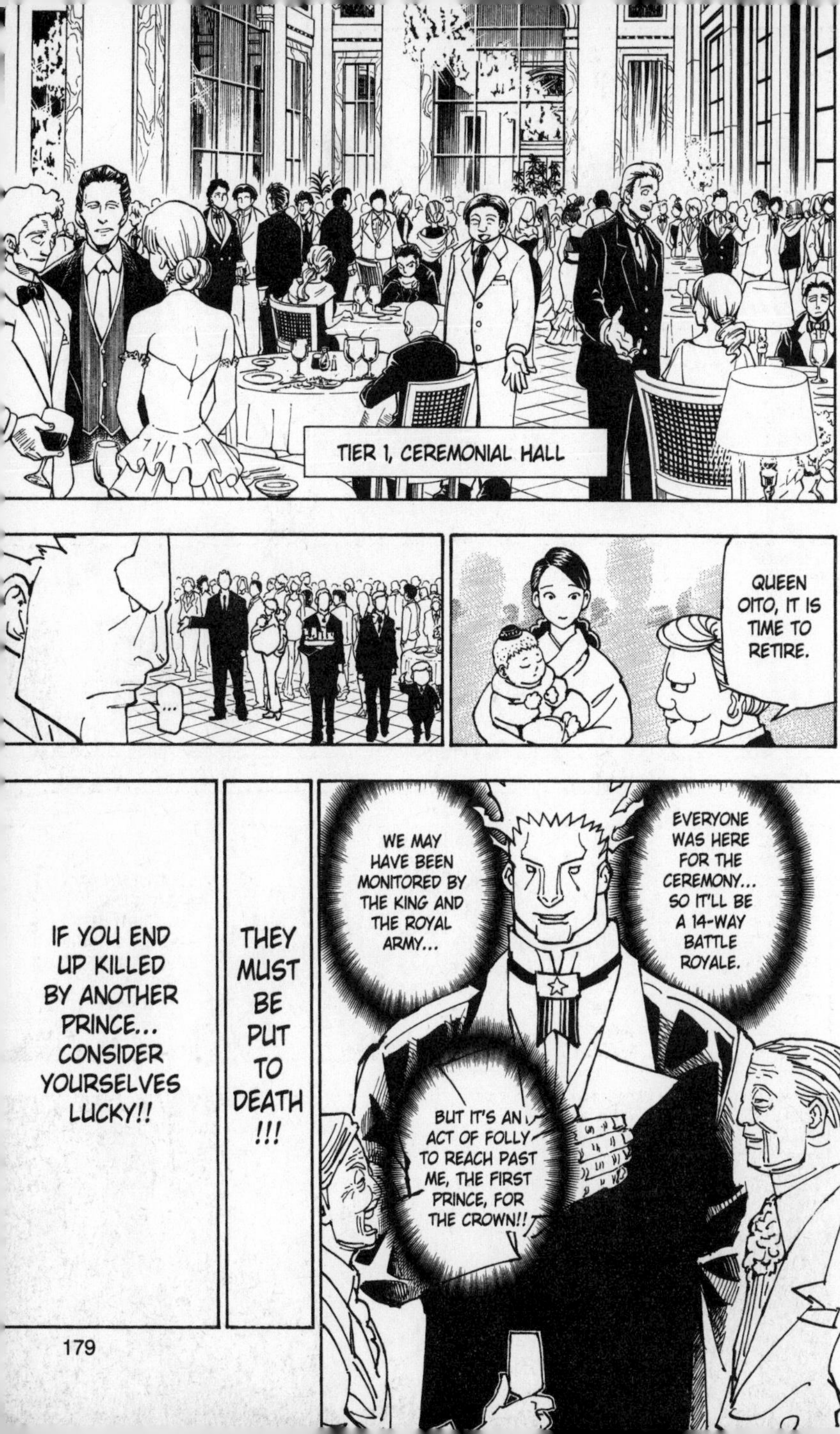
TIER 1, CEREMONIAL HALL
QUEEN OITO, IT IS TIME TO RETIRE.
...
EVERYONE WAS HERE FOR THE CEREMONY... SO IT'LL BE A 14-WAY BATTLE ROYALE.
WE MAY HAVE BEEN MONITORED BY THE KING AND THE ROYAL ARMY...
BUT IT'S AN ACT OF FOLLY TO REACH PAST ME, THE FIRST PRINCE, FOR THE CROWN!!
THEY MUST BE PUT TO DEATH!!!
IF YOU END UP KILLED BY ANOTHER PRINCE... CONSIDER YOURSELVES LUCKY!!

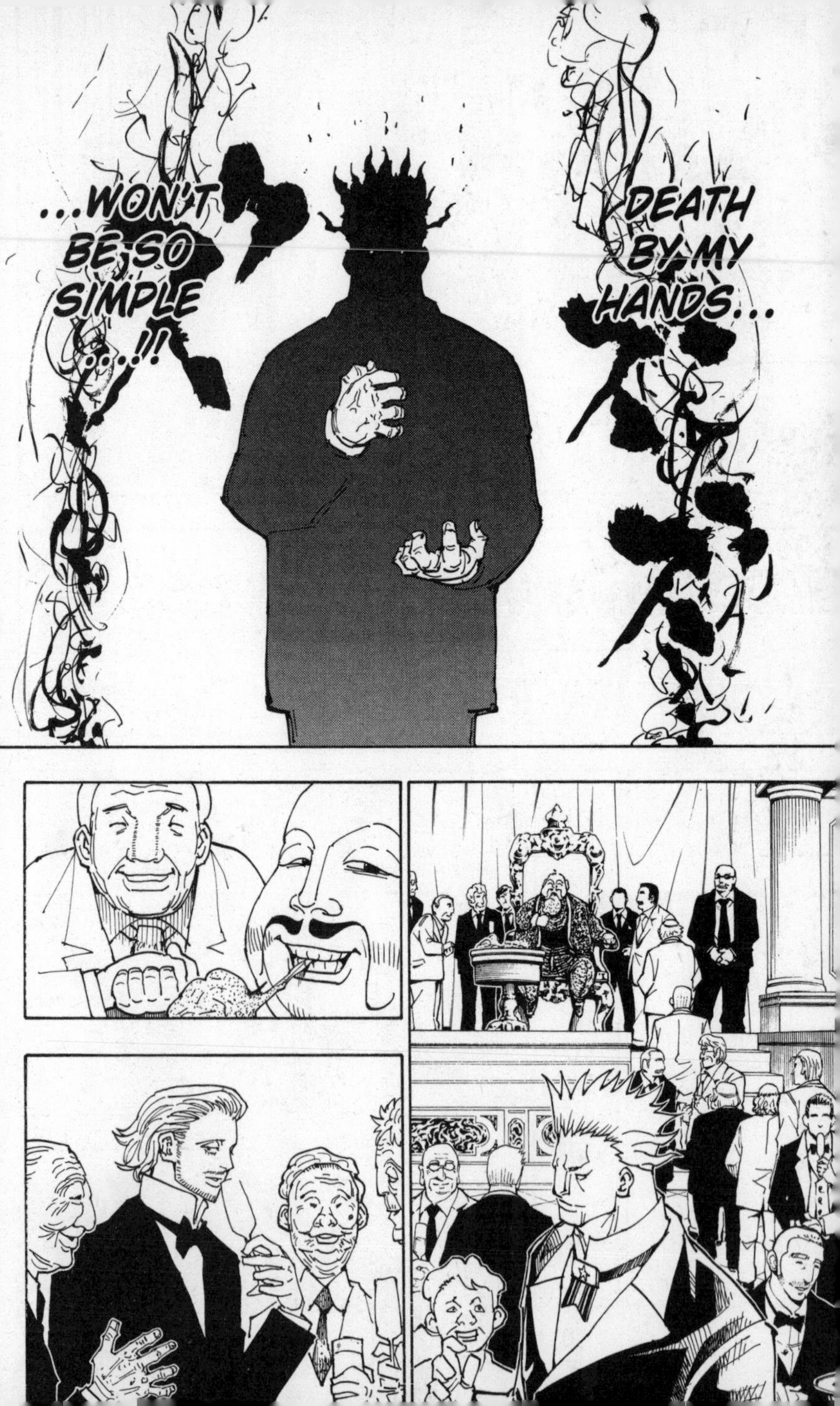
DEATH BY MY HANDS...
...WON'T BE SO SIMPLE...!!

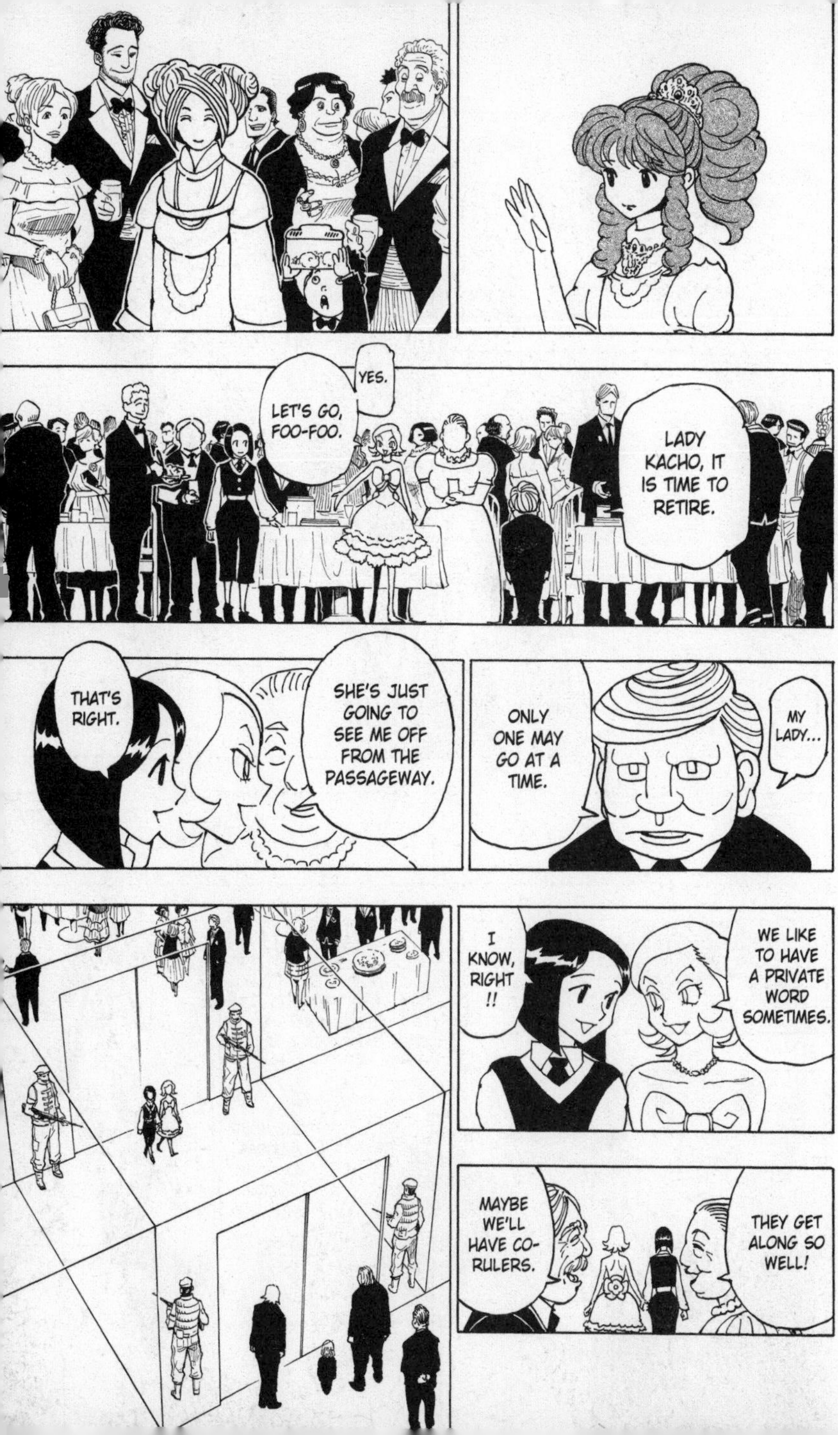
LADY KACHO, IT IS TIME TO RETIRE.
YES.
LET'S GO, FOO-FOO.
MY LADY...
ONLY ONE MAY GO AT A TIME.
SHE'S JUST GOING TO SEE ME OFF FROM THE PASSAGEWAY.
THAT'S RIGHT.
WE LIKE TO HAVE A PRIVATE WORD SOMETIMES.
I KNOW, RIGHT!!
THEY GET ALONG SO WELL!
MAYBE WE'LL HAVE CO-RULERS.

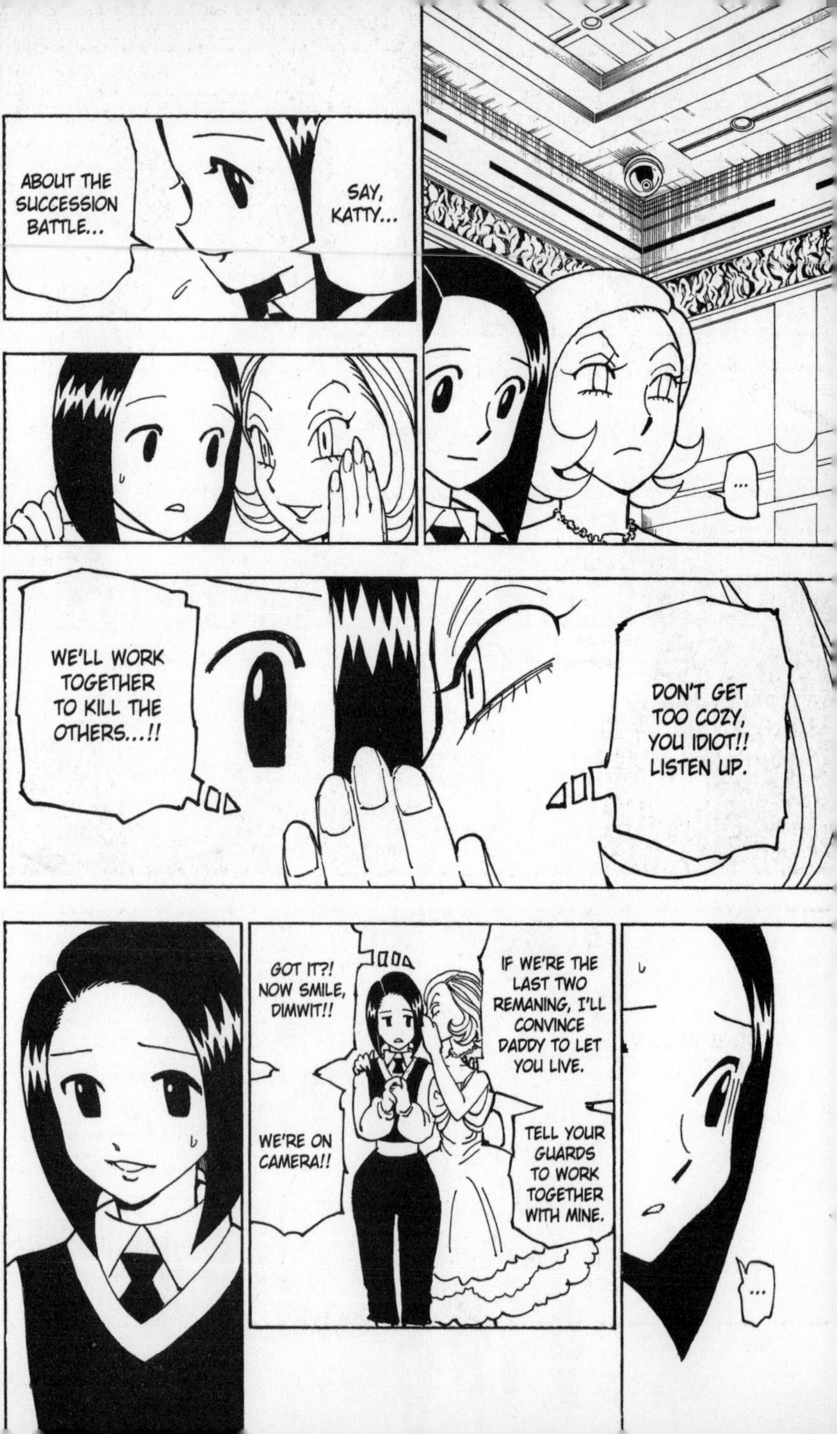
...
SAY, KATTY...
ABOUT THE SUCCESSION BATTLE...
DON'T GET TOO COZY, YOU IDIOT!! LISTEN UP.
WE'LL WORK TOGETHER TO KILL THE OTHERS...!!
...
IF WE'RE THE LAST TWO REMANING, I'LL CONVINCE DADDY TO LET YOU LIVE.
TELL YOUR GUARDS TO WORK TOGETHER WITH MINE.
GOT IT?! NOW SMILE, DIMWIT!!
WE'RE ON CAMERA!!

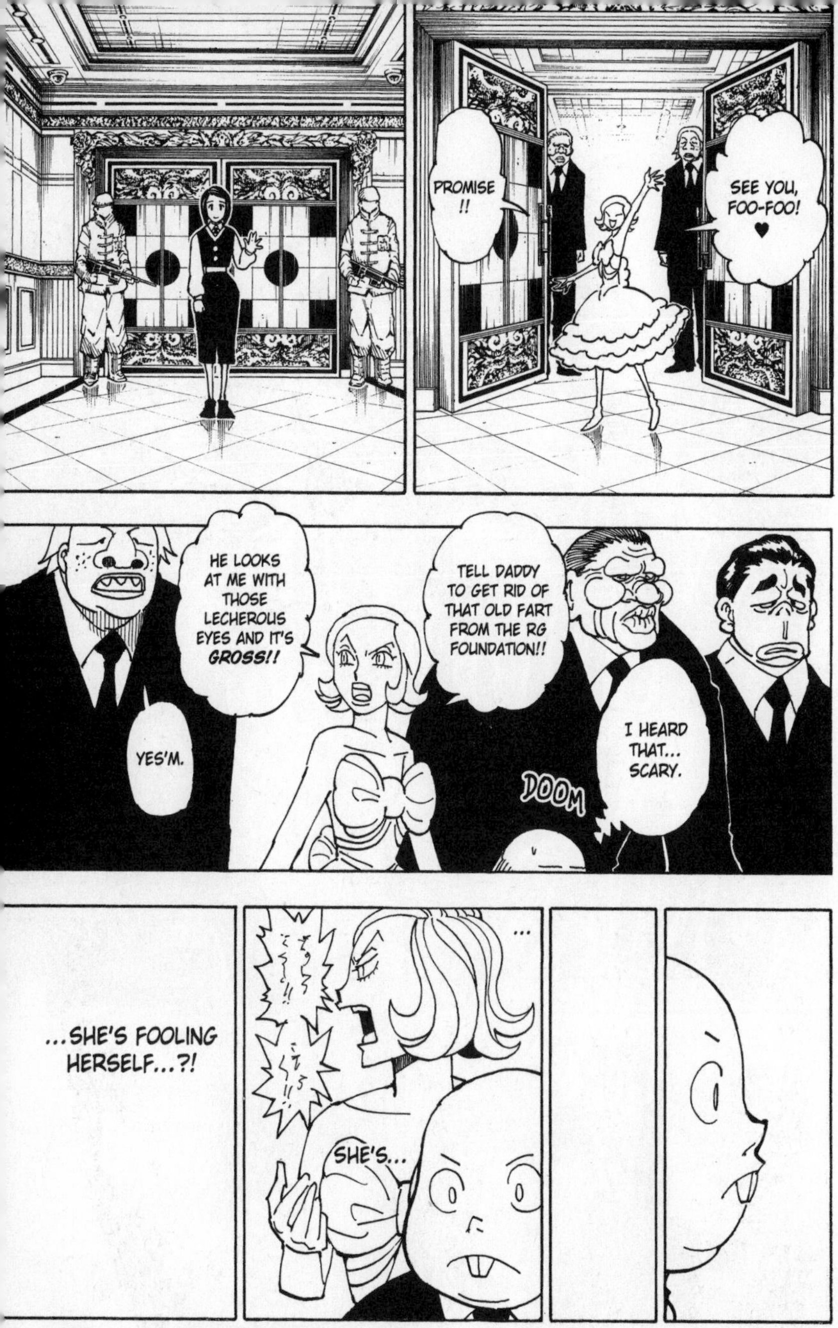
SEE YOU, FOO-FOO! ♥
PROMISE !!
TELL DADDY TO GET RID OF THAT OLD FART FROM THE RG FOUNDATION!!
HE LOOKS AT ME WITH THOSE LECHEROUS EYES AND IT'S GROSS!!
YES'M.
DOOM
I HEARD THAT... SCARY.
...
SHE'S...
...SHE'S FOOLING HERSELF...?!

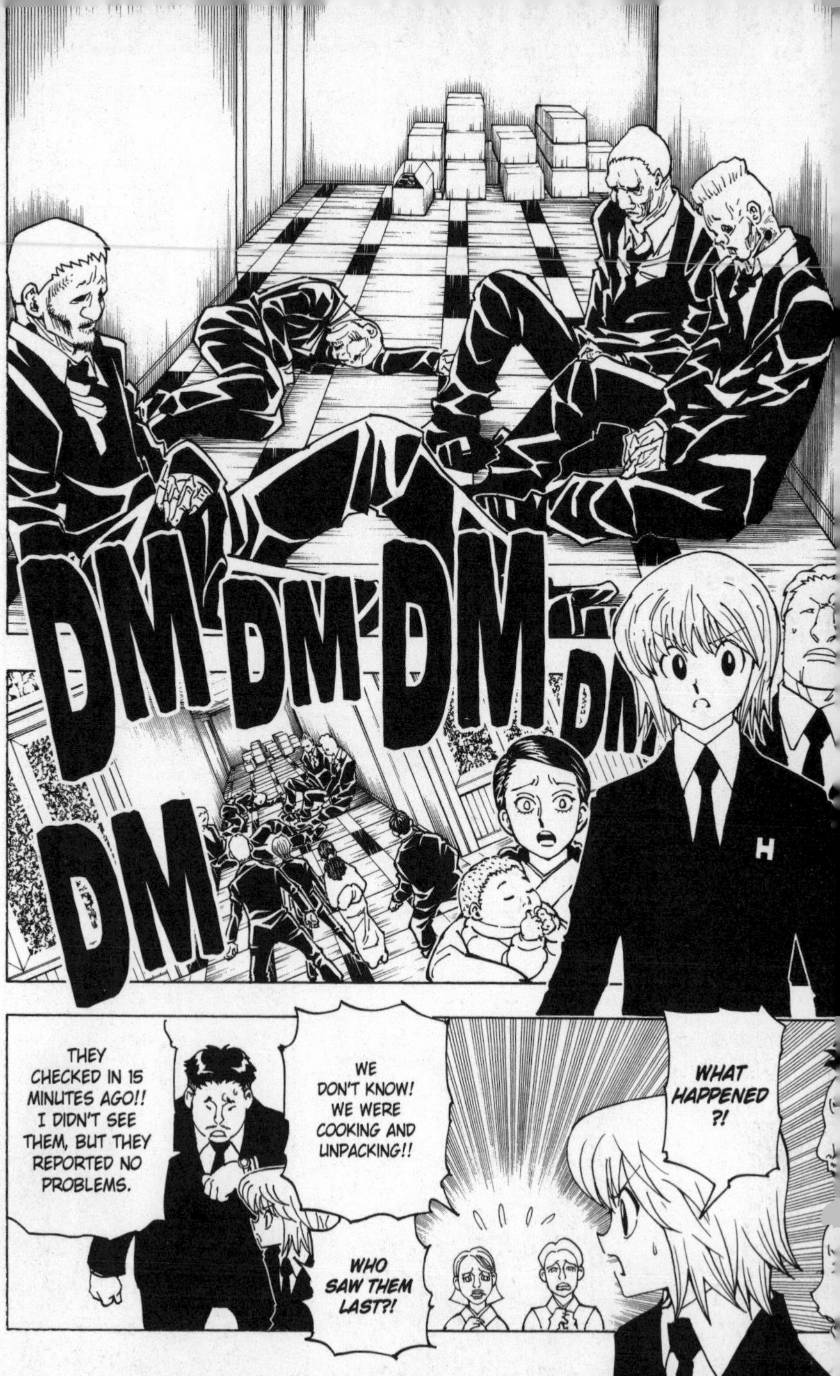

DM DM DM DM
DM
WHAT HAPPENED?!
WHO SAW THEM LAST?!
WE DON'T KNOW! WE WERE COOKING AND UNPACKING!!
THEY CHECKED IN 15 MINUTES AGO!! I DIDN'T SEE THEM, BUT THEY REPORTED NO PROBLEMS.

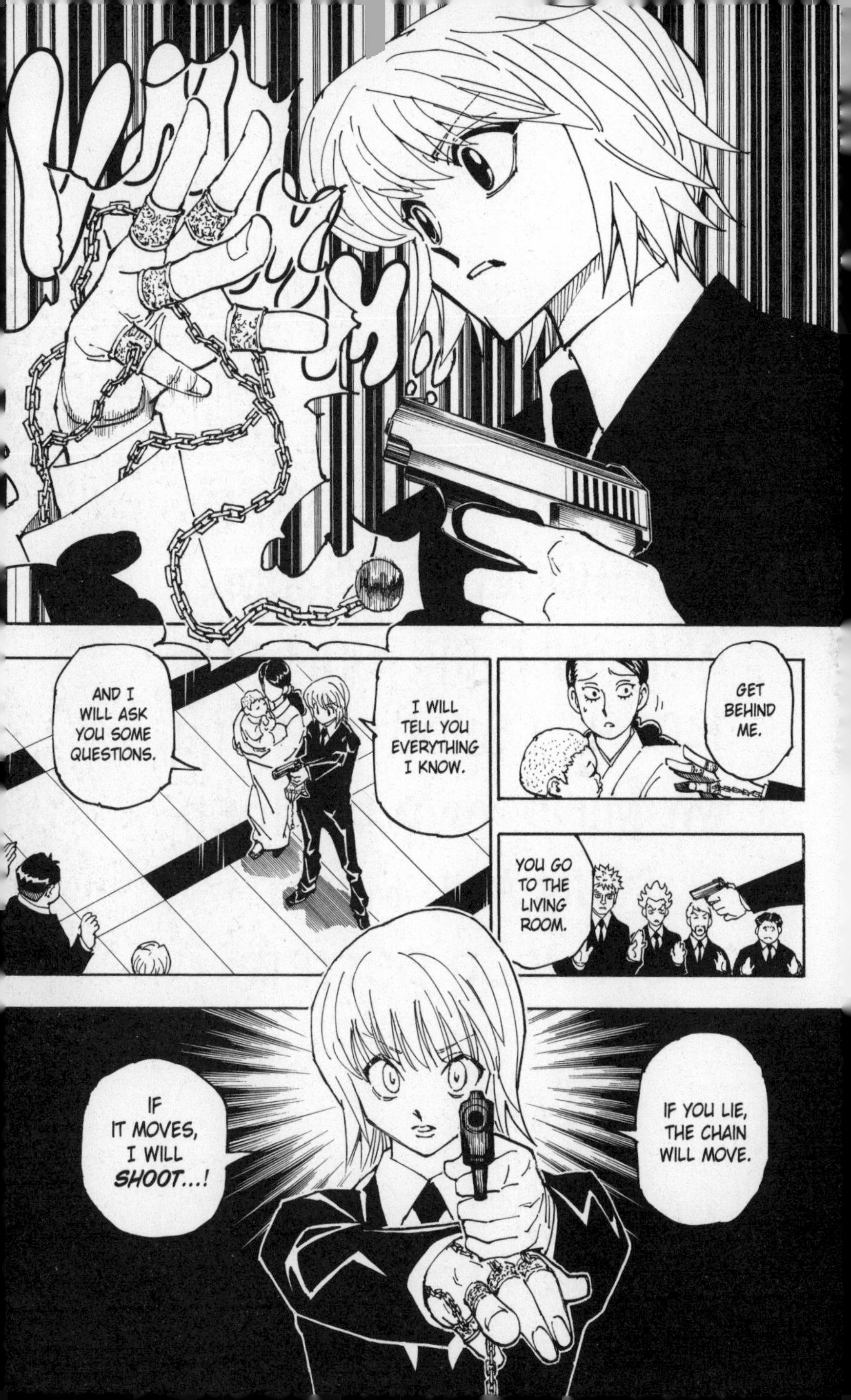
GET BEHIND ME.
YOU GO TO THE LIVING ROOM.
I WILL TELL YOU EVERYTHING I KNOW.
AND I WILL ASK YOU SOME QUESTIONS.
IF YOU LIE, THE CHAIN WILL MOVE.
IF IT MOVES, I WILL *SHOOT*...!

I DEBATED WHETHER
IT SHOULD BE "MOON
AND SUN" OR "SUN AND
MOON." I SHOUTED IT IN
MY MIND, AND DECIDED
"SUN AND MOON"
SOUNDED BETTER.

SUN
AND
MOOOON
!!!

Chapter 360: Parasite

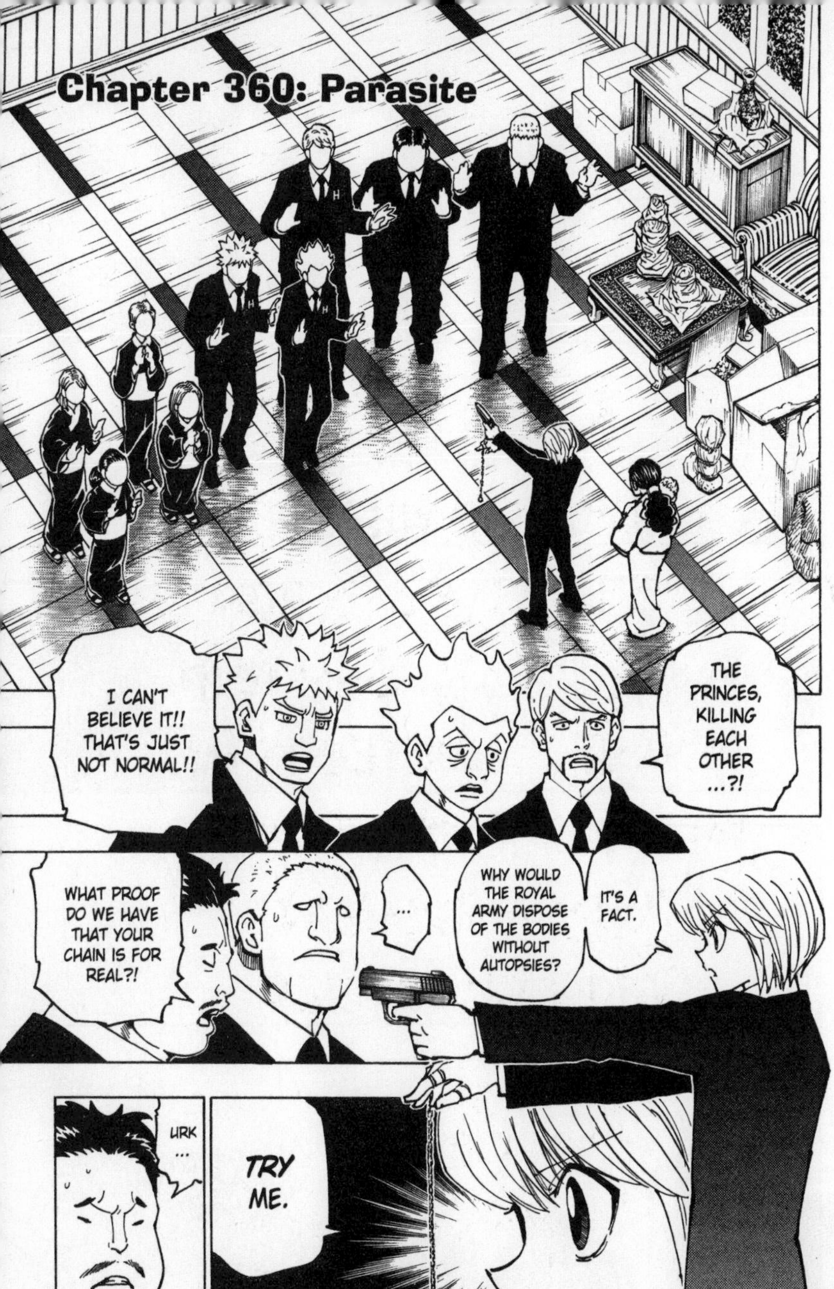
THE PRINCES, KILLING EACH OTHER ...?!
I CAN'T BELIEVE IT!! THAT'S JUST NOT NORMAL!!
IT'S A FACT.
WHY WOULD THE ROYAL ARMY DISPOSE OF THE BODIES WITHOUT AUTOPSIES?
...
WHAT PROOF DO WE HAVE THAT YOUR CHAIN IS FOR REAL?!
TRY ME.
URK ...

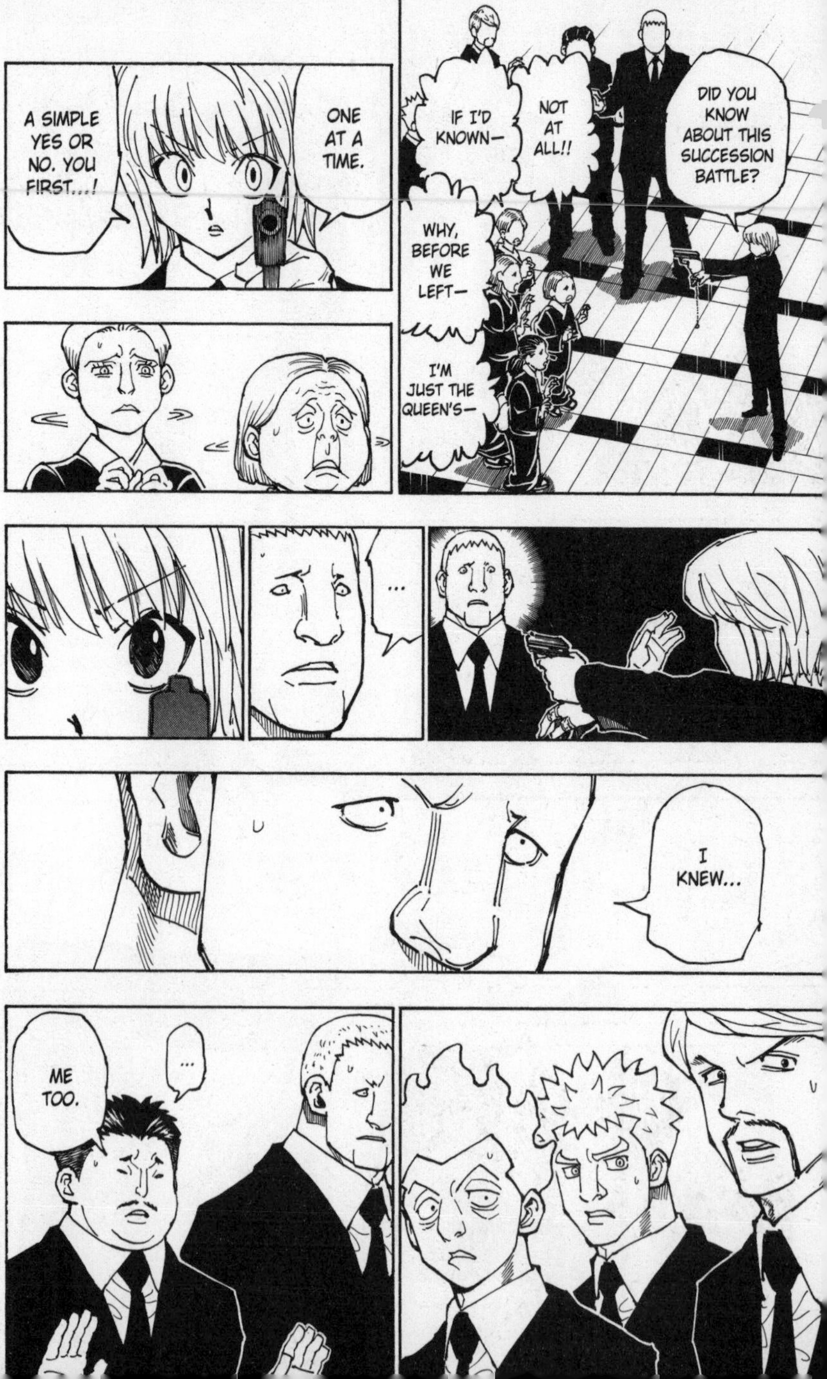
DID YOU KNOW ABOUT THIS SUCCESSION BATTLE?
NOT AT ALL!!
IF I'D KNOWN—
WHY, BEFORE WE LEFT—
I'M JUST THE QUEEN'S—
ONE AT A TIME.
A SIMPLE YES OR NO. YOU FIRST...!
...
I KNEW...
...
ME TOO.

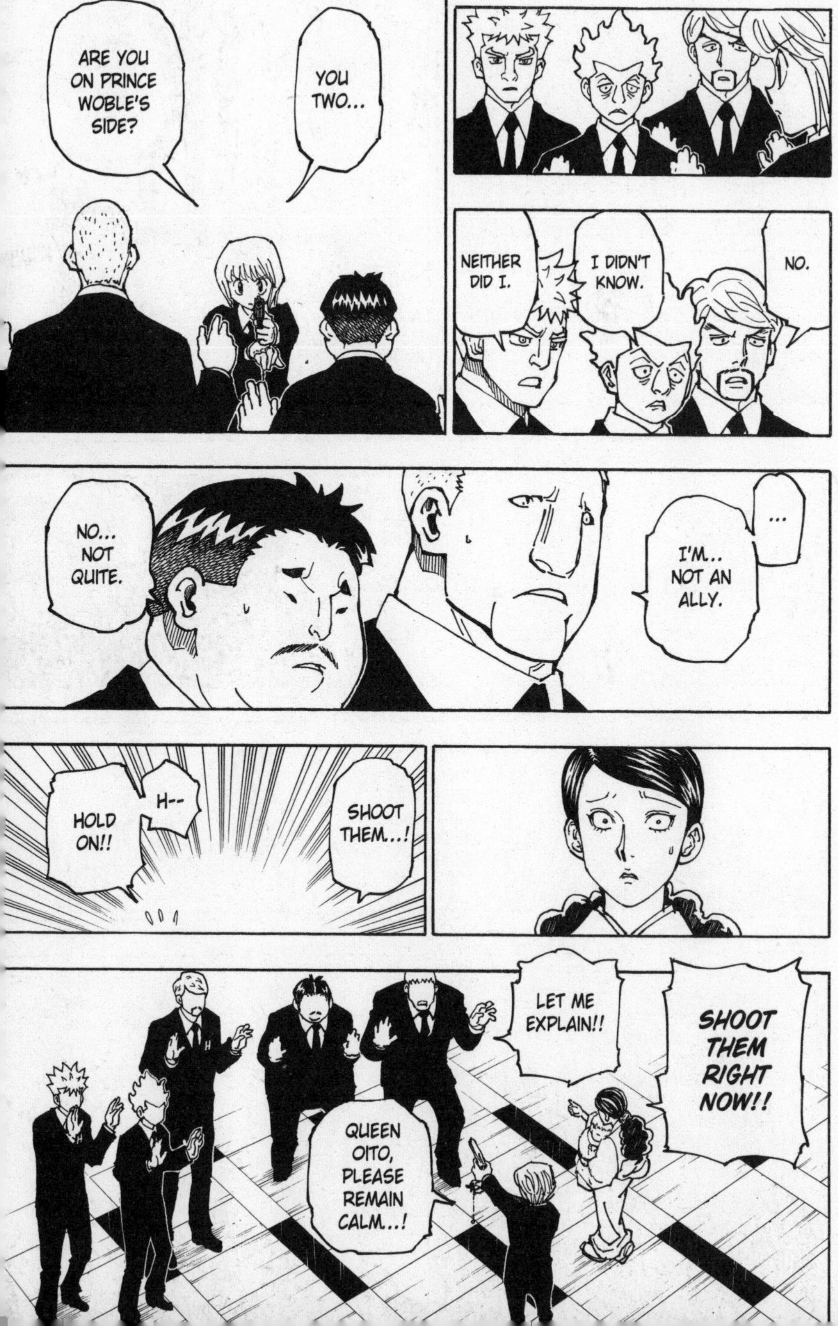
NO.
I DIDN'T KNOW.
NEITHER DID I.
YOU TWO...
ARE YOU ON PRINCE WOBLE'S SIDE?
...
I'M... NOT AN ALLY.
NO... NOT QUITE.
SHOOT THEM...!
H--
HOLD ON!!
SHOOT THEM RIGHT NOW!!
LET ME EXPLAIN!!
QUEEN OITO, PLEASE REMAIN CALM...!

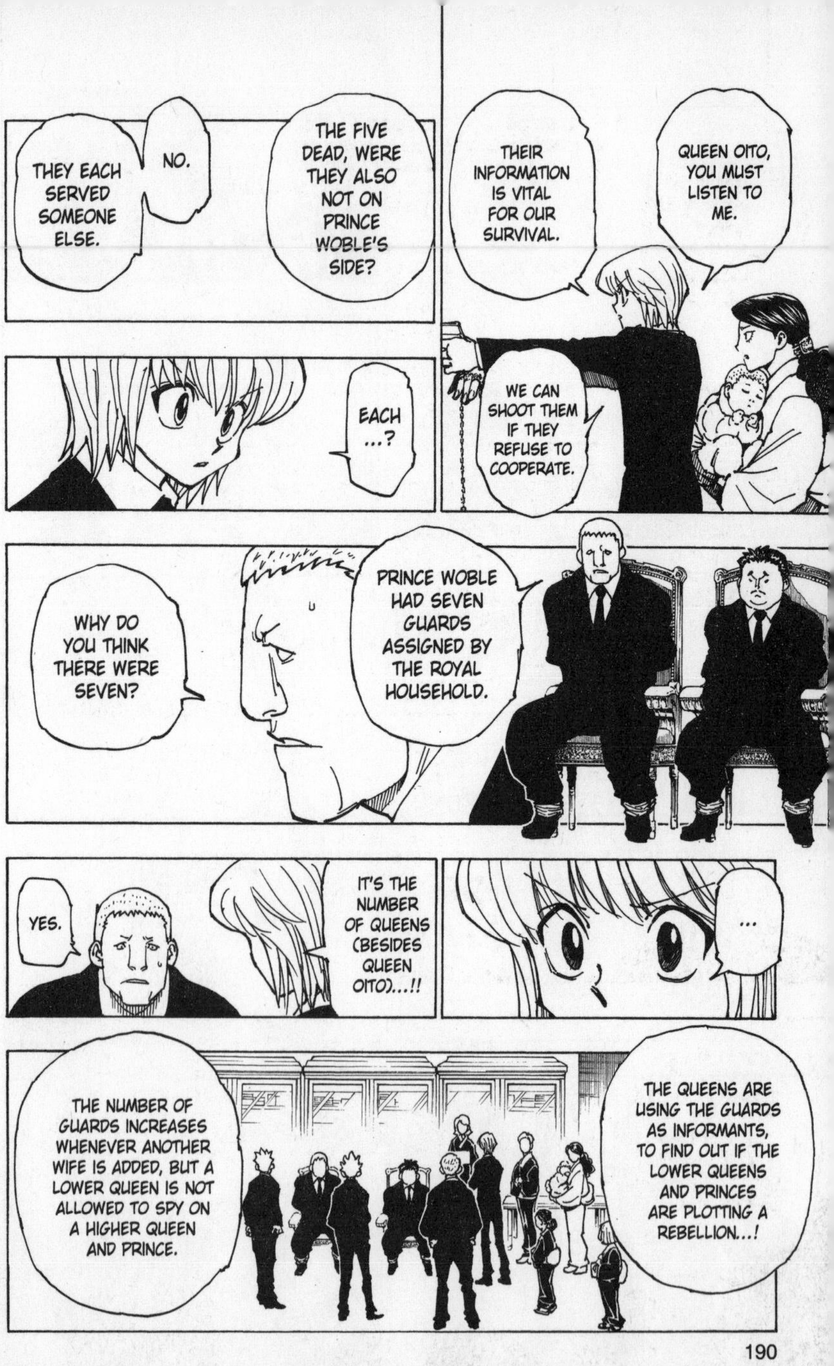
QUEEN OITO, YOU MUST LISTEN TO ME.
THEIR INFORMATION IS VITAL FOR OUR SURVIVAL.
WE CAN SHOOT THEM IF THEY REFUSE TO COOPERATE.
THE FIVE DEAD, WERE THEY ALSO NOT ON PRINCE WOBLE'S SIDE?
NO.
THEY EACH SERVED SOMEONE ELSE.
EACH ...?
PRINCE WOBLE HAD SEVEN GUARDS ASSIGNED BY THE ROYAL HOUSEHOLD.
WHY DO YOU THINK THERE WERE SEVEN?
...
IT'S THE NUMBER OF QUEENS (BESIDES QUEEN OITO)...!!
YES.
THE QUEENS ARE USING THE GUARDS AS INFORMANTS, TO FIND OUT IF THE LOWER QUEENS AND PRINCES ARE PLOTTING A REBELLION...!
THE NUMBER OF GUARDS INCREASES WHENEVER ANOTHER WIFE IS ADDED, BUT A LOWER QUEEN IS NOT ALLOWED TO SPY ON A HIGHER QUEEN AND PRINCE.

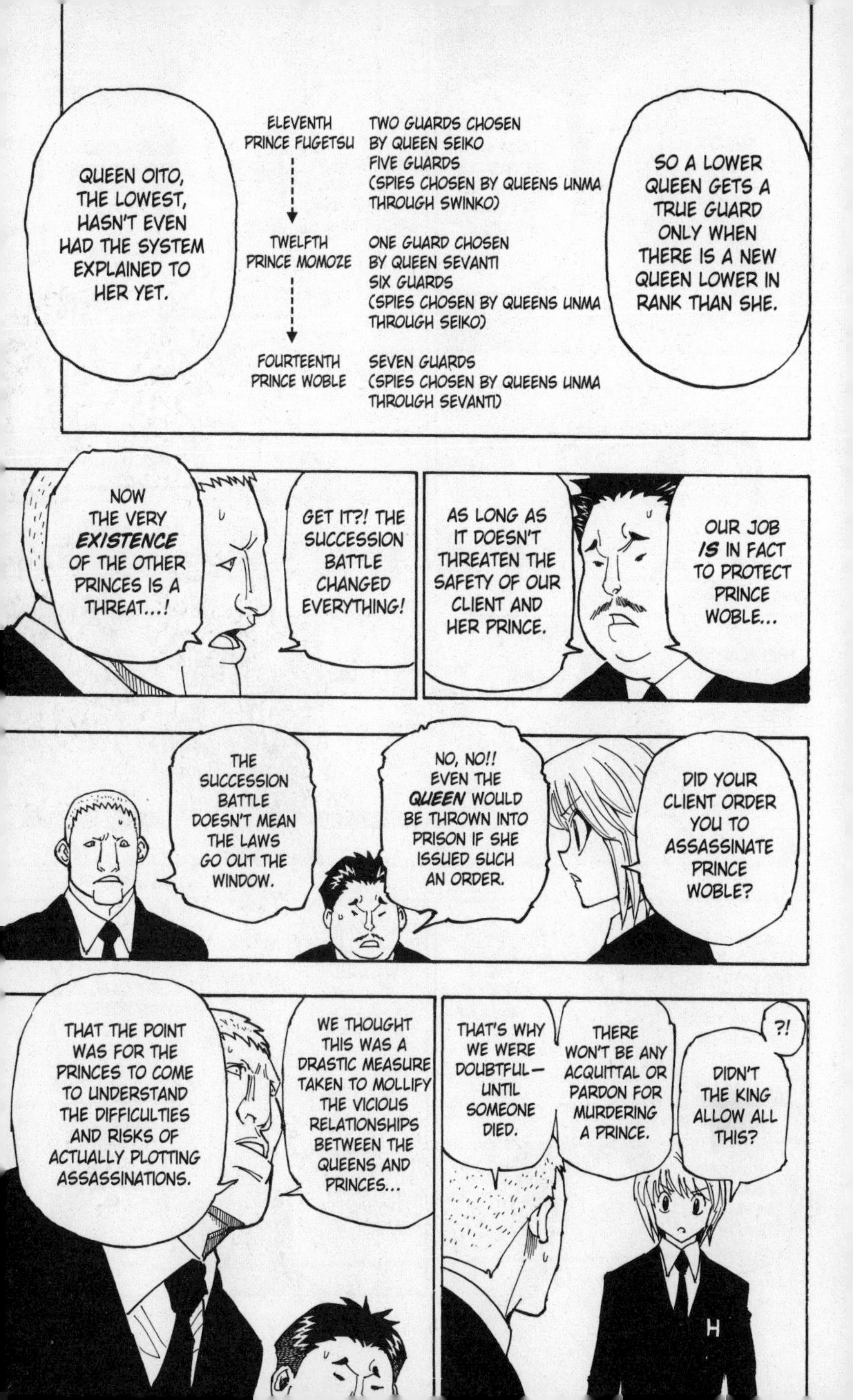
SO A LOWER QUEEN GETS A TRUE GUARD ONLY WHEN THERE IS A NEW QUEEN LOWER IN RANK THAN SHE.
ELEVENTH PRINCE FUGETSU
TWO GUARDS CHOSEN BY QUEEN SEIKO
FIVE GUARDS (SPIES CHOSEN BY QUEENS UNMA THROUGH SWINKO)
TWELFTH PRINCE MOMOZE
ONE GUARD CHOSEN BY QUEEN SEVANTI
SIX GUARDS (SPIES CHOSEN BY QUEENS UNMA THROUGH SEIKO)
FOURTEENTH PRINCE WOBLE
SEVEN GUARDS (SPIES CHOSEN BY QUEENS UNMA THROUGH SEVANTI)
QUEEN OITO, THE LOWEST, HASN'T EVEN HAD THE SYSTEM EXPLAINED TO HER YET.
OUR JOB *IS* IN FACT TO PROTECT PRINCE WOBLE...
AS LONG AS IT DOESN'T THREATEN THE SAFETY OF OUR CLIENT AND HER PRINCE.
GET IT?! THE SUCCESSION BATTLE CHANGED EVERYTHING!
NOW THE VERY *EXISTENCE* OF THE OTHER PRINCES IS A THREAT...!
DID YOUR CLIENT ORDER YOU TO ASSASSINATE PRINCE WOBLE?
NO, NO!! EVEN THE *QUEEN* WOULD BE THROWN INTO PRISON IF SHE ISSUED SUCH AN ORDER.
THE SUCCESSION BATTLE DOESN'T MEAN THE LAWS GO OUT THE WINDOW.
?!
DIDN'T THE KING ALLOW ALL THIS?
THERE WON'T BE ANY ACQUITTAL OR PARDON FOR MURDERING A PRINCE.
THAT'S WHY WE WERE DOUBTFUL— UNTIL SOMEONE DIED.
WE THOUGHT THIS WAS A DRASTIC MEASURE TAKEN TO MOLLIFY THE VICIOUS RELATIONSHIPS BETWEEN THE QUEENS AND PRINCES...
THAT THE POINT WAS FOR THE PRINCES TO COME TO UNDERSTAND THE DIFFICULTIES AND RISKS OF ACTUALLY PLOTTING ASSASSINATIONS.

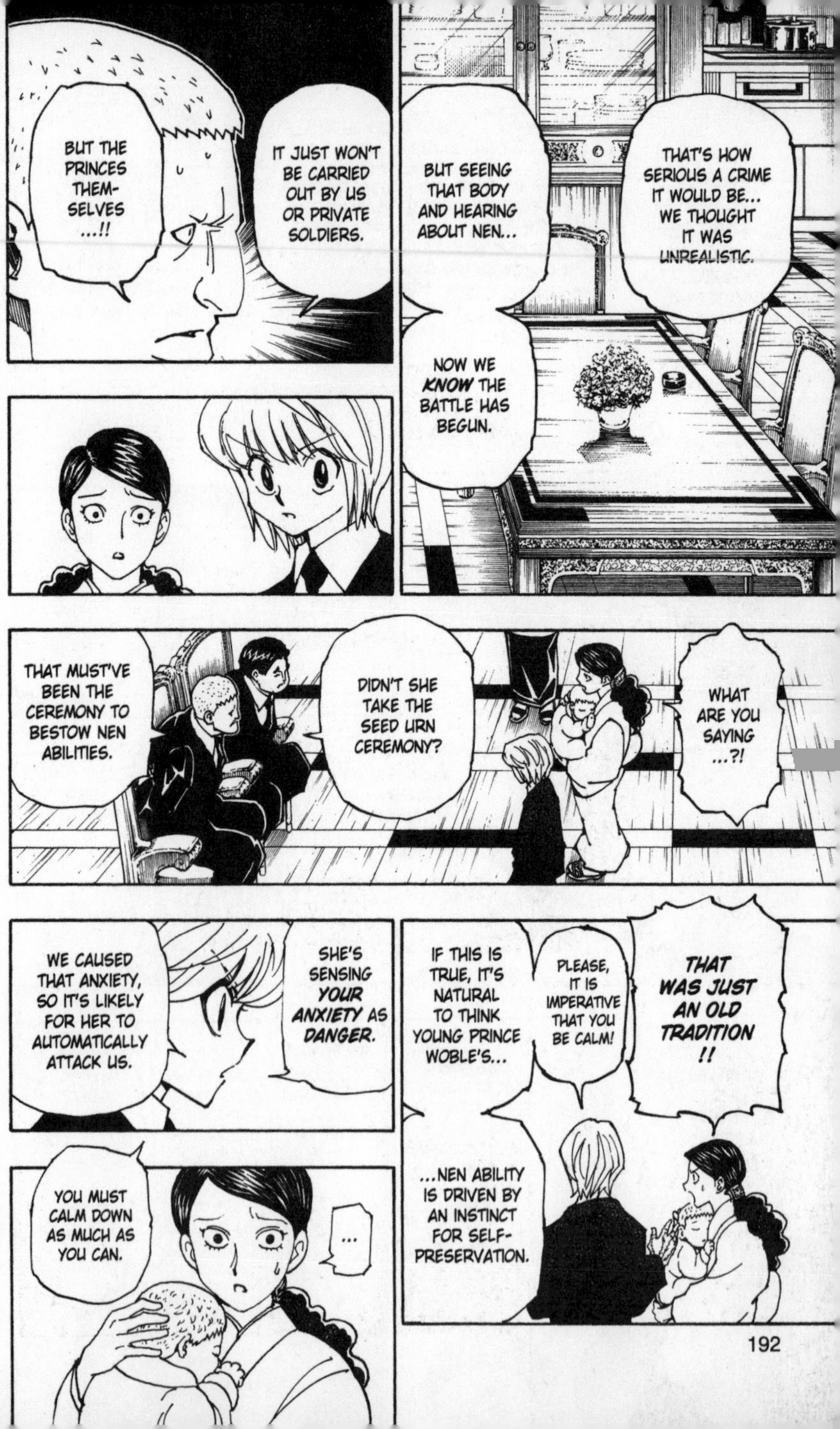
THAT'S HOW SERIOUS A CRIME IT WOULD BE... WE THOUGHT IT WAS UNREALISTIC.
BUT SEEING THAT BODY AND HEARING ABOUT NEN...
NOW WE *KNOW* THE BATTLE HAS BEGUN.
IT JUST WON'T BE CARRIED OUT BY US OR PRIVATE SOLDIERS.
BUT THE PRINCES THEM-SELVES ...!!
WHAT ARE YOU SAYING ...?!
DIDN'T SHE TAKE THE SEED URN CEREMONY?
THAT MUST'VE BEEN THE CEREMONY TO BESTOW NEN ABILITIES.
THAT WAS JUST AN OLD TRADITION !!
PLEASE, IT IS IMPERATIVE THAT YOU BE CALM!
IF THIS IS TRUE, IT'S NATURAL TO THINK YOUNG PRINCE WOBLE'S...
...NEN ABILITY IS DRIVEN BY AN INSTINCT FOR SELF-PRESERVATION.
SHE'S SENSING *YOUR ANXIETY* AS *DANGER*.
WE CAUSED THAT ANXIETY, SO IT'S LIKELY FOR HER TO AUTOMATICALLY ATTACK US.
...
YOU MUST CALM DOWN AS MUCH AS YOU CAN.

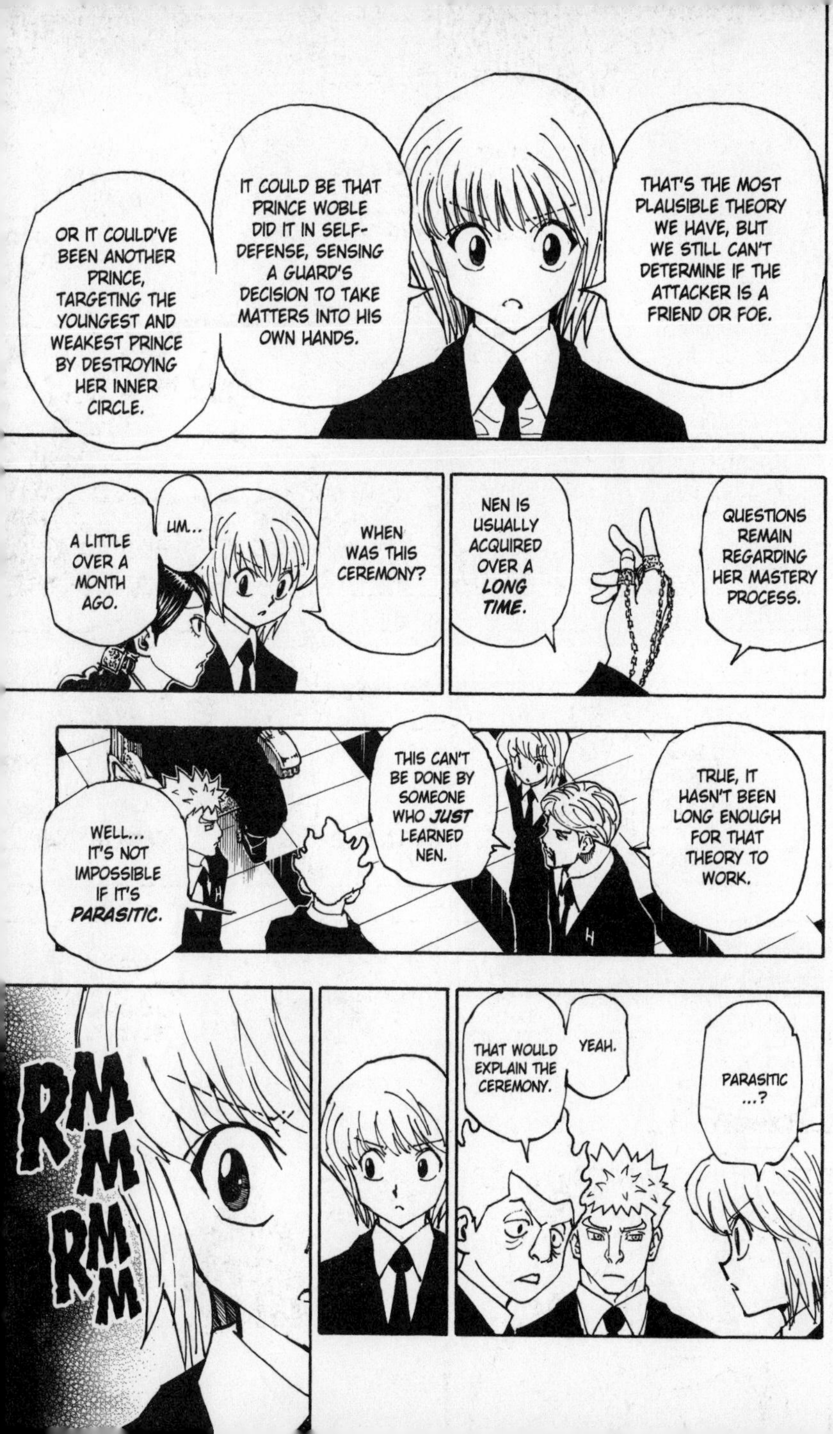
THAT'S THE MOST PLAUSIBLE THEORY WE HAVE, BUT WE STILL CAN'T DETERMINE IF THE ATTACKER IS A FRIEND OR FOE.
IT COULD BE THAT PRINCE WOBLE DID IT IN SELF-DEFENSE, SENSING A GUARD'S DECISION TO TAKE MATTERS INTO HIS OWN HANDS.
OR IT COULD'VE BEEN ANOTHER PRINCE, TARGETING THE YOUNGEST AND WEAKEST PRINCE BY DESTROYING HER INNER CIRCLE.
QUESTIONS REMAIN REGARDING HER MASTERY PROCESS.
NEN IS USUALLY ACQUIRED OVER A *LONG TIME.*
WHEN WAS THIS CEREMONY?
UM...
A LITTLE OVER A MONTH AGO.
TRUE, IT HASN'T BEEN LONG ENOUGH FOR THAT THEORY TO WORK.
THIS CAN'T BE DONE BY SOMEONE WHO *JUST* LEARNED NEN.
WELL... IT'S NOT IMPOSSIBLE IF IT'S *PARASITIC.*
PARASITIC ...?
YEAH.
THAT WOULD EXPLAIN THE CEREMONY.
RMM RMM

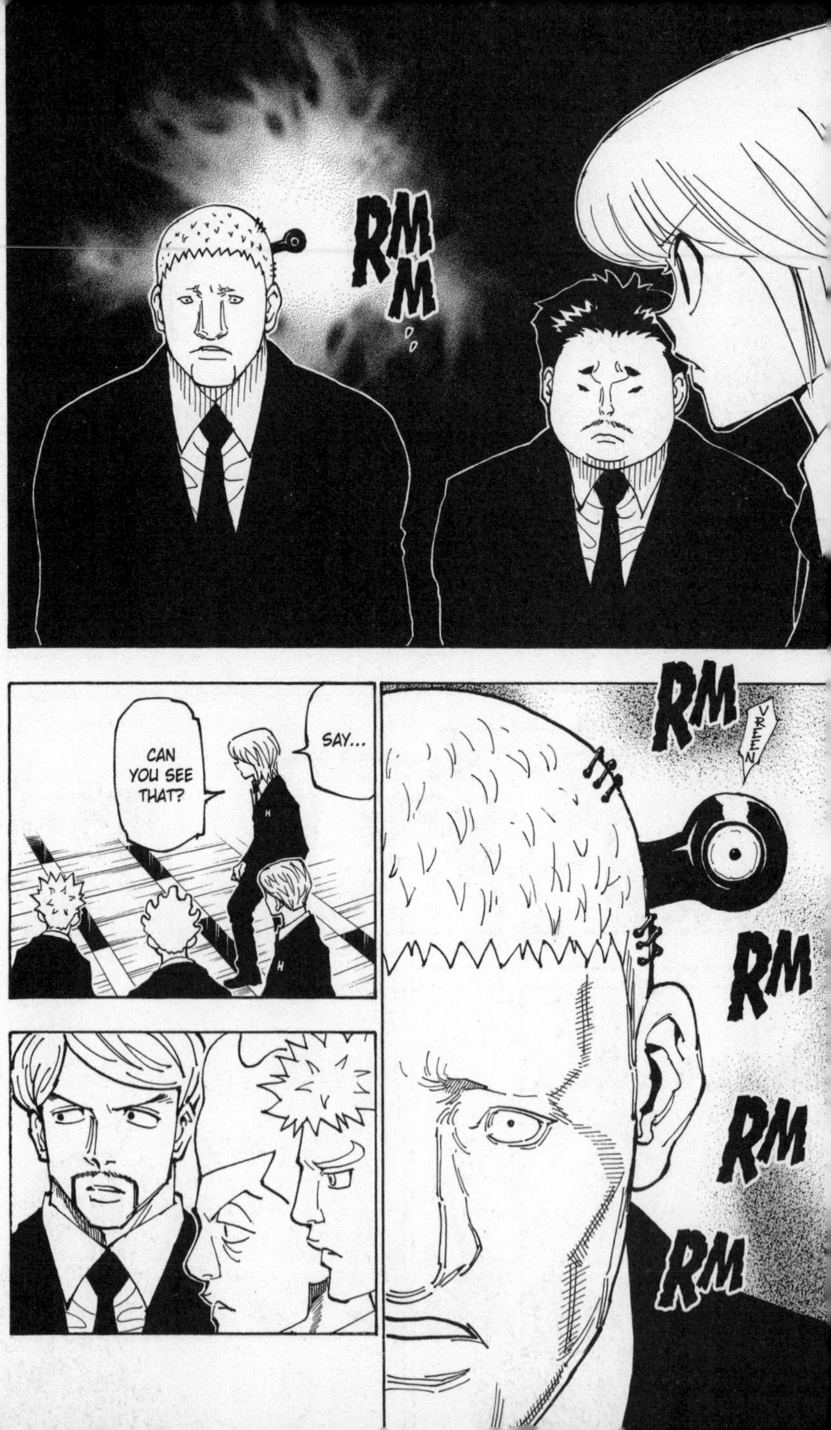
RMM
RM
VREEN
RM
RM
RM
SAY...
CAN YOU SEE THAT?

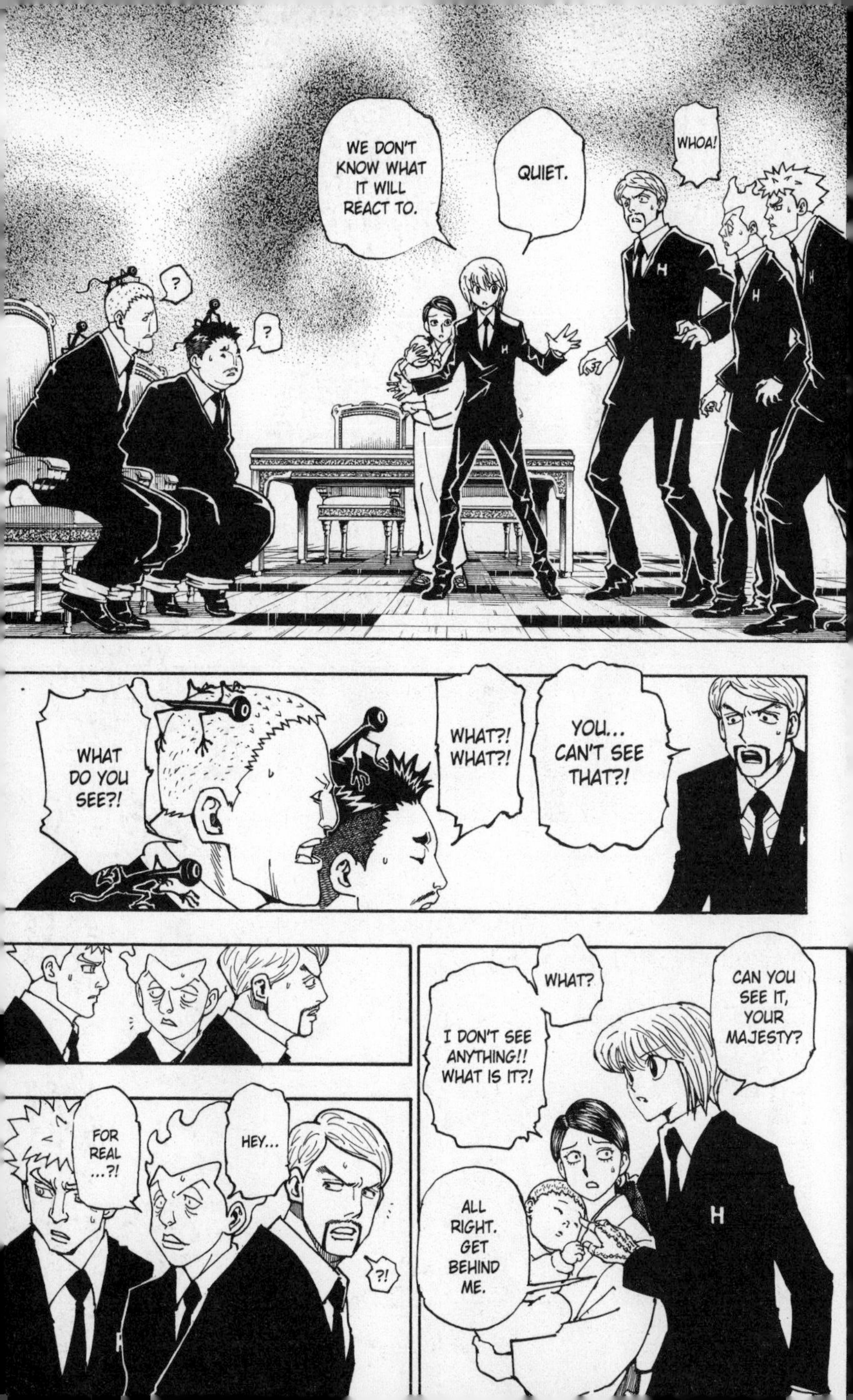
WHOA!
QUIET.
WE DON'T KNOW WHAT IT WILL REACT TO.
?
?
YOU... CAN'T SEE THAT?!
WHAT?! WHAT?!
WHAT DO YOU SEE?!
CAN YOU SEE IT, YOUR MAJESTY?
WHAT?
I DON'T SEE ANYTHING!! WHAT IS IT?!
ALL RIGHT. GET BEHIND ME.
HEY...
FOR REAL ...?!
?!

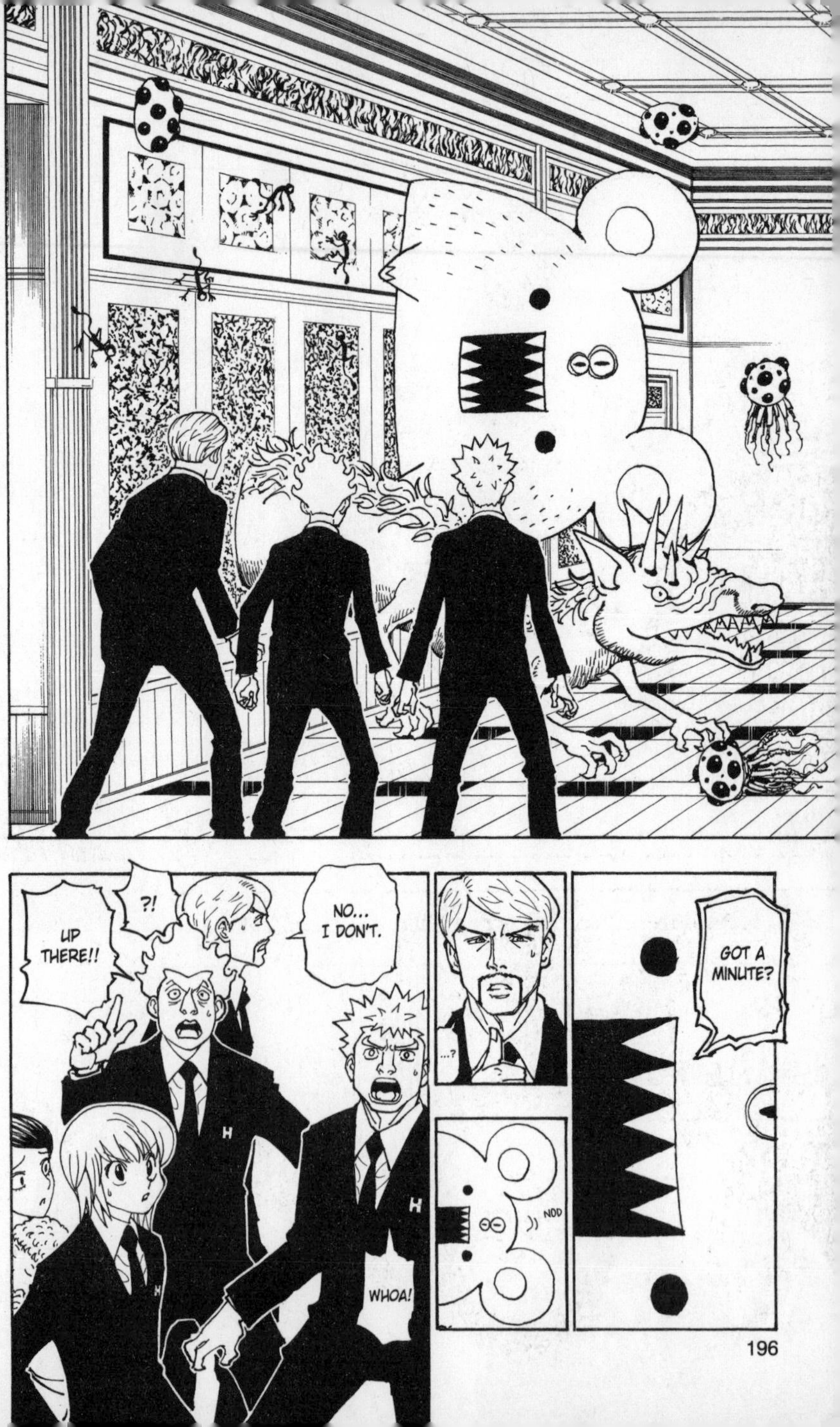
GOT A MINUTE?
...?
NOD
NO... I DON'T.
?!
UP THERE!!
WHOA!

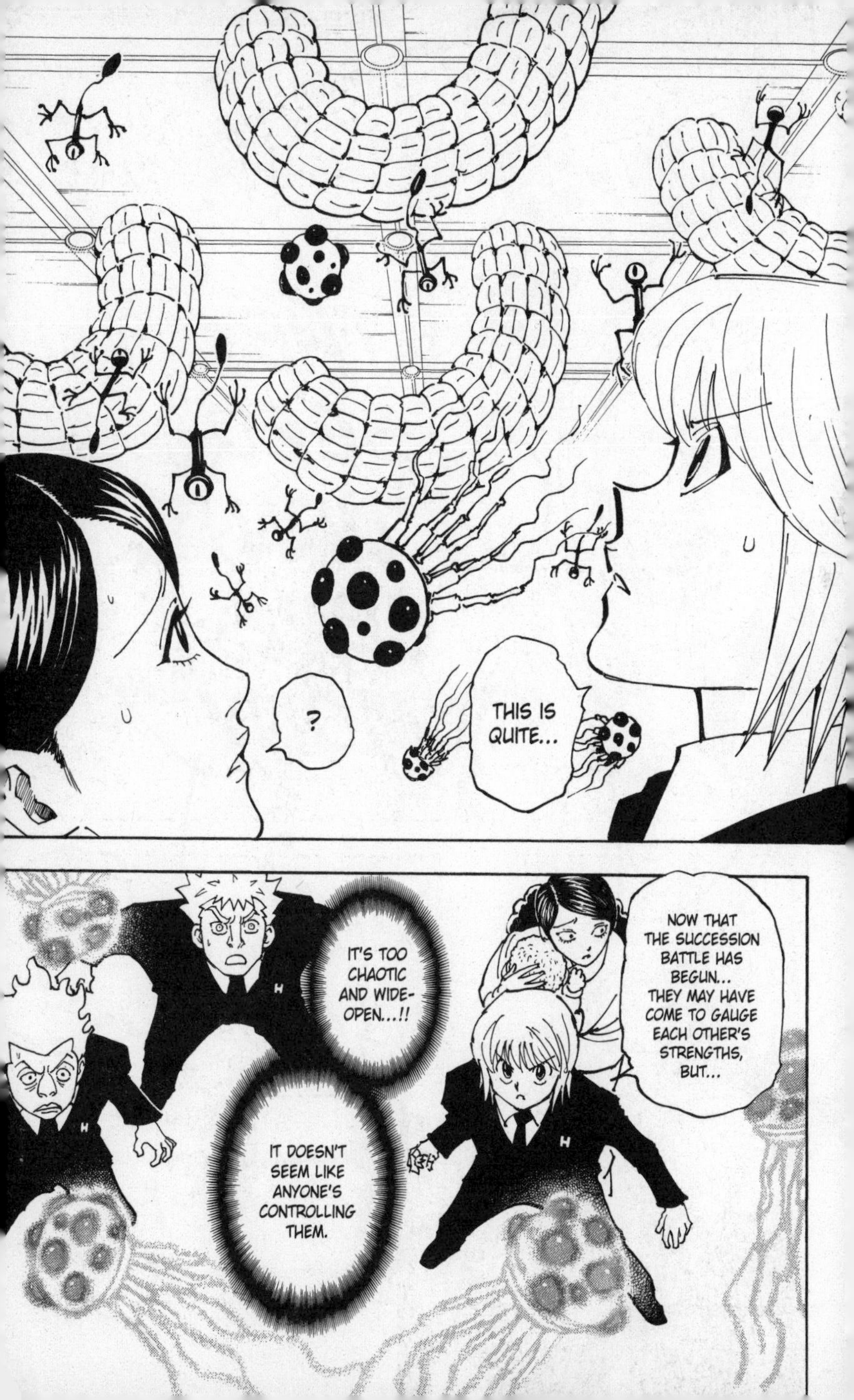
THIS IS QUITE...
?
NOW THAT THE SUCCESSION BATTLE HAS BEGUN... THEY MAY HAVE COME TO GAUGE EACH OTHER'S STRENGTHS, BUT...
IT'S TOO CHAOTIC AND WIDE-OPEN...!!
IT DOESN'T SEEM LIKE ANYONE'S CONTROLLING THEM.

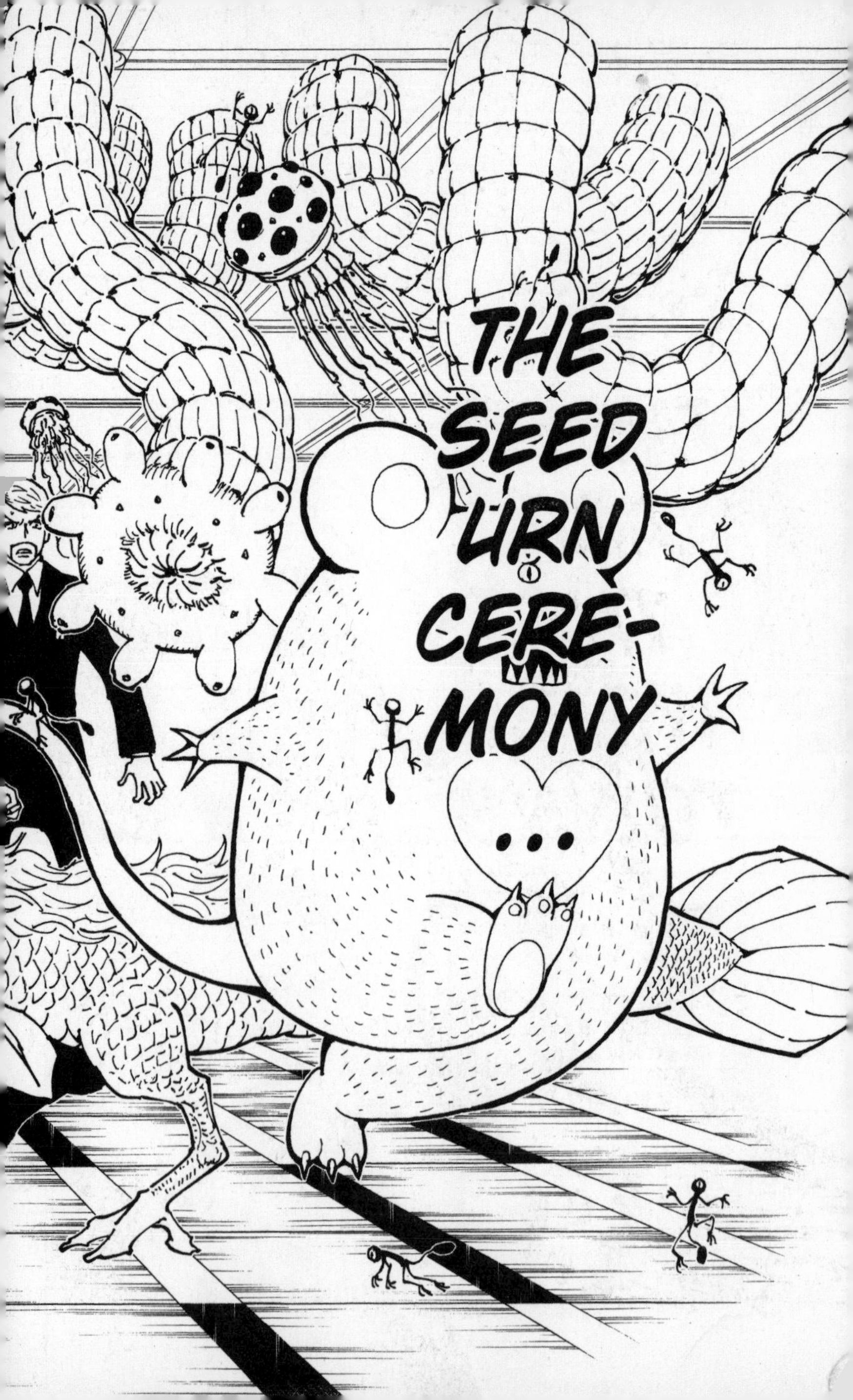
THE SEED URN CERE-MONY...

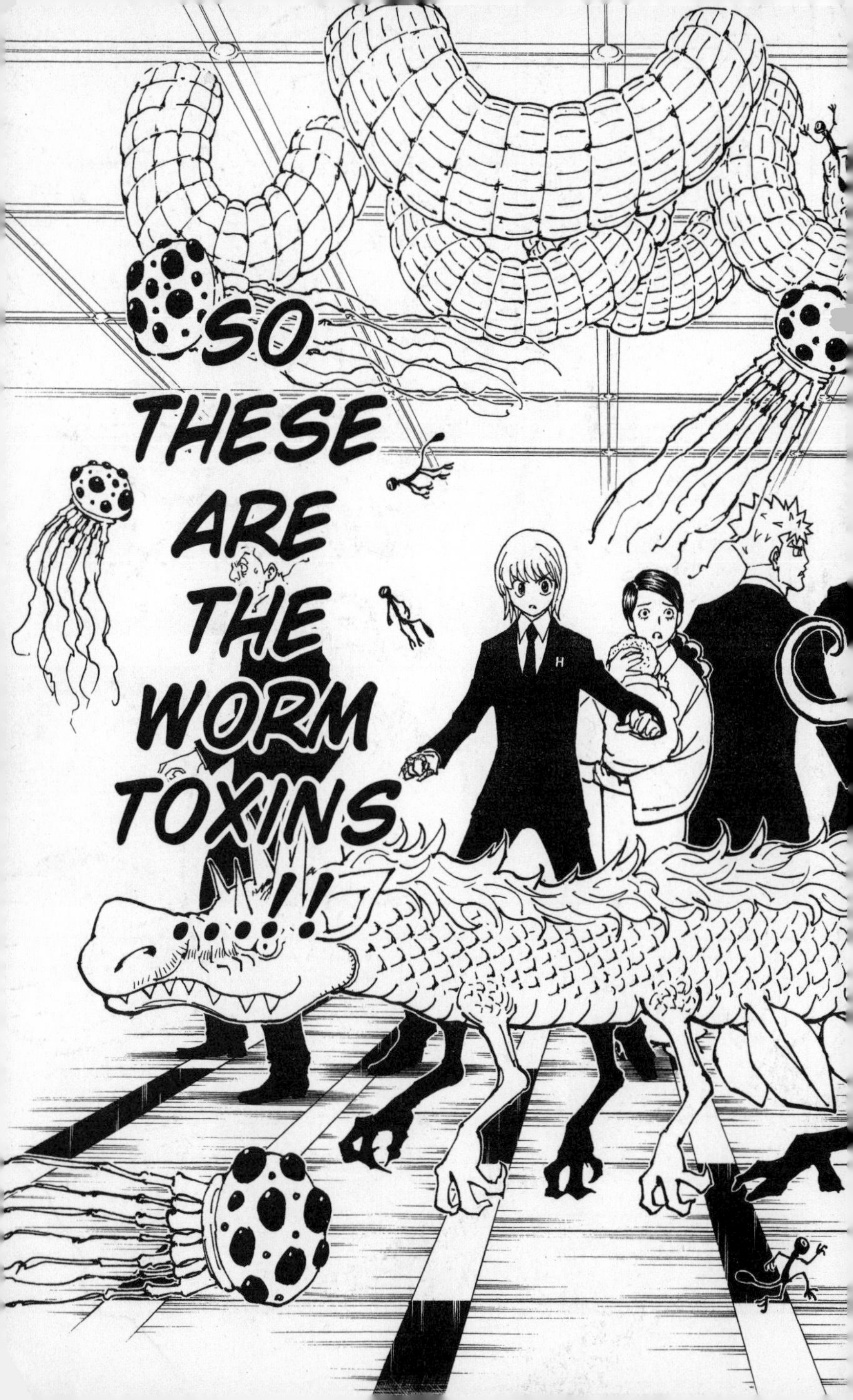
SO THESE ARE THE WORM TOXINS ...!!

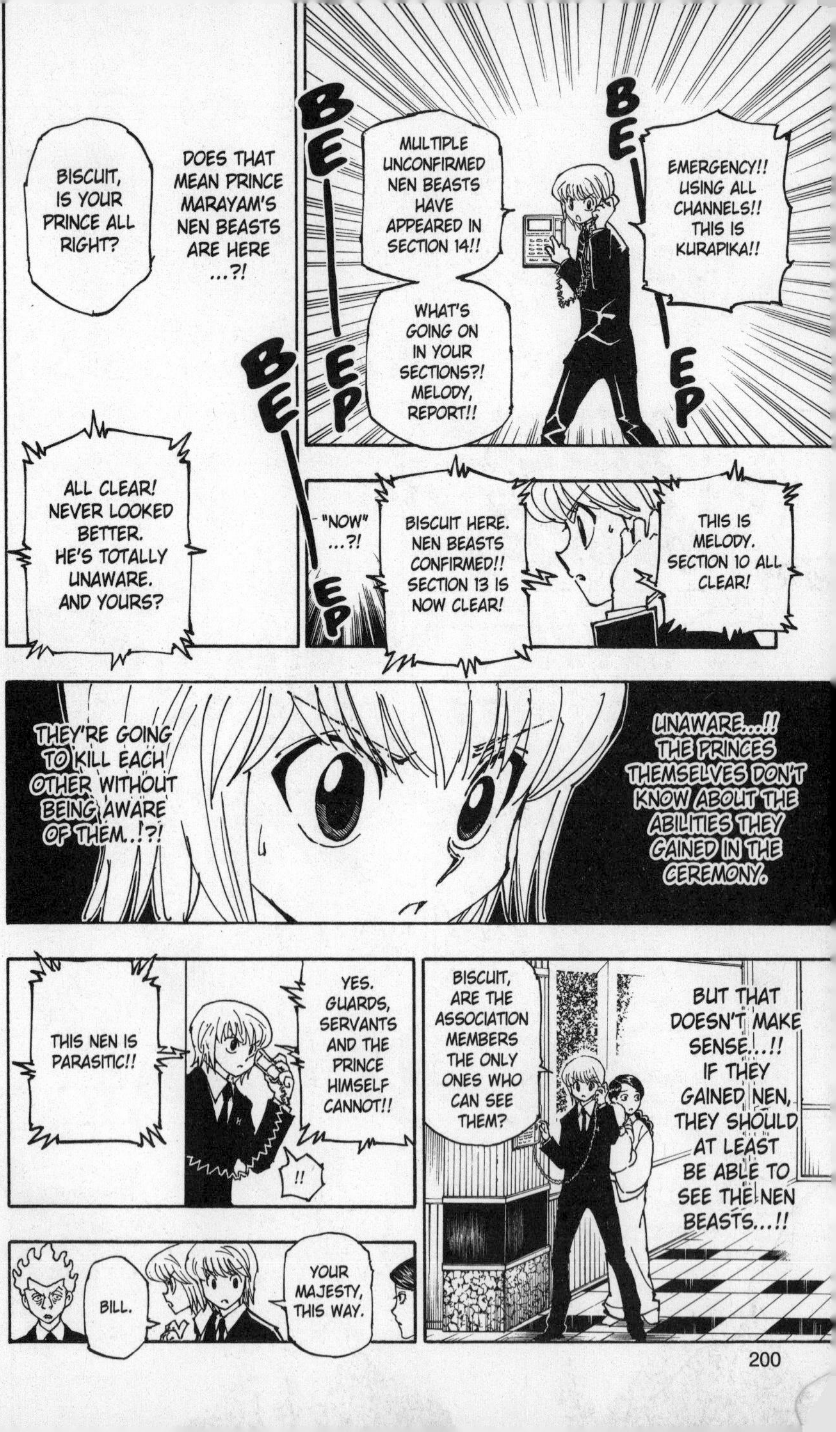
EMERGENCY!! USING ALL CHANNELS!! THIS IS KURAPIKA!!
BEEP
MULTIPLE UNCONFIRMED NEN BEASTS HAVE APPEARED IN SECTION 14!!
BEEP
WHAT'S GOING ON IN YOUR SECTIONS?! MELODY, REPORT!!
THIS IS MELODY. SECTION 10 ALL CLEAR!
BISCUIT HERE. NEN BEASTS CONFIRMED!! SECTION 13 IS NOW CLEAR!
BEEP
"NOW" ...?!
DOES THAT MEAN PRINCE MARAYAM'S NEN BEASTS ARE HERE ...?!
BISCUIT, IS YOUR PRINCE ALL RIGHT?
ALL CLEAR! NEVER LOOKED BETTER. HE'S TOTALLY UNAWARE. AND YOURS?
UNAWARE...!! THE PRINCES THEMSELVES DON'T KNOW ABOUT THE ABILITIES THEY GAINED IN THE CEREMONY.
THEY'RE GOING TO KILL EACH OTHER WITHOUT BEING AWARE OF THEM..!?!
BUT THAT DOESN'T MAKE SENSE...!! IF THEY GAINED NEN, THEY SHOULD AT LEAST BE ABLE TO SEE THE NEN BEASTS...!!
BISCUIT, ARE THE ASSOCIATION MEMBERS THE ONLY ONES WHO CAN SEE THEM?
YES. GUARDS, SERVANTS AND THE PRINCE HIMSELF CANNOT!!
THIS NEN IS PARASITIC!!
!!
YOUR MAJESTY, THIS WAY.
BILL.

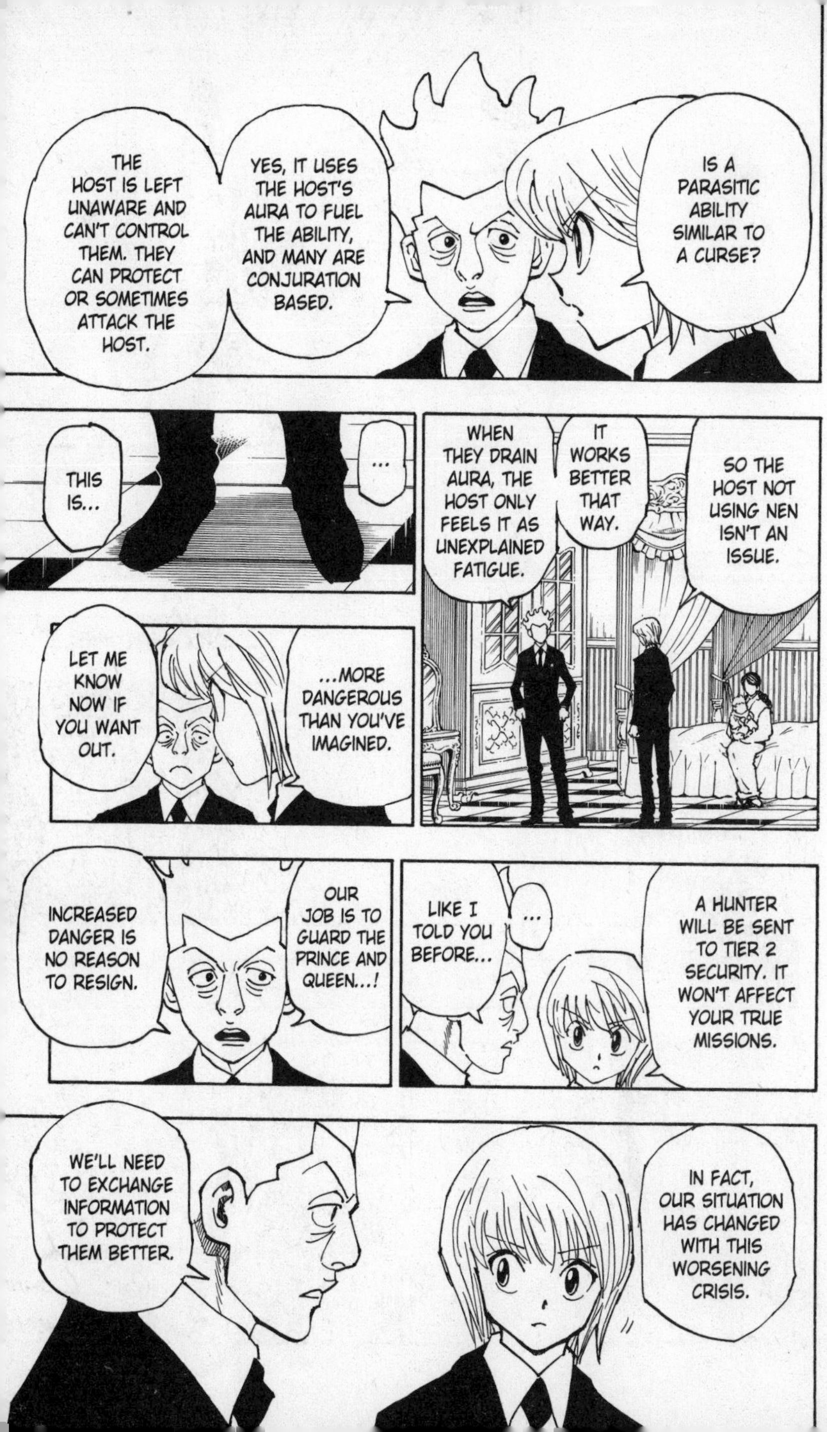
IS A PARASITIC ABILITY SIMILAR TO A CURSE?
YES, IT USES THE HOST'S AURA TO FUEL THE ABILITY, AND MANY ARE CONJURATION BASED.
THE HOST IS LEFT UNAWARE AND CAN'T CONTROL THEM. THEY CAN PROTECT OR SOMETIMES ATTACK THE HOST.
SO THE HOST NOT USING NEN ISN'T AN ISSUE.
IT WORKS BETTER THAT WAY.
WHEN THEY DRAIN AURA, THE HOST ONLY FEELS IT AS UNEXPLAINED FATIGUE.
...
THIS IS...
...MORE DANGEROUS THAN YOU'VE IMAGINED.
LET ME KNOW NOW IF YOU WANT OUT.
A HUNTER WILL BE SENT TO TIER 2 SECURITY. IT WON'T AFFECT YOUR TRUE MISSIONS.
...
LIKE I TOLD YOU BEFORE...
OUR JOB IS TO GUARD THE PRINCE AND QUEEN...!
INCREASED DANGER IS NO REASON TO RESIGN.
IN FACT, OUR SITUATION HAS CHANGED WITH THIS WORSENING CRISIS.
WE'LL NEED TO EXCHANGE INFORMATION TO PROTECT THEM BETTER.

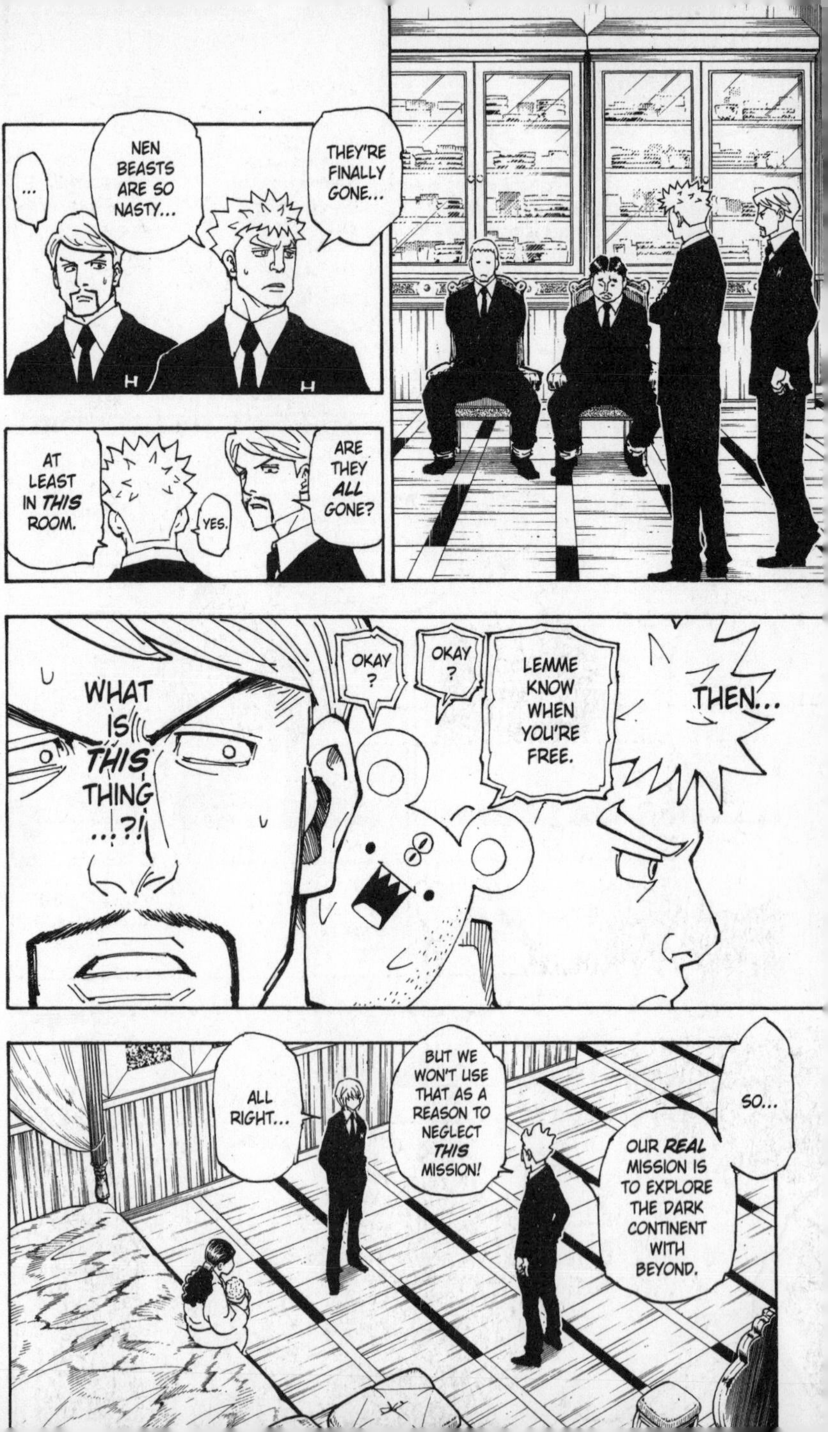
THEY'RE FINALLY GONE...
NEN BEASTS ARE SO NASTY...
...
ARE THEY *ALL* GONE?
YES.
AT LEAST IN *THIS* ROOM.
THEN...
LEMME KNOW WHEN YOU'RE FREE.
OKAY?
OKAY?
WHAT IS *THIS* THING...?!
SO...
OUR *REAL* MISSION IS TO EXPLORE THE DARK CONTINENT WITH BEYOND.
BUT WE WON'T USE THAT AS A REASON TO NEGLECT *THIS* MISSION!
ALL RIGHT...

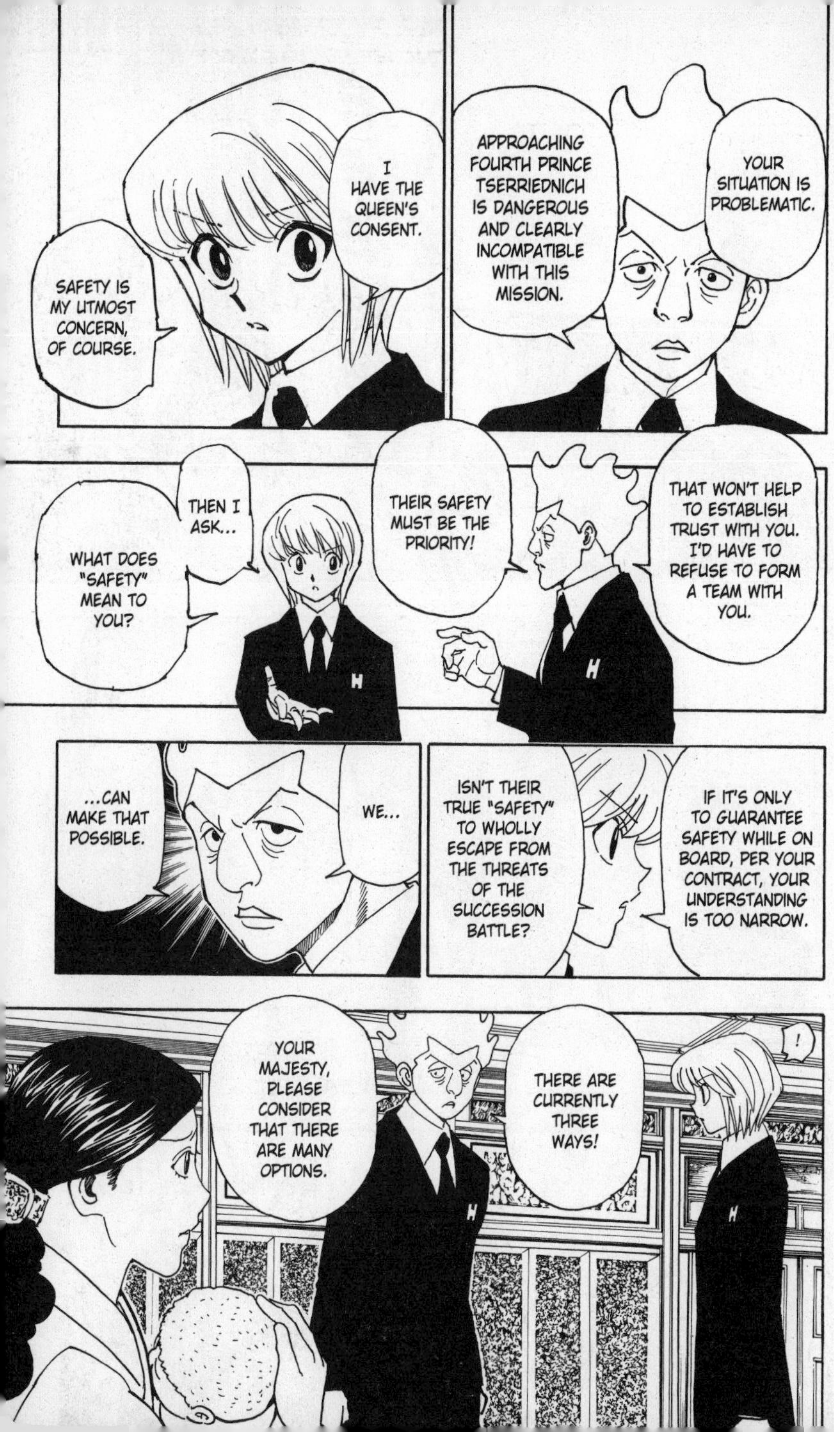
YOUR SITUATION IS PROBLEMATIC.
APPROACHING FOURTH PRINCE TSERRIEDNICH IS DANGEROUS AND CLEARLY INCOMPATIBLE WITH THIS MISSION.
I HAVE THE QUEEN'S CONSENT.
SAFETY IS MY UTMOST CONCERN, OF COURSE.
THAT WON'T HELP TO ESTABLISH TRUST WITH YOU. I'D HAVE TO REFUSE TO FORM A TEAM WITH YOU.
THEIR SAFETY MUST BE THE PRIORITY!
THEN I ASK...
WHAT DOES "SAFETY" MEAN TO YOU?
IF IT'S ONLY TO GUARANTEE SAFETY WHILE ON BOARD, PER YOUR CONTRACT, YOUR UNDERSTANDING IS TOO NARROW.
ISN'T THEIR TRUE "SAFETY" TO WHOLLY ESCAPE FROM THE THREATS OF THE SUCCESSION BATTLE?
WE...
...CAN MAKE THAT POSSIBLE.
!
THERE ARE CURRENTLY THREE WAYS!
YOUR MAJESTY, PLEASE CONSIDER THAT THERE ARE MANY OPTIONS.

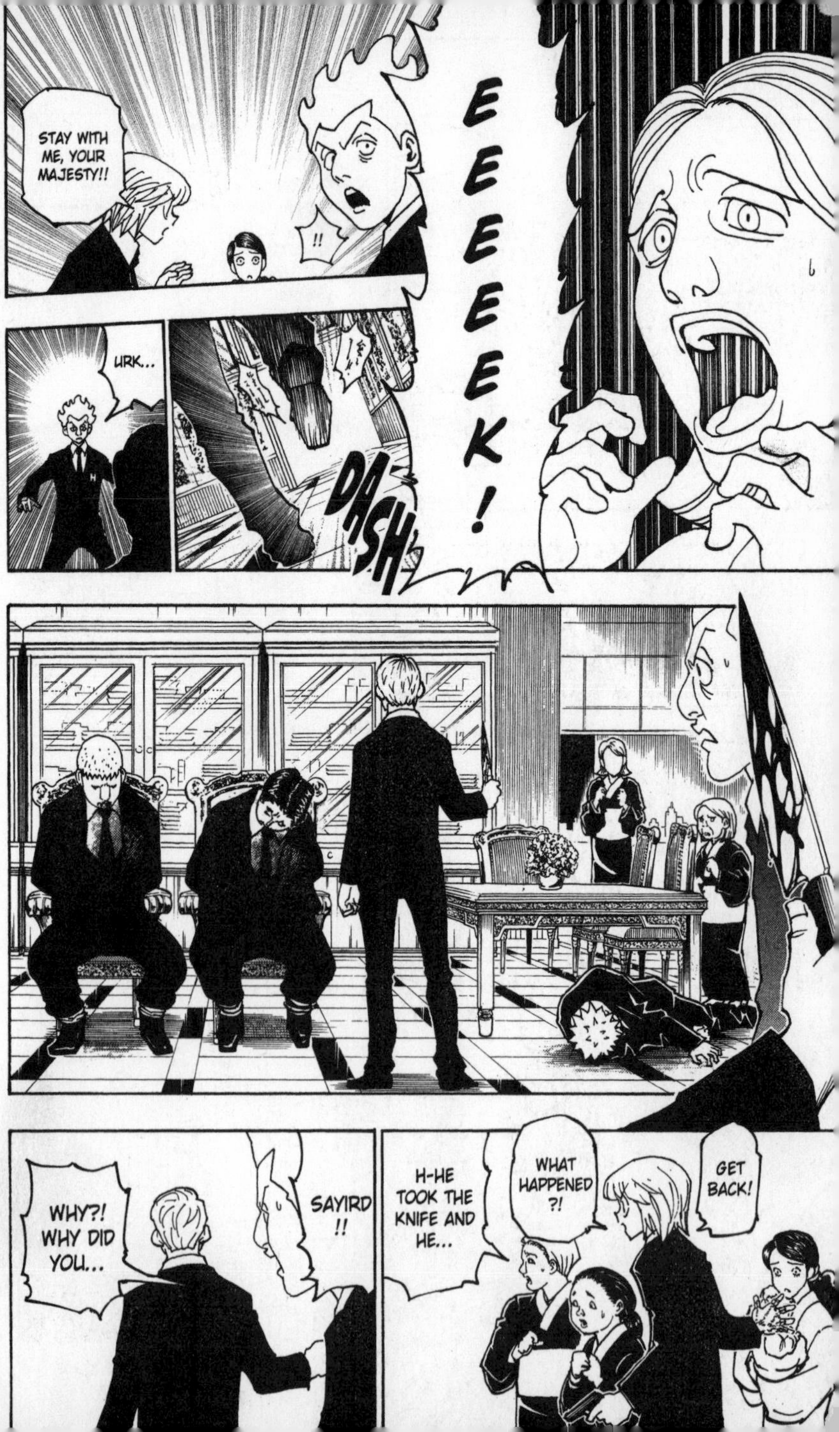
EEEEEK!
STAY WITH ME, YOUR MAJESTY!!
!!
DASH
URK...
GET BACK!
WHAT HAPPENED?!
H-HE TOOK THE KNIFE AND HE...
SAYIRD!!
WHY?! WHY DID YOU...

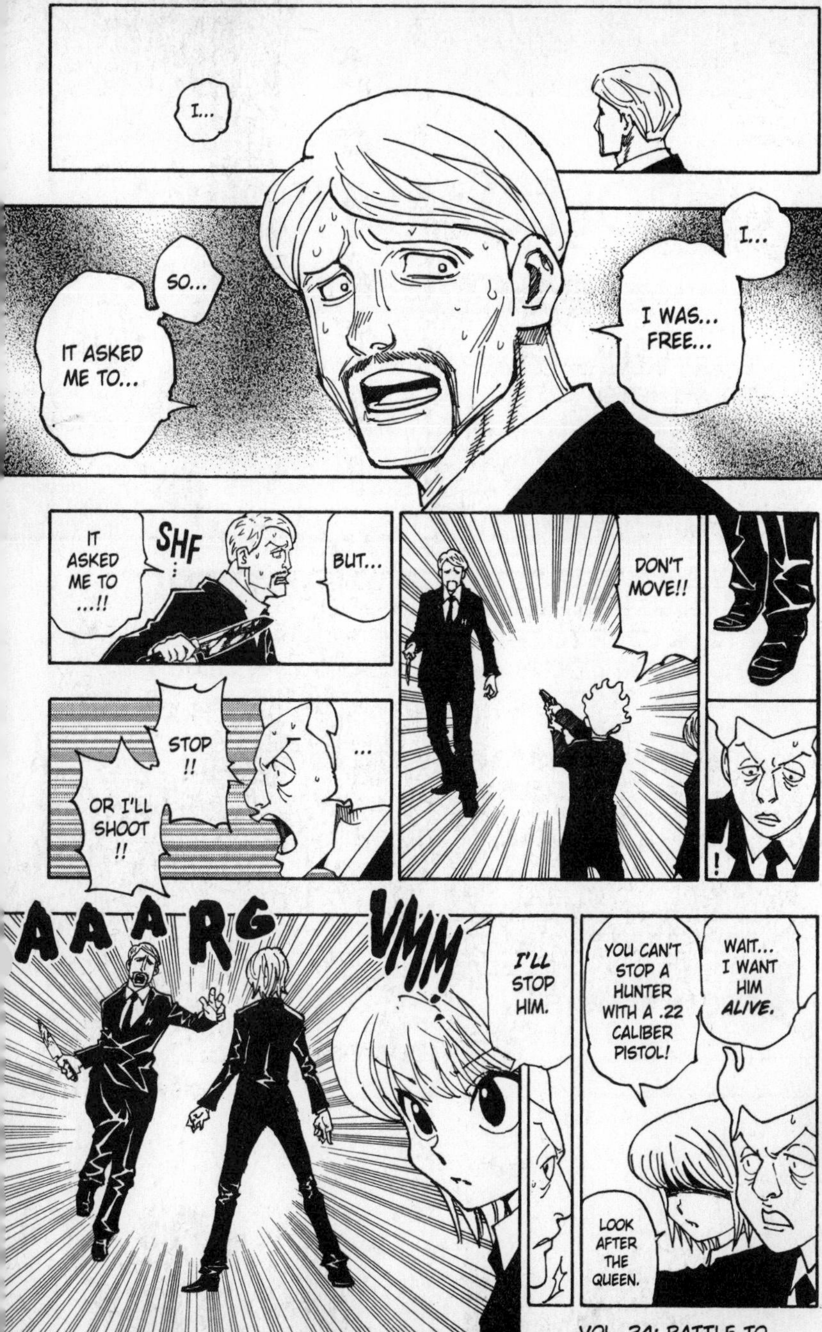
I...
I...
I WAS... FREE...
SO...
IT ASKED ME TO...
!
DON'T MOVE!!
BUT...
SHF
IT ASKED ME TO ...!!
...
STOP !!
OR I'LL SHOOT !!
WAIT... I WANT HIM *ALIVE.*
YOU CAN'T STOP A HUNTER WITH A .22 CALIBER PISTOL!
I'LL STOP HIM.
LOOK AFTER THE QUEEN.
VMM
AAARG

VOL. 34: BATTLE TO THE DEATH: END.

CHROLLO VS. HISOKA

A COMMENTARY

THERE WERE SEVERAL THINGS I WANTED TO DO WITH THIS BATTLE. FIRST AND FOREMOST, THE FIGHT ITSELF. I LOVE STORIES WHERE THE ENEMIES OF THE PROTAGONISTS FIGHT EACH OTHER. ONE OF THE MOST EXCITING ONES WAS WHEN TOSAMARU HIGH SCHOOL PLAYED BENKEI HIGH SCHOOL IN THE BASEBALL MANGA *DOKABEN*. I REALLY WANTED TO DO THAT KIND OF THING IN MY MANGA.
I TOOK CARE TO LET BOTH OF THEM SHOW THEIR MANHOOD AND ALSO PORTRAY A CLEAR, DECISIVE OUTCOME~WHILE FUN, A TOUGH THING TO DO.
THE OTHER THING I WANTED TO DO WAS HAVE SOMEONE SAY "I'LL WIN 100 PERCENT" AND THEN REALLY DO IT.
THE GUY WHO SAYS SOMETHING LIKE THAT? GENERALLY LOSES.
I REFERRED TO THE ATTITUDE ESPOUSED BY THE SWORDSMAN KOGAN IWAMOTO.
SHIGURUI IS AWESOME!!

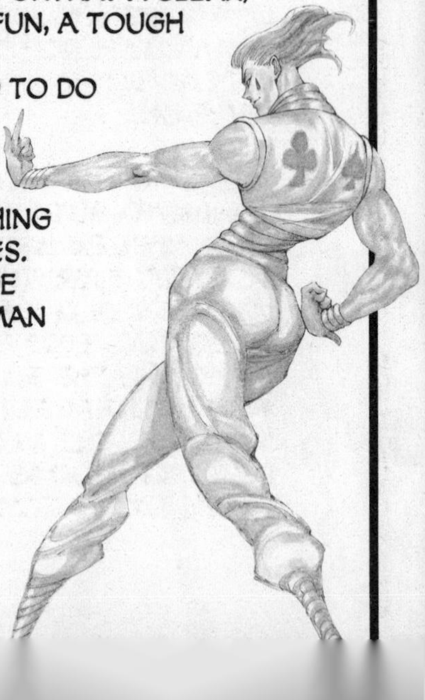

WHAT I WANTED TO DO MOST WAS TO HAVE
HIM KILL SOMEONE IN THE TROUPE. I KNEW
HOW THE STORY WAS GOING TO WORK OUT,
BUT I HADN'T DECIDED WHO HISOKA WOULD
KILL AT THE END. HISOKA WANTED TO KILL
MACHI THEN AND THERE, BUT I VETOED IT.

TO LEAD INTO THE VOYAGE ARC, I NEEDED A
MESSENGER TO DELIVER THE NEWS TO THE
OTHER TROUPE MEMBERS. HE KILLED KORTOPI
AND SHALNARK AS PART OF HIS POST-MORTEM
ANALYSIS OF HIS PERFORMANCE IN THE
FIGHT, AS WELL AS FOR REVENGE, AND I ALSO
WANTED TO SHOW HOW SERIOUS HISOKA
WAS THROUGH HIS COLD AND CALCULATING
JUDGMENT IN REDUCING CHROLLO'S ROSTER
OF ABILITIES...IS MY EXCUSE AFTER THE FACT.
IT WAS MY HUNCH THAT LETTING MACHI STICK
AROUND WOULD MAKE IT MORE INTERESTING
LATER ON.

THIS CAME UP IN MY JOINT INTERVIEW WITH
KISHIMOTO, BUT I HAVE A BLUEPRINT IN MY
HEAD WHEN I'M WRITING THE STORY, MEANING
I CAN PUT EVERYTHING INTO WORDS, AND
UPON ACTUALLY THINKING THINGS THROUGH,
I OFTEN COME TO THE CONCLUSION THAT
FOLLOWING THE BLUEPRINT IS INDEED THE
INTERESTING PATH. BUT WHEN THE DISTANT
FUTURE IS STILL MURKY, WHO YOU CHOOSE TO
SAVE OR LET GO RELIES SOLELY ON INTUITION.
I HOPE I DON'T COME TO REGRET IT...

You're Reading in the Wrong Direction!!

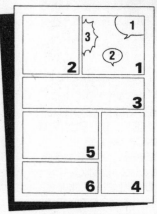

Whoops! Guess what? You're starting at the wrong end of the comic!

...It's true! In keeping with the original Japanese format, **Hunter x Hunter** is meant to be read from right to left, starting in the upper-right corner.

Unlike English, which is read from left to right, Japanese is read from right to left, meaning that action, sound effects and word-balloon order are completely reversed... something which can make readers unfamiliar with Japanese feel pretty backwards themselves. For this reason, manga or Japanese comics published in the U.S. in English have sometimes been published "flopped" – that is, printed in exact reverse order, as though seen from the other side of a mirror.

By flopping pages, U.S. publishers can avoid confusing readers, but the compromise is not without its downside. For one thing, a character in a flopped manga series who once wore in the original Japanese version a T-shirt emblazoned with "M A Y" (as in "the merry month of") now wears one which reads "Y A M"! Additionally, many manga creators in Japan are themselves unhappy with the process, as some feel the mirror-imaging of their art skews their original intentions.

We are proud to bring you Yoshihiro Togashi's **Hunter x Hunter** in the original unflopped format. For now, though, turn to the other side of the book and let the adventure begin...!

—Editor